All New, All Different?

World Comics and Graphic Nonfiction Series

Frederick Luis Aldama and Christopher González, editors

The World Comics and Graphic Nonfiction series includes monographs and edited volumes that focus on the analysis and interpretation of comic books and graphic nonfiction from around the world. The books published in the series use analytical approaches from literature, art history, cultural studies, communication studies, media studies, and film studies, among other fields, to help define the comic book studies field at a time of great vitality and growth.

All New, All Different?

A History of Race and the
American Superhero

ALLAN W. AUSTIN
PATRICK L. HAMILTON

University of Texas Press   Austin

Requests for permission to reproduce material from this work should be sent to:
    Permissions
    University of Texas Press
    P.O. Box 7819
    Austin, TX 78713-7819
    utpress.utexas.edu/rp-form

♾ The paper used in this book meets the minimum requirements of
ANSI/NISO Z39.48–1992 (R1997) (Permanence of Paper).

Library of Congress Cataloging-in-Publication Data

Austin, Allan W., author. | Hamilton, Patrick Lawrence, author.
All new, all different? : a history of race and the American superhero / Allan W. Austin,
Patrick L. Hamilton.
First edition. | Austin : University of Texas Press, 2019. | Includes bibliographical
references and index.
Identifiers: LCCN 2018051001
    ISBN 978-1-4773-1896-6 (cloth : alk. paper)
    ISBN 978-1-4773-1897-3 (pbk. : alk. paper)
    ISBN 978-1-4773-1898-0 (library ebook)
    ISBN 978-1-4773-1899-7 (non-library ebook)
Subjects: LCSH: Comic books, strips, etc.—United States—History and criticism. |
Heroes—Comic books, strips, etc.—History and criticism. | Race in literature. |
Superheroes in literature.
Classification: LCC PN6725 .A97 2019 | DDC 741.5/3552—dc23
LC record available at https://lccn.loc.gov/2018051001
doi:10.7560/318966

For Vicki, Bobby, and Hope
For Abby, Sam, Paddy, and Shelby (even though
she doesn't like superheroes)

Contents

Illustrations

Acknowledgments

Acknowledgments often seem harder to write—at least in some ways—than the book itself, given the myriad people who have helped along the way. We start, of course, by thanking those at the University of Texas Press who have helped to shepherd this book to publication. Jim Burr oversaw the project from proposal to publication, and we thank Jim for his contributions along the way. In addition, the series editors Frederick Luis Aldama and Christopher González have been incredibly supportive of our work from the start, and their suggestions have made significant contributions to an improved finished product. We also were the beneficiaries of anonymous readers who read closely, asked hard questions, and helped us to reconsider and understand in new ways just what this book might accomplish. Many thanks to Abby Webber as well, who skillfully and artfully copyedited the manuscript. We would also like to thank the various scholars whose work has informed our own over the course of this project. Both of us are also indebted to the countless writers, pencillers, inkers, colorists, letterers, editors, and others who created the comics we love and who were the impetus for this project.

We have also received significant help from Misericordia University in a variety of ways. The Faculty Research Grants Committee has steadfastly and patiently supported our long-term work, and we appreciate its willingness to conceive of this sustained project and what it might achieve. We certainly would be nowhere near publication without the committee's consistent and confident support. This project has also been supported by our department chairs, David Wright in History and Government and Becky Steinberger in English, as well as our deans, first Russ Pottle and now Heidi Manning, all of whom have provided whatever support was needed along the way. We also must thank numerous colleagues at Misericordia for their support along the way, even if they did sometimes have more fun than we might have liked with the idea of a "comic book book." We would be remiss, certainly, not to thank all of the students who have joined us over the past decade in our class on race and graphic narrative and thus have become part of the larger conversation that helped to shape this text.

Finally, a note of thanks to our families and friends. From Allan, a quick note of appreciation to Patrick. Cowriting a book presents any number of potential problems—egos, schedules, work styles, personality conflicts, and more—but writing this book has been easier than it should have been by almost any measure, and I am grateful to have you not only as a colleague but as a friend. I also must thank my parents and brother. My mother, English teacher par excellence, not only encouraged my love for literature but also supported my childhood love of comics. My father, the history teacher who encouraged my love for the past, also willingly drove me and my brother to the local newsstand regularly, where we would spend our carefully hoarded quarters on whatever brightly colored fare showed up on the comic book rack. And thanks to Phillip, who—when I was too sick to go to the newsstand—one day brought back for me a brand-new copy of *X-Men* #95, which probably, in some small way, totally changed my life, introducing me as it did not only to the X-Men but to conversations about racial difference that—somewhere, somehow—helped to shape a career devoted to the study of race and ethnicity in the American historical experience. To Vicki, Bobby, and Hope, you have—once again—been supportive beyond any reasonable expectation as this project took on a life of its own. To Vicki—who has been with me through not only graduate school but more books than she'd likely want to count—your willingness to listen to seemingly endless conversations about superheroes and their meanings when superheroes were never really your thing is so much appreciated; thanks as always for your patience and loyal support. To Bobby and Hope, who have watched me work through yet another project, thanks for your support, too, as well as numerous discussions about the matters at hand. It has been an awesome thing to write a book when you were both old enough to understand it and to want to talk about the meaning and power of popular culture (both in comics and in other forms) in American life and history. To Vicki, Bobby, and Hope, and perhaps most importantly, thanks so much for also always reminding me that there is more to life than writing books; the laughter, the trips, the goofy conversations about just about anything, and just hanging out together have all made the book endurable when it was a grind and more fun than it should have been at other times. Thanks.

From Patrick, a heartfelt thanks to Allan for his immense thoughtfulness, talent, and patience, all of which he brought to bear throughout this collaboration. Without these, this book would not exist, and our work together would not be enduring into a second decade. A further thanks also to Frederick, who (alongside Chris and all the staff at the University of Texas Press) helped bring this book to fruition and has guided me in my career since I was his PhD student at the University of Colorado–Boulder. I am also immensely thankful for the colleagues, friends, and families I have found since coming to Misericordia in 2006. Many of you—Allan, Vicki, Bobby, and Hope; Becky and Luca; Joe, Kim, Caitlin, and Molly; Justin, Alicia, and Levi; Amanda, Chris, Gabe, and Ella—have adopted me into your families, which has been profoundly important to me, particularly in recent difficult years, and I thank you all. Finally, my deepest thanks go to my family. My love for superhero comics was stoked by my parents. They bought me three-packs of Marvel Comics from the newsstands at the Thrifty market or Fred Meyer. My mom was the one who found our local comic book store in Beaverton, Oregon, and would buy me back issues if I got straight As on my report card; my dad took me to the annual comic book convention in Portland, Oregon, and, while chaperoning my choir field trip in Seattle, Washington, bought me the copy of *Avengers* #4 that would complete my collection (despite the fact that the store owner saw my enthusiasm and refused to bargain). Their memory and love live on in this book. I also want to thank my sisters, Julie and Valerie, who have always tolerated their nerdy brother and supported what I do. I love you both so much.

All New, All Different?

Introduction: Into the "Gutters"

In 1975, Marvel decided to radically revamp its tired and underperforming *X-Men* series, retaining only one of the original, all-white team members and replacing the rest with a decidedly multicultural cast. The replacements, including Russian, German, Kenyan, Canadian, Japanese, Irish, and Apache heroes, were widely promoted as an "all-new, all-different" team, and these far-reaching changes certainly paid off in commercial terms, as *X-Men* became the best-selling comic produced by Marvel for the better part of the next three decades. While the series was "all-new, all-different" in featuring a retooled squad, it also helped to break new ground in its presentation of a racially and ethnically diverse superteam. In this way, *X-Men* represented one of the early attempts within superhero popular culture—along with comics such as *Luke Cage, Hero for Hire* and the Saturday-morning cartoon *Super Friends*—to translate and even to "sell" an emerging multiculturalism that became increasingly influential after 1975. But in doing so, *X-Men*, *Luke Cage*, and *Super Friends* were not engaged in a totally novel endeavor; indeed, superhero popular culture had long been not only reflecting but contributing—progressively and regressively—to American conversations about the vexed issues of race, ethnicity, and what came to be known as multiculturalism.

Scholars, though, were initially slow to appreciate and study what superhero popular culture—comic books, television shows, movies, and so forth—might teach us about the American past and evolving ideas about race and ethnicity. As academics turned, in the last few decades, to the study of comics—the beachhead from which superheroes would launch their future multimedia empires—they tended to focus on highbrow graphic novels and theoretical analysis, preferring approaches that, for example, explored the gutter (i.e., the spaces between panels on comics'

Figure 0.1. The arrival of the "all-new, all-different" X-Men in 1975 heralded the beginning of a push to promote multiculturalism in superhero popular culture. The diverse team, however, reveals as much about the limits of multiculturalism as it does that movement's accomplishments.

pages) and the meaning that exists within or is generated by them.[1] Applying such approaches to "important" fare like Art Spiegelman's *Maus*, Miné Okubo's *Citizen 13660*, or any number of other critically acclaimed works, this original emphasis implicitly created another "gutter," that belonging to a junk culture that presented brightly colored superheroes undertaking outlandish adventures, a milieu seemingly too childish and ridiculous to merit serious inquiry.[2] This book argues instead that this relatively neglected mass culture can actually teach us an awful lot about how we have thought as well as have been encouraged to think about race and multiculturalism since the mid-twentieth century.

It has taken some time, however, for comics scholarship to catch up to this point, as early pioneering efforts are marked by their neglect of the superhero genre. The comic book creator Will Eisner's *Comics and Sequential Art*, for example, presents a master class in the art form. Here, Eisner examines comics as a unique art form with its own aesthetics that rely on the sequential juxtaposition of words and pictures to create a story. Furthermore, comics, for Eisner, have their own language, requiring the reader to interpret both visually and verbally. As a result, Eisner reminds us, comic creators must balance both the continuity of human experience and the human perception of it, which is broken up into separate segments.[3]

While theorizing about the workings of comics, Eisner wonders why comics, which enjoy substantial popularity, had been deemed largely unworthy of scholarly attention before the 1980s. His answer embodies the ways in which superheroes have been marginalized by early scholarship regarding graphic narratives. Scholars ignored comics, he argues in a blaming-the-victim explanation, in part because comics themselves had not undertaken topics meriting serious attention. By such topics, Eisner means something other than superheroes, which he holds at least partially responsible for this paucity of serious review. He proudly notes that this lack began to be redressed in the mid-1980s and after as more and more artists not only told more intellectually ambitious stories in comics but received corresponding attention and analysis.[4] This book argues that Eisner's emphasis on highbrow fare as the solution to increased scholarly attention is both right and wrong. Undoubtedly, the more "serious" works have brought heightened public acclaim and increased academic consideration. Such change does not mean, however, that the superhero comic—the lowbrow cousin of the "smart" graphic novel—deserves to remain marginalized. Instead of stopping with highbrow graphic narratives, scholars ought also to examine more consistently the gutters of junk culture, for here, too, lie important insights into the people who produce and consume such materials in great quantity as well as how those materials participate in and contribute to, to use Eisner's terms, "a wide range of cerebral topics," including race.

Scott McCloud ends up at much the same place as Eisner regarding comics in his widely celebrated book *Understanding Comics*. McCloud begins by noting that while other forms of media receive substantial critical appraisal, such attention to comics—with the exception of Eisner's work—has been lacking. Lamenting this lacuna, McCloud builds on Eisner's pioneering work to create a definition of graphic narrative: "Juxtaposed pictorial and other images in deliberate sequence, intended to convey information and/or to produce an aesthetic response in the viewer." To demonstrate the importance of this material, McCloud then takes readers on a historical tour of such narratives, starting with an Egyptian tale from 1300 BCE and working his way into the twentieth century. As he builds his theory for understanding this verbal and visual art form, McCloud is saddened that such work has largely been dismissed as mere entertainment, as if art that combines words and pictures can never be truly esteemed.[5] Like Eisner, then, McCloud laments the lack of serious attention to comics and places the blame for this sad state of affairs on popular but crassly commercial and escapist comics, among which superhero fare figures most prominently.

McCloud's explanation of how he came to love comics continues, all too clearly, to marginalize as lowbrow the superhero version of graphic narrative in trying to elevate the highbrow product. As he recounts falling in love with comics as an eighth grader and deciding to make a career in comics as a tenth grader, he writes of how he knew that the comic art form could do so much more than it had. But when he tried to explain this to others, they just laughed and didn't understand. He came to see that although comic books were capable of more, tragically, they could not escape popular understandings that reduced all such work to the margins of popular culture. To redress such misunderstandings, McCloud calls for an expanded consideration of comics that, like Eisner before him, largely dismisses the superhero fare that this book embraces. McCloud thus asks creators to produce ambitious and serious works that transcend popular conceptions of what comics are or might achieve, implying along the way that the superheroes and their ilk are an outdated art form without relevance.[6]

Given the foundational nature of Eisner's and McCloud's works, it is perhaps not surprising that scholarly work has only rather recently begun to redress this imbalance. Numerous works—Richard Reynolds's *Super*

Heroes: A Modern Mythology (1994); Gerard Jones and Will Jacobs's *The Comic Book Heroes* (1997); Ben Saunders's *Do the Gods Wear Capes? Spirituality, Fantasy, and Superheroes* (2011); Jeffrey Johnson's *Super-History: Comic Book Superheroes and American Society, 1938 to the Present* (2012); *The Superhero Reader* (2013), edited by Charles Hatfield, Jeet Heer, and Kent Worcester; *What Is a Superhero?* (2013), edited by Robin S. Rosenberg and Peter Coogan; Jill Lepore's *The Secret History of Wonder Woman* (2014); Aldo J. Regalado's *Bending Steel: Modernity and the American Superhero* (2015); and Ramzi Fawaz's *The New Mutants: Superheroes and the Radical Imagination of American Comics* (2016), to name but a few—all testify in their very titles to the greater attention the comic book superhero now receives, as well as the usefulness of superhero comics and popular culture in relation to understanding cultural issues more fully.

Those issues include racial and ethnic identity, and so, coinciding with this greater attention to the caped crusaders in general has been a consideration of superhero popular culture in relation to race. This body of work—while important on its own—demonstrates some specific patterns that our discussion attempts to redress. The majority of such works analyze black superheroes and superheroines in isolation. Jeffrey A. Brown's *Black Superheroes, Milestone Comics, and Their Fans* (2000), for example, focuses exclusively on the short-lived Milestone imprint published at DC and does not place the Milestone heroes and series within the broader historical context of superhero comics' treatment of race. A more recent work, Adilifu Nama's *Super Black: American Popular Culture and Black Superheroes* (2011), similarly narrows its focus to the positive cultural and imaginative work accomplished by black superheroes, but in its effort to laud these heroes underplays how pernicious representations simultaneously accompany their achievements. Sheena C. Howard and Ronald L. Jackson II's *Black Comics: Politics of Race and Representation* (2013) only includes, among its fourteen essays, two on black superheroes alongside a greater number of black comic strips and graphic novels. Frances Gateward and John Jennings's *The Blacker the Ink: Constructions of Black Identity in Comics and Sequential Art* (2015) does better, including among its four thematic sections one on black superheroes, comprising four essays. However, superhero comics serve in the collection as the backdrop against which other representations—including newspaper strips, war comics, Francophone comics, and web comics—stand and transcend.[7] Deborah Elizabeth Whaley's *Black Women in Sequence: Re-inking Comics, Graphic Novels, and Anime* (2016) includes two of five chapters dealing with black female superheroes, but curiously spends one of these on an analysis of Catwoman, who, for most of her representations, has been white. Michael A. Sheyah-she's *Native Americans in Comic Books: A Critical Study* (2008) moves the discussion of race in comics beyond African Americans but continues to look at one group in isolation, treating several Native American super-heroes (and even then concentrating largely on identifying stereotypes of Native Americans with little historical context). Marc Singer, in con-trast to the bulk of this work, provides a more nuanced and wider-ranging treatment of race in "'Black Skins' and White Masks: Comic Books and the Secret of Race," noting the reductive ways in which superhero comics in the 1970s and 1990s have depicted minorities and cultivated racial atti-tudes. While studies that isolate a particular ethnic or racial group make important contributions, this book takes a different but complementary approach: charting the largely unexplored terrain of a more broadly inclu-sive history of race and the American superhero, with all its complexity and contradictions. In this, we strive to present the patterns of racial and ethnic representation more generally in comics and superhero popular culture, the attitudes from which they emanate, and those they seek to cultivate.

Scholars' still somewhat qualified understanding of superhero popular culture and race is especially ironic given that racial and ethnic represen-tations were inherent, both figuratively and literally, within early comics and comic strips. As David Hajdu has pointed out, the Yellow Kid, the late nineteenth-century trailblazer for newspaper comic strips, spoke in a cli-chéd ethnic hodgepodge and hung out with others who were nothing more than gross stereotypes of Italian, African American, and Middle Eastern cultures. But though stereotypes ruled the strip (and in many ways the art form) from the start, these early newspaper entertainments also came to belong to ethnic immigrants. As Hajdu importantly notes, the "early news-paper comics spoke to and of the swelling immigrant populations in New York and other cities where comics spread, primarily through syndication (although locally made cartoons appeared in papers everywhere). The fun-nies were *theirs*, made for them and about them."[8]

As the earliest strips revolved around immigrants and outsiders, so too did the early comic book industry. In 1937, when the studio run by Will Eisner and Jerry Iger opened, it employed writers and artists who felt like outsiders: immigrants, women, native-born Americans of every ethnic stripe, and others on the margins of society. Of course, these out-siders wanted in, and, Hajdu argues, Superman represented their assimi-lation. Whereas the Yellow Kid, in at least one sense, celebrated ethnic im-migrants, Superman embodied their casting off their cultures for a more mainstream "American" identity.[9] Aldo J. Regalado echoes Hajdu, describing comics as the way in which immigrant (largely Jewish) creators "negotiated their way into the cultural mainstream" via not only their characters but, ultimately, the industry they helped create.[10] Such a development was hardly surprising, and is actually fairly typical of the immigrant experience writ large. Given how comics in general and their first superhero in particular base themselves in patterns of immigrant history and experience, scholars ought to pay even greater attention to both because they provide a unique window into evolving attitudes about race and inclusion in the United States.

Gerard Jones emphasizes such connections in *Men of Tomorrow: Geeks, Gangsters, and the Birth of the Comic Book*, his history of the early years of the comic book industry. As he writes of the superheroes' founding fathers — men of a single generation that included "Jerry Siegel, Jack Liebowitz, Joe Shuster, Harry Donenfeld, Charlie Ginsberg, Bob Kahn, Stanley Lieber, Jake Kurtzberg, [and] Mort Weisinger" — Jones emphasizes that they were all children of Jewish immigrants and thus outsiders, in some ways even within their own community. They were likewise distanced from the mainstream of US society, but Jones argues that this marginalization actually made them more cognizant of the hopes and disappointments of Americans than those in its midst. And their comics arose from this tension. Whether it was due to purely economic need or a result of seeking some kind of solace from their struggle, such men, Jones insists, created a form of popular culture that spoke to all of America's children and would later find its brand of fantasy appealing to more mature young men and women as well as adults. It was this appeal that allowed comics to persist beyond the art form's initial fascination and become part of popular entertainment and culture for the rest of the twentieth century and beyond.[11]

The end results of these founders' efforts would likely have shocked these men, as their dreams of a fantastical future not only brought them varying degrees of financial and psychological progress but also helped form what would become America's destiny. In this way, Jones contends, the early comics' creators tackled issues of gender, sexuality, power, authority, and violence with an earnestness that allowed their creations to accomplish more than even the creators themselves might have imagined possible. The superhero comic book — simultaneously base and crass but also aspirational and idealistic — thus represents incredibly fertile ground for research into how American attitudes toward gender, sexuality, and, in our case, race have both sought to shape and been shaped by the exploits of comic book superheroes.[12]

If Jones's work broadly outlines why superhero popular culture matters, Bradford Wright's *Comic Book Nation: The Transformation of Youth Culture in America* suggests how we might think differently about comic books in particular as we engage superheroes and their adventures. For Wright, comics were essential to understanding both the world around him and his place within it as he grew up. He talks about not only the escape comics provided but also how they made a large and seemingly threatening world not quite so intimidating. In other words, they helped him find both who and where he was as he matured. In this way, Wright correctly emphasizes the ways in which comic books rose above the escapism they are too often reduced to and, instead, shaped his perception of reality. Wright consequently sees comics as an important glimpse into the lives and experiences of youth, and thus urges scholars to analyze more thoughtfully comics and their history in this light.[13]

While making important points about the value of studying comic books as a means to better understand children and adolescents, Wright's approach should not, however, lead one to believe that this is all the examination of superhero popular culture is good for. Instead, while always considering the relationship of the reader to the material, one also needs to consider how comic books and superheroes can help us to better understand adults. Kids, indeed, are only part of this story in what has always been (to engage in some oversimplifications ourselves) at least a two-way conversation between the kids who consume such materials and the adults who produce them. The latter matter as well, and while the interests of children certainly have helped to shape superhero popular culture—which is, after all, produced to make money—one should not ignore the adult creators, who use comic books (and superhero popular culture more broadly defined) to share and even to sell dominant cultural ideals, including widely shared ideas about race and ethnicity within American society.

At least some creators of superhero popular culture undoubtedly understood the potential power of their work. Take Robert Maxwell, the director of Superman's radio show during World War II, for instance. When the Office of War Information asked him to dial back his "virulent attacks" against the masses of Germans and Japanese (instead of just their leaders), Maxwell refused, clearly revealing the power and obligations that he believed himself to wield. As he explained, "I can, in some small way, formulate ideologies for [millions] of youngsters. . . . I am, at the moment, teaching this vast audience to hate. . . . And, unfortunately, there is no cleavage between the individual and the state whose ideology he defends." The hate that the radio director hoped to encourage was racialized, too; as

Maxwell explained in drawing a clear line between the European and the Asian enemies, "A German is a Nazi and a Jap is the little yellow man who 'knifed us in the back at Pearl Harbor.'"[14]

Such power could more positively be wielded to encourage more accepting attitudes about race. For example, jumping forward into the twenty-first century, *Uncanny Avengers* (Vol. 1) #7 neatly presents the assumed power of popular culture when the mutant Alex Summers (a.k.a. Havok) and the human Janet Van Dyne (a.k.a. the Wasp) discuss the latter's "Unity" clothing line, which strives to make mutants mainstream via fashion.[15] As Janet explains, "Their parents may hate and fear mutants, but their kids will idolize and emulate you." Alex is less certain, worrying that the clothing line is little more than "progressive hipster propaganda. It does feel a bit . . . crass." Janet's response is telling; she argues, "Popular culture has a long history of helping ease people into accepting the different. Jazz, hip-hop, punk rock . . . music and fashion can change the world." Janet's argument not only points to the value of interracial understanding but also to the power of popular culture in helping to promote it, as the writer Rick Remender reminded his more self-aware readers that popular culture—be it fashion or comics—can both reinforce and constitute socio-cultural attitudes and beliefs, even while masquerading as entertainment.

Remender is hardly alone in such beliefs, as many of his colleagues have expressed clear ideas about the power of comic books and other forms of superhero popular culture to communicate ideas and even ideals, particularly when it comes to race and ethnicity. G. Willow Wilson, writer of Marvel's critically acclaimed *Ms. Marvel*, which features the Pakistani American Kamala Khan, expressed her awareness of concerns for how the series would portray Muslim Arab Americans. Noting that even sympathetic portrayals can end up "rehashing the same stereotypes and racist baggage that all of the unsympathetic characters have reflected," Wilson consciously strove to show otherwise.[16] Similarly, David Walker, writer of *Cyborg* for DC Comics, has spoken openly about the ways in which the character's earlier depictions and appearances emasculated and dehumanized this African American character, shortcomings Walker sought to redress in his portrayal.[17] Here, in essence, is Bradford Wright's point that comics transcend their simplistic appearance via their ability to grapple with complex topics and ideas.[18] In particular regarding their depictions of race, approaches to comics, as Marc Singer asserts, need a similar complexity, not seeing them only as passive purveyors of extant stereotypes but also as generators and promulgators of their own assumptions.[19]

Building on such an approach, one can find great meaning in superhero popular culture. The very nature of the comic book industry and its demanding production schedules connect superheroes and their adventures closely to the zeitgeist. As the writer Dennis O'Neil has explained, even if comic creators are seemingly only rushing to meet their next deadline, what comes out of this pressure cooker of creativity is something connected to "what the audience wants or actually needs," and that is comics' genius.[20] The writer Danny Fingeroth agrees. "Needless to say," he suggests, "when the Superman mythology was created, no one was imagining a serious discussion of these issues some 65 years later, and perhaps it isn't fair to scrutinize such a creation so closely. By the same token, that very lack of self-consciousness may enable us to read cultural signposts [in comics]."[21]

Comic creators have written about a more intentional process, too. For example, Fingeroth believes that superhero comics have the same potential as traditional literature to express original and transcendent ideas about humanity. In this way, "the superhero can represent a snapshot of a moment in time in a culture's development, or a broader sense of cultural identity. As a writer, I [Fingeroth] find superhero stories useful for metaphorically working out, in both literal and symbolic ways, issues that are important to me—and hopefully, to a lot of other people."[22] The longtime industry veteran Tom DeFalco agrees, writing, "Like every other kind of fiction, stories about superheroes tell us something about the human condition."[23] The scholar Adilifu Nama supports such conclusions in contending that superheroes stand as symbols for a society's morality, goodness, and justice.[24] More to our point, they don't just symbolize such societal attitudes but play a role in promulgating and thus constituting them.

These more generalized ideas about the power of superhero popular culture are applicable to issues of race and ethnicity, though not simplistically; indeed, it is no more useful to take a stance of hypercriticism than to assume an unvarying position of celebration. On the one hand, it is easy enough to point only to the shortcomings of comics' dealings with race. As Marc Singer has warned, comics can be fairly one-dimensional when tackling race, often depicting complex identities in superficial and reductive ways.[25] From the completely opposite perspective come creators like Chuck Dixon and Paul Rivoche, who have decried the dominance of what they label a liberal, politically correct outlook that dominates the industry, producing work that they term morally ambiguous and leftist.[26] Whatever their differences, both perspectives critique reified presentations that deal little with complexity.

But we must also be just as wary of unilaterally celebrating comics as we are critiquing them. Adilifu Nama veers more toward the former in what he describes as a conscious effort to move beyond the reduction of black superheroes to stereotypes. Instead, he lauds the black superheroes for their symbolic meaning and positive renderings of black identity, but does so at times in ways that too much eclipse what contrasts these celebratory readings.[27] Ramzi Fawaz likewise celebrates superhero comics for moving beyond their jingoistic roots in patriotism and nationalism as they came to embrace more "radical," internationalist, and universal ideas of citizenship encompassing a myriad of previously marginalized identity positions; however, such readings seem more based in the imagined potential of what is on the comics pages under analysis than their reality.[28] Similarly, Bradford Wright—to whom comics mattered so much as a child—concludes his book by thinking about what comics might accomplish in the aftermath of the terrorist attacks of September 11, 2001. In particular, he somewhat hopefully wonders if comics can retain their relevance in the face of such destruction and tragedy, if their imagination of fantasy worlds and scenarios can still take hold of our minds in such a starkly frightening reality.[29]

If, then, scholars are beginning to recognize what superhero popular culture might reveal about race and the myriad issues encompassed by the muddy term "multiculturalism," our explorations of these materials have just begun. The complicated relationship between superhero popular culture and race lies somewhere between the pessimism of Singer, Dixon, and Rivoche and the optimism of Nama, Fawaz, and Wright, and so too does the approach of this book. As the ensuing discussions reveal, superhero comics and popular culture reflect, produce, and contest changing—if not always evolving—attitudes toward race within US culture. Though the idea of reflection may seem more obvious, it is how that action functions in conjunction with the latter two that needs to be understood for the dynamics of race and identity within comics to be fully recognized. Comics certainly reflect societal attitudes—and the limits of those attitudes—but that is not all they do. They also, in varying and unique ways, can foster and challenge such attitudes.

In this function, the comics and other art forms we discuss are no different from any other form of literature or any other cultural production. Adam Zachary Newton, for example, locates just such a didactic purpose in the origins of the novel,[30] and work on literature from the perspective of cognitive science comes to a similar conclusion. Patrick Colm Hogan, for example, privileges literature's interaction with culture, arguing that it presents a much more comprehensive view of everyday existence than our individual and partial experience can muster. He specifically draws from Arabic literary theory, through the concept of *takhyīl*—"the simultaneously creative and mimetic imagination that guides the way we think about and react to the world"—to explain how literature shapes our attitudes and feelings toward persons in another ethnic or other group identity.[31] Similarly, Patrick L. Hamilton explicates how texts' aesthetic construction "communicate unique values and meanings. . . . They ask us to judge, value, and think about the specific issues they raise," which include issues of race, ethnicity, and identity.[32]

Comics, again, are no different in this regard; the entire furor over horror and, to a lesser extent, superhero comics fostered by Fredric Wertham in the 1950s bases itself entirely in the ability of comics to affect attitudes and values. But there are other examples, less scandalous, perhaps, but no less significant, that illustrate this power. Ian Gordon, for example, identifies this effect in the comic strips of the 1920s in relation to American consumer culture. As he points out, comic strips such as *Gasoline Alley* both reflected the growth of consumer culture by being, in and of themselves, a commodity for consumption and helped shape Americans' attitudes toward commodities. Thus, on the one hand, the strip reflected cars as a burgeoning commodity, but, on the other, it also helped shape a view of having a car as an essential aspect of American life.[33] Gordon elsewhere makes a similar argument about the comic book version of Superman, tying his popularity to how his adventures not only reflected a notion of virtue in society but also taught its audience of what such virtue consisted: "When Superman's comic book version offered a view of an American norm, it did not simply reflect that norm but was a constituent element in the creation of that vision of society."[34] Aldo J. Regalado posits a similar function for Superman and other comic book heroes in the 1930s and 1940s regarding modernity. In contrast to earlier pulp and horror novels where the modern urban landscape was something to flee, superhero comics cast it and the modernity it represented as the new American reality. The comics of this era, too, could both reflect but also question prevailing attitudes. As Regalado goes on to explicate, superheroes promulgated both faith in the New Deal safety net and skepticism toward the very government implementing it.[35]

The ability of comics to so variously shape racial attitudes has likewise not gone unnoticed, as Frederick Luis Aldama underlines in *Your Brain on Latino Comics*. Although he argues that comics do not transform their material and historical realities, they do transform—positively and negatively—the readers' imaginations in relation to constructions of gender,

race, ethnicity, and sexuality.[36] Similarly, Derek Parker Royal, in his introduction to the collection *Multicultural Comics*, avers that comics, cartoons,
and other forms of visual iconography have shaped racial attitudes—
positively and negatively—throughout history.[37] As just one example,
Superman's embodiment of the immigrant, according to Regalado, reflected the ethnic identities of his creators as well as the growing pluralist notions of US society in the mid-twentieth century. Regalado thus
celebrates how the Man of Steel shifted definitions of heroism from their
Anglo-Saxon roots and so "served both to usher in and to help navigate"
changing attitudes regarding race and ethnicity.[38]

It is within this context, then, that we approach superhero comics and
their efforts—conscious or unconscious—to shape racial and ethnic attitudes in the United States via their narrative and visual constructions.
World War II Superman comic strips and serials, for example, do not just
reflect the extant racist attitudes toward Japanese Americans that led to
their unlawful incarceration. Instead, the official furor over these comics,
which had the hero visiting an American concentration camp, aptly demonstrates the power of superheroes to shape attitudes. As Gordon Chang
observes, the Office of War Information understood this power and feared
the negative ramifications of the story, especially wary that Superman's
tale would cause readers to see the camps themselves as dens of anti-
American activity and threat, thus resulting in the need for even more
draconian actions that the government wished to avoid.[39] Here, the Superman comic strip actually surpasses the racist attitudes that led to the incarceration of Japanese Americans, creating an impression of the camps
that, government officials feared, would foster a desire for even harsher
methods.

Similarly, the black superheroes who arrived in the late 1960s and
1970s, in their sheer number, manifest the greater recognition blacks in
general both demanded and began to receive. Simultaneously, though,
they also perpetuated long-standing black stereotypes, such as what
Donald Bogle has identified as the "buck," the "coon," and the "mammy,"
among others.[40] Too, they created problematic associations of their own,
as evidenced, for example, by the intrinsic connection assumed to exist
between the black heroes. When the Falcon wants a power upgrade in *Captain America and the Falcon* #169, he instinctively goes to the Black Panther (as opposed to Cap's suggestions of the white Tony Stark or Henry
Pym).[41] When, in *Uncanny X-Men* (Vol. 1) #122, Luke Cage hears "street-
talk about a tall, regal, white-haired sister makin' the rounds" in Harlem,
he not only knows it is the X-Man Storm but shows up in time to help her

with a group of strung-out teens.[42] And when Steve Rogers—now in the identity of Nomad—searches for the missing Falcon in issue #183 of *Captain America and the Falcon*, he assumes that since Falcon "was beginning to get into black pride," he would've looked for a sympathetic ear, sending Rogers to Luke Cage's Times Square office. He thinks to himself, "Cage's color is a very slim lead, but it's all I can come up with right now!"[43] These comics, then, at the same time that they sought to challenge racism and prejudice via greater representation of blacks, also made it possible to do so and still conceive of them in stereotypical and/or homogenizing ways.

It is with this dual function—being embedded within extant racial attitudes but also promulgating unique conceptions of race and ethnicity—in mind that we approach superhero popular culture, predominantly in the form of comics but also in film and television. That such cultural products are not simply passive receptors or reflections of societal attitudes brings together, say, the competing perspectives represented earlier by Marc Singer and Adilifu Nama. Both lament the presence of stereotypes in superhero comics and popular culture, Singer because it signals the limited ways in which comics have understood race and Nama because it short-circuits a fuller understanding of the medium's and genre's potential. But how comics also help produce such attitudes speaks to the transformative potential of the superhero. If comics can so constitute limited conceptions of race that prevail within US history and culture from World War II to the present, doing so also suggests their ability to do otherwise. With this dual function in mind, then, this book attempts to move the conversation about race and the superhero forward by looking at the big picture as no one has yet. Our focus is multicultural, examining not only constructs of African Americans in superhero popular culture but also Native Americans, Asian Americans, Middle Easterners, and Latinx Americans; likewise, our focus considers not only the "big two" of Marvel and DC but also some lesser-known texts and heroes. But, perhaps most importantly, our approach is to explicate the ways in which the patterns emanating from the constructions—aesthetic, narrative, visual, and so forth—in superhero popular culture since Superman's portentous arrival in 1938 have shaped, both positively and negatively, both consciously and less so, the ways in which Americans think about such issues.

This work thus begins with the birth of the modern superhero in the mid-twentieth century, just as the world was collapsing into war. As American superheroes entered World War II, chapter 1 contends, they focused their attacks on not just a racially caricatured Japanese enemy but a racialized Japanese American foe as well. Paranoia about a presumed

internal threat reinforced and stoked fears about the war abroad to expose just where Americans stood in terms of racial justice at home as they
waged a war, at least in part, against Nazi racism abroad. Superheroes
often viciously battled both Japanese and Japanese Americans, revealing not only a similar paranoia but also its basis in the overdetermined
racist attitudes of both the creators and the broader American public that
underwrote the government's policy of exile and incarceration for Japanese Americans during the war. While some superhero fare attempted to
present a more sympathetic view of Japanese Americans, even such well-
intentioned efforts too often fell victim to stereotypes and racism. The arrival of nonwhite sidekicks in a comic book like *Young Allies* or the Green
Hornet's movie serials did little better, similarly struggling to present a
sympathetic view of racialized minorities as creators struggled to overcome racially determined views of the world. In the end, the superhero
popular culture produced during the so-called "good war" exposed and
promulgated in a highly overdetermined form the hypocrisy of an American war effort that touted freedom and equality but failed to practice
either fully.

While victory in World War II encouraged national confidence, chapter 2
suggests, Americans were soon upset to realize that the postwar world did
not look exactly like they had imagined it would. The rise of the Soviet
Union gave birth to a new kind of conflict—the Cold War—and the external battle with communism raised domestic concerns. One such worry
centered on continued racism and prejudice within the United States, an
increasingly pressing issue in the Cold War calculations of American policy
makers. This chapter explicates—in examining the two major comic book
companies and the fare they produced—a similar ambivalence that belies easy distinctions between DC as conservative and Marvel as groundbreaking. Instead, both companies generally sought safety in reified and
flattened depictions of racialized persons or tales of fantasy far removed
from contemporary worries, and thus unchallenging to the general American populace. But, it should be noted, both also took at least halting steps
toward representing a multicultural American society as well as its challenges; as they did so, superhero popular culture finally undertook a more
sustained focus on the racial challenges presented by a diverse America.

Chapter 3 examines how this emerging focus on issues of race and
equality in superhero popular culture would both become more intentional and yet remain compromised in the decades that followed. Central
to Americans' struggles in the 1960s and 1970s to achieve racial reform
was their insistence on clinging to a faith in the economic and political

structures of the United States, believing that these could ameliorate problems such as individual racism. Grounded in assumptions about the purity of America's institutions, postwar liberalism confronted racism and racial injustice but foundered as a result of its broken ideology. In conjunction, several superhero comics espoused a notion of "brotherhood" via dramatic confrontations between their established white heroes and racialized individuals and situations. At the forefront of this effort toward "relevancy" was DC's *Green Lantern/Green Arrow*, which reflected liberalism's contradictions as the heroes too often confronted racism as a moral issue of the individual conscience, leaving untouched—if not unrepresented—systematic forms of racial discrimination and injustice. Other DC and Marvel comics earnestly asserting this concept of "brotherhood" simultaneously constituted it in contradictory and heavily conditioned ways that ultimately sanction these limits as consistent with this ideal, when in fact they clearly grate against its aims.

In addition to selling "brotherhood," chapter 4 continues, superhero popular culture of the late 1960s and 1970s also strove for inclusion through the introduction of ethnic superheroes. Rising out of various civil rights efforts by African Americans, Chicanos/as, Native Americans, and Asian Americans, comics evidenced a greater awareness of nonwhite persons and communities by creating numerous nonwhite superheroes, including the Black Panther, the Falcon, and Luke Cage at Marvel, as well as Mal Duncan, the Green Lantern John Stewart, and Black Lightning at DC. Later years would see further black, Asian, Native American, and Latinx superheroes and heroines. But grating against the laudatory inclusion of such diverse heroes was the insidious nature of their representation. That the creators of these ethnic superheroes and heroines too often continued to trade in timeworn racial stereotypes and assumptions was often disguised behind the traditional trappings of the superhero genre. As well, comics themselves established reifying associations of their own running amongst and across racial categories, creating a troubling sameness in all these heroes that is similarly all too easy to dismiss as the result of generic tropes.

Chapter 5 examines the ways in which such contradictions plagued comics' efforts to wrestle with race in the era of multiculturalism. The comic book superteam before, throughout, and after the 1980s crystallized the ways in which comics (like multiculturalism) aimed for greater diversity, but did so in problematic ways. Some of these problems result from the way in which the configuration of these teams structured that diversity. Single or "token" nonwhite—and most often black—members added to established teams remained largely marginalized both within the team and literally on the page. Another trend of superhero popular culture in and around the 1980s was the interracial team up or partnership that primarily served a white audience longing for a fantasy of racial equality and harmony; however, the reality of how these partnerships remained hierarchical undermines such pleasing racial imaginings. Finally, super-hero popular culture promulgated a multicultural ethos—and its contra-dictions—in the form of more profoundly diverse superteams at both Marvel and DC, as well as the Saturday morning adventures of the Super Friends. Such teams not only possessed structural problems contradicting such inclusion but also troublingly exoticized and sexualized their ethnic (and often female) characters. As with previous iterations, these patterns paralleled multiculturalism in general, as comics, in their unique and prob-lematic ways, reinforced the very boundaries and divisions between ethni-cities and cultures they were intended to unsettle.

Faced with continuing racism despite such efforts, comic book writers and artists in the 1990s and beyond returned to the drawing board to wrestle anew with this perplexing problem. They did so in part, chap-ter 6 contends, by turning to ethnic replacement heroes. Transforming an established white hero into a nonwhite one seemingly promised a ready-made inclusivity. But carving out authentic and individual niches proved a daunting task for writers and artists, as these heroes' depictions slowly evolved alongside a maturing (if not yet matured, to be sure) national con-versation about race. When these comic books succeeded in such ways, they often did so by subverting inauthentic depictions with coming-of-age stories. Such stories, when told well, allowed for the comic book characters to become more human, moving them beyond the flattened and distanc-ing expectations of race to a more empathetic realm.

Other writers and artists of this era worked to recreate old ethnic heroes in new ways or simply to imagine a whole new universe of super-heroes. Chapter 7 examines how both approaches christened a much more self-conscious exploration and interrogation of comics' racial past. Up-start companies like Image Comics and Milestone Comics, to varying de-grees of success, probed this past in order to less superficially confront and depict race. Back at Marvel and DC, creators in the 1990s and early 2000s went back to the 1970s and updated classic blaxploitation heroes like Black Lightning, Luke Cage, and the Black Panther, rebirthing these heroes by directly engaging with their problematic pasts and thus, at times, tran-scending them. The more successful of these efforts created human and empathetic characters that gestured toward a growing tolerance in the early twenty-first century, albeit a tolerance that continued to betray clear limits.

A closing coda takes up how, in recent years, superhero popular culture, once again mainstream in American culture, has continued to pursue greater diversity. DC and Marvel have made multiple relaunches of their comic lines, often in conscious (if not always thoughtful) response to growing demands for diversity. Superheroes have likewise become plentiful on the small and large screens, where the positive moves and backward steps originally exhibited in comics have persisted. All this has occurred in a social and political context where issues of race (not to mention gender, sexuality, and class) remain flashpoints within US society, and thus the shaping power of this popular culture remains as relevant and complicated as it was when it began.

CHAPTER 1

"World's Finest"? The Wartime Superhero and Race, 1941–1945

The story of superhero popular culture—both in general and in relation to race and ethnicity—began as the world was collapsing into war in the late 1930s. When Superman received a starring role in the debut issue of *Action Comics*, in June 1938, he became an overnight sensation. The series (featuring one Superman story per issue) sold about 900,000 copies per issue, easily eclipsing the industry average. Superman's solo title, which debuted in June 1939, did even better, selling an average of 1.3 million copies per issue. This success allowed DC to expand into other media, too, eventually selling a comic strip to the McClure Syndicate, cutting a deal with Fleischer Studios to make a cartoon version of Superman for the big screen, and launching a radio program.[1] As the Man of Steel rose to superstardom, DC's owners looked for the next big thing, tasking the artist Bob Kane with developing a new superhero. Kane went to work with the writer Bill Finger, and the two created Batman, who debuted in 1939 in *Detective Comics*, a comfortable home for the Dark Knight and his adventures prior to, like Superman before him, headlining his own solo title in the spring of 1940. Perhaps inevitably, given their individual success, Batman and Superman joined forces in 1941, when DC Comics launched *World's Finest*, a ninety-six-page quarterly that presented separate Superman and Batman stories.

This was only the beginning for the rising superhero industry. Led by Superman and Batman, the comic industry was booming by the early 1940s, with sales figures—reaching fifteen million per month—that shocked adults. No printed material on the shelves came close to matching such numbers; "what had been a small corner of the junk culture industry in the summer of 1938, of far less concern than pulps or books or even children's story magazines, had become, in two years, the greatest unifying element of American childhood."² As DC looked to exploit the market, the company released *All Star Comics*, featuring the Justice Society of America (JSA), which included characters such as the Flash, Hawkman, Doctor Fate, the Spectre, Green Lantern, Doctor Mid-Nite, the Atom, Starman, and Sandman; in 1941, a female hero, Wonder Woman, finally debuted and eventually joined the JSA. Other companies, inspired by the money to be made hawking comics to kids, entered the field, too. In 1941, Ace Comics began publishing the adventures of Captain Courageous in various titles, and in 1944 Blazing Comics presented the short-lived exploits of the Green Turtle. Most importantly in the long run, a young pulp publisher named Martin Goodman launched a new comic book company in 1939. While the start-up would appear under a series of at least eight different names (including, among the better known, Timely, Atlas, and, two decades later, Marvel) in an attempt to circumvent tax laws, the new company introduced a host of wartime heroes, most prominently Captain America, created by the writer Joe Simon and the artist Jack Kirby. In 1941, Goodman's company also teamed up a group of teen sidekicks that included Cap's Bucky and the Human Torch's Toro, bringing the youngsters together in *Young Allies*.³

The boom in comic books as the world collapsed into war was not coincidental. Companies connected their superheroes to the war and patriotism for both commercial reasons and a real desire to contribute to the war effort. When the Office of War Information (OWI) requested that entertainment producers conform to government guidelines, comic book companies quickly agreed to work to raise morale, encourage Americans to cooperate with and participate in the war effort, identify the threat of the Axis powers, and educate Americans about their country's war aims. The OWI also asked that the popular media highlight a harmonious melting-pot society in the United States, and publishers were more than happy to oblige this request as well. Pushed along by critics who worried about the effects on children who read such violent, hypersexualized tales, industry leaders were more than ready to indulge a jingoistic patriotism during the war.⁴ In this way, what superheroes accomplished was twofold: they offered their audience exciting tales of violence and destruction but also made that conflict appear manageable and controllable. Not surprisingly, comic book sales climbed further in the early war years, read by not only kids but also US servicemen (with the *New York Times* estimating that one out of every four books shipped to a soldier was a comic book).⁵

Comics creators were similarly invested, joining the war before the United States officially did. This is hardly surprising, given the fact that many of the creators were Jewish liberals who were appalled by the Nazis. Kirby, for example, had Americanized his given name (Jacob Kurtzberg) to express his Americanism. He later recalled how Captain America arose because "the opponents of the war were all quite well organized. We wanted to have our say, too." With his patriotic uniform knit together from the forms and colors of the American flag and his self-sacrificing patriotism, Captain America exemplified the comic book response to the war. Captain America did such a good job of standing up to the Nazis that the German American Bund, a pro-Nazi organization in the United States, organized a large hate-mail campaign against the comic book. The group also made obscene and threatening phone calls to the publisher. One threat was deemed serious enough for the staff to receive police protection. A new genre of jungle comics also appeared, warning that the Allied empires were often the first line of defense against Axis aggression, and Will Eisner was soon suggesting in "Espionage" (a story that appeared in *Smash Comics*) that the threat was creeping ever closer to American shores.[6]

Across his media incarnations, Superman more tentatively engaged the conflict, doing so most prominently on the covers of his comic books, which became newsstand posters encouraging the purchase of war bonds and stoking patriotic pride. Inside, the comics rarely engaged the war. When they did, the stories took absurd twists. One comic strip, for example, saw Superman saving Santa Claus from the clutches of Hitler, Mussolini, and Hirohito. (Santa, after his rescue, delivers an empty box to Adolf!) Another adventure, told before the Nazi invasion of the Soviet Union transformed the latter into an American ally, featured Superman arresting Hitler and Stalin for their crimes.[7]

Part of how comics hoped to combat the Axis menace was by calling for inclusion, as the OWI had requested. The JSA, for example, warned that the Nazis hoped to exploit class and ethnic divisions in the United States. As the comic reminded readers in one issue, "the United States is a great melting pot, into which other races are poured—a pot which converts all of us into one big nation!" That story concluded with a simple message for Hitler: "You can't beat that combination, Adolf. . . . It's too strong!" A Golden Age Green Lantern story, "A Tale of a City," promulgated a similar message; it opened with the hero "sponsoring a multicultural Christmas radio program, which features a chorus made up of children of different races and ethnic groups." They are interrupted by a rude, elderly, and obviously ignorant woman who says that they should not celebrate Christmas because "they ain't all real white 100% Americans [because their] color is wrong and their religion is wrong and most of them is foreigners anyway."

Green Lantern angrily responds, "How dare you talk like that in America! You're a fool! And there are many fools in America who think like you!" In this exchange, the comic both communicated an inclusive vision of US society while also checking those that might not share it.[8]

Such sentiments as those expressed by the JSA and Green Lantern, however, would prove more the exception than the rule governing wartime superhero popular culture. Alongside such affirmative and inclusive visions of American identity and culture, a comic book industry dominated by immigrants and ethnically marginalized Americans produced far more superhero adventures that fed into a racialized wartime hysteria and buttressed notions of white American superiority. The relationship between white superheroes and racialized minorities thus exposes the vexed nature of an American wartime liberalism that often touted freedom and equality but failed to practice either fully at home.

Americans, Race, and World War II

While developments during World War II led some Americans to see a high tide for racial equality, others saw such optimism as little more than national self-delusion; whatever one's position, the debate suggests the complicated relationship between wartime liberalism and race. Those understanding a more progressive version of wartime race relations, John W. Jeffries argues, now talked about America's multiethnic makeup as an orchestra or a salad, with each ethnic group contributing to the larger whole but now no longer assumed to assimilate as "100% Americans." These new ideas reflected a belief that Americans benefited from such differences, as well as the tolerance requisite for such appreciation. These new theories of American identity and unity allowed, it would seem, each group to retain an ethnic identity while also being part of the national whole. This more inclusive identity manifested on the big screen in a host of war films that featured multicultural platoons. Indeed, Jeffries writes, "Every squad and every ship's compartment, so it has seemed in memory and the movies, had someone named Kelly, and Goldstein, and Kowalski, and Jones, someone named Tonelli, and Larsen, and Sanchez, and Schmidt, perhaps even an Indian called 'chief'—Americans all, from Brooklyn and Dixie and from all across the land, joined in common cause."[9] Such inclusion was mirrored in the language of countless wartime laws passed by Congress that promoted equality while prohibiting discrimination.[10]

A more complicated reality, however, revealed the clear limits of attempts to achieve such high-flown inclusive ideals. As Roger Daniels has argued, important contradictions existed between these lofty liberal goals and the methods with which the American government waged war, contradictions made clear by the treatment of African Americans and Japanese Americans. While Daniels notes that the war would eventually generate progress toward civil rights, it accomplished little in and of itself that was significant and lasting. Wendy Wall agrees with Daniels that the wartime promotion of tolerance was limited; she argues that due to a linking of tolerance and unity that allowed for the condemnation of bigots but not the critique of federal policies or entrenched power structures, "the promise of the wartime discourse on pluralism and consensus was limited when it came to the nation's racial minorities—particularly Japanese Americans and blacks." Indeed, she contends, in many cases those pushing for racial equality "were dismissed as troublemakers, traitors to an 'American Way' that often put civility and social harmony above all else."[11] Even Jeffries, though a bit more open to the idea of important wartime change, cites any number of examples that belie a total transformation in racial attitudes. For some groups—he notes specifically Polish Americans, Mexican Americans, Native Americans, and Jewish Americans—important progress seems to have occurred. None, however, saw only triumphs during the war; instead, most struggled with mixed results that derived naturally from vexed American attitudes about race.[12]

Shortcomings involving racial equality thus affected a wide range of groups, but a brief discussion of Japanese Americans and African Americans in particular helps to set the general wartime atmosphere, in all its complexity. Japanese Americans found themselves racially defined as a threat to their fellow Americans and their country.[13] After the Japanese attack on Pearl Harbor, panic and fear gripped the American public, and on the West Coast that panic and fear focused on Japanese Americans. The Federal Bureau of Investigation immediately rounded up about 2,200 Issei (or first-generation Japanese Americans) whom it deemed suspicious. But these arrests did not calm pressure for further action, and calls for a more draconian program echoed throughout the media, western statehouses, and the broader public.[14] Critics of Japanese Americans eventually found General John L. DeWitt, commander of the Western Defense Command, receptive to their pleas. DeWitt advocated American concentration camps based on explicitly racist reasoning in defining the American enemy, explaining that "[a] Jap is a Jap. . . . It makes no difference whether he is an American citizen, he is still Japanese."[15]

On February 19, 1942, President Roosevelt signed Executive Order

9066, which allowed the government to forcibly exile all Japanese Americans living on the West Coast and then incarcerate them in ten concentration camps run by the War Relocation Authority (WRA). The government's decision, it should be noted, ran counter to reports from the FBI, the Office of Naval Intelligence, and others that doubted the necessity of incarcerating about 120,000 Japanese Americans (two-thirds of them native-born American citizens; the other one-third were denied citizenship by American law). The government moved ahead anyhow, grounding its actions, according to a later government report, in wartime hysteria, racism, economic competition, and early Japanese victories in the Pacific theater. The presidential order did not name Japanese Americans specifically, but DeWitt targeted only them.[16] While the government quickly abandoned the term "concentration camp" in describing these detention facilities, euphemisms should not mask the unpleasant reality that Japanese Americans now faced: incarceration behind barbed wire.

While African Americans did not face exile and incarceration during the war, failures in racial democracy—chief among them continuing segregation and job discrimination, especially in expanding defense industries—were all too apparent. The union leader and racial activist A. Philip Randolph, for example, planned a march on Washington to protest such discrimination, knowing that Roosevelt wanted to avoid the embarrassment it would bring. Leveraging the president's desire to assert moral leadership abroad, Randolph won important concessions from the White House, although not civil rights legislation, which both men knew had no hope of passing Congress. In return for Randolph calling off the march, Roosevelt, on June 25, 1941, issued Executive Order 8802, the first time the US government put forth a policy of nondiscrimination in employment. The executive order also created the Fair Employment Practices Committee. While an important symbol, to be sure, the committee had only the power of "moral suasion" and, as a result, often faced intractable resistance from employers, unions, and laborers. Ultimately, some jobs were opened to African Americans in this way, but often such gains were only "of a token variety."[17]

Outside of employment, African Americans faced a host of other wartime issues not unfamiliar to American history. The military, no matter how much Hollywood tried to wish the problem away, remained segregated throughout the war. At home, frustrations rooted in the African American exodus from the South that generated increasing competition for jobs and scarce urban housing exploded into a series of race riots, the most significant of which occurred in New York City and Detroit. In response to such maltreatment, some black newspaper editors organized what they called the "Double V" campaign, which suggested the need to win a war not only abroad but also at home. This campaign was loud enough to concern the president, who asked his Justice Department to initiate conversations, but only concerning how to curb their efforts.[18]

Superhero popular culture worked within this racially contested atmosphere throughout the war. On the one hand, it reflected and helped to propagate lofty liberal ideals that suggested a society moving toward inclusion and an increasing appreciation of diversity. In this way, it could be just as high-minded as the most optimistic celebrant of acceptance. On the other hand, superheroes far more often revealed and helped to reinforce racist reasoning and outlooks that undermined the best of intentions. Superhero popular culture presented a series of arguments that supported the exile and incarceration of Japanese Americans and, in the arguments' prevalence, reveal the comics creators' wartime paranoia about Japanese and Japanese Americans as overdetermined. And even as superhero popular culture sought to reflect a more inclusive society via the use of ethnic characters and sidekicks from a range of backgrounds, it did so in ways that reinforced and thus left functioning notions of white American superiority. Ultimately, these denizens of the funny pages and screen exposed and furthered the complicated and contradictory relationship between American liberalism and race during World War II.

Profiling a Racialized Enemy: Superhero Popular Culture and Japanese Americans

Whatever the best intentions of the OWI and comic book industry leaders, American superhero popular culture, particularly following the Japanese attack on Pearl Harbor on December 7, 1941, was more often hateful than idealistic in its treatment of Japanese Americans. The comic book writer Roy Thomas, reminiscing about the Golden Age of comics during which the superhero "really came into his own," notes that while some comic books provided Americans with hope after Pearl Harbor, racism also seeped into these adventures, leaving us, if we choose, to "wrangle endlessly with 20-20 hindsight over how reprehensible (or forgivable) . . . references . . . to 'Japs'" were. But the ramifications of superhero popular culture's depiction of Japanese and Japanese Americans exceed what Thomas laments here. For, on both page and screen, the creators of this period unleashed a torrent of starkly stereotyped and thus demeaning depictions of this racialized enemy in what came to be presented as a battle of "good versus evil—America versus Japan!"[19]

Such problematic depictions began with the erasure of any distinction between Japanese and Japanese Americans. The stark presentation of a clash between good and evil in the Pacific left little room for nuance regarding Japanese Americans, despite those widely held aspirations of an inclusive unity at home. Indeed, comic representations of Japanese Americans, even those attempting to toe the government's line on distinguishing between Japanese and Japanese Americans, most often blurred any discernible difference between the overseas enemy and Japanese Americans via a crude racial profiling that marked anyone of Japanese descent as suspect. In the summer of 1943, for instance, the *Superman* newspaper comic strip ran a story line that saw its titular hero visit Camp Carok, an American concentration camp, and thwart Japanese and Japanese American attacks. In doing so, the strip displayed the power of profiling by focusing on teeming hordes of disloyal Japanese Americans working in close connection with Japanese villains, suggesting that all Japanese Americans were disloyal, a reality highlighted when Lois Lane echoed the WRA's oft-repeated mistake of equating the locked-up Japanese Americans with prisoners of war.[20] Only at the very end of this story would the strip attempt to distinguish loyal Japanese Americans. In the last panel of the story arc, Superman directly addresses the reader. "It should be remembered," the Man of Steel intones, "that most Japanese Americans are loyal citizens." Reciting the standard WRA message, Superman informs readers that Japanese Americans were serving in the military and working in factories. In addition, Japanese Americans had committed no single act of sabotage.[21] While such a message might have made it easier for all involved to sleep at night, the story line leading to it hardly supported such a conclusion. Indeed, in the two months between the introductory and concluding panels, the story line failed to present even one loyal Japanese American.

The ubiquitous use of "Japs"—the universal wartime racial epithet that blotted out any difference between Japanese and Japanese Americans—in superhero popular culture provided another means of obliterating such distinctions. In 1942's "Japoteurs," an episode of the Superman animated serial produced by Fleischer Studios, Lois radios for help after a superbomber has been hijacked by Japanese Americans, whom she bluntly labels "Japs." In the opening strip for the Man of Steel's adventure at Camp Carok, to cite another example, the epithet was used to refer to all who lived in "a typical Jap relocation camp" because, the military guide explains, it is difficult to distinguish between "loyal Americans of Jap ancestry [who] are indiscriminately mingled with enemy sympathizers who would be glad to sabotage our national welfare at the first opportunity," and Japanese, who were represented by "the Jap government."[22] Underlying the racist term was a racial connection that made all Japanese—even native-born American citizens—suspect. The 1943 Batman serial used the racial epithet to similar effect, often referring to Japanese Americans as "sinister Jap" spies as the Dynamic Duo took on a Japanese American saboteur, Daka. In one scene, a kidnapped white woman can only exclaim, in shock and horror upon meeting Daka, "A Jap!"[23]

Consequently, Japanese Americans appeared on the comic page and movie screen as essentially Japanese and, as a result, disloyal. Such disloyalty added another dimension to what superhero popular culture taught its audience about this racialized foe. This unrealistic fear had been stoked by high-ranking government officials. Perhaps most famously, in the months after Pearl Harbor, California Attorney General Earl Warren warned that the Pacific coast presented an inviting target for Japan and, also, that the absence of Japanese American sabotage to that point provided convincing (though counterintuitive in retrospect) evidence of a well-coordinated plan for widespread subversion when the "zero hour" arrived. "To assume that the enemy has not planned fifth column activities for us in a wave of sabotage," he told a congressional committee, "is simply to live in a fool's paradise." Such attitudes placed Japanese Americans in a catch-22 position, their loyal actions serving only as further proof of their disloyalty.[24]

Superhero popular culture took up this theme and ran with it, not only repeating but exacerbating the myth of a traitorous and well-organized Japanese American enemy. The narrator in *Young Allies* #3 warns readers that "even in this great land which is America, sinister forces are loose, seeking to destroy the freedom we so cherish!"[25] The Black Dragon Society, featured in much of American popular culture and highlighted in the Justice Society of America's wartime adventures, became a well-known example of such alleged Japanese American perfidy. In *All Star Comics* #12, for example, members of the JSA go to war with the Black Dragon Society, which was, in the dehumanizing words of Roy Thomas well after the fact, "spreading its evil tentacles abroad."[26] The 1942 comic book describes how the evil society, with its "fanatical assassins and spies," holds Japan in thrall, just as it hopes to conquer the Pacific. The Black Dragon Society, the narrator later warns, has "fanatical members . . . scattered throughout the world, ready to strike and kill at [its] bidding."[27]

Such well-organized and disloyal efforts took forms other than the Black Dragon Society. Superman confronted a similar problem in the funny pages when Lois and Clark discover "serious trouble" at Camp Carok. Superman quickly realizes that the imprisoned Japanese Americans "couldn't have received their weapons without outside help," suggesting widespread plans as well as a support network. Later, the villainous Sneer orders all of his numerous Japanese American henchmen to speak in English, explaining, "If we are to conquer this country we must understand its language and customs well."[28] Batman also found himself facing down not just the violence-crazed Daka but the villain's League of the New Order, comprised of "dishonored" white men who now worked for the Japanese American traitor. The league, it turned out, represented a wide and very tightly organized conspiracy (the existence of "Section 50" suggesting at least forty-nine other such groups), with multitudinous plans to wreak havoc.[29]

Superman's and Batman's adventures reinforced this widely broadcasted image of Japanese American disloyalty by tying it to a feigned patriotism, making their treachery all the more malevolent. The cartoon "Japoteurs," a tale of Japanese American subversion and sabotage, made this point clearly as it opened by presenting newspaper coverage of the test flight of the "world's largest bombing plane." The camera then pans to a Japanese American saboteur in his office, focusing eventually on a picture on the wall that drives home Attorney General Warren's concerns about the untrustworthiness of Japanese Americans. In the light of day and for all to see, the poster presents the Statue of Liberty, an apparent sign of the saboteur's assimilation and even his celebration of American ideals. By night, however, and hidden behind drawn blinds, the image shifts, the rising sun replacing the Statue of Liberty and revealing the Japanese American's true, and most assuredly disloyal, intentions.[30] The *Superman* comic strip reinforced this familiar message while the Man of Steel is undercover at a villainous meeting. When a gong sounds, many of the seemingly "white" men in the room pull off plastic masks to reveal that they are really Japanese Americans.[31] The *Batman* serial also showed how patriotism masked foul intentions when the barker outside the Cave of Horrors run by the Japanese American villain lures people in by talking about kicking in tax monies to support Uncle Sam's war.[32]

In depicting what were portrayed as well-established patterns of disloyalty, superhero popular culture taught its consumers that one simply could not trust Japanese Americans to mean what they said. In the *Batman* serial, the aforementioned barker for the Cave of Horrors—a front for Japanese American perfidy—demonstrated this lesson clearly. He sells the show as a "patriotic duty" by arguing that seeing the grisly reality of the enemy will help the United States win the war. Ratcheting the jingois-tic rhetoric ever higher, he urges passersby to see why the United States is fighting and encourages "every man, woman, and child [to] aid in this war effort." Daka likewise embodies a more generalized duplicity, often say-ing things he clearly doesn't mean. Whenever he apologizes with a stilted "so sorry," for example, viewers understood his treacherous sarcasm. The villain's oh-so-polite references to "Miss Page" (Bruce Wayne's girlfriend, Linda) likewise plainly (if poorly) masked his malevolent intentions for her and her country.[33] Superman faced similar challenges in his cartoon adventure when the Japanese American saboteur negotiates with the kid-napped Lois as his collateral. Although Superman meets his enemy's con-ditions, the Japanese American — as all in theaters must have expected — drops Lois to her seeming death anyway (although Superman does, of course, rescue her in the nick of time before doling out a well-deserved beating to her captor).[34]

Much of World War II–era superhero fare further reinforced the dan-gers that Japanese Americans allegedly presented by casting them as a racialized threat. One dimension of this threat was their being wholly "other," a dimension often signaled by various framing devices. Through mise-en-scène framing, for example, "Japoteurs" immediately suggests this danger, its title frame, with bamboo-style lettering, announcing their menacing difference, a message reinforced by the ominous, clashing gongs that begin the episode.[35] Captain America's wartime adventures framed a similarly threatening internal presence when the star-spangled adven-turer has to journey to "the mysterious Oriental section of the city."[36] The wartime *Batman* serial did the same by presenting an abandoned Japa-nese American neighborhood. Here, cameras panned across a run-down version of a "Japantown," filled with Japanese-language signs as well as abandoned shops that suggest poverty, filth, and danger. The narra-tor pressed the point, lest any viewers miss it: "This was part of a foreign land, transplanted bodily to America and known as Little Tokyo. Since a wise government rounded up the shifty-eyed Japs it has become virtually a ghost street, where only one business survives, eking out a precarious existence on the dimes of curiosity seekers." Clearly endorsing exile and in-carceration as a security measure against scheming Japanese Americans, the serial hinted ominously of danger in the one remaining business, the "Cave of Horrors" run by a saké-swilling, traitorous Japanese American: the aforementioned villain of the piece, Daka.[37]

This Cave of Horrors crystallized both the disloyalty and the otherness that superhero popular culture overemphasized during the war. Daka's exhibit seemed a patriotic tourist attraction, promising "one thousand shocks" for a mere ten cents, plus an additional penny for Uncle Sam. Hidden behind such false patriotism, the cave was ominous. Those brave enough to tour the cave saw a bright pair of animalistic eyes peering at them out of the darkness. Customers then strolled through a wax-statue history of atrocities, starting in the present with Japanese soldiers armed with bayonets forcing a white soldier to dig a hole, then threatening a well-dressed white woman, and finally harassing a white soldier imprisoned in a tiny, inhumane cage. The tour ended with a caveman standing over the lifeless body of another that he had just clubbed to death, presenting a direct comparision of the Japanese enemy to violent, prehistoric man. Just past the caveman, a hidden door led to the villain's headquarters. The path to Daka's lair thus literalized these twin tropes of the Japanese American threat: allusions to Japanese and Japanese Americans as perpetrators of wartime atrocities who hide behind a carefully constructed veneer of faked 110-percent patriotism and as wholly unlike the white American viewer.[38]

This framing of Japanese and Japanese American "otherness" did not end with the Cave of Horrors, nor in fact with the *Batman* serial. Daka's actual headquarters is decorated in a heavy-handed "Oriental" style that belies his faked patriotism and loyalty. A huge Buddha-like statue looms over the room, which is filled with smoking incense to heighten its foreignness. In a separate hideout—the foreign-sounding Sphinx Club—Daka likewise surrounds himself with burning incense, "Oriental" screens, and another huge golden statue. Similar framing appears in the comic strips, as Superman traces the plotting of Japanese Americans in Camp Carok to "a large Oriental rug establishment" in a nearby city. This headquarters, much like Daka's, emphasizes the un-American qualities of its inhabitants: the rising sun dominates the back wall, and the entire lair is covered in very foreign-looking Japanese script.[39]

Inhabiting such racialized spaces were racialized bodies that had long existed in the popular American imagination and that comics likewise deployed. Representations of Asians in popular culture had, from the start, presented derogatory and limiting images. As Robert G. Lee has shown, public displays of an exoticized China and its people were popular in the United States as early as the late eighteenth century. In 1784, for example, the Peale Museum featured weapons, utensils, and a feet-binding display in its Chinese exhibit. By the turn of the century, various museums added clay and wax Chinese figures to such displays, making Chinese individuals a part of these curiosities. None other than the master showman P. T. Barnum himself popularized Ah Fong Moy, a Chinese woman "always robed

in resplendent silks and often seated among luxurious Chinese furnishings," at his own American Museum starting in 1834.[40] Twentieth-century
popular culture carried such images forward, with Hollywood productions
featuring the villainous Fu Manchu. Comics like *Flash Gordon* and *Terry
and the Pirates* reiterated this danger from the East in presenting characters like Ming the Merciless and the Dragon Lady that traded in such
timeworn tropes.[41]

The foundational creators of the nascent superhero popular culture
drew on the power of such tropes. Superman's creators, Jerry Siegel and
Joe Shuster, had dabbled in such types before striking it big with the Man
of Steel. As a child, Siegel had been drawn to pulp magazines, which featured threatening "Orientals" alongside gangsters and alluring ladies.[42]
One of Siegel's early stories (dating to January 1933) included a scene
where — in the racially loaded language of the day — a "Chinaman and Jap,"
among others, are transformed into "hate-filled wolves" who attack each
other. Siegel and Shuster fully embraced anti-Asian racism in a 1937 issue
of *Detective Comics* that included their Slam Bradley, the epitome of white
courage and strength, taking on "a horde of evil Chinese." The hero takes
on the revealingly named Fui Onyui, at one point flinging the sinister villain about "by the end of his pigtail." Slam later takes the battle into "a hidden catacomb under the streets of Chinatown," where he mixes it up "with
a mob of Celestials." Throughout, Joe Shuster's artwork expressed "absurd
glee in the image of Slam whipping identical, ball-headed Chinese stereotypes through the air by their preposterously long queues."[43]

Siegel and Shuster, second-generation Jewish immigrants from the
lower middle class, have often been lauded for bringing their ethnicity to
Superman in positive ways that turned the Man of Steel into "an allegory
that echoed for immigrants and Jews; the strange visitor who hides his
alien identity so as to be accepted by a homogenous culture."[44] But their
ethnic background also seems to have predisposed Siegel and Shuster to
a competitive perspective toward other ethnic groups. In this way, Superman's vicious war against Japanese Americans might have represented, at
least in part, an attempt by Siegel and Shuster to stake a claim to being
"100% Americans," for both themselves and their immigrant community.

In doing so, Superman's creators reflected a history in which new immigrants from different countries often found themselves pitted against
each other as well as immigrants who had arrived a few generations before. Many recently established groups saw advancement as requiring outcompeting and even oppressing others. Fitting in, it turned out,
often meant adopting nativist attitudes that connoted an "insider" status.

Ronald Takaki has summarized this story in the historical experiences of Irish Americans and African Americans. Although the two groups initially existed in a similar social sphere—carved out by white attitudes that painted both groups as savage, less than human, unintelligent, unruly, and more—Irish immigrants often quickly adopted antiblack attitudes. Forced to start at the lowest forms of work, Irish newcomers won jobs, in part, by playing up their "whiteness" in contrast to African Americans. As Takaki sums up, the Irish, under attack by nativists as aliens, worked to assume an insider status by staking a claim to whiteness while simultaneously attacking African Americans, in the process transforming themselves into Americans.[45]

Given the deep roots of anti-Asian images and ethnic competition, it is hardly surprising that wartime comics also emphasized the racial difference of Japanese Americans through their appearance. Superman most explicitly did so in the funny pages when he needed to infiltrate a gang of conniving Japanese Americans. To accomplish his mission, Superman, with "the aid of his amazing muscular control," transforms himself from a valorous, square-jawed white hero into an untrustworthy, squinty-eyed, yellow villain. His racist transformation complete, the Man of Steel even takes on a Japanese accent, proudly declaring, "It's easy—to make myself—look like a Jap. Take a-lookie at the new Watasuki!"[46] Likewise, in "Japoteurs," the villain's treachery is made clear from the start by his buckteeth, thick glasses, and Fu Manchu mustache.[47]

In addition to physical appearance, superhero popular culture set Japanese Americans off as different and dangerous by playing up audio cues or signifiers. In the *Batman* serial, Daka giggles malevolently when he considers feeding white Americans to his pet crocodiles. Batman later senses Daka's "otherness" over the telephone, describing his "strange voice" to Robin. When Daka is mistaken for part of the Cave of Horrors, uncomprehending tourists mock his strange accent.[48] The "other's" accent also revealed evil intentions. In "Japoteurs," for example, the Japanese American saboteur utters incomplete sentences in a thick, almost indecipherable accent, revealing his subversive plans in choppy sentences. "Hehehe," he cackles awkwardly at one point as he prepares to steal a new American superbomber, adding that "well-placed bomb will stop pursuit." Japanese Americans in the *Superman* strip sound almost exactly the same, repeatedly mangling the English language and stiltedly exclaiming things like, "Honorable eyes must be lying!"[49] Captain America's comic book adventures, unable to rely on audio cues, made do as best they could by placing putatively Japanese symbols next to the villain's words, reinforcing the baddie's otherness.[50]

Alongside the threat their wholly different natures presented, Japanese and Japanese Americans were also bluntly described and visualized as sub-human. References to them as "yellow" were a clear giveaway of their difference. Thus, Starman went off to battle "yellow men," among the most innocuous example of such language. A kidnapped inventor ratchets the racist rhetoric higher, referring to his assailants as "yellow babies!" In another JSA story featuring the Sandman, a captured scientist refers to an enemy as a "yellow bully!" Later in that same issue of *All Star Comics*, the Spectre describes the Japanese as "yellow punks." To these were added near-constant references to Japanese and Japanese Americans as animals. As Japanese bombers attack a defenseless Filipino hospital in *All Star Comics*, one doctor describes the enemy as "inhuman beasts," a motif repeated seemingly endlessly during the war. Doctor Fate later identifies the enemy as "buzzards," while Wonder Woman commands, "Come along little yellow doggie!" The Spectre employed a comparison to sharks instead, describing Japanese as their "human cousins."[51] In the newspaper strip, Superman uses terms like "rats" and "skunk" to belittle his opponents,[52] and the *Batman* serial did much the same, noting in its opening that its heroes would respond wherever crime might raise its head like "a maddened rattlesnake."[53]

Working hand in hand with these descriptions was the dehumanized visual depiction of Japanese and Japanese Americans across wartime superhero popular culture. The Justice Society confronted an enemy presented in these terms. In one adventure, Doctor Fate battles Japanese soldiers that bare large, almost horselike teeth. In another, a profile presents an enemy more apelike than human, a distended jaw jutting forward to highlight his simian features. Later in the same issue, the JSA's Spectre pursues a racialized group of enemies. Aboard a submarine, an angry, porcine interrogator promises a kidnapped inventor that if he fails to cooperate, his assailants will treat him so badly that "death [will] seem a pleasure!"[54] When Captain America takes on the League of the Unicorn — which has emerged from "the dark recesses of barbarian Japan," intending to "kill and torture [and] play havoc with human lives"—the villains are just as dehumanized: their demonic leader (who turns out to be a white man in disguise at the story's end) possesses huge fangs, bulging, bloodshot eyes, and a unicorn-like horn protruding from his forehead. The cover of issue #13 featured a larger-than-life enemy, wearing thick glasses while sporting a scraggly mustache and clawlike hands. Later in the issue, the leader, King Unicorn Zong, looks like a vampire, a barely human monster craving always more and more white blood. Cap also has to battle a "powerful giant" Japanese foe who looks more apelike than human.[55] Star-

Figure 1.1. The Young Allies went to war against a clearly dehumanized enemy meant to intimidate and even terrify young (as well as not so young) readers. As the bat-like enemy lunges at the reader, his loathsomeness is clearly displayed, calling readers to support a war effort meant to protect Americans from such despicable enemies.

man went to battle against a clearly subhuman lot; in one panel, they are shrouded in shadows, with simian skulls, buckteeth, and clawlike hands. In that same issue, the Atom faced similarly styled villains when confronting an advancing horde of soldiers in the jungles of the Pacific theater. In one panel, the enemy flees from American forces, looking more like cats than human beings. In another, the hero smashes together two apelike skulls.[56]

This emphasis on the enemy as animals carried on when the best-known sidekicks of the wartime era teamed up in the *Young Allies* series. While many illustrations of the enemy might be analyzed, one particularly startling example depicts a Japanese soldier as bat-like, with pointy ears and sharp fangs, lunging out of the panel directly at the reader, creating a sharp sense of fear and loathing. In another, the enemy sports a Fu Manchu mustache on a leering, apelike face that brandishes fangs.[57] The Young Allies reinforced such images by referring to the enemy as "rats." In an even more striking example that combined the typical cave-like hideouts of the enemy with their animalistic nature, the Young Allies stumble across a huge, "secret pipe of disaster" that funnels Japanese soldiers into Alaska. As the enemy troops emerge in the continental United States, a Young Ally screams, "Greetings Mole — get back in your hole!"[58]

Furthering the references to these racialized enemies as subhuman were descriptions and depictions of them as devils or demons. Batman, for example, upon discovering that Daka has kidnapped a white woman, exclaims, "Why you Jap devil!" The serial narrator reinforces this point, wondering, "What deviltry does [Daka] plan?"[59] These comparisons were often delivered ironically by the enemy, too, whose constant references to superheroes as "devils" could only have provoked skepticism on the part of consumers. When Hawkman confronts a planned invasion of the United States, he attacks a Japanese soldier, who screams in fear, "Eaagh—a devil man is after us!"[60] Given the context of the comic and the war, readers understood very well who the devil actually was: the racialized enemy. The motif was repeated in the *Batman* serial, when, after our hero has escaped one of Daka's traps, the villain says that Batman is either a "magician" or a "devil," once again reflecting the accusations back upon the accuser.[61] The same pattern appeared in Superman's comic strip as, for example, a Japanese soldier who is being pursued by the Man of Steel warns, "That demon is overtaking us"; certainly, no American during the war saw Batman or Superman as the "demon" in these scenes.[62] Captain America's creators engaged in similar rhetorical strategies that reflected accusations back upon the Japanese enemy. In his battle with the League of the Unicorn, Cap confronts Zong, who refers to our hero as a "devil," although readers clearly understood Zong to be the true source of evil in the tale.[63]

The pervasive depiction of the Japanese enemy as hyperviolent added yet another dimension to the overdetermined threat they represented. As Superman sarcastically explains while Japanese American thugs try to take him out in a hail of gunfire, the traitors are "downright generous with [their] bullets." His opponents do little to contradict the Man of Steel's judgment, with one threatening to "cut [him] to ribbons!"[64] On the silver screen, Batman faced a similar foe who raged and lusted for violence. Daka berates his underlings and giggles at the thought of inflicting violence on whites during an attempted train bombing, gleefully asking, "How many were killed?" Daka is also content to learn that his own men have suffered death, a "small price" to pay for defeating (he mistakenly thinks) Batman and Robin.[65] King Unicorn Zong, when confronting Captain America, is much the same. When one intended victim does not immediately perish, Zong orders his followers, "Finish him . . . with torture!" When he later plots to wreck a train carrying Chinese royalty, Zong celebrates the deaths of all on the train, demonstrating his lack of regard for human life.[66] All of these racialized villains loved mayhem, death, and violence—for some, the more exotic the better: Daka, for instance, favors feeding white victims to his voracious crocodiles and murders more creatively when necessary, describing his specially made "Medusa" cigarettes as "a special brand" designed to off a potential squealer in his jail cell before he can turn state's evidence.[67]

And, when things go bad, the enemy's love for violence and disregard for human life could lead to suicide tactics. In the *Superman* comic strip, for instance, a flashback shows the Japanese villain, the Leer, having failed in his mission to sabotage the United States, committing suicide with "the laughing death."[68] The Japanese propensity for suicide also suggested their ability to make weapons of themselves. In "Japoteurs," the villain, realizing that he will never get the stolen superbomber to Japan, sabotages the control panel, leaving the plane and himself to plummet toward a densely packed city.[69] The violent Japanese and Japanese Americans are also willing to sacrifice the lives of their compatriots when necessary in suicide attacks. Daka again has no qualms about sacrificing his servants' lives for the greater cause, for example when ordering one to jump senselessly to his death during a rooftop brawl with Batman and Robin.[70]

The combination of a propensity for violence and a widely presented fake loyalty ultimately resulted in broad fears of Japanese American treachery, yet another theme, and one easily enough derived from what many Americans understood to be the Japanese sneak attack on Pearl Harbor. Comic books occasionally made clear reference to the attack. The Justice Society of America, for example, went to war after "a treacherous, sly attack upon the Pearl Harbor naval base by Japanese bombers." Much like all Americans, the narrator continues, the heroes responded to "the savage challenge" with "righteous indignation" as they demanded "their chance to fight for the country they love best." To emphasize the treachery of the attack on Pearl Harbor, Hawkman later responds to "a smashing Jap raid [that demolished] many planes!"[71] *Captain America* presents the message as directly as possible in issue #13, the cover sporting a "Remember Pearl Harbor" logo and promising that this was an "All Out for America Issue!" The cover art featured Cap punching out a Japanese general as he exclaims, in a broadly shared public sentiment, "You started it! Now—we'll finish it!"[72] Clearly, Pearl Harbor was not forgotten.

The motif of treachery also played out in allegorical stories featuring Superman, a well-understood stand-in for America. Throughout his wartime adventures, Superman faced an onslaught of sneak attacks that symbolized not only Japanese evildoing but also American resilience. Japanese American traitors attack Superman from behind in "Japoteurs," seemingly seeing this as the only way to overcome his prodigious might.

Figure 1.2. Sneak attacks were ubiquitous in wartime superhero popular culture, making clear references to Pearl Harbor and a broadly understood propensity in Japanese and Japanese Americans for treacherous violence. Here, Doctor Mid-Nite not only points out such treachery but also contrasts it to a sense of "fair play" in the United States.

Similar attacks happen throughout the comic strip as well, with one particularly bloodthirsty attack aimed at slicing open the hero's throat with a circular saw (an ineffectual attack, it turns out, on a man as strong as steel). In another clear parallel to Pearl Harbor, even a short-term success on the part of Japanese Americans has little long-term effect. In one case, Japanese Americans spring a surprise attack on Superman at Camp Carok, burying the Man of Steel under a pile of scrap wood. Although the villains brag, "Behold the highly vaunted Superman falls victim to Japanese ingenuity," they are dead wrong in asserting that this is only "added proof that America is destined to become a vassal state of Japan!"[73] Instead, Superman quickly dusts himself off and moves on to rooting out the large conspiracy.

Superhero popular culture replayed racialized treachery in the form of sneak attacks against other white heroes, too. As Doctor Mid-Nite explains upon observing a Japanese soldier attacking an American infantryman from behind, this is "their favorite sneak play!" Springing into action, Doctor Mid-Nite chastises the attacker, demeaningly lecturing, "Here, little fellow! You mustn't play like that!" This theme was then rehashed throughout the JSA's battles against the Japanese American enemy, with attack after attack being launched in sneaky ways.[74] Batman faced a similarly deceit-ful foe in Daka, who uses a trapdoor in his headquarters' floor to send un-suspecting victims to their deaths in the jaws of his pet crocodiles. Timely Comics presented a familiar treacherous threat to Captain America and his sidekick Bucky. The opening scene of their battle against the League of the Unicorn presented a full-page splash featuring a demonic enemy hold-ing a hatchet to Bucky's throat. As Cap sprints to his sidekick's rescue, a line of horned Japanese thugs approaches him from behind, clearly har-boring the most malevolent intentions. The second page drives the point home as viewers watch as what our heroes call an "Oriental," who refuses to join the nefarious league, flees in terror, only to be stabbed in the back by an operative wearing a horned helmet. As Cap and Bucky arrive, at-tempting (too late, it turns out) to save the life of the victim, another gang member charges Captain America from behind, but our hero pivots, and the menacing horn shatters on his shield.[75] Like Superman, too, these superheroes ultimately triumph over such nefarious methods.

Besides such manufactured treachery, wartime superhero popular cul-ture also played on Americans' perceptions of the Japanese and Japa-nese Americans as a very real threat to the continental United States. When Superman eavesdrops on the Sneer, for example, readers of the funny pages learned that a soon-to-come attack on American troops in the southern Pacific "will forerun the actual invasion of America itself!"[76] Such an attack, of course, would begin on the Pacific coast, and *All Star Comics* #11 ominously depicted "crowded [Japanese] troopships near the West Coast," with the enemy hoping that the sneak attack will inspire so much fear that "there will be no [American] resistance." Issues #11 and #12 presented more clearly defined attacks against San Francisco, a city threat-ened by "a ripsnorting spy ring." No matter how unrealistic an invasion of San Francisco was in the real world, the comics presented dramatic dan-gers as "a fleet of deadly Japanese aircraft carriers" moves into position to attack. Doctor Fate pitches in farther up the West Coast, helping to defend American bases in Alaska. The hero arrives in time to help stem the tide, and Doctor Fate shakes a confession out of a captured soldier: the Japa-nese want to use Alaska as a base to invade Canada (a threat, readers must have understood, to the United States as well). Having won the battle, Doctor Fate reminds readers of the need for sustained vigilance. "Well, that's the end of the Jap reinforcements," he explains. "Alaska is safe, at least for the time being."[77]

The threat moved inland as well, suggesting that all of the United States—and not just the West Coast—faced danger from the racialized enemy. The Spectre, for example, has to save Chicago from a "rocket-bomb," which he redirects to Japan. Hawkman has to protect New York City from an even more fanciful weapon—"a gigantic propeller guided by the human brain"—that could, somehow, destroy cities. Hawkman, in typical superheroic fashion, arrives just in time, summoning hawks to catch and dispose of the bombs dropped by the propeller.[78] The heroes' inevitable victories notwithstanding, such comics clearly communicated a clear and present danger to the United States.

And, finally, the comics and movie serials extended this racialized threat to white women. Already mentioned was Lois's capture and use to (if only temporarily) thwart Superman in "Japoteurs." Japanese soldiers similarly threaten Lois in another *Superman* cartoon, "Eleventh Hour," in which she and Clark have gone to Japan to cover the war. Each night at eleven o'clock, however, Superman sneaks out and commits sabotage ("good" subversion in this case, as opposed to that of the "Japoteur"). The Japanese military then abducts Lois and threatens to execute her if Superman commits any more subversive activities. After he does, the Man of Steel flies to the rescue, saving Lois at the last minute from a firing squad, the leader depicted impotently in shadows with a droopy, phallus-like sword. Back home in the United States, Lois was repeatedly threatened in the comic strips, too, taken hostage at the start (and then saved by Superman) and kidnapped later and thrown down a dry well to her seeming demise (only to again be rescued). The racialized threat to white women was highlighted in the *Batman* serial, too, as the Cave of Horrors presented three Japanese soldiers, one with a bayonet, threatening a well-dressed white woman. Bruce Wayne's girlfriend, Linda, is similarly repeatedly menaced, constantly under siege in this film as Daka and his men kidnap her, spy on her, and assault her, knocking her unconscious at one point.[79]

Thus wartime superhero popular culture's depiction of Japanese and Japanese Americans was manifold in its approach. After erasing the differences between both groups and thus positioning Japanese Americans outside of America, comics, cartoons, and movie serials presented both as disloyal, wholly other, dehumanized, violent, and treacherous. Bradford Wright explains that "perhaps more than any other medium, comic books proved uniquely suited to portray the Asian enemy as many Americans saw him,"[80] but the implications of these portrayals go even further. What the superheroes' wartime adventures presented about Japanese and Japanese Americans was, in a sense, the sum of Americans' fears regarding this perceived threat, thus both rendering that wartime hysteria but also implicitly revealing its ultimately overdetermined nature. In its excess, superhero popular culture managed to put on page and screen all that Americans felt toward Japanese and Japanese Americans, making them a crucible that distilled for its audience all that fed into the illegal incarceration at home.

Profiling Racialized Allies and Normalizing White Superiority

At the same time that superhero popular culture contradicted liberal ideals of equality and the wartime emphasis on inclusivity in its myriad problematic depictions of Japanese Americans, it also expressed a recurring theme of white American superiority. Indeed, the denigration of Japanese and Japanese Americans just discussed had always — at least implicitly, and often explicitly — set off white Americans as inherently "better than" their racialized enemy. But this white superiority also factored into what were intended as more sympathetic portrayals of other racial and ethnic groups as well as the nonwhite sidekicks who would eventually debut in this era.

The Chinese were one such group whose depictions served to reinforce white American superiority. As a result, superhero popular culture presented Chinese characters in a purportedly new light that actually remained rooted in problematic stereotypes and misconceptions. The Chinese — now an ally for whom old images of sinister and mysterious bad guys ensconced in Chinatown's opium dens, laundries, and chop suey shops no longer fit — were now seen as peaceful if simple people living in a burgeoning democracy. Whatever improvements such change might have suggested, the comics, at the same time, implicitly suggested Chinese inferiority to whites, resulting in humiliating stories that saw the Japanese easily infiltrating Chinese groups and that witnessed the Chinese remaining reliant on whites, in one case even submitting to training from women, a revealing example given gendered hierarchies of the era.[81]

The *Superman* comic strip embodied such negative representations lurking beneath well-intended praise for Chinese Americans. During the course of Superman's comic-strip war against Japanese Americans, Lois and Clark begin a campaign in the *Daily Planet* that attacks Japan and supports China. Their activism leads to a visit from the "mayor of Chinatown," Lum Wong, who explains, "The Chinese citizens of this city, pleased with your articles, wish you to take part in tomorrow's great bond-selling parade." Lum Wong wears a traditional Chinese robe and hat to the meeting. While the mayor's language is a bit stilted, reinforcing his wardrobe's sense of difference, it is not mangled like the English spoken by Japanese Americans in the strip, and the bond drive demonstrates his clear com-

Figure 1.3. Superhero popular culture hoped to elevate the status of some nonwhite groups in American society, but often undermined its efforts by using such groups to further highlight white superiority. The *Superman* comic strip did so by presenting loyal—but not equal—Chinese Americans, who appear as good citizens but remain mired in racialized depictions, here emphasizing not only differences in clothing but also a sexualized understanding of nonwhite women.

mitment to his adopted country, thus putting the Chinese on a more elevated footing. However, there were limits to such elevation. At the parade the next day, drenched in "Oriental" imagery—pajama-like clothing for women (which Lois adopts, too), Chinese language signs, and whatnot— a Chinese woman dances provocatively, thrusting her breasts forward at the reader.[82] In such an exotic locale, Chinese Americans could demonstrate their loyalty, but only in a manner that continued to mark them as different and lesser.

The second-class citizenship of Chinese characters (and people) appears all the more clearly if one accepts Gene Luen Yang's argument about the history of the Green Turtle, a short-lived wartime superhero. Yang believes—admittedly relying in part on rumors that have never been verified—that the Blazing Comics hero was secretly Chinese. Created by the artist Chu Hing for the publisher Rural Home, the Green Turtle debuted in 1944. Hing apparently wanted the character to be Chinese, but the publisher insisted he be white. The Asian American artist quietly rebelled, always obscuring the hero's face and refusing to share his origin story,

leaving open the possibility that he was indeed Chinese. Hing might have
even hoped, Yang surmises, that the demeaning portrayal of the Japanese
enemy in the comic would help gain his character broader acceptance. Yang
suggests that the "unnatural pink" color of the superhero's skin served as
the publisher's insistence on "just how Caucasian this hero is supposed to
be." As a result of this conflict, the Green Turtle's comics "read like Hing
and his publishers are wrestling within the art itself, through the compo-
sitions and colors and hidden details." If the Green Turtle was in fact Chinese, his obscured racial identity reveals a continued lack of racial progress
in wartime America, even as the apparent struggle over his identity leaves
room for problematic attitudes to appear contested.[83]

Native Americans came off no better. In *All Star Comics* #12, Doctor
Fate's adventure took him out west, where he ran afoul of a Native American tribe, who, after defeating him in battle, make sure he is all right. Why
such sympathy for their vanquished enemy? The Indians, it turns out,
have attacked Doctor Fate unwillingly. As the chief unhappily explains,
"We have turned into traitors to America—but if we rebel, those yellow
men will kill our wives and children!" A brave adds, "And those little yellow
men will continue to use us to their foul advantage!" Doctor Fate's ensuing
adventure then sketches a familiar story of an inferior, nonwhite people
who want to help whites but cannot because their families are held hostage by the Japanese, who continue to act barbarically in taking the war to
women and children (and not just soldiers).

This story's climax further underlines such inferiority. As Doctor Fate
confronts the enemy on his own, the Native Americans, inspired by the
white hero, realize that Doctor Fate, in their chief's words, "is fighting
our fight! He fights for our country and for our families! Are we cowards?
Better to die fighting, than to live in fear." Inspired, another exclaims, suc-
cinctly capturing both the Native Americans' backwardness and their re-
deemable qualities, "Ugh! We fight!" Together, Doctor Fate and the Native
Americans defeat the Japanese "punks," and the white hero then allows
the Native Americans to free their families. At the story's end, Doctor Fate
tells a military officer, "I brought you some volunteers, major. . . . These
Indians ought to be great fighters in the Asiatic jungles!"[84] This happy ending reinforced common themes of white superiority and the ability of nonwhites—with proper inspiration and supervision in the right context, of
course—to aid the war effort, but in an obviously paternalistic and con-
descending manner.

The *Batman* serial presented the same double-sided message regarding
Native Americans. In the race to find radium for a destructive gun, Daka's

gang members rush to a mine, stopping at "Steve's Indian Trading Post," a run-down roadside shop operated by a Native American. The gangsters abuse the proprietor, derisively calling him "Sitting Bull." In hot pursuit, the good guys arrive soon after the gangsters leave. Steve greets them with mangled English, further indicating his outsider status: "Me Steve. What you want?" He then stereotypically tries to sell some hand-carved wares, stiltedly asking Bruce's girlfriend, Linda, "You buy, pretty lady?" The travelers eventually realize that Steve knows about the mine, which he calls simply a "cave," the concept of mining apparently being too sophisticated for him to grasp. Steve then provides directions that seem pretty straightforward, if uncertainly delivered: "Cabin on . . . [pause] . . . right road, cave in mountain, left road." While lacking elegance, the directions seem clear enough, but Dick Grayson (a.k.a. Robin) complains that Steve is "clear as mud." Before they set off, Bruce buys a couple of handcrafted goods, telling Steve to keep the change. Stereotypically honest, however, Steve insists on making change, explaining, "Indian no take gift."[85] Again, Native Americans could contribute to the war effort, but only with substantial and much-needed guidance from whites.

Perhaps not surprisingly, attempts to treat Japanese Americans more sympathetically in comic books foundered on similar problems, successfully introducing loyal and even heroic Japanese Americans, but only in subordinate roles that reminded readers of their inferiority and potential treachery. The fullest treatment of this subject came in the lesser-known adventures of Captain Courageous.[86] While well intentioned, one story in *Four Favorites* #9 proved particularly problematic. Here, creators presented a fairly nuanced view of exile and incarceration that expressed sympathy for its victims but ultimately reinforced Japanese Americans' subordinate status as well.

Captain Courageous's tale went to great lengths to present a positive view of at least some Japanese Americans. The story did so by showcasing a loyal Japanese American boy, Niki, and his parents, who have been locked up at the Santa Anita racetrack. When Niki struggles to understand why his family has been incarcerated, his dad explains, as some in the Japanese American community did during the war, "The country that your mother and myself came from is at war with America. And we must stay here in order that we may help America win!" Niki asserts his Americanism to contest this point: "But I'm an American, I was born here! My teacher told me that!" His father agrees, "That's right, Niki," but explains, in the twisted logic of the wartime era, "and if you're a good American, you'll stay here and not go home—there are bad Japanese who want to harm

America—that's why we've been sent here, to keep us away from bad Japanese, so we can help America win the war!"

Niki, a teenage boy dressed in the American style (a stylish yellow sweater over a collared shirt and a pair of knickers), becomes the key symbol of Japanese American loyalty in the story. After leaving camp to retrieve his dog, Butch, he hitchhikes back to town, his travels allowing him to further affirm his Americanism. As he walks along, Niki says to himself, "I like America and baseball and don't believe any of that crazy hari kari stuff that Mr. Gichi tried to teach me!"—thus proving his assimilation, although here in contrast to less acculturated members of his ethnic group. The comic further underlines this point when a white driver pulls over to pick Niki up and exclaims in shock that he's "a Jap"; Niki takes offense. "I am not!" Niki replies. "I'm as much an American as you are!" The somewhat dubious driver agrees to help Niki, and their ensuing conversation wins him over: Niki is indeed a real American, as clearly demonstrated by his talking about baseball—the national pastime, after all—as he is dropped off. To the comic's credit, the initial depiction of Niki offered a clear contrast to how Japanese Americans had been previously depicted in comics, not to mention how they were viewed in US society.

The ultimately mixed message of the comic book arrived, however, clearly in Niki's Uncle Saki, who has been forced to work for the traitorous Captain Nippo but eventually sides with the United States. In doing so, he puts a bow on this adventure's moral about Japanese American inferiority by emphasizing his need to prove himself loyal, a need similarly underlying Niki's assertions of his American identity. As Saki and Niki chase Captain Nippo, who plots a submarine attack, Saki explains that he will "have to take my punishment." When they spot the sub's periscope, Saki's intentions become clear; he dives off the boat, explaining, "I go to commit hari kari the American way!" and blocks a torpedo tube with his body. As a result, when Captain Nippo orders the sub to fire, the vessel destroys itself. Niki confirms his uncle's heroism, noting that he always knew Saki was a "good American," and Captain Courageous explains, paraphrasing President Roosevelt's own words, that "Saki did it the hard way, but he proved that being a real American is a state of mind, not a color of skin!" Niki then drives the point home: "Gee, any American would have done the same thing!" Saki's and by extension all loyal Japanese Americans' need to demonstrate their loyalty puts conditions on their status as Americans, which by implication determine them as lesser.

All Star Comics #12 followed a similar pattern.[87] As the Atom goes about trying to circumvent a plot to steal American technology, a Japanese

American calls out to him. The so-called "Yankee Jap" immediately asserts his loyalty to the United States to the initially dubious Atom: "Well, you needn't worry—I'm Japanese all right, but I was born in America and I love this country as much as you do!" He goes on to explain, in a now-familiar theme of Japanese American untrustworthiness, "There are many more Japs like me—unfortunately, imperial Japan has put the pressure on us and we've been forced to work against Uncle Sam." The loyal Japanese American then leads our hero to the saboteurs' lair, earning the Atom's patronizing praise—"Say, that's right on the beam, fella!"—and again demonstrating the lesser status of Japanese Americans. Further true to the theme of white superiority and nonwhite inferiority is the fact that the Atom fights off the Japanese American enemy alone.

Superhero popular culture's implicit basis in white superiority was further revealed by the introduction of nonwhite sidekicks both in comics and on the big screen. Wartime superhero popular culture unsurprisingly produced no nonwhite superheroes and only a few nonwhite sidekicks, a fact that itself speaks to this stark reality. These characters, exemplified in comic books by the Young Allies' Whitewash Jones and on the silver screen by the Green Hornet's Kato, fell well short of promoting equality and acceptance. Instead, such newcomers found themselves unceremoniously shunted into sidekick roles, steeped in stereotypes that limited their agency.

For instance, Whitewash Jones, as Michael Uslan has written, appears from our contemporary perspective to be no more than a conglomeration of the basest stereotypes regarding blacks that had been portrayed throughout twentieth-century American popular culture. Whitewash thus arose from the classic comic stereotype of the "pickaninny" and the well-established cinematic figure of Stepin Fetchit.[88] When initially introduced by Captain America's sidekick, Bucky, Whitewash is described as a kid "who can make a harmonica talk!" Whitewash adds, "Yeah man! I is also good on de watermelon!"[89] The reader thus "knew" Whitewash from the start as a stereotype and not a human character, and he kept readers in that comfortable zone throughout the adventures of the Young Allies, always speaking in a mangled dialect and sporting thick lips, overexaggerated facial expressions, and outrageous hats. In retrospect and despite what appear to be his creators' intentions, it is difficult to find much progress in a sidekick's sidekick burdened by such racialized ideas; in many ways, Whitewash undermined any sense of real progress for African Americans during World War II.

In addition to a basis in black stereotypes, the comic also asserted

Whitewash's inferiority. Whitewash might have been presented as a hero, but his constant expressions of fear (in a stilted dialect) made him distinctly inferior to his peers. When the Young Allies need to traverse a graveyard to pursue German spies, Whitewash is terrified. Talking to himself as he flees in terror, Whitewash says, "Get movin' feet! Ah ain't going in dere!" He then calls out to his teammates, "Ah suddenly remembah'ed, fellas. Ah-Ah gotta run a' errand fo' mah mammy!" Forced into the graveyard by teammates who insist that ghosts don't exist, Whitewash can only wishfully interject, "Ah-ah-ah hope de g-g-ghosts know dat!" He later screams in fear, "Gosteses! This place am haunted!" Whitewash does little better when confronting living threats. When natives attack in a later issue and his white teammates jump bravely into battle, he says, "This is a nightmare . . . I hope!?!" In issue #3, Whitewash again tries to duck a frightening confrontation, lamely explaining to his teammates, "Oh, oh, Ah just remembered Ah got an appointment elsewhere."[90]

In addition to his distinct lack of courage, Whitewash Jones's mistake-prone adventuring further reduces his status as a Young Ally. While Whitewash does indeed make contributions that help his team defeat the enemy, his help is often accidental. For example, he helps his teammates out of one jam only because he is well behind the others in getting down a tunnel because "mah pants got caught." When he sees spies with guns advancing on the others, he panics. "Lawdy!" he exclaims, "Ah gotta d-do s-sumpin' t' help muh buddies!" Seeing nothing to do except pull a lever—which he ridiculously hopes will call the police—Whitewash yanks the handle, triggering the headquarters to self-destruct. Distracting the spies, the calamity allows the Young Allies to escape.[91]

Whitewash is further diminished due to his lack of intelligence. Indeed, he is played throughout—to comic effect, the creators seem to have hoped—as a dim-witted kid. He gives away the Young Allies, stowaways on a ship, when a suspicious crew member demands they answer his call. Whitewash responds, none too cleverly, "It am only us mice, suh!" The team is, it goes without saying, discovered. After the Young Allies arrive in France, Whitewash reveals his lack of worldly sophistication (as well as, perhaps, the racism he has internalized growing up in America) when he asks, "Is dere darky French kids?" When the team then tries to communicate with a non-English-speaking French soldier, Whitewash can only contribute, "Ah'm not hep to yo' jibe!"[92]

Finally, Whitewash's dialect and appearance prevent him from being considered an equal, as defined by the dynamic, intelligent whites who are. Stranded in Europe, the team has to raise money. They decide to organize a variety show, and Whitewash appears in exactly the role readers would have expected, as "Growlo, the Ape-Man." Throwing himself into his role, Whitewash acts like a monkey—bowing his legs out and scratching at his armpits—while clamoring, "Ook- Ook-." When the teammates later have to take up jobs aboard a ship, Whitewash assumes the segregated role for blacks in the "scullery," cooking for the crew with enthusiasm: "Dinnah am served," he calls out. "Last one down gets a rotten egg!" He takes his "street" style into scraps as well, saving a compatriot from a German soldier's attack by pulling the infantryman's hat down over his eyes while exclaiming, "You all ain't wearin'g yoah hat right! Let me show you how, Harlem style!"[93]

Much like *Young Allies* failed to elevate Whitewash Jones to a position of equality in superhero popular culture, the Green Hornet's wartime serials failed to advance the position of Asian Americans in its presentation of Kato, the title character's Korean sidekick.[94] Played by Keye Luke, a Chinese-born American actor, Kato seemed, on the surface, to represent progress. He is a scientific genius who provides the Green Hornet with an array of sophisticated gadgets. From the start, *The Green Hornet* emphasized Kato's scientific brilliance, opening the serial with Britt Reid (a.k.a. the Green Hornet) praising Kato for his "scientific knowledge" and describing him as a "wizard" after testing a sleeping-gas gun. Kato's intelligence, viewers learned in *The Green Hornet Strikes Again!*, is even more widely respected by the scientific community, and in this second serial he also explains the technology behind a new antiaircraft bomb to the Green Hornet.[95] Kato is more than just a thinker, however; he also proves himself an excellent field operative, repeatedly cracking safes and, when the Green Hornet needs backup, employing an effective (if stereotypical) kung fu fighting style to quell criminals.[96] In these aspects of his character, Kato clearly seems intended to embody a more substantial equality with, if not superiority to, his white comrade.

But it is in Kato's relationship with the titular hero that the subordinate status of Asians—and thus the superior position of white Americans— appears more predominantly. As a result of Kato's contributions and their shared past, the Green Hornet clearly has warm feelings for Kato, even if he does not often express them. The close relationship manifests, for instance, as an injured Kato convalesces in Reid's apartment following an explosion.[97] At the same time, however, Kato remains always a sidekick, spending most of his time as a valet and chauffer. In embracing his role as a manservant, Kato's depiction mitigated what progress he could represent, as his docile nature (as he willingly submits to white leadership) and fierce loyalty to his white benefactor, who had saved his life in Singapore years ago, render him wholly subordinate.[98] Throughout both serials, Kato dutifully obeys orders, never questioning his mentor's instructions, which almost always leave him in a supporting role as the Green Hornet takes on the bad guys by himself.[99] In addition, Kato is marked as lesser by his mangled use of the English language. Throughout, Kato's stilted speech patterns are punctuated with mispronounced words, often stereotypically using *r*'s for *l*'s. To cite just two examples of an ongoing pattern, early in *The Green Hornet*, Kato thanks his boss for saving "my rife" and then, upon rescuing a woman, says, "The porice! We must get rady into our car quickry!" Kato highlights his foreign, kung fu fighting style by noting that a karate chop to one villain will "pararyze" him for thirty minutes.[100] Whatever "advances" Kato represented for nonwhite Americans thus were distinctly limited, as was he in the eyes of superhero popular culture.

Conclusion

When *World's Finest* finally brought Superman and Batman together in its stories in 1954, their teamwork was a logical conclusion to the heroes' earliest adventures, as Superman and Batman had actually been battling, as we have seen, similar enemies since the earliest days of World War II. Indeed, even when waging separate battles against the forces of evil, the "World's Finest" headliners—along with any number of lesser-known white heroes and their occasionally nonwhite sidekicks—had worked to keep the United States safe after the surprise attack on Pearl Harbor. In doing so, however, the superhero popular culture comprising these characters both reflected and helped to constitute a basic conundrum facing American society during World War II: honest hopes for inclusivity existed alongside the realities of a racism that specifically resulted in the exile and incarceration of Japanese Americans and more generally precluded equality for nonwhites.

Such contradictions ultimately feed into a cruel irony of the wartime era: that the purportedly virtuous white heroes could perpetrate the very actions and crimes for which their racialized foes were condemned. Thus, readers cheered on the Sandman in *All Star Comics* as he grabbed a gun on a Japanese aircraft carrier and turned it on its owners. As he exclaims, "This ought to make those shrimps sorry they started this!" the narrator notes that his "aim is true," while the reader sees the silent but very bloody deaths of four enemy sailors.[101] Superman also went to war with a lust for violence that contemporary readers might find surprising. When his disguise is about to be blown in one strip, he grins in eager anticipation of the beating he is about to deliver. In another, he notes that he has "lost [his] temper" after Japanese submarines attack him from behind, and the Man of Steel promises, "You'll be sorry." He then chases down the attacking fleet, playfully calling, "Yoo hoo! Wait for me!" Although Superman still sounds playful as he catches the first submarine, declaring, "Tag! You're it!" what follows is anything but playful as our hero embeds the submarine in the ocean floor before proceeding to do the same to all the subs in the fleet. Superman then swims off on his mission, leaving the stranded sailors to die slow and tortuous deaths (off panel, of course) as their submarines run out of oxygen.[102] Likewise, Wonder Woman leaves others to a watery death when she sabotages a Japanese landing party at sea. As she moves on, the readers can only assume that the Japanese troops will meet their own watery doom.[103]

Given the reality that celebrated such brutalities on the part of "good" (and white) heroes but disparaged similar behavior on the part of "bad" (and nonwhite) enemies, it is no wonder that wartime comics, as much as they might have intended otherwise, did little to promote a viable version of an inclusive and egalitarian United States, preferring instead to present a lily-white definition of the "World's Finest." If superhero popular culture intended to present the multiethnic United States as an "orchestra," it showcased a band that produced disharmonious and cacophonous tunes. If it hoped to present a diverse "salad" of ethnic and racial groups, it produced a dish with rotten ingredients. These failures, emblematic of broader social struggles to address racial inequality effectively and not all that surprising in the wartime context, had important long-term implications for superheroes, Americans, and race, setting the stage for continued struggles to square American ideals with American realities that plagued not just superhero popular culture but all of American society in the aftermath of World War II.

CHAPTER 2

Struggling for Social Relevance: DC, Marvel, and the Cold War, 1945–1965

In the twenty years that followed World War II, Americans found themselves plagued by uncertainty. On the one hand, an optimism that had taken hold even before the war held a continuing power. Henry Luce, for example, in penning "The American Century" for *Life* magazine, published on February 7, 1941, had urged Americans to "accept wholeheartedly our duty and our opportunity as the most powerful and vital nation in the world . . . to exert upon the world the full impact of our influence, for such purposes as we see fit and by such means as we see fit."[1] Luce's essay embodied Americans' faith in their ability to shape the global destiny, and many Americans might have hoped that total war would produce total peace and a boundless prosperity based upon an international system increasingly shaped by and even modeled on American democracy and capitalism. On the other hand, such confidence and ambitions were rather quickly shaken, as the world that began to take shape didn't look quite like what Americans had envisioned. As the Soviet Union rose to superpower status, Americans felt anxious, for if the "American century" were not going to come off, what would? Could they really expect the "American way" to triumph in an emerging Cold War? Could anyone really have control in the atomic age as technology moved ahead so quickly and destructively? These concerns shaped domestic conflicts as well, one of which focused on continued racism and prejudice within the United States, even after a war fought against Nazi racism. How would Americans reform race relations? Would they even try? Such daunting questions must have left Americans with mixed feelings as they embarked on their postwar lives.

Superhero popular culture reflected and stoked this ambivalence as it struggled for its very survival in the years following World War II. Faced with increased competition from romance, crime, and horror comics, mounting political pressure from another Red Scare, and an anticomics crusade in the mid-1950s that cast an unfriendly glance at superheroes even as it primarily targeted horror comics, publishers of superhero comics, led by DC (which dominated the shrinking market with Superman and Batman), looked for safety from political storms. They did so by taking a childish turn, eschewing—much as the larger society did—controversial issues for stories that focused instead on fantasies seemingly far removed from contemporary anxieties. In contrast to this status quo of safe and childish fare was a second tack that prevailed during this same period. Atlas Comics became Marvel Comics and revived its superhero line in the early 1960s and took the lead with stories that more directly addressed contentious social issues, including racism and prejudice.

But while it seems easy to critique DC for its conservative bent and to laud Marvel for its liberal challenge to inequalities, the place of comics in the Cold War era is considerably more fraught, particularly when it comes to race and ethnicity. Paralleling the ambivalence more broadly abounding within postwar American society and culture is an ultimately uncertain treatment of race at play in what *both* companies produced in the two decades following World War II. Reflective, for example, of the anxieties about and limitations surrounding social—and particularly racial—reform, safety in comics in part hinged upon reified depictions of racialized characters. Nonwhite individuals and cultures, in this regard, were regularly homogenized as ignorant, backward, and little more than exotic backdrops for various heroes' adventures. At the same time, however, a glimmer of something more emerged at both DC and Marvel as well. Comics, especially by the early 1960s, began to promote a more inclusive agenda as the civil rights movement gained strength.[2] Incorporating diversity within fictional universes and at least starting to confront issues of inequality and discrimination, superhero popular culture began to address the racial challenges presented by a multicultural America.

Americans, the Silver Age, and the Politics of Safety

As a growing anxiety overtook a triumphant American mood in the mid- to late 1940s, comic companies confronted a political context that hardly promoted or encouraged any kind of social criticism, especially in regard to the United States' racial shortcomings. In the immediate postwar years, instead, Americans moved decisively away from reform. Anticommunism and a Red Scare resulted in a more conservative orientation that blocked the possibility of building on the New Deal. In this way, while women and laborers might have held hopes that 1930s-style reform would return after the war, inequalities instead ruled.

The antireform spirit had important consequences on efforts to improve race relations, too, where heightened expectations of equality required both continued protest from below and positive responses from the government. The push from below occurred as a long list of civil rights activists, such as J. A. DeLaine, Ella Baker, Amzie Moore, Septima Clark, Fred Shuttlesworth, and Harry T. Moore—often forgotten today—called for change.[3] They found their calls blocked, however, by whites who responded with a variety of tactics that ranged from violence to subtle resistance. President Harry Truman's response was, at best, mixed: the president voiced support for civil rights but didn't always follow through. As the NAACP's Walter White explained, "We deliberately and consciously avoided asking for a conference to hear Mr. Truman tell us that [he was] for civil rights. . . . The time has come for him to do something . . . instead of telling us how he feels personally." Emblematic of many Americans, the president seemingly preferred, when possible, to ignore race as a systemic national concern. As a result, by the end of the 1940s, African Americans had seen little concrete change in their circumstances.[4]

The 1952 election of Dwight Eisenhower as president of the United States did little to change matters. Pressure from activists eventually forced federal action, most prominently with the Supreme Court's decision in *Brown v. Board of Education* in 1954. Here, responding to new legal arguments that no longer relied on the *Plessy v. Ferguson* precedent of separate but equal but instead now asserted that segregation denied rights to citizens, the court's ruling to desegregate public education seemed revolutionary. But, as the historian William Chafe clarifies, this decision was insufficient absent accompanying governmental action and direction; without these, it was little more than words. Such support, unfortunately, did not come; the Supreme Court delayed a year before explaining—and then only ambiguously—how desegregation would proceed, and Eisenhower refused to use his moral authority and political power to support the decision. Lacking a strong emotional or intellectual commitment to fighting segregation, the president acted only after provoked by the Little Rock crisis in 1957. It was, Chafe concludes, simply not enough.[5]

The point was reinforced in American foreign policy, which struggled in the 1950s to assert world leadership against Soviet charges of racism. The United States attempted to address such concerns at the 1958 world's fair in Brussels, creating "Unfinished Business," an exhibit that acknowledged racial problems in America but showed the nation progressing toward a democratic integration. Despite the seemingly positive effects of the exhibit, American racists convinced Eisenhower to revise and eventually scrap it, suggesting the power of racism in the worst years of the Cold War.[6]

In addition to the indirect effects of such political uncertainty, economic instability directly impacted the comic industry as well. Superhero comic book sales had begun to slip as the war came to an end. In response, characters became "safer" by championing American ideals, avoiding controversy, and trumpeting a traditional American exceptionalism. Declining sales also encouraged publishers to diversify their lines by adding crime, romance, and horror titles. This shift left only a handful of superheroes — A-list stars like Superman, Batman, and Wonder Woman — on the newsstand, all now decidedly aimed at a juvenile audience. This need to improve sales in the early years of the Cold War likewise precluded any honest attempts — likely to ignite controversy — to address issues of race. Playing it safe to protect sales, publishers largely ignored the nascent civil rights movement in the early 1950s, presenting only stereotyped images of nonwhites as background color, hapless victims, comic relief, or deceitful and brutal enemies.[7]

Along with slumping sales, a simmering prewar anticomics movement came to a boil after 1945; its growing notoriety further limited whatever social commentary creators might have attempted. The initial attack had been launched in May 1940, when Sterling North of the *Chicago Daily News* complained of "mayhem, murder, torture and abduction — often with a child as the victim, Superman heroics, voluptuous females in scanty attire, blazing machine guns, hooded 'justice' and cheap political propaganda . . . on almost every page." DC — understanding the very real threat presented by North — created standards to make Superman's tales more palatable to such critics, turned to mad scientists and the like for its villains (as opposed to a plethora of corrupt industrialists in the earlier issues), and made sure to emphasize the upright qualities of Superman, who, his owners now ostentatiously emphasized, purveyed wholesome qualities, morality, and traditional values, such as self-reliance. The arrival of World War II provided the logical climax to such changes, as DC now sought to make the Man of Steel also synonymous with American democracy.

North's campaign, while quickly overtaken by the events of World War II, nonetheless blazed a trail for a range of postwar crusaders who increasingly connected comics to rising worries about juvenile delinquency. Although statistics did not bear out such anxieties, a variety of groups — including the press, community organizations, and government agencies—began to target comics as a source of trouble, even after a number of publishers established advisory boards (staffed by psychologists, teachers, and welfare workers) designed to ward off such attacks while appealing to parents. Early industry responses to such challenges proved thoroughly inadequate, however, as by 1948, adolescents, under adult supervision, lit comic books ablaze in massive bonfires "disturbingly reminiscent of Nazi book-burnings."[8] Such alarm did not bode well for the industry.

The situation had become even bleaker by the mid-1950s when academics and politicians again took aim at comics. Echoing earlier worries about violence, sex, and propaganda, these concerns reached a crescendo in the work of Fredric Wertham, a psychiatrist and longtime liberal crusader against the evils of comic books. Among a long list of such evils, Wertham included racism.[9] He also attacked DC's flagship character, Superman, for promoting a violence evocative of that which had led to the rise of fascism and World War II. DC's other mainstays—Batman, Robin, and Wonder Woman—were attacked for promoting homosexuality, often via scurrilous readings of what appeared both on and off the page. In response, publishers quickly promulgated a new and more restrictive Comics Code—the primary goal of those leading the 1954 US Senate hearings focused on this very issue—and beefed up their advisory boards. The results were stultifying: comics were now reduced to, at most, kiddie fare and, even more perniciously for the industry, potentially an outworn fad. Though the newly established Comics Code might have prevented further public outcries and consequent legal action, it also established reductive attitudes toward comics that, in many ways, persist to this day.[10]

In this constrictive environment, DC's new Silver Age heroes debuted and prospered. The first, a new Flash (who was secretly the police criminologist Barry Allen), arrived in 1956 and was soon followed by new versions of Green Lantern (Hal Jordan), Hawkman, and the Atom that would join Superman, Batman, and Wonder Woman. All represented an "unvarying" type of hero: "a positivist in a positivist world, using reason and knowledge to master an ultimately knowable universe and thus restore our unquestioned status quo to proper order."[11] These new series presented an orderly world challenged only by goofy villains who were easily defeated.[12] These superheroes supported authority and a bland consensus grounded in anticommunism, affluence, and faith in the American way that would only be furthered once they joined together in a new team book, *Justice League of America*.[13]

Such superficial consensus and supposedly nonoffensive fare, however,

Figure 2.1. Typical of 1950s fare, *Superman's Girl Friend Lois Lane* uses ethnicity only to add background color and to play for laughs, reflecting a broader social desire to defuse issues of race in the Cold War United States. Lois's comments in this way reflect broadly shared longings for "safe" conversations about race that continued to look backward— instead of forward—in treating prejudice and inequality.

remained grounded in problematic portrayals of race. In a variety of ways, nonwhites and their cultures were reduced to no more than a demeaning backdrop for the heroes' adventures. A quick perusal of a collection like *Superman in the Fifties*, described in its foreword by the comic book writer Mark Waid as "the best and most important Super-tales of that seminal decade," reveals Metropolis to have been almost entirely white; when nonwhites appeared, they often served a comic effect. For example, *Superman's Girl Friend Lois Lane* had the titular reporter covering a professional wrestling event. The match pits "Hairy Sam" against "Injun Ike," the latter stereotypically sporting a Mohawk and beating his chest at his moment of triumph. As they grapple, an old lady screams, "C'mon, Injun! Scalp him!" and Ike does just that, ripping a wig off of Hairy Sam's head. Lois sees right through the "sport," knowingly observing that wrestling—and the ethnic color that spices it up—is nothing but "colorful comedy designed strictly for laughs! The crowd eats up every slap-stick routine!"[14] Superman's earliest televised escapades suggested a similar lack of diversity.

Much like the comics, the introduction to each week's episode of the *Adventures of Superman* television show, starring George Reeves in the titular role beginning in 1952, showcased an entirely white cast of Metropolis citizens. Nonwhites appeared in individual episodes, but usually only as exotic—and threatening—backdrops. In "Treasure of the Incas," for instance, the show rendered Peru and its people a threatening realm. The villain, an evil-looking, heavily accented man with a scarred face, spices his language with foreign words. Lima, this story's setting, is nothing but adobe buildings, stucco facades, and Spanish-language signs. Once outside the city, Lois Lane and Jimmy Olsen confront a barren and arid countryside, which becomes especially threatening after they are chained and left for dead in the tradition of a "barbarous custom" of the Incas.[15]

Batman and Robin introduced 1950s comic book readers to a similarly exotic version of the Middle East in a story titled "Bodyguards to Cleopatra."[16] The comic's cover presented brown-skinned Egyptians, with a sexualized Cleopatra in the foreground, sitting on a luxurious couch, wearing ostentatious jewelry, and dressing provocatively, her low-cut blouse highlighting her curvaceous figure. Two slave girls, dressed in bras and skirts, fan her obsequiously. In the background, having traveled to the distant past, Batman and Robin slug it out with Egyptians, who wear horned helmets and skirts. Inside the comic, the natives are now colored white, just like our heroes, although the visual message deviates in no other way: Cleopatra now lounges on a bed provocatively, while evil, shirtless men sneak up on our heroes from behind.

Wonder Woman carried on in the same way, her creators safely distancing her (and themselves) from social concerns, if nonetheless still tripping over issues of race.[17] Her tales rarely even glanced at race at home and often employed images of the "other" for background color only. In this way, stereotypes of the Middle East added an exotic element to the Amazon's adventures. Middle Eastern bazaars launched two such tales, the first involving Steve Trevor and a flying carpet that he buys from a stereotypical salesman in "the mysterious East." Readers later visited an Egyptian bazaar inhabited by a similarly depicted peddler, portrayed with missing teeth, a fez-like hat, and a striped robe.[18]

Asia and South America also served as convenient and colorful backdrops for Wonder Woman's adventures. For example, she toured the Pacific in 1959 when natives invited her "to attend the New Moon Dances on Pearl Island." Surrounded by locals dressed in stereotypical Polynesian fashion—the men are shirtless and adorned with flowered headbands; the women wear bright, floral-print dresses and ankle bracelets, with flowers in their hair—Wonder Woman enjoys the festivities until a tidal

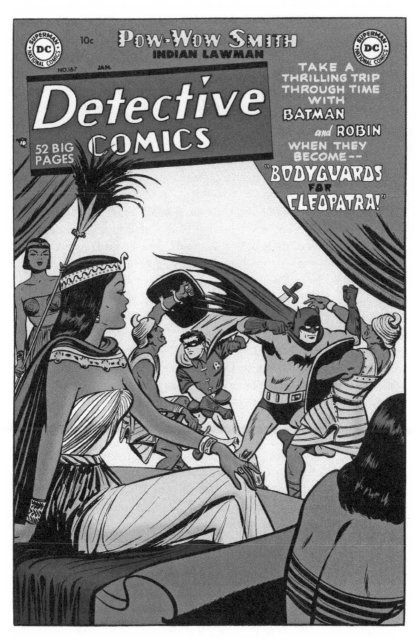

Figure 2.2. Sustaining patterns established during World War II, comic creators of the 1950s continued to trade on stereotyped visions of nonwhite sexuality. As a result, gender and race worked in tandem to define and limit nonwhite characters in powerful ways. Here, Cleopatra serves as little more than a sex object for the heroes and readers to ogle.

wave threatens. In another tale, an alien invasion of South America brings the Amazon into contact with "jungle natives!" The locals, faces brightly painted, embrace the powerful newcomer. "You great magic," one says in broken English. "We take you to mighty chief!" At the village, a typically thatched-hut affair, loinclothed and naïve natives worship an alien invader, seen as the one that "wise men tell about for many moons!"[19]

Even when stories elevated nonwhite peoples and cultures from such background roles, they remained homogenized in their depiction. Practically unvaryingly, comics presented nonwhite individuals and communities as backward and helpless. "Superboy and the Sleeping Beauty" presented just such a view of nonwhites, in this case Africans, as part of a convoluted plot involving Lana Lang being accidently poisoned by a dart from a blowgun. The depiction of the African tribe underscores the ridiculousness of their beliefs. Warned by the opening narration that this "voodoo poison" comes "from the darkest Africa," readers learn that Superboy must locate "pygmy voodoo doctors" within three days to save Lana's life. As he arrives in what he describes as "darkest Africa," Superboy locates the tribe, where "a screaming witch doctor sends ripples of superstition through huddled pygmies." Further belittling their superstitions is the witch doctor Wamba's warning: "Only I keep the night demons from flying into your huts to torment you!" Throughout, the Africans appear easily fooled and superstitious. Alongside this portrayal of their ignorance, the comic also emphasizes their inferiority; the natives attack Superboy, but their blowguns are no threat to our hero. Wamba, acceding to Superboy's obvious superiority, agrees to help, leading him to the antidote that saves Lana.[20]

The televised adventures of the adult Superman were often no different. For example, Afro-Caribbean people were flattened demeaningly in "Drums of Death." Here, Perry White's sister has disappeared in Haiti, leaving behind only a scrap of silent film featuring shirtless natives beating ominously on drums. Perry rightfully doesn't trust the "voodoo doctor" in the film, thus privileging his white sensibilities, and sets off to investigate. Additionally, a local official informs Perry that voodoo is no longer practiced in Haiti, except by the "ignorant"; the near-constant presence of voodoo drumming in the soundtrack not only belies his optimism but implies the widespread persistence of such ignorance. To similar effect are the repeated appearances of natives, all dark, sweaty, shirtless, and talking in broken English.[21]

If Superman's televised adventures set their sights on so diminishing peoples of African origin, Batman's postwar adventures similarly targeted

Native Americans. In 1954's offbeat tale "The Origins of the Bat-Cave," the discovery of a shard of Native American pottery—bearing an ominous inscription, "Death to the man of two identities"—sends the Dynamic Duo three hundred years into the past.[22] Batman and Robin arrive to a dramatic scene, with "two Indians on the warpath after [a] white man!" Our heroes jump to rescue the latter, Jeremy Coe, whom the plot reveals as the man noted in the pottery shard, a frontiersman who has been painting himself red to pose as an Indian. Coe has been forced to such subterfuge by the "redman's attacks on the western-most colonies," which have become "more and more savage." Coe being too injured to continue, Batman takes his place, painting himself red, dressing in Indian-style garb, and donning war paint.

Batman's execution of this racist subterfuge ultimately functions to diminish his Native American foes. He successfully spies on the "war council" until a freak rainstorm washes his paint off; but when the motley throng of Native Americans—all loincloths, spears, and war paint—attack, Batman slows them down with some "batarang magic." The Indians' amazement as the "batarang" flies off and then returns underlines their ignorance. Outnumbered and in need of help, Batman then uses his cape to send up bat-shaped smoke signals, which terrify his opponents. As one laments, "Man-who-looks-like-bat has powerful medicine! He calls upon great spirits!" The Native Americans' terror and wonder combine to reinforce their inferiority in relation to the hero. Despite their numbers, they are wholly in his power, unable to do more than gawk at his abilities that, from their ignorant standpoint, smack of magic.

Batman's interactions with Native Americans in the contemporary world proved little better in presenting them as equals.[23] "Batman—Indian Chief" begins when the Dynamic Duo discover their reservation counterparts: Chief Man-of-the-Bats and Little Raven. As they talk to Great Eagle (a.k.a. Chief Man-of-the-Bats) and his son, Little Eagle (a.k.a. Little Raven), the Dynamic Duo learn that these two have developed their alter egos, modeled on Batman and Robin, to battle criminals like Black Elk, who has "been terrorizing the countryside." However, Great Eagle was injured in his most recent clash and cannot go out in public as Chief Man-of-the-Bats without being recognized.

This problem leads, inexorably, to Batman and Robin impersonating Chief Man-of-the-Bats and his sidekick, as the hero again dons redface, this time adding an ornate feathered headdress. But Great Eagle also avers that Batman "must perform only in Indian fashion" to sell his impersonation. The ensuing adventure makes clear that "Indian fashion" is once again lesser. When Robin suggests using the Batplane, his mentor reminds him that "we've got to handle this like Indians—remember!" They then track the bad guys without technology, reinforcing an anachronistic view of Native Americans that relegates them to a primitive lifestyle. This point is furthered when the trail goes cold. While Robin despairs, Batman perseveres, reminding his protégé, "Again we've got to play Indian! Great Eagle would find the trail. . . . So will we!" The latter statement—as well as the duo's entire masquerade—makes clear that anything their Native American imitators can do, Batman and Robin can likewise do (and probably do better), giving the latter a pronounced superiority over the former. The story's end did little to alter this depiction. After Batman triumphs, he and Great Eagle warmly shake hands. On the one hand, this brief closing sequence seemed to suggest some matter of equality between Batman and Chief Man-of-the-Bats. But on the other, Batman has really done all the work. Not only that, but the Dark Knight's assistance was necessary; he pitches in to help the Sioux when they cannot help themselves. Though the circumstances between these two adventures may vary somewhat— the Caped Crusader replacing a white man in the first and a Native American man in the second—what remained consistent between them was a belittling reification of Native American individuals and communities as ignorant, backward, and, in the end, in need of benevolent white help.

The final member of DC's "Trinity," Wonder Woman, would tread similarly problematic ground in her postwar adventures. In "The Secret of Volcano Mountain," for instance, Wonder Woman is called into action to battle an alien invader against which the native locals are totally helpless. One pleads, "Help us, Wonder Woman!" Another begs, "Save us!" A third makes the point clearly: "Only you can do it!"[24] In addition to such helpless depictions of nonwhite peoples, when ethnic characters did appear in sustained roles, Wonder Woman's creators made them puerile and dependent, most obviously with the arrival of Mister Genie. Mister Genie dresses in curly-toed boots and a giant turban, his protruding belly and prominent mustache further marking him as different. The character also speaks in stereotyped language that reinforces his difference, shouting out things like, "By the beard of Allah!" and "By the beard of the Prophet!" Even though typically paired with Wonder Tot, a toddlerized version of Wonder Woman, Mister Genie is the one infantilized, always playing the child in ironic need of Wonder Tot's paternalistic guidance and help. He cries and throws tantrums to get Wonder Tot to play with him, and these playdates always turn into adventures that terrify the "cowardly" Mister Genie.[25]

HAVE PITY ON ME, *WONDER TOT!* DON'T LET ME SPEND ANOTHER THOUSAND YEARS IN HERE! LET ME OUT! AND I PROMISE YOU, ON MY OATH AS A GENIE, THAT I WILL GRANT ANY WISH OF YOURS! PLEASE, *WONDER TOT!* PLEASE!

Figure 2.3. Comic creators sometimes reified nonwhite characters by turning them into helpless children in need of a white savior's guidance and help. Mister Genie demonstrates this approach directly, often seeking the support of Wonder Tot. In combination with visual cues of his Middle Eastern otherness, readers "understood" the character almost as soon as he appeared on the page.

Such demeaning representations would not remain consigned to the 1950s. Ethnic characters in *Wonder Woman* took a more ominous turn with the arrival of Egg Fu in 1965.[26] This Chinese villain neatly fused racial anxieties with Cold War concerns as Steve Trevor undertakes a clandestine mission "behind the Chinese bamboo curtain," thus moving Wonder Woman out of the fantasy world of Wonder Tot, Mister Genie, and the like, to address, at least for once, real-world concerns. In the process, the story presented echoes of nuclear worries brought to a crescendo by the Cuban Missile Crisis, as well as older images of the "Oriental" enemy. In this way, Egg Fu became a classic, if short-lived, villain, an "Oriental mastermind" who represented "a greater threat to the free world than an exploding sun!"

The Egg Fu saga showcased the Chinese threat to the United States in terms familiar to any reader of World War II–era comics and their similar depictions of an Asian threat. The Chinese are treacherous: early on, the story warns of a threat to the continental United States, as three Chinese saboteurs approach the coastline. This trio's dialogue likewise emphasizes their difference by way of a mangled accent: "Speak Amelican—Wong! Or you'll attlact suspicion—!" Further demonstrating their inferiority, Steve Trevor easily handles "these chopstick Charlies" when they confront him and Diana, until they suddenly explode. Steve immediately understands what has happened and makes clear Chinese inhumanity: "Th-they're boobytrapped! To prevent anyone from capturing them alive! How do you fight a country that thinks nothing of human lives?" Wonder Woman further warns, "What a relentless foe we face—who has no more regard for human life—than if it were paper confetti!" Thus, from its very start, this *Wonder Woman* plot grounded its depiction of the Chinese in timeworn images of the Asian: treacherous, inhuman, and inferior.

Commanding these mindless servants is Egg Fu, "the most baleful brain that had ever been steeped in Oriental cunning for the sole purpose of annihilating the free world." He is likewise steeped in the same Orientalist depictions as his followers. His bragging about his nefarious plans presents his treachery and inhuman disregard for life, pitched in the same mangled dialect as his men: he crows about his "doomsday locket which will wipe out the entire Amelican Pacific Fleet at one blow!" He further explains, highlighting his clear sneakiness, "The Amelicans would be warned if the locket were fired at rong range! So—we will wait until their fleet comes too close for them to escape annihilation! And our scout planes ladar warns us that will be vely soon! Heeeee—ho!" The second issue of this storyline continued to remind readers of this racialized threat with bamboo-style lettering as the cover announced "the most startling villain ever devised" in a "tale of unbearable menace!"[27] Here, our heroes battle their way through hordes of treacherous Chinese soldiers, facing trap after trap. In the climactic battle, Egg Fu is defiant but also defeated: he strains against Wonder Woman's lasso and shatters, leaving Wonder Woman to deliver the moral: "Egg Fu was destroyed by force! The same kind of force he would have used against innocent people!"[28] But this climax also implicitly reinforces Wonder Woman's superiority and Egg Fu's inferiority: the former has to do little but hold her lasso to defeat the self-destructive latter.

As DC survived with its safe approach, other companies struggled to find a footing in the market by similar means. Martin Goodman's Timely line (soon to adopt the moniker Marvel, but in the early 1950s publishing as Atlas) attempted a superhero revival rooted in the Cold War between 1953 and 1955. Reasoning that his heroes had done well in World War II combating Axis enemies, Goodman hoped for a repeat performance, this time against Communist foes. Goodman thus launched new books for World War II classics like Captain America, the Sub-Mariner, and the Human Torch, enlisting his heroes in an aggressive anticommunist campaign. Here, Captain America returned as a "Commie Smasher" who defended the United States against Communist agents bent on betraying America. It was clumsy stuff, and the heavy-handed fare failed to sell to a dwindling audience.[29]

Beyond its graceless plotting, the Atlas-era resuscitation of these heroes remained grounded in the same problematic portrayals as did DC's characters at the dawn of this Silver Age. Captain America, for example, contrasted white and American progress with the exotic and inferior "other" in 1954's "The Girl Who Was Afraid." An early image in this tale included a pyramid in the background, reminding readers of Egypt's storied past, juxtaposed with a car in the foreground, suggesting perhaps a country and culture moving forward. The tale introduces Adu Bey, an Egyptian who loves America, by emphasizing his subordinate status. "America is great," Bey exclaims. "She is wonderful! I like her people and I want them to like me!" He also hopes, "Maybe I can flee to your land someday . . . and they will take me because I have been generous with you, eh?" Bey's over-the-top adulation and cloying sycophancy not only make Bucky suspicious but explicitly mark the Egyptian as inferior. Bey ultimately turns out to be a good guy, however, helping Cap and Bucky uncover and defeat a Red plot against freedom. But while Bey's valor suggested that nonwhites could be heroes, the Egyptian remains hardly the equal of whites. Instead, he mistreats women and repeatedly acknowledges his subordinate position to whites.[30] In an adventure in China titled "The Green Dragon," Captain America and Bucky would confront yet another clearly inferior foe. In this tale, Cap and Bucky have to recover a stolen list of Chinese soldiers who have defected to the United States. Investigating against an exotic background of Buddha statues, "Oriental" screens, and Chinese architecture, Cap and Bucky manage to outsmart and outfight inferior Chinese soldiers.[31] Once again, what was not white and American was reified as an exotic and inferior "other."

But while one may not be quite so surprised that such insensitive depictions persisted in Atlas Comics prior to its becoming Marvel, it is perhaps somewhat shocking to see them and other problems persist following the much praised rebirth in the early 1960s. In some cases, nonwhites didn't even show up in the background of early Marvel fare. Jack Kirby's urban streetscapes, for example, suggested an America populated exclusively by whites. Thus, when superheroes act in the city, they are backgrounded by

Figure 2.4. While Marvel often receives praise from critics for engaging social issues, including race, in the 1960s, its work at times looks little different from the more commonly maligned DC. The Human Torch's sojourn to Africa, for instance, resulted in a wide range of stereotypical and reductive images.

well-to-do, white crowds. In panel after panel, white men dress in suits and fedoras while well-manicured white women wear stylish dresses. The absence of nonwhites is striking, revealing the unexamined ways in which stereotypes continued to influence creators who were simultaneously trying to make progressive statements about race.[32]

As was the case with their competitors at DC, Marvel often presented nonwhites—when they did actually show up—as little more than an exotic backdrop. Indeed, blatantly racist and reductive images arose when Marvel heroes traveled to Africa. When the Human Torch ventures into a "dense African jungle," he is immediately surrounded by spear-wielding Africans. The natives wear animal masks, and one is mostly covered in leopard skin, with white war paint complimenting his tusked and feathered headdress.

The warriors, colored a dusky gray/black for their skin tone, carry over-sized shields, one of which sports an abstracted skull. When the natives attack, they swarm all over the Torch, defeating him and then taking him back to their primitive, thatched-hut village. Here, a native, with his chest painted yellow and long feathers in his hair, leans back and eats fire. Another image presents a savage African leader shouting in anger, his snarling lips revealing crooked teeth.[33] Marvel's new heroes also catered to ideas about the exotic East and in particular Egypt, where they presented all the standard motifs. When the Fantastic Four find themselves traveling into the past to ancient Egypt to confront the time-traveling conqueror Rama-Tut, their adventure hits on myriad exoticizing tropes: pyramids in the background, evil leaders in garish headdresses, and Sue Storm all sexed up in a clingy, yellow Egyptian dress.[34]

Similarly exotic—as well as erotic—images suffuse the pages of *The Invincible Iron Man* when Tony Stark battles Hatap, "the mad pharaoh." In the present, Stark watches an objectified belly dancer, dressed skimpily in a green-and-pink bra and a low-cut pink skirt, a red gem in her belly button. After traveling into the past, Iron Man meets Cleopatra, who reclines on her bed to receive him, her low-cut blouse and naked thigh reinforcing her exotic allure. Her actions have the same resonance as her appearance: at one point she suggestively promises Iron Man "anything . . . any wish" if he will defeat Hatap, and near the story's end, Cleopatra throws herself at Iron Man in thanks, noting that she has "lost my heart to you," as the hero fades away, pulled back to the present.[35] Not only trapped in the past, Cleopatra and Egypt as a whole remain trapped in an Orientalized, exoticized portrayal.

And as was again the case with DC heroes' exploits, those at Marvel regularly relied on an assumed inferiority of nonwhite peoples and cultures. A persistent motif in the depiction of Egyptian people in *The Fantastic Four* is their superstitious—and thus ignorant—nature. When Rama-Tut arrives in this past, the baffled natives run about, hither and yon, shouting, "Oh, wonder of wonders! What miracle is upon us?" Even after being blinded by his crash-landing, Rama-Tut easily subdues "the dazed natives." The arrival of Marvel's "First Family" to this same past prompts like reactions: when the superstitious natives see the Human Torch fly through the sky, they can only register his presence as "an omen from the gods!"[36]

Much like Egyptians, more generic Middle Easterners were also presented in demeaning ways by Marvel. For example, Doctor Doom's endless plots against the Fantastic Four included one absurd scheme in which he builds a machine that amplifies the powers of petty criminals by a factor of twelve. He uses the machine on Yogi Dakor, a circus performer known as "the fire-proof man," who is presented in blatantly ethnic terms, wearing a turban and a scraggly goatee. When he confronts the Human Torch, Yogi Dakor poses as an emissary from the "maharajah" and addresses our hero as "Sahib Torch." To similar effect, when Sergeant Fury and his commandos venture into North Africa, they find alluring women but also angry men who resent the commandos' attention to the local women, exhibiting their upset by uttering things like, "By Allah!" Once Fury and his men convince the natives that the Nazis are the real enemy—demonstrating the necessity of their benevolent white guidance—the nonwhite locals pledge a new allegiance.[37]

A similar pattern emerges in the pages of Marvel's *The Avengers* series. The villainous Baron Zemo, living "deep in the wilds of a South American jungle," reigns, not unlike Rama-Tut, as the "undisputed ruler" of an ashy-gray group of shirtless natives who dress in short, bright skirts and carry countless spears. Zemo's dominance over what he calls the "worthless fools" is clear, and they scatter quickly to bring him the "tribute" he demands. When Captain America arrives to battle Zemo, his presence only further plays to the natives' generalized weakness. Cap, using his shield to deflect their bullets, dismissively declares that he won't "be beaten by some aborigine with a pop gun!" He further outwits the natives, using a pole to jump over them as they comically crash into each other.[38]

Thus, Atlas/Marvel tread new but no less problematic ground—at least in comparison to DC, if not historically—in its homogenization of Asian peoples and cultures. Whether Chinese, Japanese, Korean, or Vietnamese, Marvel creators painted them—literally and metaphorically—with the same brush that had formerly been reserved for Japanese and Japanese Americans during World War II and subsequently extended to the Chinese via Egg Fu at DC. The Korean War, for example, brought the Human Torch and his sidekick, Toro, to the peninsula, where they ran into North Koreans steeped in recognizable racialized tropes. The enemy is untrustworthy and easily identified by their appearance, including an unearthly yellow color as well as slapdash uniforms that look more like oversized pajamas than military dress. The North Koreans speak with heavy accents, further highlighting their difference; they taunt the heroes after dousing their flames, "Now you never get peekie at Pongtu where we have many 'Melican prisoners not reported to U.N. peoples!" A second Korea-based tale presented the Human Torch with the chance to save a white woman menaced by North Korean captors, thus playing to the racialized threat of rape.[39]

Captain America also applied these same racialized motifs to various Asian settings in the mid-1950s. In "Kill Captain America," Cap's North Korean antagonists lurk in a cave, are colored the unearthly yellow preferred by Atlas for Asians, and, of course, are up to no good, working with drugs to brainwash American POWs. Captured by the guerilla Kag, Cap is forced on "the march of death," arriving at a village full of weasellike enemy soldiers. Cap physically bests the North Korean fighters and then defeats Kag, who attacks—unsurprisingly—from behind. In another 1954 story, Cap reinforced a final World War II theme, facing off against a mob of North Korean POWs who resemble mindless zombies.[40] Captain America's exploits led him into Indochina, too, in a propagandistic story that covered the same narrative and visual ground. Here again, Cap and Bucky face a brainwashing operation, this time one that forces captured Americans to spout anti-American messages on the radio. Colored an unearthly yellow and dressed in disheveled pajamas—just like their evil Korean counterparts—the subhuman Indochinese enemy forces white men to act against their country. While Cap and Bucky ultimately free the American victims, the story clearly suggested the need for sustained vigilance against this revived "yellow peril."[41] More to the point, in its mirror-image treatment of the Indochinese, this tale demonstrates the subsuming Orientalism that reified all Asians.

The Chinese threat arrived most fully on American shores in the pages of *Yellow Claw*, which debuted in 1956. The titular villain, in the hands of Al Feldstein and Joe Maneely, appeared as a "Fu Manchu clone" grounded in World War II–era racism.[42] The Chinese in general represent a hybrid threat of race and Communism in "The Coming of the Yellow Claw" as they pursue the titular villain's assistance in destroying the United States "from within [as] the lowly termite crumbles into dust the most majestic structures!" The Yellow Claw himself, still offstage, crystallizes such ominous threats from the East, as legend tells of his "strange and mysterious power" and terrified locals only whisper his name, "as though it were the very name of death itself!" When the Yellow Claw finally appears, he certainly looks the part that World War II comics had imagined for the Japanese enemy—with his long mustache, pointy, bat-like ears, and talon-like fingernails—which was now transferred to all Asians.[43]

If one had hoped these base generalizations would cease with the Marvel rebirth, such hopes would be dashed. Given its World War II setting, it is perhaps unfair to expect much in the way of progress from *Sgt. Fury and His Howling Commandos*, as it relied on images and rhetoric drawn directly from that bygone era. Although Fury and his men typically fought in the

Figure 2.5. The Yellow Claw embodied a revived fear of the "yellow peril" in 1950s America. Drawing on a deep history of anti-Asian sentiment in the United States as well as in the comic book industry, the Yellow Claw was dehumanized, treacherous, and deadly.

European theater, "On to Okinawa" took our heroes into the Pacific, where they were ominously warned, "Japs are different from Nazis! It's not the same kind of war." Another story reinforces the enemy's subhuman nature and tactics as a soldier describes "trees . . . crawlin' with Japs!" The appearance of the Japanese enemy relied on other such stereotyped images, with thick glasses and buckteeth featuring prominently. When Fury needs to infiltrate the enemy, he dresses one of his men in a Japanese uniform and then uses makeup to literally turn him yellow. As a finishing touch, Fury orders the impersonator to use "some goo at the corners of each of [his] eyes to make 'em slant!"[44] In spite of its later creation, *Sgt. Fury* falls back on the racist depictions of its setting.

More might have rightly been expected from those heroes set in the present. If less explicitly racist than *Sgt. Fury*, however, Marvel's 1960s headliners still evince the same homogenizing approach to Asian characters, fictional or otherwise. The Hulk, a hero grounded in a countercultural challenge to authority and facile Cold War assumptions, seemed to present hope for more progressive portrayals of Asians.[45] The comic, however, instead presented stories like "The Hordes of General Fang" that promulgated depictions of Asian inferiority and helplessness that echo those of nonwhites in DC's Silver Age fare.[46] This tale is set in "a tiny Asian village in the principality of Llhasa," where news of General Fang's approach arrives on horseback in this primitive society. The message raises despair among the villagers, who help the reader better understand the utter helplessness of the locals, dressed in the most ridiculous hats and living in pre-modern conditions. As one bluntly laments, "The hordes of General Fang! We are doomed!" The leader of Llhasa, the Lama, reinforces the point, glumly observing, "Alas, I feared it was only a matter of time before he plundered our helpless land! . . . Our only hope is to appeal to the outside world for help!" The Llhasans' plight thus only serves to further homogenize Asians and nonwhites as helpless without superior—and, ultimately, white—assistance. Iron Man's origin presented his Asian enemy—the Vietnamese—in similarly pejorative terms.[47] The text at times reduced the Vietnamese antagonists in general to a subhuman status, for example when Iron Man refers to them as "murdering swine." The images of the specific Vietnamese enemy buttressed this language, as Don Heck drew heavy bags around the villainous Wong-Chu's eyes, making him look all too pathetic, a message reinforced by the sweat pouring profusely down his face as he realizes he is finally confronted by an enemy who is not so helpless.

The Hulk and Iron Man's erstwhile teammates in the Avengers also faced an amalgamated Asian villain, the Commissar.[48] Set in the fictional "Communist-ruled puppet state of Sin-Cong," a revealingly named locale, our story begins with Major Hoy and the Commissar seizing control of the territory. Major Hoy looks just as any reader of early 1960s comics would have expected, his fist raised in anger in front of his sunken cheeks, scrag-

Figure 2.6. The Avengers' adventure in Sin-Cong introduced another in the long line of homogenized Asian villains, as the Commissar embodied the "yellow peril" much like the Yellow Claw had. Such villains continued to trade in timeworn and racist stereotypes that survived even as comic creators increasingly desired to address issues of race.

gly mustache, and fangs. When one villager protests that their American "friends" have helped to feed and clothe them, the massive Commissar strikes fear into the natives by throwing boulders impossible distances and smashing rocks with his inhumanly powerful punches. As the story's introduction concludes, the silhouetted figure of the Commissar looms over the hapless villagers, who bow down to him, his "forbidding shadow fall[ing] over his helpless subjects and spread[ing] like a virus across the conquered land." Confronting the Avengers (now comprising Captain America, Hawkeye, Quicksilver, and the Scarlet Witch), the Commissar simultaneously serves as a personification—and thus continuation—of that overdetermined Asian threat that appeared decades earlier. Back-grounded by a Sin-Cong palace decorated with dragon-faced arches and exotic architecture, the Commissar is ensconced in Orientalist imagery. He likewise proves treacherous, whether by attacking the Avengers from behind or forcing each male Avenger to fight him one on one, lest the Scarlet Witch be killed, in a series of battles in which he cheats. Adding to how his gigantic and thus monstrous form dehumanizes him is the reve-lation that the Commissar is no more than a robot controlled by Major Hoy. The fictional nature of the Commissar, Hoy, and Sin-Cong thus speaks to the racialized imagining of Asians at Marvel as a conglomeration of stereotypes that signals how all of such descent were subsumed and homogenized.

Marvel's own apotheosis of so "Oriental" an enemy—Iron Man's arch-foe, the Mandarin—arrived by similarly conscious design in the adven-tures of Iron Man. Stan Lee, looking back in 2005, explained, "I always wanted to create an inscrutable, mystical Asian villain since, as a teenager, I was turned on to a series of books featuring one of evildom's most clas-sic bad guys, a dude named Fu Manchu. . . . I guess you could say that our Mandarin was my tribute to frightful, fiendish Fu Manchu."[49] The convo-luted origins of Lee's uber-villain, ensconced in the typical rhetoric asso-ciated with the implacable "Oriental" enemy, came in early 1965.[50] Intro-duced by a cover featuring a looming Mandarin, larger than life, with long, outstretched arms grasping across the Great Wall of China to ensnare Iron Man, the villain's origins included just about every trope of the "Orient" as threat. His father, "a direct descendent of Genghis Khan," had tragi-cally "married beneath him[self]," tying himself foolishly to "a high born Englishwoman!" Clearly, the Mandarin explains to Iron Man, the gods "must have been displeased," because an "idol" toppled over and killed his father on the very day his ill-fated son was born. When his mother soon after died of a broken heart, the Mandarin was given to his aunt, an angry woman who raised the child "to hate the world" while teaching him "the sciences of the world . . . the arts of warfare . . . and the subtle crafts of villainy!" After losing his family's wealth, the Mandarin eventually stumbles across a flying saucer with alien technology in the form of ten rings that will allow him to become "master of earth!" A perfect blend of "Oriental" antiquity, Asian perfidy, and alien technology, the Mandarin now emerged as a quintessentially overdetermined "yellow" threat to "white" America.

Set in "the remote vastness of Red China"—or, as later noted, the "seething, smoldering, secretive Red China"—the Mandarin's adventures also presented a fully dehumanized enemy.[51] As Tony Stark notes, taking on the enemy is "like walking into a dragon's mouth." In the hair-raising conclusion to *Tales of Suspense* #54, the Mandarin stands seemingly triumphant, and the viewer sees a landscape image of the outside of the Mandarin's stronghold late at night. Here, silhouetted by a full moon, a coyote, fangs bared and head reared back, howls at the moon.[52] Later in the story line, the Mandarin, shown throughout with wickedly crooked teeth, appears apelike, hunched over the ruins of his ill-earned high-tech equipment.[53] The foreign and even inhuman appearance of the enemy was reinforced in another story by juxtaposed panels midadventure, one presenting the Mandarin in all his evil bluster, the next contrasting the enemy with a calm, cool, and collected Iron Man, whose piercing blue eyes shine through his mask.[54] As the antagonist lurched through story after story, often hunched over menacingly as he attacks Iron Man, his appearance continued to reiterate the monstrous threat that he—and the Asians he stood for—posed.[55]

The Mandarin's Chinese underlings, for their part, also suggested the inhuman and servile qualities of the Asian other. The baddie, indeed, has a seemingly endless army of faceless men willing to sacrifice their lives for his self-interested cause. These storm troopers at times appear with almost featureless faces, the Mandarin looming over them as their absolute master. In a later story, although the Chinese are colored "white" like Stark, their dress—consisting of the long-established funny hats, earrings, pajamas, scruffy facial hair, and ammo belts—continued to set them apart, highlighting their profound difference from their white adversaries.[56]

Finally, the Mandarin's actions confirmed that the threat of the "yellow peril" remained a pressing concern for the American public. First and foremost, the Mandarin, like all the Asian comic villains before him, often plots sneak attacks. The villain also relies heavily on advanced and nefarious technology, for example in deploying a magnetic weapon and a paralyzer ray in his battles versus Iron Man. When using the latter, the Man-

Figure 2.7. The apotheosis of the "yellow peril" villain, the Mandarin joined characters like the Yellow Claw, Major Hoy, and the Commissar in reifying Asians as less than human, conniving, threatening, and evil. Such portrayals belie commonly held assumptions about the wholly progressive nature of Marvel's 1960s fare. Here, the contrast between the white Iron Man's bright blue eyes and the thoroughly racialized Mandarin suggests that a racial hierarchy still holds power.

darin reveals his truly barbarous self, leaving our hero alive momentarily because he wants "to toy with you a little longer first!" In addition to his technological prowess, the Mandarin is also the self-described "greatest karate master the world has ever known!"[57]

Consequently, though Marvel might at first appear to have played it less "safe" than the DC comics of the postwar era and Silver Age, the company's fare was no less predicated on reified and homogenized depictions of nonwhite "others." Even as comics changed in response to political and economic constrictions both within and without the comics industry, they remained, at best, stagnant in how they depicted nonwhite individuals and communities, reflecting and reinforcing a broader cultural ambivalence about race in the United States. The fact that "playing it safe" in comics during the Cold War era often relied on pernicious, homogenized depictions of Asians, Native Americans, and other nonwhites as ignorant, backward, and helpless is, however, only one side of comics' engagement in US society of this time, and thus reflects just one side of the American ambivalence in this era.

The Other Side of the Coin: Steps toward Social Relevance in Comics

If broad social factors existed that discouraged the comics industry from addressing racism, no less broad societal changes, climaxing in the 1960s, also cultivated an atmosphere in which publishers could pursue less timid stories. The changes began—at least from the broader public's perception—in 1955, when Rosa Parks refused to give up her seat on a Montgomery bus, sparking a boycott that would last 381 days. The boycott changed everything, although perhaps many did not understand this immediately. Still, as local African Americans organized to sustain what would be a long challenge, it became clear just what they were willing to risk (in terms of jobs, comfort, and even personal safety) to protest inequality. The boycott also generated an increasing belief in the ability to create real social change and introduced new leaders, including Martin Luther King Jr., to a broader public. In early 1960, grassroots activism took a second important step in Greensboro, North Carolina, when four black students at North Carolina A&T College courageously started the sit-in movement at their local Woolworth's. As the movement grew, reaching more than a thousand protestors by the end of the first week, observers could sense the discontent and rage that continued to permeate the black community even after *Brown v. Board of Education*, and even more so as sit-ins spread quickly beyond Greensboro. The subsequent founding of the Student Nonviolent Coordinating Committee (SNCC) suggested that these kinds of protests were not one-offs; a revolution was at hand.[58]

Such pressures from below eventually brought establishment responses, if only haltingly. John Kennedy found himself forced to act by the growing movement, despite his general indifference to racial issues as a congressman. The ambitious politician had only sought advisors with ties to the black community when it became clear he would run for president. His narrow victory in 1960 came in part from African American voters, but the new president followed in the pattern of his bipartisan predecessors, failing to live up to his rhetoric. He seems, William Chafe observes, to simply have lacked any particular commitment in this regard. This changed, finally, in 1963, when police brutality against nonviolent protestors moved Kennedy to deliver his famous address on civil rights and to propose a bill to ameliorate such problems. Kennedy's assassination, however, left the problem with Lyndon Johnson, whose fixation on consensus drew him to address issues of race. He had begun to do so, in fact, even before becoming president, selfishly seeing the need to break free from stereotypes about southerners if he were ever to win the office. This kind of political calculation also seems to have informed Johnson's actions as president, with Chafe arguing that the new president leveraged the demands for civil rights to transform his party from the regional interests that hemmed it—and, perhaps more importantly, him—in.[59] Thus, while the Civil Rights Act of 1964 and the Voting Rights Act of 1965 stand as landmark legislation, Johnson's commitment seems too self-interested to suggest a complete reorientation of liberal beliefs about race.

Within this societal and political context, some of DC's superhero fare of the Cold War era diverged from the rest to treat issues of race and ethnicity more effectively. Indeed, at least some at DC seem to have felt unhappiness as their heroes moved into fantasy worlds divorced from the realities confronting their readers in the postwar era. For example, in 1949 DC began devoting one page in all of its books to calls for tolerance, cooperation, and civic engagement. The very next year, it ran a one-page story starring the Man of Steel that called for racial and religious tolerance. Similarly, 1951's "Know Your Country" saw Superboy promoting diversity since "no single land, race, or nationality can claim this country as its own." In 1952, Superman intervened after a white child got credit for the heroic actions of a black one, teaching a lesson on prejudice in the process. But while Superman spoke out against racism in such educational features, he did not address such issues in his comic book adventures, marking the clear limits of the company's activism.[60]

If Superman's comic books dodged serious critiques of race, his appearances in other media were more ambitious, albeit mixed in their efforts. The *Adventures of Superman* radio show proved its willingness to address discrimination in "Clan of the Fiery Cross," a June 1946 program that saw the Man of Steel take on a Ku Klux Klan–like enemy. The program allegedly revealed Klan passwords in Georgia, among other secret information. The forthright critique of racial prejudice in the show has inspired many stories, some perhaps apocryphal, about the effects of Superman's battle. One such story suggests that the Georgia Klan tried to arrange a boycott of the show; another claims that the radio show caused Klan membership to decline.[61] The televised *Adventures of Superman* likewise had high-flown goals, as expressed by George Reeves, who portrayed Superman: "We're all concerned with giving kids the right kind of show. . . . Our writers and the sponsors have children, and they are all very careful about doing things on the show that will have no adverse effect on the young audience. We even try, in our scripts, to give gentle messages of tolerance and to stress that a man's color and race and religious beliefs should be respected." While Reeves and the show's creators might have been inspired, at least in part, by a desire to make the show "safe"—and thus marketable—for kids, the emphasis on tolerance hinted that the show might move beyond the comic books in its treatment of race.[62]

Such hopes were realized in "The Riddle of the Chinese Jade," which managed to present Chinese Americans as human beings instead of stereotypes.[63] Though this episode opens with predictable bamboo-style lettering that introduced the title, and suggested Chinese primitivity in such aspects as Chinatown's lack of phones and abundance of caves, underneath this typically "Oriental" frame existed glimmers of hope for equality. A curio shop owner, Lu Sung, and his niece, Lilly, are solid citizens who want to assimilate. When Lois and Clark visit to cover the story of Lu Sung's donation of a valuable jade statue to the National Art Museum, they discover that the curio shop proprietor is an excellent American in the making, dressing in an American-style suit and learning English. When he promises our reporters, in his typically stilted fashion, "a scoop of news," he kindly takes Lois's paternalistic correction—"a news scoop"—and goes on to praise "this great country" for all it "has done for me and my people!" Lois can only beam: "Lu Sung, I am proud and happy to know you."

Even the ethnic villain in this piece, Harry Wong, comes off as a surprisingly sympathetic character. He plots with Greer, a white thug, to steal the jade statue but wrestles with feelings of guilt. Harry ultimately goes along with the heist because he feels that the jade belongs to his fiancée, Lilly, too, and he wants her (and, of course, himself) to benefit from the wealth it might bestow. The climax of this plot, however, further underlined Harry's less stereotypical nature. He eventually bails on the plan, but Greer wants to finish the heist. The two men struggle, but Greer knocks Harry out and beats Lilly into unconsciousness, too. After Superman saves the day, the episode ends with a twist. Harry deserves punishment, but the white detective decides not to arrest him. Although he has never taken the law into his own hands in this way, the detective explains, his sympathy for Harry leads to a deal: if Harry will testify against Greer, he will not be prosecuted. Leaving aside the procedural issues with the episode's conclusion, it stands out for its more humane treatment of Chinese Americans.

Like Superman, Batman's postwar comic book adventures evinced little

Figure 2.8. For all its reliance on the politics of safety, postwar DC fare would make both subtle and more direct efforts to confront issues of racial discrimination. Here, in a quiet and unobtrusive (and, thus, perhaps more effective) way, Gotham appears a more diverse city than it had once appeared, if only in a limited way.

interest in directly tackling issues of race and prejudice, although an occasional story hinted at themes of tolerance.[64] Gotham City, like Metropolis, was populated largely by white citizens, although occasional glimpses of nonwhites did occur. "The Phantom of the Library," for example, suggested that a more multicultural society existed—if clandestinely—in Gotham. Here, the reader sees the room for "Foreign Language Books." Captured in one solitary panel, four men sit engrossed in their books, each apparently reading in his native language. While one presents no clear nationality, the others have ethnic markers. One has arched eyebrows and slanted eyes, hinting at his Asian background. Another wears a pale-blue, American-style suit, but his fez suggests his Mediterranean or Middle Eastern origins. The final man wears a turban. While such characters don't appear on Gotham's streets, they could be found—for a panel, at least, and perhaps a bit too trapped in racialized appearances—hanging out at its library.[65]

Gotham City would appear much the same way in the 1960s *Batman* television show, as crowd scenes and public settings were, for the most part, populated solely by whites. In "Nora Clavicle and the Ladies' Crime Club," for example, the crowd at a luncheon is wholly white, as is the crowd at a bank in "The Entrancing Dr. Cassandra" and a group of soldiers in "Penguin Sets a Trend." Blacks would show up in limited roles—as part of a film crew in "Penguin Is a Girl's Best Friend" or a member of the Joker's gang in "The Joker's Flying Saucer"—and other nonwhites appeared as stereotypical villains: the Asian scientist Lotus in "Louie's Lethal Lilac Time," the Native American Chief Standing Pat in "The Great Escape," or Fernando Rodriguez Enrique Dominguez, a Latino member of the same gang as the chief, who played against—but no less reinforcing—type with a British accent and heightened vocabulary.[66]

Batman's adventures in the 1950s provided one more positive look at an Asian American. In "The Man behind the Red Hood," Batman meets Paul Wong when the Caped Crusader teaches a criminology course at State University. Wong—a vision of assimilation in his letterman's sweater, shirt, and tie—is very sharp, picking up clues in crime scenes and earning Batman's earnest praise. But Wong misses clues as well (no one is, after all, as good as Batman), and he is embarrassed when Batman offers help. In the end, Wong and the other students prove their mettle, helping the Dark Knight solve the mystery, suggesting a kind of equality and acceptance rarely seen in DC's postwar comic books.[67]

Similarly humanistic depictions of nonwhites were to be found at Atlas, even in the otherwise scurrilous *Yellow Claw*. Set against this series' compilation of "Oriental" treachery and "yellow peril" hysterics was a Chinese American FBI agent, Jimmy Woo, who served to remind readers that not all Chinese were the enemy. Along with Suwan, the Claw's grandniece, who is driven by her conscience and growing love for Woo to assist him, the agent repeatedly frustrates the villain. Woo and Suwan make a startling transformation in *Yellow Claw* #2, when Atlas dropped the use of its standard unearthly yellow and instead colored the two valorous Chinese Americans white, providing a visual cue to the series' recognition of their humanity. The point is driven home in a panel that juxtaposes the newfound whiteness of Woo and Suwan with the Yellow Claw's animalistic hand, sporting sharpened fingernails and colored yellow.[68]

A similarly somewhat progressive image of Chinese Americans also appears in *Captain America* #77, which begins on an ominous note: "Death stalks Chinatown! It is the long arm of the Chinese Communists, reaching from the homeland clear over to haunt and threaten the loyal Chinese Americans in New York's Chinatown! Who can stop it? Who can halt the dread menace of . . . the Man with No Face!"[69] However, such threat soon proves an exception to this setting; as Cap explains to Detective Wing, a Chinese American, "I don't have much occasion to be asked to help out in

Chinatown! Your people are a pretty law-abiding group, Wing!" While Cap maintains a somewhat paternalistic relationship with Wing, not unlike his other Cold War brethren, throughout the story, the praise he shares matters, especially given how rare such evaluations were elsewhere in the comic book industry.[70]

From these initially halting steps toward tolerance and equality, the nascent Marvel Universe that debuted under and was driven by the writer Stan Lee and the artists Jack Kirby and Steve Ditko brought a more pronouncedly reformist sensibility to comics. Their heroes, indeed, brought something new to comics. The arrival of the Fantastic Four was the first to portend something different, and other new superheroes soon followed. The Hulk arrived next, followed quickly by Spider-Man. Building on these early successes, the Marvel creators quickly populated their universe, adding characters like Thor, Ant-Man, Nick Fury, Iron Man, Wasp, Hawkeye, Daredevil, and others. Throw in a couple of heroes reborn, including Captain America and the Sub-Mariner, and the universe grew further. The core heroes came together as the Avengers, and Marvel introduced a second team book featuring a group of young mutants, the X-Men.[71]

As its heroes struggled with personal problems and Cold War concerns, Marvel's new protagonists raised—if slowly and inconsistently—the possibility of a new approach to race. Marvel's antiestablishment if apolitical comics were the first to include black civilians. Furthermore, Stan's Soapbox, a monthly column that allowed Lee to speak out on whatever was on his mind (often in promotional ways, of course), buttressed this approach to race as Lee made calls for a broadly defined tolerance.[72] Lee's columns reflected what he saw as the ethos of Marvel's creators. As he later described, his company had "no official party line" in terms of politics, but "most of our writers are young, idealistic, and passionately liberal." Artists, Lee added, include "every shade and facet of the political spectrum, and that's the way it should be. After all, the Marvel Bullpen is really America in microcosm, and I figure that, like our nation itself, we should be strong enough and wise enough to tolerate every type of ideology." Within this inclusive vision, Lee stressed, "the only philosophies that have no place at Marvel are those preaching war or bigotry."[73]

Such a general philosophy of tolerance at Marvel seems to have reached even the story lines most unlikely to be sympathetic to such a message. Under the creative partnership of the writer Roy Thomas and the penciller Dick Ayers, the *Sgt. Fury* title included a 1967 story focused on a Japanese American soldier that contrasted its predominantly problematic approach to this ethnic group. In this tale, Jim Morita arrives to Fury's squad, only to be confronted by two obviously racist soldiers who refer to the new arrival as "Slanty-Eyes" and threaten to "show 'im what we do with his kind back where we come from!" When Morita protests by noting that the soldiers have confused him "with the rats that bombed Pearl Harbor," Fury looks on from a distance, giving "the Nisei a chance to show what he can do!" As a physical confrontation occurs, the racists go on to call Morita a "little man" and "Hirohito." Morita schools his antagonists—in both the English language and combat—deploying unmatched martial arts skills. Fury then intervenes, forcing the unthinking soldiers to apologize. So far, so good; the antiracist message is clear enough. However, the story then undermines some of its intended good with an ending that presents Morita as the dispenser of fortune-cookie wisdom—"as a wise man once said, it's better to die on your feet than to live on your knees"—that reduces him to stereotype. He—and not whites—also assumes responsibility for "fixing" racism; as he explains to Fury, "I kind'a figure it's my job to change their minds, anyway!"[74]

But the progress at Marvel goes beyond one such dramatic scene; other, more sustained signs of hope started to appear, especially in titles like *The Amazing Spider-Man*. Created by Stan Lee and Steve Ditko, the titular angst-ridden teenage hero appealed to youth coming of age amid Vietnam, civil rights, and a spirit of revolution.[75] Spidey's book also promoted racial inclusiveness, quietly approaching the topic in what might have been Marvel's most effective (and, perhaps not coincidentally, least preachy) manner. In these pages, hints of the ways in which a comic book might more effectively address socially relevant topics in the mid-1960s appear to careful readers, as Ditko presents subtle but important depictions of a truly multicultural and even integrated America. Unlike the street scenes of Kirby, Ditko's backgrounds include a wide range of African Americans that, even though not fully fleshed out as characters, present as a simple assumption the idea that the United States was a multiracial (or at least biracial) society, a quiet but revelatory change in comic book storytelling.

African Americans thus show up in any number of roles. Black kids, for example, appear in numerous ways. In one issue, three youths witness an embarrassing moment for Spider-Man, who trips and tumbles into the water. As he emerges and refuses autographs, an African American teenager whispers to his white friends, "I haven't got the heart to tell him that we're Human Torch fans, anyway!"[76] Slightly older African American youths share Peter's high school graduation, their excited parents beaming with pride as their children graduate from what appears to be a harmoniously integrated school. These black students follow Peter as he moves to

Figure 2.9. The *Amazing Spider-Man* artist Steve Ditko quietly presented readers with a vision of a multicultural America by including nonwhites in the background of scenes, such as this one, a depiction of Peter Parker's graduation from high school.

Empire State University, too, hanging out with whites on campus, suggesting an easy acceptance. When protest breaks out on campus, the protestors are an integrated bunch, suggesting that reform appeals to all Americans, regardless of color.[77]

The presence of African American adults further reinforces this message of racial inclusiveness, suggesting that the integration of childhood seamlessly transitioned into equality as adults. On the streets, African American background characters join whites in complaining about the tragically misunderstood Spider-Man, one noting that our hero is "getting on my nerves!"[78] Black professionals populate other parts of *The Amazing Spider-Man*, further reinforcing a message of integration. J. Jonah Jameson's offices at the *Daily Bugle*, for instance, employ numerous black professionals, including the prominent and ever-present supporting cast member Robbie Robertson, long-suffering aide-de-camp to the blustering Jameson. More strikingly, when Peter's Aunt May is hospitalized with a rare and potentially fatal blood condition, a black doctor reveals the good news of her cure.[79]

The pages of *Sgt. Fury and His Howling Commandos* put to the fore another African American character, the soldier Gabe Jones, in 1963. Joining an integrated unit that included the Jewish Izzy Cohen and the Italian American Dino Manelli, Jones played an equal and more crucially humanistic role in the platoon from the start, a two-page splash that introduced the diverse Howlers. Shown with his most iconic symbol, his trumpet,

Jones's biography reinforced the message: "'Gabe' used to blow the sweetest trumpet this side of Carnegie Hall! Now he gives out with the hot licks on the field of battle . . . but his notes are just as true, and his hands and heart as steady as ever!"[80] Outside of battle, Jones longs for the good old days when he could dedicate his life to music, wistfully remarking at one point, as he raises his trumpet to his lips, "Man, would I like to be wailin' with Jonah Jones back at the Embers right now!" He is excited as the Commandos arrive at a town in the battle zone, exclaiming, "Man, I've been waiting a long time for this visit to town! Hope they have a good jazz combo somewhere!"[81]

Additionally, Jones often plays the role of hero, unlike his World War II–era predecessors like Whitewash Jones who served only as comic relief. Thus, Jones fights effectively, even when playing his instrument. At one point, with the Commandos under siege, Fury rallies his men around the trumpet, ordering Jones to "keep tootin'. . . . C'mon you guys—let 'em know we're here—howl, blast ya—howl!!" As Jones's musical stylings rally the Commandos, he simultaneously knocks a Nazi unconscious with the butt of his rifle.[82] Similarly, in "Lord Ha-Ha's Last Laugh," Jones blows his trumpet to draw a Nazi attack, which he rather easily overcomes, dodging bullets and tossing a grenade back at his enemies while mocking them: "Where'd you learn to shoot, man? In a penny arcade?" As he throws the Nazi grenade back at his combatants, the writer Lee (through the voice of Jones) takes on the race issue directly, posing American racial egalitarianism against Nazi racism as Jones ironically hollers, "Heads up, master race!"[83] Jones's ultimate heroism is demonstrated by his willingness to sacrifice his own life courageously in a suicide mission (that he miraculously survives), here even more nobly transcending the goofball antics of his World War II predecessors.[84]

In case readers missed the underlying messages of racial equality in the first five issues of *Sgt. Fury and His Howling Commandos*, Lee and Kirby made the point explicitly in "The Fangs of the Fox," the first of several such sermons on tolerance that would likewise pepper the Marvel fare of the early 1960s.[85] Here, readers met George Stonewell, who steps in to replace Dino Manelli, who has broken his leg. From the get-go, the narrative establishes Stonewell as a racist. When he meets Manelli, he refuses to shake his hand after identifying him as an "Italian." He is similarly rude to the Jewish Izzy Cohen. Not surprisingly, Stonewell has a stormy meeting with Jones, whom the former is stunned to see in the barracks. In contrast, Stonewell responds much more positively to the WASP-ish Rebel Ralston—a polite greeting along with the observation, "Glad there's one of my kind in this squad!"—and to Dum Dum Dugan, to whom Stonewell remarks, "I was gettin' worried about this squad after meetin' some of the others!" Stonewell's obvious racism would spill over onto the battlefield as well. Both Jones and Cohen confront Stonewell when on two separate occasions he disobeys orders from Fury. Appalled that Jones "put your hands on me," Stonewell promises to "get ya for that!" Stonewell takes similar offense at Cohen, exclaiming, "No guy named Cohen talks to me like that! I'll put you in your place, you punk!"

If such scenes, perhaps heavy-handedly, make clear the bigotry Stonewell both possesses and represents, others served to ironize his intolerance. For example, a captured Nazi overhears Stonewell's diatribes and tries to recruit him to fight for Hitler, arguing, "It is our side you should be fighting on! The side of the superior Aryans! For we do not allow inferior races to mingle with us—to be part of our culture! That is why we cannot lose the war! That is why we are always triumphant!" Stonewell refuses; he may be a racist, but he has "no use for Nazis, either!" Later, when Nazi soldiers encircle him and Cohen, the fault lines of Stonewell's racism are again exposed. As the pair stand together, Cohen quips, "I notice you ain't complainin' about my religion all of a sudden!" Finally, when Stonewell is injured and needs a blood transfusion, his rare blood type is matched only by Jones, who readily volunteers to donate his blood. The narrator makes clear this irony, describing Stonewell, as he is transferred to another command, as a "man whose heart was filled with bigotry—with hatred—whose life was saved by the two men he most despised." In the end, "The Fangs of the Fox" left readers with hope for change in the kinds of Americans Stonewell embodied. Leaving, Stonewell shares his new address with Cohen and Jones. This leads the soldiers to wonder if they did, perhaps, get to Stonewell after all. Fury then delivers the moral of the story: "The seeds of prejudice, which takes a lifetime to grow, can't be stamped out overnight—but if we keep trying—keep fighting—perhaps a day will come when 'love thy brother' will be more than just an expression we hear in church!"

Fury's pontificating in *Sgt. Fury and His Howling Commandos* was just a start; more fully developed sermons would develop in comic books starring the X-Men and the Fantastic Four, such moralizing becoming another means by which early Marvel promoted tolerance and equality. The former was the less effective of the two, a flawed but truly sincere attempt to address social concerns about race via stories of genetic difference. In the pages of *X-Men*, Lee allowed Professor X to explain why a secret school to train mutants was necessary: "When I was young, normal people feared me, distrusted me! I realized the human race is not yet ready to accept those with extra powers! So I decided to build a haven . . . a school for X-Men! . . . Here we stay, unsuspected by normal humans, as we learn to use our powers for the benefit of mankind . . . to help those who would distrust us if they knew of our existence!" In this passage, Lee paralleled "extra powers" to racial and ethnic difference, the one being slow to receive acceptance in the Marvel Universe and the other, in our own. Professor X would also serve as foil to the mutant villain Magneto (and vice versa), inviting comparisons to Martin Luther King Jr. and Malcolm X.[86]

It is in this latter parallel that Lee tripped over his own racial metaphor, often producing stories that blamed the victim for racism and discrimination by making mutants the criminal aggressors. The archvillain Magneto exemplified this problem, arguing against Xavier's goal of a "golden age" of human-mutant cooperation by contending that the "humans must be our slaves! They are not worthy to share dominion of earth with us!"[87] Lesser mutant baddies echoed similar themes. The Vanisher clearly sees mutants as racially superior, telling a group of nonpowered humans, "It is only fitting that homo superior should be served by the inferior homo sapiens! Therefore, I shall allow you to become my lackeys!"[88] Similarly, Mastermind expresses a complete disregard for lesser humans, expressing his anger in an argument by telling Quicksilver, "I shall destroy you now as easily as I might destroy a mere homo sapien!"[89] Even the X-Men felt similar frustrations with humanity. In issue #8, the Beast—out of costume in responding to a sudden emergency—finds himself accosted by a human mob. When he arrives back at the mansion in tattered clothing, the Beast angrily announces, "I'm through risking my life for humans. . . . For the same humans who fear us, hate us, want to destroy us! I think Magneto and his evil mutants are right . . . homo sapiens are just not worth it!"[90]

Lee's most obvious attempt to address difference in the early issues of *X-Men* arrived in a three-part story spanning 1965 to 1966. In the first part of this epic tale, Lee introduces readers to Dr. Bolivar Trask, a leading anthropologist, at a press conference.[91] There, Trask makes an ominous pronouncement that again underlines mutation as a metaphor for difference: "We've been so busy worrying about cold wars, hot wars, atom bombs, and the like that we've overlooked the greatest menace of all! Mutants walk among us! Hidden! Unknown! Waiting—! Waiting for their moment to strike! They are mankind's most deadly enemy! For only they have the actual power to conquer the human race! Even as we speak, they are out there—scheming, plotting, planning—thinking we don't suspect! But, there is still time to smash them—if we strike now!" The next panel shows newspapers rolling off the presses with headlines screaming, "Mutant Menace!" Professor X again provides a more tolerant counterpoint. He goes on television to debate Trask, presenting a message that, though it does not convince an angry and frightened public, serves as an extratextual paean for tolerance over fear and hatred. "Before giving way to groundless fears," Xavier remonstrates, "we must first consider — what is a mutant? He is not a monster! He is not necessarily a menace! He is merely a person who was born with different power or ability than the average human!"

The rest of the story functioned to undermine the position Trask represented, not unlike *Sgt. Fury and His Howling Commandos* did with Stonewell, by highlighting its irony. Trask unveils his plan to deal with the so-called mutant menace, his robotic Sentinels, but his creations turn on him, a first hint at what the wages of such bigotry can be. As the story moves forward, Trask eventually realizes this very moral. As he eventually concludes, "I had wanted to help humanity — to fight the mutants!! What a fool I was!! What a blind — dangerous fool!"[92] Trask then confronts the Master Mold, which makes Sentinels, arguing, "No! No! I was wrong! I realize that now! They aren't menaces to mankind — it's you who are! [The X-Men] mustn't be harmed —!" Realizing that he has "created an evil far greater than the menace it was built to destroy," Trask wrecks the Sentinel-creating machinery because he doesn't want to see all of mankind enslaved and destroyed — not, importantly, just to protect mutants. Trask dies while destroying all the machinery and the Master Mold, and his demise allows Lee to impart the lesson at the story's end: "Beware the fanatic! Too often his cure is deadlier by far than the evil he denounces!"[93] Here, though Lee can be accused of reducing a fanatic's desire to subjugate those genetically different from himself to a lesson of one man's moral failings, the metaphor of bigotry and racism's self-destructive consequences also operates within the narrative.

Lee and Kirby were more successful in staying on track with the arrival of the Hate-Monger, a villain whose very identity and mission required a sustained focus on difference, in *The Fantastic Four* #21.[94] As Lee later recalled, this story "meant a lot to me, because it was the first full-length feature to openly and forcefully attack the evils of bigotry and racial hatred. In a way, I feel it helped set the tone for what would later become the Marvel Creed of Humanism!"[95] The issue opened with a splash page showcasing the Hate-Monger, robed in purple with a KKK-like hood, holding a burning torch in one hand. The accompanying text, in prose less bombastic than Lee's usual style, read simply: "The editors predict that this is the most unusual, thought-provoking tale you will read this season! We believe you will agree!" In case fans might turn away from this relatively pedestrian opening, Lee also opined that this story was "destined to become a Fantastic Four classic!"

The scene then shifts to the Baxter Building, where the Fantastic Four learn about the Hate-Monger in the newspaper. In response to the rioting that the villain is causing, the Thing (a.k.a. Ben Grimm) is angry, noting, "That crumb who calls himself the Hate-Monger has been causin' trouble wherever he goes, and nobody can stop him because he's too smart to break any laws!" Reed Richards concurs, emphasizing that the Hate-Monger is "the most dangerous type of menace! He preaches class hatred, race hatred, religious hatred!" Sue Storm, playing the role of the one whose ignorance needs correction, cannot understand why her teammates care, saying that "his activities don't concern the Fantastic Four!" At this point, the narrator critiques Sue, intoning that she will quickly learn "how completely wrong her casual comment is!" This brief tableau established the story's moral continuum, between those, like Sue, who are willing to ignore such bigotry, and those, like Reed and Ben, who are not.

The story would go on to confirm Reed's fears, at the same time giving a sci-fi but no less metaphorical twist to how such racism can easily spread. When the team comes across a rally led by the Hate-Monger, they find him surrounded by a crowd chanting, "Down with all foreigners! Down with everybody who disagrees with us! Hail the Hate-Monger!" The villain, leaning with menace over his podium, snarls, "Those who are not with us are against us! They must be destroyed!" He then goes on to preach, "We must drive all the foreigners back where they came from! We must show no mercy to those we hate!" The Hate-Monger's power is palpable, as he "seems to have the crowd in a trance! They—they're actually agreeing with his un-American sentiments!" As it turns out, the Hate-Monger is swaying Americans to racism and hatred with more than just words; he also has invented an "all-powerful H-ray" that can turn anyone into a hateful person. Indeed, this even includes the Fantastic Four, who, when zapped by the H-ray, "begin to fight among themselves! Not the good natured bickering which their fans know so well, but a different type of conflict, filled with hostility and raw hatred!" Though perhaps too facilely generalizing a specifically racialized bigotry into hatred, the story does serve to emphasize the fears of how easily such intolerance can ensnare.

The climax of the story presents yet another instance of Lee's somewhat saccharine sermonizing. The Fantastic Four, finally cured of the H-ray's effects, ultimately take the battle to the Hate-Monger. In a panic, the villain fires his H-ray wildly, accidently shooting a couple of his soldiers, who now see that they've been tricked by the Hate-Monger, whom they shoot and kill. When his mask is pulled off, the story provides its final twist: the Hate-Monger is really "Adolf Hitler! The mad Fuehrer! The most evil human being the world has ever known!" Final clarity is lacking, however, as Reed points out, "Actually, we'll never know whether he was the real Hitler, or one of the many doubles the Fuehrer was reported to have!" Nonetheless, Reed can now deliver the parting moral of the story: "Until men truly love each other, regardless of race, creed, or color, the Hate-Monger will still be undefeated! Let's never forget that!" The narrator then reinforces the point, arguing that "Reed Richards' words never shall be forgotten! Not while the stars and stripes still wave! Not while America endures!" Though the jingoistic celebration of America perhaps clashes with the events of the story—which saw those very Americans swayed to forget what the story claims they shall not—as well as the country's own racial history, there is no denying that this tale of the Fantastic Four, like those in *Sgt. Fury and His Howling Commandos* and *X-Men*, made strident use of the comic page to elicit tolerance and antiprejudicial feelings in its readers.

Conclusion

Reed's clarion call for racial equality belied, however, a decidedly mixed message from Marvel, despite signs of racial progress in the early 1960s. *The Fantastic Four Annual* #3, which presented the long-awaited marriage of Reed and Sue, made the point clearly. To make a long story short, Doctor Doom, archnemesis of the Fantastic Four, is unhappy and plots to ruin the big day. As a result, the issue becomes a kaleidoscope of Marvel heroes and villains, the former thwarting the latter's myriad plots to stop the wedding. The Mandarin makes a brief appearance, furtively looking around a corner and attacking the X-Man Angel from behind. The African American Gabe Jones arrives on the last page of the story as a bouncer, keeping unwanted guests out.[96] Even in the aftermath of Lee's call for racial inclusiveness, the Marvel Universe consisted of loads of white characters and only two nonwhites important enough to make even brief appearances. Marvel still had a long way to go.

It is hardly surprising, given the ambivalence within US society in the twenty years following World War II, that what the comic book industry produced at the same time was equally ambivalent: both plagued by stereotyped and demeaning representations of nonwhites and their communities while peppered with calls for tolerance and more progressive images. The arrival of Marvel in the early 1960s, and, to a lesser extent, concomitant work at DC, suggested a watershed of sorts in the comic book industry vis-à-vis race that coincided with the growth of the civil rights movement. Although scholarly work often traces the rise of "social relevance" in comic books to the early 1970s (and specifically to *Green Lantern/Green Arrow*, which will be addressed in the next chapter), this earlier work heralded important—if incompletely realized—change. That the growth came slowly made sense, as not long prior, DC and Marvel (as Atlas) had been relying on long-held images of race. Still, the early 1960s suggested that race might be addressed in more (self-)conscious and progressive ways. Others would soon jump into the breach, heralding even more significant progress but also continuing problems in the conversation about race both in comics and in society at large.

CHAPTER 3

"We're All Brothers!": The Ideal of Liberal Brotherhood in the 1960s and 1970s

A black teenage couple — Rick and Linda — experience car trouble as they drive in the suburbs. Two pudgy white motorcyclists see the couple and conclude that their arrival is the first step toward integrating the white neighborhood. The two bikers harass the couple to teach them to "stay on their own side of town," so Rick draws their attention while Linda goes for help. Rick leads the two men into a construction site and to the sixth floor of a partially constructed building. As they pursue Rick, though, the bikers trip and fall off the side of the unfinished high-rise; one manages to grab the edge of a girder while the second clings precariously to him. As they call for help, Rick returns and reaches to help them. As he does so, one of the white men asks why he's saving them; Rick replies, "Cause we're all brothers no matter what color we are!" The bikers, having learned their lesson that being prejudiced is a "pretty dumb stupid thing" and can make you do some "pretty dumb stupid things," resolve to help the couple with their car.

Such is the plot of "Prejudice," from Season 1 of *The All-New Super Friends Hour*, which aired on Saturday mornings throughout the fall of 1977. Part of each hour was a short episode like "Prejudice" featuring the Wonder Twins, Zan and Jayna, as well as their space monkey, Gleek. In this episode, the heroes are alerted to Rick's danger by Linda, and the duo save the bikers at the last minute.[1] The significance of this episode is two-fold. First, it serves as an example of how superhero popular culture of the 1960s and 1970s began to confront even more earnestly and intentionally the realities of racism and prejudice in the United States. Second, it is emblematic of the ideology underlying these encounters. Specifically, the events and moral of this Saturday-morning parable embody a notion of "brotherhood" that existed in US culture throughout the 1960s and into the mid-1970s.

Rooted in what historians describe as the "liberal consensus" of the postwar era, this notion treats prejudice and racism as an issue of the individual white conscience; that is, racism and discrimination emanate from individual whites—as opposed to, say, being entrenched in the economic, political, and social structures of US society—and thus the key to correcting prejudice is to "fix" these flawed individuals. In "Prejudice," this correction occurs through blacks proving themselves to whites, specifically when Rick elects to save the bikers despite their harassment of him. Not only does Rick thus come to occupy the moral high ground—saving his oppressors when they would likely not have done the same—but he does so out of, and thus gives voice to, a vague notion of "brotherhood" within which whites and blacks can become friends and equals. But the onus for change is put first on Rick and thus blacks in general: within this brotherhood myth, blacks must prove themselves worthy—morally and ethically—to foster a parallel change in racist white individuals that is imagined as the solution to the racism and discrimination that is assumed to exist solely within the hearts and minds of some flawed individual whites.

The superhero comics of the 1960s and 1970s, as they began more intentionally to confront racial issues, promulgated this liberal myth of "brotherhood." Veering from the more overtly racist depictions of blacks, Asians, and Native Americans that existed during and following World War II and building on the hints of change in the early 1960s, comics creators sought even further to challenge such stereotypes and change the minds of readers by confronting established white heroes with both racially charged situations and racially marked individuals. Surpassing the metaphorical or sermonizing tales of their first halting efforts to address race more progressively, superhero comics now dealt directly but no less dramatically with more concrete encounters with bigotry and racism. Most emblematic of this effort was the *Green Lantern/Green Arrow* series by the writer Dennis (Denny) O'Neil and the penciller Neal Adams, a series that was then (and is still today) hailed for its pioneering efforts to bring "relevancy" to the comic page via its treatment of not only racism but a plethora of social ills. Other series published before and after *Green Lantern/Green Arrow*—from DC's *The Flash*, *Justice League of America*, *Superman's Girl Friend Lois Lane*, and *Teen Titans*, to Marvel's *The Avengers*, *Amazing Adventures*, *Daredevil*, and *Iron Man*—further testify to their creators' similarly laudable aims. However, if the superhero popular culture discussed in the previous chapter revealed a broader ambivalence at large within Cold War US society about race, these later efforts indicate the inherent limitations of the very myth comics creators ended up promoting and constituting, the very same limitations that undermined postwar liberal ideology and its efforts against racism and discrimination more generally.

Postwar Liberalism: Consensus, Contradiction, and Comics

Writing about the American society of the 1950s, the historian James T. Patterson captures a confidence and optimism brimming on the surface of this decade: "The whole world, many Americans seemed to think by 1957, was turning itself over to please the special, God-graced generation—and its children—that had triumphed over depression and fascism, that would sooner or later vanquish Communism, and that was destined to live happily ever after (well, almost) in a fairy tale of health, wealth, and happiness."[2] This ebullient sense of America's prospects—grating as it does against the realities of Cold War America previously discussed—stemmed from the economic and political success accomplished by World War II. Both the Great Depression and Nazi Germany had been defeated as a result of American intervention, ushering in an apparent age of political and economic confidence that helped to generate unity. Prospering economically, assuming a leadership role in world politics, and forming a bulwark against the rising threat of Communism, Americans in the 1950s seemed united by not only a common set of goals but a political, economic, and social belief in their country's fairy-tale destiny.

This ubiquitous faith and confidence is commonly referred to as the "liberal consensus." Underlying this consensus was a common set of assumptions: the superiority of and symbiosis between capitalism and democracy, fierce anticommunist sentiment, and, most importantly, a belief that the problems in America were neither structural nor requiring radical change.[3]

Thus, at the heart of this consensus lay, as the British journalist Godfrey Hodgson recognized, an inherent conservatism. "For all its belief in innovation," he writes, "American society . . . was still conservative. People wanted change; they did not want to be changed. Or, rather, they changed their clothes, their cars or their homes more easily than they changed their assumptions, their attitudes or their beliefs."[4] Put another way, to the extent that Americans might have valued an abstract ideal of reform, such change remained relatively superficial. After all, if the essential structure of society was deemed sound, then no grand reforms were needed, just specific and discrete efforts to address what Americans perceived as anomalies rather than endemic problems.

In other words, though Americans might have valued an abstract ideal of reform, at the same time, they placed limits on change. This ideological construction thus made it "possible to support the Civil Rights movement ardently and avoid radicalization." As Marianne DeKoven further summarizes, "It appeared to be just a question of overcoming local, (what then seemed) residual, antiquated racism—manifesting itself as segregation and remediable by integration—with determination at the national level."[5] William Chafe sums up the consequences for various social reform efforts: "Throughout the postwar years, liberal reformers had acted on the belief that the basic economic and social structure of America was sound. Within this framework of beliefs, social categories such as race, class, and gender were perceived as incidental barriers to equity."[6] Similarly, Lewis M. Killian explains how, though "a national orgy of guilt and fear . . . provided the catalyst for the passage of the Civil Rights Act of 1964 and the Voting Rights Act the next year," the "basic economic changes required if laws mandating desegregation and equal opportunity were to have more than a minimal effect had not come about."[7]

The pursuit of racial equality under the auspices of this postwar liberalism proved to be particularly limited by its inherent contradictions. According to Carol Horton, in *Race and the Making of American Liberalism*, postwar liberalism based itself in a generative and inspiring rhetoric of racial equality that conceived racism in abstract terms.[8] In particular, liberalism understood racism and discrimination in *moral* terms, with particular and problematic consequences. By casting racism as morally incompatible with the ideals of American society, liberalism reduced the scope of the problem. Specifically, it cast discrimination in the binary terms of white against black, as well as making it a matter of intent. That is, dealing with racism became a matter of addressing individual racists and discrete acts of discrimination.[9]

Horton alludes to the specific consequences of liberalism's moral understanding of racism. For one, such a conception proved inadequate to redress the complexities of racism precisely because it neglected the structural forces creating segregated and economically disadvantaged ghettos. Second, it put focus on only certain forms of discrimination and racism. Complementing liberalism's neglect of structural discriminatory forces, then, was a parallel concentration on discrimination as only stemming from discrete individuals.[10] As a result, racism was reduced to a moral struggle individual whites must overcome; the emphasis thus turned away from reforming the structures of American society toward instead reforming individuals' blinkered moral consciences.

The comics of the 1960s and 1970s that dramatized racial issues within their pages, and thus sought to confront racism and discrimination, based themselves in the same limited and contradictory liberal understanding that pervaded postwar American society. Such contradictions were emblematized by O'Neil and Adams's *Green Lantern/Green Arrow*, published by DC Comics from 1970 to 1972. They were further promulgated throughout the 1960s and 1970s in various superhero comics that crystallized their own version of "liberal brotherhood." Comics specifically preached a contradictory and heavily conditioned tolerance that presented, as sufficient in and of itself, only a moral judgment of the forces underpinning racial discrimination within American society.

Frustrated Aims: Liberal Understandings of Race in *Green Lantern/Green Arrow*

Though published serially between 1970 and 1972, the thirteen issues of *Green Lantern/Green Arrow* by O'Neil and Adams were rooted consciously within the liberal spirit and legacy of the 1960s. O'Neil explicitly identifies the title's basis in this spirit. For one, he puts the origin of the series squarely within that decade, writing that how the series came to be "has to do with those years marked indelibly, in Day Glo, on the soul of anyone who experienced them, the praised and damned Sixties." In particular, O'Neil casts his opportunity to write the series as his chance to carry on in the spirit of the 1960s counterculture. Locating himself on the periphery of 1960s social issues—"I signed petitions. I went on marches. I argued against the war and supported Martin Luther King."—O'Neil grasped *Green Lantern/Green Arrow* as "an opportunity to stop lurking at the edges of the social movements I admired and participate by dramatizing their concerns."[11] In these and similar statements, O'Neil reveals an origin story for *Green Lantern/Green Arrow* that firmly places its effort to cultivate social awareness within the legacy of the 1960s, even if its actual publication was later.

The series, as well as O'Neil and Adams, continues to be hailed for bringing such social awareness to comic books. Reviews in the *Wall Street Journal* and *Newsweek* contemporary with the run's publication noted the series' "self-consciously leftist" exploration "of political and social issues" and lavished praise on it "for questioning old assumptions and challenging established authorities instead of endorsing traditional American values."[12] More recently, the series has been celebrated for rescuing comics from the ghettos of mere entertainment and kiddie fare; comics, it showed, could instead communicate and protest the ills of American society.[13] O'Neil and Adams's *Green Lantern/Green Arrow* in many ways established the standard by which other comics' efforts to deal with racial and social injustices are framed and judged. It thus stands as a crucial benchmark within comic book history, in many ways embodying the self-conscious and earnest ambitions of many comic creators to so use their work as a kind of sounding board for social progress.

O'Neil sought to achieve his aims via the title's contrasting titular characters: Green Lantern, the test pilot Hal Jordan, who had been given, by the Guardians of the Universe, a ring capable of projecting anything his mind could construct; and Green Arrow, a former millionaire industrialist turned vigilante Robin Hood. For O'Neil, Green Lantern functioned as a "crypto-fascist; he took orders, he committed violence at the behest of commanders whose authority he did not question. If you showed him a law being broken, his instinct would be to strike at the lawbreaker without ever asking any whys." Green Arrow, in O'Neil's hands, became "a lusty, hot-tempered anarchist" who served as the counterpoint to Green Lantern's model citizenry.[14] The first issue, #76, immediately established their contrast, as Green Lantern unknowingly rescues a corrupt slumlord from outraged citizens, and Green Arrow quickly confronts him with the urban realities of poverty and racism. This confrontation continues in three classic and oft-reproduced panels that consequently frame both comics' and scholars' treatments of race in comic books: an "ancient black man" confronts Green Lantern, telling him, in the first panel, "I been readin' about you . . . how you work for the blue skins . . . and how on a planet someplace you helped out the orange skins . . . and you done considerable for the purple skins! Only there's skins you never bothered with—!" He continues his lecture in the second panel: ". . . the black skins! I want to know . . . how come?! Answer me that, Mr. Green Lantern!" In the third panel, all Green Lantern can do is hang his head in shame and stammer, "I . . . can't . . ."[15] Green Lantern's and Green Arrow's actions subsequent to this confrontation then become the tableau through which the former hero attempts to redeem himself and O'Neil and Adams dramatize social concerns— comprising (but not limited to) racism, urban and rural poverty, corporate greed, political corruption, environmental degradation, overpopulation, and drug addiction—for their young audience.

However, when it comes to race, the creators simultaneously exhibit the limits of the liberal ideology their comic attempted to spread. Like Horton and others describe of liberalism, *Green Lantern/Green Arrow* ultimately succumbs to the contradictions inherent within that moral conception of racism, matching in many ways liberalism's inspiring visions and sweeping rhetoric as well as its inherent limitations. In this way, the lauded creators also located discrimination within particular individuals whom the heroes subsequently attempt to "reform." These reduced understandings are almost immediately on display in the remaining events of the series' first issue. Green Lantern, following his "revelatory" confrontation with Green Arrow and the ancient black man, pleads with Jubal Slade, the slumlord he previously rescued, but to no avail. Green Arrow, on his own, attempts a sting to gather incriminating evidence on Slade, but fails as well. In the end, the two heroes join forces to dupe Slade into confessing his criminal activities to the district attorney.[16] In all these efforts, the comic crystallizes the cause of urban racism and poverty in only one villainous individual, Jubal Slade.

Moreover, Slade is but the first instance in the series' pattern of condensing racial and social problems into discrete individuals in need of correction. The run's second issue depicts Green Lantern, Green Arrow, and a Guardian in mortal guise arriving at the company mining town of Desolation, run by the villainous Slapper Soames. By issue's end, Soames and his ex-Nazi enforcers have been defeated, but the entrenched poverty and economic deprivation remain after the heroes depart. In issues #78 and #79, the heroes intervene to assist Native Americans, but only by dealing with a local biker gang that harasses them, thwarting the genocidal intentions of the cult leader Joshua, and, finally, fighting to save the Native Americans' land from Theodore Pudd and Pierre O'Rourke, a corrupt union official and a claim jumper. Later issues depict similarly narrow efforts, as the heroes confront a drug dealer (issues #85–86) and then a white supremacist congressman (#87). In each of these encounters, the heroes consistently limit their efforts to removing only these wrongdoers from the situation, rather than addressing the larger economic and political problems faced by their victims. By reducing these problems to an individual, Manichean morality (in which clearly distinguished "good" and "evil" clash and the former triumphs), *Green Lantern/Green Arrow* produced an understanding of social issues hemmed in by liberalism's limits.

Further problematizing the inability of *Green Lantern/Green Arrow* to transcend the ideological limits of postwar liberalism, the series at times clearly acknowledges more structural or systemic causes of racism and other social problems. For example, at the start of the series, Green Arrow gives Green Lantern a "guided tour" of the impoverished reality about which he has heretofore been ignorant. Here, the panels depict the

Figure 3.1. Reflecting the limits of liberal understandings of reform, *Green Lantern/Green Arrow* avoids structural problems in choosing instead to focus on corrupt, immoral individuals. Here, Dennis O'Neil and Neal Adams capture the consequences of such individuals' actions: the bad guy has been defeated, but the people whom he had oppressed remain oppressed and without any seeming hope for the future. While the comic acknowledges this reality, the heroes choose not to address it, preferring to look for a more beautiful version of America elsewhere.

crumbling exterior stoop of the tenement building, with its exposed brick and broken railings; inside the dilapidated building are graffiti-filled walls, trash-strewn floors, and a ramshackle staircase, as well as the mostly black adults and children living there.[17] These issues of tenement life—the deteriorating and hopeless conditions that are visually communicated in this sequence of panels—are beyond the immoral actions of one slumlord, though that, unfortunately, is how they are ultimately conceived by the heroes and their creators.

A similar conflict between imagery and plot appears at the end of the heroes' sojourn in Desolation. In the final two panels, the pair witnesses the miners — shrouded in somber blacks, yellows, and oranges in the next-to-last panel — returning to their jobs. When Green Lantern celebrates the workers' triumph, Green Arrow cynically replies, "Look at them . . . injured . . . grieving for lost friends and family . . . nothing to look forward to except more poverty . . . and ignorance . . . you call that winning?!" Here, where Green Lantern proclaims victory, Green Arrow sees little to celebrate, acknowledging the systemic economic issues that remain entrenched. However, despite their differing assessments, both heroes' reactions are the same: they turn away from this explicit evidence of systemic poverty and deprivation, piling into a pickup truck and continuing their journey west. Green Arrow himself declares as they turn away from Desolation, "Come on . . . let's go find the pretty part of America!"[18] Though he brings recognition to these larger issues, he also reveals how the heroes and their creators have no intention of addressing the broader systemic issues they confront, which require further-reaching if not radical solutions.

With issue #79, the series makes clear who is responsible for such change, placing that burden on nonwhite individuals. Exposed to the poverty and deprivation of a Native American reservation, Black Canary, Green Arrow's paramour who joined the trio one issue earlier, voices what the creators imagine as a solution to the Native Americans' needs: "They need something no one can give — They've been under the white man's heel for so long they've lost faith in themselves — They no longer believe in themselves as a tribe — a society — or even as human beings!"[19] Here, the problem stems from Native Americans themselves. Their loss of faith as individuals and as a people constitutes the root of their impoverished existence. This understanding of the situation thus leads Green Arrow to disguise himself as the tribe's legendary chief, Ulysses Star, and to paternalistically chide the Native Americans into action. "You were once a proud people . . . a great people . . . and you can be again!" he lectures them. "First, though, you have to stop playing doormat for O'Rourke and Pudd . . . and be willing to fight for your rights!"[20] As Green Arrow makes clear, the Native Americans — and no one else — have an imperative to change, but only because the comic reduces their situation so that the onus for change is not on US society but on the tribe.

A corollary to this reduction is how the series diminishes the effect of racism and other social issues on its white heroes and the "establishment" they represent. They face what amounts to only a personal moral quandary. The immediate effect on Green Lantern is to doubt his former moral certainty. As Hal recites the vow that recharges his ring—"In brightest day, in blackest night, no evil shall escape my sight! Let those who worship evil's might, beware my power—Green Lantern's light!"—he ruminates, "How often have I made that vow . . . and until today, I believed what I was saying! But evil was all around me . . . disguised as familiar everyday persons and places!"[21] Here, Lantern demonstrates how his awakening has launched him into a world of moral and ethical uncertainty. The expression of such uncertainty repeats throughout the first half of the series whenever Lantern recharges his ring. In Desolation, he similarly thinks, "I used to speak that oath with pride . . . with conviction! But now . . . I'm not convinced of anything!"[22] He makes almost identical statements as he attempts to intervene in the Native Americans' land dispute,[23] and when he and his companions strive to help an overpopulated planet.[24]

Such doubt similarly plagues Green Arrow throughout the series. To convince Green Lantern to join him, Arrow exhorts, "Remember America. . . . It's a good country . . . beautiful and fertile . . . and terribly sick!" He goes on to say, "There's a fine country out there someplace! Let's go find it!"[25] Here, Green Arrow clearly expresses his need for redemption, and such a need is reiterated throughout the narrative. The opening caption of the second issue points to the heroes as "searching for America! . . . Seeking an answer, a creed, an identity!"[26] Issue #79 concludes with the Guardian's summative wish: "I pray you find the splendor in yourselves . . . before it is too late!"[27] Here, the sickness within America gets translated into a loss of self that Green Arrow, like the supposedly more naïve Green Lantern, experiences.

The course, then, of the series becomes resolving these individual dilemmas. By the midway point of the series, Lantern appears to have resolved his uncertainties. He recharges his ring without giving any voice to the doubts he previously held. And when asked by his girlfriend, Carol Ferris, about the unlimited power at his command, Lantern somberly explains, "Those days are gone . . . gone forever—the days I was confident, certain . . . proud to be a servant of the Guardians! I was so young . . . so sure I couldn't make a mistake! Young and cocky, that was Green Lantern—Well, Carol, I've changed! I'm older now . . . maybe wiser, too—Yeah, maybe wiser . . . and a lot less happy—!"[28] Encapsulated here is the apparent upshot of all that Green Lantern has experienced and confronted: he feels both wiser and sad. However, the development this statement implies is not as profound as O'Neil and Adams intend. His exposure to racism, as well as to other social problems, remains firmly couched in an internal moral and ethical conflict he as an individual must reconcile, and little more. What has changed about Green Lantern are his moral and ethical intentions—hence his purported "wisdom"—but such "development" belittles the social realities prompting it.[29]

Green Arrow's redemption comes in issues #85–86, a two-part story line often singled out from the run for its treatment of teen drug use. In this plot, Arrow's neglect of his ward, Roy Harper (a.k.a. the archer and Teen Titan Speedy), leads Harper to substitute heroin for his mentor's friendship.[30] The end of the second issue provides the payoff, as a newly clean Harper arrives to tell Green Arrow off: "Drugs are a symptom . . . and you . . . like the rest of the society . . . attack the symptom . . . not the disease!" But though the series here again acknowledges much larger issues than individual failings undergirding teen drug use, it skirts them in providing a narrative of individual redemption. The final panel's image of a tearful but smiling Green Arrow indicates the pride he now feels in his young ward and, apparently, in himself.[31] Like his partner, Green Lantern, Green Arrow finds the redemption he sought all series long, replacing the sickness and uncertainty he felt with pride and self-congratulation.

Green Lantern's and Green Arrow's character arcs thus promulgate the limits within liberalism in its privileging of this narrative of individual redemption over broader social change. As Cyrus R. K. Patell describes, liberalism often deploys specific, individual stories as part of its political discourse, but such use falls short of addressing the larger social context within which those individual narratives occur.[32] Such oversimplification is rife within *Green Lantern/Green Arrow*. All the heroes ultimately do is realize a moral good about themselves; they do very limited actual good within their comic world. Beyond taking down a few corrupt individuals, they do nothing to positively affect racial and social inequities. The inner city remains impoverished and hopeless, Desolation remains as blighted a community as it ever was, the Native American reservation remains impoverished and deprived, and the victims of such structural oppression have sole responsibility for solving their struggles and deprivation. All these elements of the narrative communicate how particular individuals are responsible for the problems and their solutions, rather than how such interlinked issues as racial discrimination and economic exploitation are, in both their conception and solution, to be understood at a more societal and structural level.

Yet, the text repeatedly asserts a significance or profundity to their effort. The final panel of issue #79—with the floating Guardian near the somnolent bodies of Green Lantern and Green Arrow amidst a mountainous vista—conveys a solemnity that, on the one hand, suggests how the "hard-traveling heroes" (as they are sometimes called) have achieved resolution. But such a visual coda grates against Green Lantern's question two panels prior: "We had a real down-home brawl, Oliver . . . but we didn't settle anything, did we?"[33] Green Arrow makes a similar statement at the end of issue #86, after the drug dealer Salomon Hooper has been brought to justice: "Hooray for us! We squashed one worm! How many others are infesting this stinking world . . . peddling misery?"[34] Such instances, where the characters and series acknowledge the limits to what these tales represent, reinforce the fact that they ignore the implications of those limits. Green Lantern's rhetorical—and thus unanswered—question applies not only to that specific adventure but to the series as a whole. Though their personal needs might have been satisfied, those of the communities they encountered, and indeed those of the peoples giving impetus to their quest, remain unmet.

If *Green Lantern/Green Arrow*, then, is the standard by which comics are judged in their representations and dealings with racial and social injustices, that remains a low standard indeed. Jane Smiley, writing about Mark Twain's *Adventures of Huckleberry Finn*, decried that novel's low standard for dealing with racism, stating that "the entry of Huck Finn . . . sets the terms of the discussion of racism and American history, and sets them very low" by only locating its solution within a form of personal transformation.[35] O'Neil and Adams's *Green Lantern/Green Arrow* similarly set a low standard for the discussion of racial and social injustice, as their lofty aims are ultimately frustrated by the liberal ideology within which they construct the series. By establishing individual transformation and redemption as the terms constituting what the series laudably identifies as necessary change, *Green Lantern/Green Arrow* unfortunately found itself circumscribed by postwar liberalism, limiting what it ultimately strove to communicate to its audience.

Contradictions in the "Brotherhood" Comics of the 1960s and 1970s

Though *Green Lantern/Green Arrow* is often singled out for its efforts to make comics "relevant," it was not the only, nor the first, comic series to so earnestly confront racism and prejudice, just the most celebrated. At both DC and Marvel, multiple series featured stories and plotlines that brought a variety of heroes into contact and at times into conflict with black, Asian, and Native American individuals and communities. These encounters, like those in *Green Lantern/Green Arrow*, implicitly or explicitly invoked an ideal of brotherhood, suggesting that whites and nonwhites could come together in equality. *The Flash* (Vol. 1), in issues #180–181, implicitly represents such brotherhood with the arrival of its hero, in his civilian identity of Barry Allen, to Tokyo and specifically his egalitarian friendships with the police detective Captain Hash and the film director Hideki Toshira. Similarly, in *The Avengers* (Vol. 1), when Hank Pym/Goliath hires the black Bill Foster as his lab assistant, the two are so perfectly matched—so equal—that Foster anticipates Hank's thoughts.[36]

Other comics more explicitly invoked this ideal, the title of *Daredevil* (Vol. 1) #47, for example, proclaiming, "Brother, Take My Hand!" *Justice League of America* (Vol. 1) #57 presents a similarly titled story, "Man, Thy Name Is Brother!," and features a cover on which Native American, black, and Indian youths hold hands beneath the figures of Green Arrow, the Flash, and Hawkman, as well as an interior splash page featuring all six characters walking arm in arm.[37] Comics further communicated this "brotherhood" ideal by ending their stories with a reinforcing moral. In the closing panels of *Justice League of America* #40, Batman asserts that "men must be educated to understand that one man is very much like another!" and Martian Manhunter immediately adds, "The old saying that all men are brothers under the skin is true!"[38] At the conclusion of *Superman's Girl Friend Lois Lane* #110, which depicts Lois's efforts to care for an abandoned Native American baby, Lois retorts to those who would question her efforts, "My heart and Little Moon's are the same color!"[39] Similarly, at the end of *Daredevil* #47, Willie Lincoln, a blind black man, expounds to his Seeing Eye dog, "Y'know, boy—just a short time ago I thought I'd really hit bottom! But then I found me a friend—and cleared my name! Now even without my eyes—I'm looking forward to tomorrow—for the first time! I feel like I'm part of the human race again! Murdock [a.k.a. Daredevil] never made a big deal about it—but, when you get down to where it's at—maybe that's what brotherhood is all about!"[40] As such explicit declarations—along with the more implicit representations—make obvious, comics and comic creators in the 1960s genuinely sought to espouse equality and tolerance.

But whether implicit or explicit in their promulgation of "brotherhood," these comics all similarly betray the limitations inherent within the ways comics realized this ideal. Ironically, the putative heroes in these tales are often guilty of the same prejudices against which they fight, a complicity

Figure 3.2. The theme of multiracial brotherhood dominated comic books in the 1960s and 1970s. While interracial amity appeared in many depictions, like this one, the conditional quality of such brotherhood hardly suggested equality was at hand, no matter the good intentions of writers and artists.

that the moral logic of these tales encompasses but also implicitly absolves. Racial stereotypes also contradict the tenets of "brotherhood"; even while espousing lofty aims of tolerance and equality, comics depicted nonwhite characters in subordinate and/or demeaning ways and positions. Consequently, it was as if comics were telling their audience that "brotherhood" could be achieved, but without any acknowledgment of whites' culpability in its lack or any substantive shift in how whites thought of those different from them. In general, these contradictions parallel those limitations within postwar liberalism, but are also the unique manifestation of how comics textualized its version of those shared ideals.

The Avengers and the Inhumans featured in *Amazing Adventures* are emblematic of how such comics' unintended irony betrays a contradictory moral logic. In *The Avengers* #32–33, the team—at this time comprising Captain America (Steve Rogers), Goliath (Hank Pym), the Wasp (Janet Van Dyne), and Hawkeye (Clint Barton)—confronts the Sons of the Serpent, a white supremacy group targeting blacks and immigrants. At the same time, the generically Asian General Chen[41] has arrived in America to address the United Nations and condemn the United States; by story's end, the Avengers, initially pretending to join the Serpents, thwart the group's attempt to take over the United States and expose Chen as their leader, the Supreme Serpent.

Through this plot, however, *The Avengers* ends up condemning its villains for actions similar to those of the team. This inherent contradiction appears clearly in two juxtaposed scenes in the story line's second issue. In the first, General Chen condemns the United States' military action abroad while also allowing, as Chen declares, "hate-mongers in your own land!!" Immediately following this declaration is a thought bubble, from one of the US representatives, making clear the general's insidious intent: "I thought so! The whole purpose of Chen's visit here is to win a propaganda victory—and the Serpents are handing him one, on a silver platter!"[42] Emphasized here is Chen's secret purpose, and the series clearly intends its reader to perceive Chen's villainy—which also trades in time-worn Asian stereotypes—as based in his use of deception. However, the Avengers deploy similarly deceptive means. Immediately following the scene at the UN, an angered Bill Foster confronts Goliath and the Wasp, who are "to be the guests of honor at the next rally of the Sons of the Serpent."[43] Though the pair reassure Foster that all is not what it seems, they stop short of fully revealing their plan to defeat the Sons of the Serpent out of concerns for his safety. But whereas General Chen's deceptions were villainized just prior to these exchanges, the Avengers' copycat methods receive no such moral condemnation. The heroes' deceptions are a means to a noble end, while those of the Serpents and their leader speak to their ignoble nature.

But even more contradictory is the larger moral message regarding racial "brotherhood" promoted throughout the two-issue story line. Specifically, the writer Stan Lee and the penciller Don Heck strove to communicate the idea that those who allow, by their own inaction, such racism and discrimination to continue are as morally responsible as those hate groups represented by the fictional Sons of the Serpent. As the Serpents attack an immigrant named Gonzales, an elderly white couple watches through their apartment window. While the husband stammers, "We—we have to do something—!" his wife tells him, "No! Come away from there! It's dangerous to get involved!" The caption above the subsequent panel, in which a beaten Gonzales slumps against a brick wall, makes clear the creators' opinion of whites like this couple: "Thus, we take our leave of Henry and his wife—two less-than-admirable citizens who feared to get 'involved.'"[44] Clearly, the narrator's righteous critique of the couple emanates from their explicit choice to avoid helping Mr. Gonzales, and thus their allowing such attacks to continue.

But Henry and his wife are not the only characters in the story subject to this critique. In fact, the titular heroes themselves are as much—if not more—subject to such a criticism, although none is forthcoming from the self-righteous narrator. The Serpents' attack on Bill Foster outside Hank Pym's lab precipitates the Avengers' involvement; watching the attackers' ship fly away, Goliath, with fist raised, vows, "There's no place on earth that can shelter you from the retribution of—the Avengers!"[45] However, as much as this statement expresses Goliath's and the team's willingness to combat the Serpents, other statements by the heroes belie this claim. For one, when Goliath initially discovers Foster after the attack, he immediately recognizes the serpent-shaped staff left behind as the group's calling card. This reveals, of course, that Goliath was aware of the Serpents prior to this specific attack—and failed to intervene. Similarly, when Goliath and the rest of the Avengers discuss the Serpents, Captain America notes, "There's a strange, mysterious pattern to their activities! They're rich—well-organized—and they operate on a national scale!"[46] Again, Cap, like the remaining Avengers, has not been oblivious to the Serpents' prior attacks, but the team has—until now, and only when it directly impacts them—let the racist group continue to pursue its reprehensible agenda, not unlike Henry and his wife, whom the team is clearly meant to contrast.

Further underlining this contradiction is Captain America's subsequent

Figure 3.3. A repeated hypocrisy in comics of the 1960s and 1970s often went unacknowledged. While both violence against nonwhites and a refusal to intervene to prevent such violence were criticized, as depicted here, superheroes themselves were sometimes guilty of not stepping in to help the oppressed. In this way, *The Avengers* set the stage for the limited activism of superheroes during this era.

visit with the SHIELD[47] leader Nick Fury, who explains, "We've been ga-therin' info about those crumbs for months! . . . I planned to tackle 'em after I dusted off an outfit called AIM—but now me 'n my boys are kinda busy with some other stuff. So, if you and them costumed cut-ups of yours wanna go after those belly-crawlin' creeps, I'd be much obliged, mis-ter!"[48] Not only does Fury pass the responsibility for confronting the Ser-pents and their racism, but he further makes clear that getting involved is a lower priority than defeating not only the evil scientists of AIM but some vague "other stuff" with which he is "kinda busy." As the story ironi-cally makes clear, Henry and his wife are not the only characters that can be morally impugned for their inaction. The heroes and institutions that should, ostensibly, contrast this couple have likewise let the Serpents continue their efforts unimpeded, thus contradicting the moral at the heart of this story about "brotherhood."

Roughly five years later, similar ironies and contradictions would permeate another attempted realization of "brotherhood" at Marvel. *Amazing Adventures* #6–8 (published bimonthly from May through September of 1971) featured the royal family of the Inhumans: their king, Black Bolt; his queen, Medusa; and fellows Karnak, Gorgon, and Triton. Created by Stan Lee and Jack Kirby during their run on the first volume of *The Fantastic Four*, the Inhumans lived in the city of Attilan, hidden in the Himalayas. This story line saw them forced, by Black Bolt's mad brother, Maximus, to leave their "Great Refuge"—Black Bolt, due to amnesia induced by his brother, and the remaining royals in an effort to locate the lost king, who eventually turns up in the tenements of San Francisco. Their resulting encounters with humans provide the means by which the story's creators—the writers Roy Thomas (#6 and #8) and Gerry Conway (#7) and the artist Neal Adams—explicitly promoted an ideal of "brotherhood." For example, as the members of the royal family find themselves under attack by Chinese soldiers, the aquatic Triton dives into the ocean, giving him an occasion to ruminate on humanity's inherent brotherhood: "Here . . . the sea's turmoil is a natural one. Here . . . man battles the elements—not himself. And though there be humans and In-humans . . . both are truly men."[49] Man's conflict and "inhumanity" toward other men, unlike the sea's turmoil, is inherently unnatural. It is a battle against "himself," man and, in this case, Inhuman being brothers within a larger humanity. Karnak draws a similar conclusion when he and his family members arrive on a private California beach only to be immediately accosted by a group of bodybuilders. He remarks, "From one land to another—and here . . . the tale is the same. It saddens me. They act like children."[50] Again, the comic uses one of the Inhumans to indict mankind for violence directed against its own, finding it contradictory to man's inherent brotherhood.

However, the story simultaneously ironizes and thus contradicts the logic of this moral. There is a crucial difference between the violence the Inhumans confront from the Chinese and that presented by the bodybuilders: the former is instigated by the Inhumans themselves. The splash page of issue #7 foregrounds the seemingly unconscious bodies of Gorgon, Karnak, Medusa, and Triton following the crash of their vehicle; in the background, a civilian leads Chinese soldiers to the crash site. Though one soldier sees the Inhumans as monsters, the captain does not, ordering his men to put down their weapons. However, this action gets misinterpreted by the Inhumans, and they immediately attack the soldiers.[51]

Figure 3.4. Depictions of the inner city were constant companions of stories about race in the 1960s and 1970s. While scenes such as this one suggested, perhaps, broader structural concerns in need of being addressed, the comics themselves rarely addressed such issues.

Consequently, those condemning mankind for its violence, the Inhumans themselves, can be condemned just the same for not living up to the brotherhood ideal they and the comic espouse.

Further underlining the Inhumans' own lack of brotherhood are their prejudices toward nonwhites. As Triton races away from the battle with the Chinese and into the sea, he comments about how the formerly un-inhabited island has changed: "Now . . . it seems infected with scurrying humans."[52] Not only does Triton cast humanity as a disease, but his—and thus his creators'—characterization of the Chinese as "scurrying" plays into stereotypes of the Chinese and other Asians as vermin. Later, when the family is led by Medusa to the tenements, inhabited in these panels by several black men and children, in which Black Bolt is lost, Gorgon whispers, "Medusa—why did you pick this place? I feel . . . most uncomfortable." Karnak snaps back, "Quiet, Gorgon, you always feel uneasy . . . among humans."[53] Gorgon is, apparently, particularly uneasy in this black neighborhood, a prejudice that, in how it remains unchallenged within the comic, troubles the brotherhood moral at its center.

Similarly troubling is how comics allowed stereotypes and other racially based assumptions to continue functioning within this ideal of "brotherhood," ostensibly setting the former up as not inconsistent with the latter. Various stereotypes about Native Americans appear in comic book depictions across titles. In *Justice League of America* #57, as Green Arrow works with a young Apache, Jerry Nimo, to track down the crooks that framed him, Jerry demonstrates numerous stereotypes commonly associated with Native Americans. He can track "oil droppings" from the crooks' car, a skill for which Green Arrow praises the young man: "Jerry, you should be proud of your Apache heritage! Your ancestors were renowned for their exceptional tracking ability." Additionally, Jerry demonstrates the stereotypical enhanced senses of Native Americans: when the trail is obliterated by wind, he can still follow it by smell.[54]

The depiction of Native Americans in *Superman's Girl Friend Lois Lane* #110 — tellingly titled "Indian Death Charge!" — is similarly stereotypical. Lois and a group of tourists travel to a Santa Fe reservation to watch a Puebloan rain dance, and when the Pueblo people appear, the majority of them are shirtless with feathers in their hair.[55] Furthermore, when the scene shifts back to Metropolis to a protest of Lois's adoption of the Native American "papoose" Little Moon, the protesting Native Americans are even more stereotypically garbed, wearing full feathered headdresses and fringed leather shirts and vests. A stereotypical affinity with nature is likewise part of the Native Americans' depiction. As their leader, Johnny Lone Eagle, explains to Lois their conflict with the "white man," he emphasizes the latter's destruction of the environment — from the hunting of the bison to polluting the rivers and rampant deforestation. Finally, when

Figure 3.5. While comic books in the 1960s and 1970s promoted a brotherhood meant to transcend racism and discrimination, the presentation of this theme often undermined itself via its grounding in antique and stereotyped understandings of nonwhites. Here, Lois Lane demonstrates her brotherhood with Native Americans, cooperating to help them but betraying stereotyped understandings that grated against the theme of brotherhood.

Lois and Johnny work together to communicate the Native Americans' story, they do so via Lois translating the smoke signals Johnny creates in a three-panel sequence.[56]

In *Teen Titans* (Vol. 1) #24, Wonder Girl, Robin, Kid Flash, and Speedy vacation at a Native American–run ski ranch, a trip that provides the setting for a barrage of ethnically derisive humor. As they first meet Eddie Tallbow, who runs the ranch, he explains to them how "it's going to take a lot of wampum to pay the mortgage on this place—!"[57] As the Titans assist Eddie in tracking a lost group of skiers, not only does Eddie express his growing superstitions—"My people's medicine man, old Charlie By-and-By, warned me. . . . He said this real estate was haunted! I'm beginning to believe it!"—but also he gets chided by Robin for losing his "Indian instincts" and needing the Titans to find the skiers' trail. On the same page, another panel depicts Wonder Girl (Donna Troy) groaning "UGH!" in response to another of Robin's puns, followed by Eddie's comment, "Say, I didn't know you spoke Indian, Donna!"[58] As much as this story features the (white) Titans working together with Eddie Tallbow—and thus provides another implicit image of "brotherhood"—the ways in which the story uses Eddie, and the Native Americans he represents, as a comic figure derides him and contradicts the story's putative aims.

Like Native Americans, blacks remained stereotyped in comics even as they were being celebrated as "brothers." With *Teen Titans* #25, the creators launched a story line in which the white members of the Titans—Wonder Girl, Kid Flash, Speedy, Hawk, and Dove—give up their costumed identities to work for the philanthropist Loren Jupiter to, as he explains, "combat the new problems of tomorrow" and "challenge the unknown in man himself[:] . . . the mysteries of riots, prejudice, and greed."[59] Here, this series wears its noble intentions on its sleeve, much like *Green Lantern/Green Arrow* would. The heroes' first mission takes them to Hell's Corner and a meeting with Mal Duncan, an African American teen who will join the team in its mission. However, Mal's depiction allows multiple stereotypes to persist. Donald Bogle describes the black stereotype of needing to "overprove," or demonstrate equality by proving superior to whites, that Mal aptly embodies.[60] He has a constant need to prove himself, as evidenced by his refusal to don one of Jupiter's drab uniforms until "he's earned the right to wear one,"[61] or by not only completing the same tests as the Titans but also sneaking aboard an unmanned spacecraft headed to Venus. At the same time, Mal also evokes the stereotypical comic figure of the "coon," or "the Negro as amusement object and black buffoon."[62] In this case, Mal's plan backfires, as he ends up stranded in space and needing the Titans to rescue him. As a result, he appears completely ineffectual and—not all that unlike his World War II predecessors—a buffoon. A later story depicts Mal trapped back in prehistoric times, a predicament that is the result of his unknowingly—and comically—walking into the midst of a time experiment conducted by Jupiter; all the oblivious Mal can do before being sucked back into the past is utter a startled "Hunh?"[63]

Mal's appearances further reinforce a stereotypical inferiority as, despite the team—and comic—paying lip service to his equal position, he actually occupies a secondary status to the white Titans. In *Teen Titans* #35–36, Jupiter and the Titans travel to Italy, but Mal is left behind.[64] In *Teen Titans* #44, when the team reunites following an almost three-year hiatus from publication, Mal remains subordinate. He complains, "Makes me wonder why I've been trekking here every week to check all the equipment Mr. Jupiter gave us when he closed shop!" Unlike the other Titans who went on with their lives, Mal was not only "left minding the store" but also was completely neglected by his erstwhile teammates: "Some team! You guys coulda dropped me a post card or somethin'! Sure—you were busy—but I never heard from anybody!"[65]

And even when Mal adopts various superheroic identities, he remains staunchly in a second-class position. First, he dons both a strength-enhancing exoskeleton as well as the abandoned costume and identity of the Guardian; however, Mal is put in his place by the archer Speedy after one throw-down: "Yeah, for a second-rate super hero, he did a great job!"[66] Later in the same issue, Mal gains his own unique powers and identity: after defeating the Angel of Death in a boxing match refereed by the archangel Gabriel, Mal receives Gabriel's horn, which, when blown, makes him the equal of his opponents. But even this ability only reinforces Mal's secondary status. The first time he blows the horn, as he prepares to pursue the Wreckers, it literally transports the other five members of the Titans—Kid Flash, Wonder Girl, Robin, Speedy, and Aqualad—to him.[67] Unlike the white heroes, who easily defeat their foes, Mal's eventual victory is prolonged in its achievement, hinting at his continued status as a lesser and secondary member of the team.

Such stereotypical and, more importantly, persistent inequality is also expressed in the opening sequences of *The Avengers* #73. Prior to the commencement of the main plot, the issue presented a two-panel sequence of the African-born Black Panther's journey to the United States. As he leaves Africa, he remarks, "They call it the dark continent . . . but now it blazes with the pulsing light of knowledge . . . of self-awareness! Yet, somehow, it is no longer home to . . . the Black Panther!" At the same time as the Pan-

Figure 3.6. Conflicted understandings of racial and ethnic difference could appear within the same panel of a comic book, whatever the good intentions of its creators. While the text here suggests (if somewhat paternalistically) "progress," in the form of knowledge and self-awareness in Africa, the images continue to emphasize Africa's primitivity in both the subject matter as well as the shaded presentation.

ther's dialogue speaks to the advancement of Africa—from darkness to light and, implicitly, from ignorance to knowledge/self-awareness—the visual depiction of the continent emphasizes primitivity. Appearing in both the foreground and background are shirtless blacks carrying spears, surrounded by jungle; and though the Panther speaks to a movement out of a metaphorical "darkness," with the exception of one of the Africans—who is only seen from behind—all the others appear only as blacked-out shadows. The second panel only adds to a depiction of Africa's and blackness's inferiority. In it, Black Panther has reached the United States, and as he flies over an airport with clearly defined roads and buildings—all markers of "civilization"—he remarks, "This is home now to T'Challa, son of T'Chaka! A land of complexity and contrast . . . of triumph and of sudden tragedy! But, above all, as rich with beckoning promise as any new-born nation!"[68] Inherent within T'Challa's comments and the juxtaposed panels is a contrast to the detriment of Africa and blackness. The United States possesses a complexity and richness that make it the Panther's new home, but this statement implicitly identifies Africa as lacking these qualities, an assumption that in its reliance on stereotypical black inferiority clearly grates against the supposed equality "brotherhood" promised.

But the most virulent and pervasive contradictions of this "brotherhood" ideal are to be found in the treatment of the Japanese characters in a two-part story in *The Flash* published in 1968. The plot gestures toward such "brotherhood" as Barry and Iris Allen reunite in Japan with two of the former's friends: Captain Hash of the Tokyo police and the "ace director of Nippon artfilms" Hideki Toshira.[69] Again undermining the symbolism of their friendship is the comics' stereotypical and dehumanizing depictions of the Japanese characters. The main villains of the piece—Baron Katana and his sword-wielding second-in-command, Daisho—appear manifestly subhuman. Separate panels provide close-ups on their faces: Daisho appears ratlike, with an elongated skull, slit eyes, a long, sharp nose, and buckteeth, while Katana is also rodent-like in appearance.[70] But the villains aren't the only Japanese characters to suffer from such racist physical depictions. Captain Hash bears a more apelike appearance, while Toshira is a full head shorter than the white Barry Allen. Between their verminous

Figure 3.7. Japanese villains of the 1960s and 1970s were often not all that far removed from their World War II counterparts. Here, Daisho and Katana seem to have emerged straight from an early 1940s tale, appearing dehumanized, untrustworthy, and violent.

and simian faces, yellow skin, and diminutive stature, the Japanese characters—villainous and heroic alike—are thoroughly dehumanized.

Katana and his associates are further dehumanized by their clear lack of any regard for human life. At the end of the prologue, Katana orders Daisho to take care of the remains of a defeated samurai warrior, which the ever-faithful Daisho does in the next panel, throwing the body unceremoniously off a cliff and into the sea below.[71] Not long afterward, two Japanese fighter-jet pilots attempt to assassinate Barry Allen by launching heat-seeking missiles that target not only our hero but Hash and Iris Allen as well; the racialized bad guys are obviously unconcerned by the potential for collateral damage.[72] Similarly, once his samurai warriors are fully trained, Katana launches them (literally, as they have jet packs) at a small Hokkaido police outpost, and the terrified screams of the policemen as well as the warriors' own "banzai" cry makes clear their inhuman nature and murderous intent.[73] Ultimately, Daisho and his warriors are revealed as truly inhuman—they are secretly androids—a revelation that only completes their dehumanization.

As well, stereotypical associations and assumptions about Japan and the Japanese appear throughout the tale. Japan itself is presented, in a typically Orientalist fashion, as a setting of sensual delights. As Barry and his wife, Iris, arrive, Hash recalls Allen's last visit and how both he and Allen took part in various "delights" offered to single men.[74] Barry and Iris have a brief opportunity to experience similar delights in the present, as they attend a sumo match and drive down the neon-lit streets of Tokyo at night on their way to meet Toshira.[75] Japan also embodies a sense of mystery and evil in the story. Katana's castle, the Black Heron, sits upon an island cliff, its foreboding presence looming over the fishing village below. Inside, the Flash contemplates the eerie nature of his surroundings: "Creepy pad . . . all these silent Japanese-butler ancestors lining the walls! Poor dads . . . hung in the closets! Wish they'd closed them!"[76]

But such mystery is not limited to the Japanese landscape and setting; the characters as well are ensconced within a motif of deception. Katana jealously guards his secrecy, whether it be allowing the shrimp fishers on his island "their innocent pursuits [rather] than arouse suspicion by barring them," obscuring his ancestral connection to the Black Heron castle through a dummy corporation, hiding behind a screen door as Daisho engages the Flash in battle, or, his ultimate secret, building an army of samurai warriors—including Daisho—that are secretly robots.[77] But such mastery of deception and secrecy proves, again, hardly unique to the story's nonwhite antagonists. The protagonists Hash and Toshira, for example, collaborate to expose Katana's presence at the Black Heron, the latter pretending to use the island as a film location and the former disguising his police force as extras. And in a minor subplot, the female officer Tushi twice disguises herself, once as Barry Allen (at Iris's request to protect his identity) and later as one of the film's samurai extras to hide the fact that she is protecting Allen's dual identity.[78] All the comic's Japanese characters thus practice secrecy and deception.

By far, though, the most problematic representation of the Japanese in *The Flash* involves language, as a back-and-forth between dialogue and editorial captions serves only to further demean the Japanese characters. When Hash initially welcomes the Allens, it is with, "Hai! Is esteemed ferrow criminorogist Barry Arren-san! Wercome to Japan," which a caption clarifies as "Difficurty of pronouncing 'L's' in Japanese ranguage!"[79] Conversely, but no less insultingly, when the female officer Tushi speaks in grammatically correct English, the editors chime in to explain: "She talks Engrish real 'straight,' huh, keeds? A graduate from U.C.L.A., natch!"[80] The second issue's depiction of Baron Katana also emphasizes his similarly broken dialect. When Daisho asks him to kill the Flash, the baron replies, "Rater! First, must rind out who he is ... who sent him!" which is accompanied by the following caption: "Baron arso talks bad the Engrish!"[81]

But the incessant in-text captions are but a prelude to a text page titled "Meet Frank Robbins" in place of the second issue's usual letters page. Here, Robbins introduces himself while mimicking the dialect of the characters. He opens by stating how he is "eminentry quarified" to write comics and how he studied English "in order to accomprish later success," mentions his collection of antique weapons, "incruding a suit of Samurai armor, as worn by our rittle friends," and ends with the following "apology" and teaser:

> Please forgive any rapse into Japanese during this biography ... my typewriter keeps rapsing into "R" instead of "R" ... see? There it goes again! Have to sneak ... up ... on ... the ... "L" Ha! Did it!
>
> Now, before it sneaks up on me ... better sign off! Keep tuned in for the exciting death-defying adventures of ... FLANK LOBBINS! OWTCH! Hit me when I wasn't looking![82]

Not only does the text mimic the stereotypical dialect of the characters, but it evidences various ethnocentric assumptions on Robbins's part. He actually refers to this broken dialect as Japanese, betraying his belief in the racist dialect's authenticity. He similarly plays on the stereotypes of secrecy, as he not only has to "sneak up" on the "L" key of his typewriter but is taken unawares by the dialect, in the same way that Katana and other Japanese characters in the story practice sneak attacks.

As much as Robbins appears to use his autobiography—and likely the comic itself—to demonstrate his self-assured understanding of the Japanese culture and people, it rather exhibits his stereotypical and dehumanizing view of the Japanese, one which, like so much else in *The Flash* and other comics of this age, virulently contradicts their supposed aim of "brotherhood." But what is even more problematic is how, as presented on the pages of these comics, such depictions do not appear inconsistent with such ideals as tolerance, equality, and ultimately "brotherhood." Instead, the net effect of this fare from DC and Marvel was to implicitly put forth that such contradictions and racial stereotypes can remain wholly consistent and operative within this ideal. In sum, the comic book version of "brotherhood" implicitly sanctions much that actually contradicts that very ideal.

The Conditions for Change in "Brotherhood" Comics

Besides constituting their version of "brotherhood" so as to encode and thus absolve these contradictions within it, the version of this ideal within the DC and Marvel comics of the 1960s and 1970s comes heavily conditioned. Specifically, the comics place responsibility for its achievement less on the whites promoting it and more on the nonwhites, thus continuing the idea established via Jim Morita in *Sgt. Fury and His Howling Commandos*. In doing so, comics reflect and end up promulgating on their pages assumptions underpinning liberal understandings of the civil rights movement, which, according to Carol Horton, saw a change in African American consciousness as a required initial step. African Americans, according to this belief, lacked a sense of self-worth, a condition that needed repair first in order to then cause whites to realize blacks' equality.[83] The implications of what Horton describes are many. This liberal conception of change is predicated upon an initial transformation of African Americans. They need to be raised up to a state of self-worth and pride. Too, progress can occur only after blacks change. This assumption conceives of whites' responsibility for racism and discrimination as distinctly limited. They only have to change subsequent to blacks'—and by extension Asians' and Native Americans'—transformation into something, for lack of a better term, worthy.

Such conditions would replicate themselves in a variety of specific forms throughout the "brotherhood" comics of the 1960s and 1970s, beginning with various representations of the need for blacks and other nonwhites to change. In *Justice League of America* #57, when Flash encounters the recently fired Joel Harper, a black man, Joel makes clear how he attributes his firing to the racism of his former boss: "He fired me, Flash— because I'm colored! I betcha I wouldn't have been canned—if I'd been a white boy!" The Flash responds by diminishing Joel's feelings, telling him, "Joel, don't feel that way! Everybody has ups and downs in life."[84] Here, Flash implicitly admonishes Joel to change: he is wrong to feel he has been singled out due to race, as the hero offers him a platitude. Green Arrow's interaction in the same issue with the Native American Jerry Nimo conveys a similar message. When Jerry explains that he dropped out of school due to the discrimination he faced as an Apache, Green Arrow is likewise dismissive, telling him, "You're meeting up with prejudice—and you're no exception there!"[85] Here, the hero puts the onus on nonwhites not only to change but also to realize that their experiences of racism are nothing unique.

Similar conditions placed on nonwhites are found scattered throughout various other "brotherhood" comics. In *Teen Titans* #26, where the team first meets Mal, their friendliness meets his angry rebuffs, but by the issue's end, Mal instead needs to prove he belongs with the team.[86] Likewise, at Marvel, Thor intervenes in the Inhumans' confrontation with Lionel Dibbs, a black man with an artificial hand that can transform into a gun, who plans to raze his childhood home to the ground in protest of its conditions. Thor, seeking to get Dibbs to listen to reason, implicitly identifies Dibbs's anger as the obstacle to a peaceful solution.[87] Daredevil, too, in his encounter with Willie Lincoln in "Brother, Take My Hand!" serves as an implicit critique of the black man's despair. Though cleared of all charges, Willie remains despondent; in response Daredevil, as Matt Murdock, reveals not only his own blindness but how it pushed him to become a "top lawyer in the country."[88] Here, comics presented an indictment of blacks' own attitudes—in this case, Willie's hopelessness and despair—as the obstacle that must first be overcome.

Lois Lane's encounters with nonwhites in her spin-off series, *Superman's Girl Friend Lois Lane*, likewise convey a message that such change to end racism has to begin with nonwhites. Her claim at the end of "Indian Death Charge!" that she and Little Moon have the same blood is as much, if not more, a message to the Native American characters as to any white characters.[89] But it is her encounter with the African American population

Figure 3.8. As Matt Murdock (a.k.a. Daredevil) lectures Willie Lincoln about overcoming his hopelessness, the hero makes the familiar point that blacks must first fix themselves before any improvements can be made in their individual lives. Such sermons distanced whites from responsibility for racism in American society and suggested that whites were happy to fix such problems, but only after nonwhites made the necessary changes in themselves.

of Metropolis's "Little Africa" four issues earlier, in issue #106, that provides one of the more (in)famous depictions of this condition. In "I Am Curious (Black)," Lois intends to write about Metropolis's black neighborhood, Little Africa. However, she finds her intentions repeatedly thwarted. Whether approaching a group of black children, knocking on the door of a tenement apartment, eating at a coffee shop, walking on the street, or looking at a black baby in a stroller, Lois is rebuffed and met with suspicion by any black inhabitants she meets. Even an initially welcoming blind woman shuns the reporter when she starts to talk: "When she heard me speak . . . she knew I was white!"[90] A black man leading a meeting on the street voices the attitudes underlying these reactions, as he takes Lois as a symbol of their oppression: "Look at her, brothers and sisters! She's young and sweet and pretty! But never forget . . . she's whitey! She'll let us shine her shoes and sweep her floors! And baby-sit for her kids! But she doesn't want to let our kids into her lily-white schools! It's okay with her if we leave these rat-infested slums! If we don't move next door to her! That's why she's our enemy!"[91] It is these attitudes—the suspicion and anger that blacks harbor toward whites—that the story will argue must change.

Fomenting this necessary attitudinal change is a physical (and temporary) transformation that Lois herself undergoes. Using Superman's Plastimold Machine, she changes into a black woman and returns to Little Africa. Though she encounters some hostility and suspicion from whites—a formerly friendly cabdriver races past her as she hails him, and the whites on the subway stare at her[92]—the vast majority of her return serves to point out the wholly different way she is treated by the black community, and thus its hypocrisy. She returns to the slum tenement where her knock was previously rejected and now finds welcome and a cup of hot coffee. Similarly, the black street speaker—here identified as Dave Stevens—sidles up and lays a line on her, far from the hatred he spewed at her before.[93] Both sequences highlight the black characters' own biases against whites, and thus their inherent contradictions. As much as they suffer from discrimination based solely on the color of their skin, they practice a similarly race-based discrimination as exposed by their wholly opposite reactions to a white and then a black Lois.

It is the latter discrimination—that of blacks toward whites—that the climax and denouement of the plot highlight as needing to change. For one, the racism toward blacks from whites goes wholly unaddressed. More centrally, the comic's final stages make clear—both in terms of plot and visual imagery—that blacks' own prejudices and hypocrisy need to be overcome first. When Dave Stevens is shot and needs a blood transfusion, Lois conveniently matches his blood type. Following the procedure, Lois returns to her original skin color, at precisely the moment that Stevens wants to meet the woman who saved his life. Lois worries, "He called me whitey! His enemy! Wh-what will he say now?" Superman then voices the story's problematic moral: "If he still hates you . . . with your blood in his veins . . . there may never be peace in this world!"[94] Here, the potential obstacle to a vaguely defined "peace" is Stevens's continued hatred toward Lois and thus, symbolically, blacks' biases against whites. These biases are what need to be overcome, not only because Superman declares it so but because white attitudes are left unchanged in the story: those prac-

Figure 3.9. In seven panels, *Superman's Girl Friend Lois Lane* presented the standard message of racial progress, which required African Americans to change in order to achieve brotherhood, represented here by a handshake bathed in a warm light. Once Dave Stevens overcomes *his* prejudices, rapprochement with whites is possible.

ticing discrimination disappear from the narrative unchallenged and unchanged, and Lois, though temporarily black, remains what she always was: a well-intentioned (if misunderstood) white liberal.

The story's final page, a sequence of seven silent panels, visually conveys this message. As Lois approaches his hospital bed (panel 1), Dave Stevens stirs (2), turns to look at Lois's face (3), and then appears shocked: his eyes widen and his mouth opens (4). In the next panel (5), his shock changes into a beaming smile directed at Lois, and he then extends his hand toward her (6). The final panel (7)—and closing image of the tale— depicts Lois's and Dave's hands joined in front of a beaming glow of light.[95] This sequence, as celebratory in intent as it might have been, captures the "brotherhood" ideal's inherent condition that blacks and nonwhites in general must first change. It is Dave Stevens who changes, his hatred and suspicion replaced by friendliness. It is also he who extends his hand first, as the panel clearly shows his arm to be more fully extended toward Lois's than hers is to his. The only obstacle this sequence and the story as a whole represents as existing and being overcome is blacks' suspicious and ultimately hypocritical attitude toward whites. "Brotherhood" requires that Dave—and those like him—change.

In addition to requiring this change in black attitudes, comics asserted a corollary one: the need to trust in the inherent goodness of whites and their intentions. Implicit within the idea that nonwhites must develop a sense of self-worth and humanity to change whites' minds is that *only* such a development is necessary to effect the change. In other words, but for the attitudes and behaviors of nonwhites, whites are inherently open to ideas of equality and "brotherhood." Such an idea appears both explicitly and implicitly in many comics. It is, for instance, explicit in Flash's advice to Joel Harper, as he literally tells the lad, who rails against his white boss, to "give him time to cool off! When he realizes what a hero you were, he'll give you back your job!"[96] Even more clearly making such a claim is the Hawkman sequence in this same issue. Accompanied by Snapper Carr, Hawkman intends to investigate the reasons behind Harvey Young, a "young philanthropist," giving up on aiding India's poor. What Hawkman finds provides the moral: Young is leaving because his efforts have met suspicion and violence from both the Basas and Uttars, warring tribes that, as Young himself explains, have "forgotten . . . the talks I gave them on the brotherhood of man!"[97] They have, in other words, failed to recognize Young and his partners' good intentions. Similarly, Johnny Lone Eagle and Dave Stevens in *Lois Lane*, Mal Duncan in *Teen Titans*, and Willie Lincoln in *Daredevil* have to accept the good intentions of their white, liberal benefactors.

Here, comics deviate from and fall shorter than the civil rights movement, where a goal was to change whites' minds. No such transformation is envisioned in these comics. Instead, whites are already predisposed to recognize the humanity of blacks and other nonwhites. Whereas, then, the liberal assumptions undergirding the civil rights movements at least required parallel transformations in whites and nonwhites (however naïve such requirements might have been), the ideal of "brotherhood" in the comics of the 1960s and 1970s only required one half of this equation.

The "brotherhood" ideal in comics similarly required nonwhites to avoid certain actions. Direct, political action was no means to achieve such equality. One of the most thoroughgoing critiques of direct action in general appears in an earlier issue of *Justice League of America*, deceptively titled "Indestructible Creatures of Nightmare Island!" Though the title of issue #40 may belie its brotherly intentions, its opening caption manifests these clearly:

Conscience is many things, say the philosophers. He who heeds its voice is a virtuous man. Were some man to build a machine which could compel men to heed the "still small voice" of conscience, then he might make earth into a utopia!

Or—suffer the same terrible fate that overtook Andrew Helm when

he attempted to give his native planet a conscience and drew the Justice
League of America into the eerie case of the . . . INDESTRUCTIBLE CREA-
TURES OF NIGHTMARE ISLAND![98]

Though seeming to value the concept of conscience, this preamble also appears to question the feasibility of compelling conscience, its results being
posited as either "Utopia!" or nightmare. Helm's "Corti-Conscience Machine," intended to stimulate humanity's conscience, runs wild after its
creator's death, causing mankind to behave immorally, and so the members
of the Justice League combine to disrupt its effects. Having successfully
done so, the team provides the issue's moral, critiquing the flawed belief
of Helm: "Too bad he couldn't have lived to realize that conscience cannot
be forced on a man!" declares Superman, and Wonder Woman adds, "It
must come as a result of understanding between men!" The disembodied
astral form of Helm concurs: "Sigh! I've learned my lesson! Now if all other
people on earth could do the same—I'd feel my invention served its part
in the betterment of mankind!"[99] Though ending, once again, on a note of
"brotherhood" (or "understanding between men"), the means to such an
end remain fundamentally passive. Just as nonwhites before were admonished to trust in the good intentions of whites, whites and nonwhites here
are similarly warned against compelling conscience, an implication-laden
moral that seemed to undercut any active effort to address even the moral
conception of racism assumed by the "liberal consensus."

This moral conception of racism and discrimination—perhaps best
represented in *Justice League of America* #40 by Wonder Woman literally
hauling a Latin American dictator before a list of moral rules ("Treat your
neighbor as you would be treated! A job for every man! No laws that aid
only the rich!") that she has written in stone like a chalkboard for him
to read[100]—further circumscribes what actions can be taken by casting
them as products of discrete situations and/or individuals. As a result of
this conception, and of superhero comics' own simplistic morality of good
versus evil, the "brotherhood" comics of the 1960s and 1970s, like *Green
Lantern/Green Arrow*, treat racism and discrimination as intentional acts
by individual wrongdoers or villains. Wonder Woman's education of the
dictator is one such example, implying as it does—perhaps contradictorily—that morality can be taught (and therefore imposed). Likewise, one
of Helm's first examples of what his machine will correct is seen in a panel
depicting an African American couple being blocked from voting. Helm
declares, "No longer shall citizens be deprived of the right to vote,"[101] but
such a claim focuses on one particular and discrete instance of discrimi-

nation that will be resolved, not the ways in which discrimination may be built into the structures of US society.

A similarly narrow focus on discrete individuals pervades the "brotherhood" narratives in other comics. Two adventures of the Teen Titans saw the teammates set their reforming sights on individuals as the source of racism. In *Teen Titans* #30, racism is wholly concentrated in one individual—Hargood P. Tout—who is, by story's end, revealed as a criminal and hauled off to jail. Similarly, when the Titans visit the town of Fairfield in *World's Finest* #205, the town's prevalent racism is identified as the product of one man—Richard Handley—whose mind linked with an alien computer to give birth to this burg and its attitudes. The original Sons of the Serpent arc in *The Avengers* similarly casts racism as an aberration, whether via repeated mentions of racism as a "poison" or the revelation that the group is secretly headed by a foreign national, both of which portray their bigotry as something foreign to US society rather than endemic to it.[102]

Conclusion

Though the majority of these "brotherhood" comics published in the 1960s and 1970s fell short of their ideological aims due to their various contradictions and conditions, at least one tale suggested the potential of comics to transcend these limits and address racial issues with significant complexity. That comic is *Iron Man* #27—"The Fury of the Firebrand"—from July 1970. The story's conflict revolves around a new community center that Tony Stark, via the Iron Man Foundation, is helping to construct in the fictional midwestern metropolis of Bay City. The project is opposed by a group of black protestors planning a sit-in at the construction site, a group that the villainous Firebrand attempts to goad toward more violent action. By story's end, Stark's partner, the Bay City councilman Lyle Bradshaw, has been exposed as using the construction project to line his own pockets, and Firebrand's plot has been thwarted, though the villain himself escapes.

Threaded through this plot is a critique of the very ways in which white liberals have sought to address racism and discrimination. In particular, the comic speaks to how the complexities of the post–World War II black ghetto transcend the very discrete and narrow efforts made, in the spirit of liberalism, to improve those conditions. The community center at the heart of this story's conflict is the symbol of this point. Stark has tabbed

Figure 3.10. *Iron Man* #27 stands out in the 1970s for its more complex, if ultimately unfulfilled, take on systemic issues of race in American society. Unlike most comic books of the time, this one allowed African Americans a voice to critique feel-good liberalism and its limited solutions to widespread problems.

Eddie March, a black former boxer who briefly filled in as Iron Man until a blood clot in his brain forced him to give up fighting of any kind,[103] to direct the center. Eddie, though hesitant about taking the position, initially demonstrates hopes for the effect of the center on his old neighborhood. As they drive into the Bay City tenement, March comments, "But here's a place that hasn't changed . . . the north side! It looks just as bad as when I was a kid! Buildings and faces without hope . . . a spankin' new community center plunked in the middle of this is sure gonna cause some excitement!"[104] Here, even though surrounded by and cognizant of the hopeless conditions of this tenement, March naïvely believes that the construction of a single community center represents a significant contribution to the neighborhood's improvement. When the pair arrive at the construction site, they are confronted not only by the black protesters but also with a contrasting attitude. As one protester declares, "Maybe a community center is good for a lotta white consciences, but it ain't what the blacks on the north side want!"[105] The protester makes clear that the community center represents a less than substantial contribution to improving conditions in this ghetto, functioning as a salve for the white conscience, and thus capturing the ways in which liberalism generated such well-meant but symbolic and thus ultimately limited gestures. By defining racism and discrimination in discrete and narrow ways, liberalism also narrowed the scope of its own action.

This critique expands over the course of the issue, as Eddie interacts with Helene Davis, a black protester he rescued when violence broke out at the site. As Eddie challenges her militant stance, Helene even more thoroughly undercuts the well-intended liberalism Eddie evidences. When Eddie seconds his earlier claim, stating that the "community center could be one bright spot in all the squalor, Helene!" she retorts, "Why must we settle for any squalor?" Her answer cuts right to the heart of the problem: the community center, and the liberal spirit supporting it, fails to change the prevailing conditions of the ghetto in any substantive way. As they approach a boarded-up market, Helene continues:

> Look at this! This could be a black business bringing money into the community, hiring black men and women who are jobless now . . . ! Instead, it's a firetrap in the making, owned by a white slumlord no one ever sees or knows! Most of the money for this community center goes to a white realty firm for the property and a white construction company to build it! Suppose we got the money instead of the center? It could be used to set up businesses like I said . . . create jobs . . . ! It would be an investment! We could pay it back! That's what we're fighting for![106]

Whereas many of the other "brotherhood" comics of the 1960s and 1970s held up such narrow and discrete efforts and gestures for celebration, Helene's monologue at least voices the contrasting position: that such efforts do more for those whites behind them—morally and economically—than for the black and other nonwhite communities they putatively aim to help. By the end of this exchange, Eddie has been convinced, further highlighting the poverty of his earlier belief, as well as the liberalism motivating it.

But though *Iron Man* #27 affirms this criticism of the liberalism behind "brotherhood," it in the end swerves away from the full implications of the ideas it has expressed. By issue's end, both the councilman's and Firebrand's efforts have come to naught, and the conflict between the protestors and Stark has been mollified. Though no longer willing to serve as the center's director, Eddie does accept the vaguely defined position of "fighter" for Stark's Iron Man Foundation, and ends on a note of brotherhood, telling Stark that "with your help and Helene's [the result of his new position] should be somethin' good!"[107] But in an issue that pointed out the emptiness of vague and symbolic efforts in contrast to the practical realities blacks face, the incoherent nature of Eddie's job and the "somethin'" it will produce seem a step backward. In the end, despite the potential of its earlier scenes, *Iron Man* #27 turns to a self-assured and empty moral confidence that things have "worked out" because one evildoer has been thwarted. The ending, like postwar liberalism, thus revolves around a very discrete instance of wrong, but the comic deserves some credit for raising the larger and more complex questions and realities surrounding race that often went unaddressed even in this well-intentioned phase of comics' social awareness.

The same empty moral hand-wringing and self-serving congratulation displayed in *Iron Man* frustrates so many other of this era's earnest efforts to address race and preach tolerance. *Justice League of America* #40 concludes with Green Lantern's claim that "until [the ideal that 'all men are brothers'] is properly understood, there will always be injustice in the world!"[108] Such a statement, however, absolves the heroes of needing to take any action: they will do nothing because nothing can be done until such understanding—which cannot be compelled—is reached. Likewise, in *Justice League of America* #57, the heroes can only imagine a world of such understanding; as Snapper Carr ponders, "What a world it will be when mankind—is kind to man!"[109] Other comics conclude with even less concrete but just as irresponsible morals. The Teen Titans conclude that Richard Handley, the man whose biases permeated the town of Fairfield, "sure was a lot of things! But, then, I guess we all are,"[110] a statement as vague as it is empty. As well, *Teen Titans* #41 saw the following conclusion drawn after the defeat of a slave-catching ghost pursuing Mal Duncan: "Man's inhumanity to man—history is filled with terrifying examples—right to the present day! But, sometimes there is help." But the only "help" in the story is a "singed, half-torn apart straw doll" that comes to life via an inexplicable kind of voodoo/magic, a form of help not practically applicable to reality.[111] The three-part Inhumans feature in *Amazing Adventures* ends with a reporter's sign-off—"And that was our world today. How was yours?"[112]—that just reports the goings-on as facts and nothing more. Finally, the concluding revelation of Chen's leadership of the Sons of the Serpent in *The Avengers* #33 leads to a conclusion that affirms the purity and sanctity not only of America's institutions but also of America, its creed, and its people: "That's the courage of a free country," Captain America bloviates. "Any man has a chance to sway us—any man may be heard! And it's also our strength—it's the creed by which we live!"[113]

These concluding morals are ultimately hollow in how they absolve whites of responsibility for the social crises of racism and discrimination. For all that they tried to combat these plagues, the comic creators' faith in the purity of the United States and its structures, as well as their discrete and thus narrow definition of what gives rise to these issues, remained largely steadfast. More crucially, their comics communicate in a myriad of ways not only these same assumptions but also that the latter were not inconsistent with achieving a long-sought-after ideal of "brotherhood." Thus, though the sheer plethora of comics engaging in such consciousness-raising efforts in these decades—from *Green Lantern/Green Arrow* to *Flash*, *Justice League of America*, *Superman's Girl Friend Lois Lane*, and *Teen Titans* at DC, and *Amazing Adventures*, *The Avengers*, *Daredevil*, and *Iron Man* at Marvel—marks significant progress from previous decades, that progress is to some extent qualified by the ideological limits within which their plots, dialogue, and images remain constrained and constrain themselves.

CHAPTER 4

Guess Who's Coming to Save You? The Rise of the Ethnic Superhero in the 1960s and 1970s

Starting in the late 1960s, mainstream comics experienced a veritable ex-plosion of ethnic characters. The sheer number of such superheroes rep-resented a real and valuable kind of progress. Adilifu Nama, for example, celebrates the arrival of black heroes—by far the largest in number—as erasing the distinction between the "popular and the political," as comics and superhero popular culture began to "boldly engage the racial tensions that America was experiencing."[1] Such significance extends to all the non-white heroes to debut during this era; as Frederick Luis Aldama notes, tra-ditionally marginalized groups now found their identities acknowledged and given a greater share of the spotlight.[2] Undoubtedly, creators saw a need—based on events and trends in the larger society—to acknowledge and address racial imbalances in their work through diverse additions to their pantheons of heroes. The arrival of diverse characters, in fact, repre-sented a second tactic employed by comic book creators in the pursuit of "relevancy," complementing the "brotherhood" ideal popular in the mid-1960s and early 1970s.

In adding copious new ethnic characters, comic book creators seemed, however, to understand inclusivity as a sort of numbers game, as a matter of simply adding "more," with sometimes some but often too little thought given to the actual portrayal of the individual nonwhite characters who arrived. Foreshadowing the ofttimes shallow nature of the coming 1980s multiculturalism, many creators seemed to believe, in other words, that just *having* multiethnic characters sufficed to address racial shortcomings in comics. In this way, even as black, Native American, Asian and Asian American, and Latinx heroes and heroines began fill up comic book pages, creators—whatever their good intentions—consistently failed to escape the gravity of deeply entrenched and long-held American notions of race.

In this effort to diversify, black heroes led the way, with the Black Panther playing the pioneering role in 1966. Others—including the first African American hero, the Falcon (1969), and the first headlining black superhero, Luke Cage (1972)—arrived soon after at Marvel. DC introduced Mal Duncan in 1971; the Green Lantern John Stewart in 1972; Tyroc, the first black member of the Legion of Super-Heroes, in 1976; and then its first headlining black superhero, Black Lightning, in 1977. Other notable black superheroes to debut include Marvel's Blade (1973), Brother Voodoo (1973), and Black Goliath (1975). Black women also arrived, if belatedly. Marvel's Misty Knight, a former cop turned private detective with a bionic arm, first appeared in 1975. Two months later, Marvel debuted the X-Men's Storm, who would become its most prominent black female. At DC, Nubia arrived in the pages of *Wonder Woman* in 1973. With Nubia playing the role of an antagonist, DC's first black female hero would appear in 1977, when Karen Beecher adopted the costumed identity of Bumblebee.

The era also featured the first appearances of several Asian, Latinx, and Native American heroes and heroines. The Japanese mutant Sunfire appeared, initially as a villain, in 1970, and made subsequent guest appearances before briefly joining the X-Men. Marvel's most prominent Asian character, Shang-Chi, the Master of Kung Fu, arrived in 1973. Marvel also introduced Mantis, a half-Vietnamese barmaid/prostitute who joined the Avengers in 1973. DC debuted the original Karate Kid (Val Armorr), the son of a Japanese crime-lord father and an American secret-agent mother, who joined the Legion of Super-Heroes in 1966, and Lady Shiva, who arrived a decade later. A small number of Native Americans also began to populate the comic book page. Marvel's first Native American superhero— the Red Wolf—actually debuted twice in the 1970s: first, as the twentieth-century Cheyenne William Talltrees in 1970, and second, as Talltrees's nineteenth-century predecessor, Johnny Wakely, in 1971. The revamped *X-Men* title also featured—at least briefly—the Apache John Proudstar, a.k.a. Thunderbird, and, in 1979, Shaman, the Sarcee member of the Canadian superteam Alpha Flight. Having already established Chief Man-of-the-Bats, DC introduced the Native American Dawnstar in 1977; she hailed from the planet Starhaven, colonized by Native Americans after their kidnapping by aliens in the thirteenth century. Finally, the 1970s provided a couple of Latinx heroes: the Puerto Rican White Tiger, who debuted in 1975, and the Spanish American El Águila, who appeared in 1979.

This sudden presence of ethnic superheroes coincided with a growing awareness of ethnic individuals and communities on the part of the predominant American society and culture. Such awareness was largely fostered by the ethnic activism of the 1960s and 1970s, beginning with the black civil rights movement. As the efforts of black activists participating in sit-ins and freedom rides grabbed the nation's attention, newspapers and televised news programs made blacks' efforts a part of American daily life, convincing a growing number of whites to participate in the struggle. Too, blacks themselves shrugged off their characterization as victims, demanding that things change in asserting their own agency.[3] Concomitant with that increasing awareness of blacks' suffering, struggles, and voice was an awareness—and a demand for an awareness—of their individuality.

Demands for similar recognition permeated the civil rights efforts of Mexican Americans, Native Americans, and Asian Americans during this period. The birth of "Chicanismo" denounced assimilation and birthed "La Raza Unida" as a unified voice.[4] The development of this militant voice also defined a wholly separate Chicano subjectivity and identity,[5] cementing an awareness of this presence in American society. Similarly, Native Americans in 1961 crafted the Declaration of Indian Purpose as a call for self-determination and, by the end of the decade, would form the American Indian Movement (AIM) to protest more militantly an assimilation they feared would rob them of their cultural and individual identity.[6] As early as 1948, Japanese Americans had successfully overturned the Alien Land Law, a success followed in 1965 by the overdue removal of long-extant restrictions on Asian immigration into the country.[7] These demands and successes by Chicanos, Native Americans, and Asian Americans, like black civil rights efforts, contributed to white Americans' growing awareness of nonwhites as unique individuals and communities with their own identities and cultures.

Films of the 1960s and 1970s not only manifested this growing awareness of—and interest in—ethnic individuals and communities, but also established limitations to their representation that would influence comics. Like black civil rights efforts, black films in the 1960s opened white Americans' eyes to a different view of blacks: no longer feeling the need to prove their worth, no longer submissive and passive, but now angry and bitter. Similarly, black films of the 1960s confronted white Americans with a world they had formerly been blind to that included "ghettos, whores, hustlers, addicts, pimps, and pushers, a world of racist sickness, of oppression, of black despair and rage."[8] Here, black films paralleled black civil rights efforts to shatter preconceived and paternalistic understandings about blacks and the environments in which they lived. By the 1970s, however, this "black world" would be wholly exploited and commodified in the form of "blaxploitation" films that traded in familiar stereotypes of blacks—most prominently, the brutal black "buck"—and linked the concept of "blackness," and thus black identity, with "the trappings of the ghetto: the tenements as well as the talk, the mannerisms, and the sophistication of the streets."[9]

Filmic representations of Asians, Native Americans, and Latinos were similarly problematic. Like black films, Asian-centered movies of the "kung fu" variety exploited and flattened ethnic identity. Movies likewise appropriated and homogenized Native Americans as at peace with nature, impoverished, oppressed, and mystical, recycling the image of the noble savage.[10] Representations of Latinos were just as limited. Here, the "Hollywood social problem film" offered only two empty resolutions: a return to the barrio and its deprivation or successful assimilation, with a coinciding loss of ethnic identity.[11]

Even more insidious was how such films masked their trading in these timeworn types. As Donald Bogle observes regarding the history of black film, the basic black stereotypes—the "tom," the "buck," the "coon," the "mammy," and the "tragic mulatto"—were often camouflaged by various "guises." That is, the audience was deceived into not perceiving the traits of a particular stereotype via the "guise," or role, within which the type was subsumed. For instance, black butlers and maids remained loyal "toms," lazy "coons," and boisterous "mammies," but the servant role overpowered the perception of the type, repackaging it insidiously. Such repackaging occurred from the start. D. W. Griffith's *Birth of a Nation*, for instance, obscured "bucks" and "tragic mulattoes" by depicting them as villains. "Toms" and "coons" became jesters in the 1920s, while, from the 1930s through the 1960s, all black types appeared as servants, entertainers, and "problem people" before finally emerging as militants. Such surface change proved deceptive, as audiences were lulled—and perhaps lulled themselves—into thinking that representations of blacks were changing. Though dressed up in new roles, the same stereotypes—not only about blacks but about all nonwhite individuals and communities—persisted under the "guise."[12]

The new ethnic superheroes of this era found themselves similarly mired in persistent stereotypical representations, whose usage in comics generally has not gone unremarked. Will Eisner, for example, justifies the use of visual stereotypes as "an accursed necessity" resulting from a need, he theorizes, for comics and cartoons to communicate efficiently to their reader via simplification.[13] Derek Parker Royal pursues the implications of this alleged requirement, pointing out that such reliance on stereotypes potentially betrays prejudices within creators as well as readers and can easily veer into degrading representations, particularly in the context of race/ethnicity.[14] Jared Gardner, in the context of Asian American representation in comics, further unpacks the use of these—and by extension other—racial stereotypes. He points out how comics have historically perpetuated imagery of Asians as, in one way or another, an invading mob, but he also credits comics—particularly narrative/sequential ones versus single-panel comics and cartoons—for their ability to unsettle such visual depictions.[15] Stereotypes—visual, as these theorists concentrate on, or nonvisual—remain at best a double-edged sword in comics, a reality made clear by the new nonwhite heroes of the 1960s and 1970s. These comics relied heavily on established racial stereotypes while simultaneously promulgating racialized associations of their own, both of which can be easily missed and dismissed as part of the trappings of superhero comics; thus, the reality of this stereotyping persists behind the camouflaging function of guise. In doing so, comics—whatever the good intentions of their creators and whatever the value in the increased number of nonwhite superheroes—demonstrated their ability not only to replicate pernicious thinking about racialized others but also to insidiously mask this dehumanizing process.

The Emperor's Not-So-New Clothes: (Dis)Guising Cultural Primitivism in Ethnic Superheroes

Several of the ethnic superheroes to debut in the late 1960s and throughout the 1970s were based in some of the most primordial stereotypes, what M. H. Abrams defines as "cultural primitivism." As Abrams describes, cultural primitivism values the natural and nature over the man-made or artificial. Problematically, cultural primitivism values the lives and existence of the "primitive," for lack of a better term, as superior to those of individuals living in the modern, "civilized" world. Their isolation from the modern, then, is what makes them and their way of life better.[16] The perpetuation of this stereotype has important ramifications. W. Lawrence Hogue, for instance, explicates one ideological function of such primitive depictions, to which he assigns the term "racial tradition." For Hogue, modernity—white, European, urban, and capitalist—objectifies what is different from it as completely homogenous, isolated, and premodern. At the same time, those "others" are also integrated into capitalism as material and labor resources.[17] Thus, cultural primitivism/racial tradition valorizes primitive or premodern cultures, but only does so in a way that relegates them and their people to anachronism and exploitation. Implicit within Hogue's ideological conception is Western capitalism's dependency on nonwhites as material, ideological, and psychological resources. In his critique of Joseph Conrad's *Heart of Darkness,* the Nigerian novelist Chinua Achebe expresses another implicit aspect of this stereotype: an underlying desire in the West for Africa to serve as its "foil" to better highlight Western "grace." But at the same time, Africa evokes a sense of disquieting familiarity to the West, reminding it of its own "darkness." For Achebe, the predication of European/Western superiority upon a contrast with African barbarity and savagery also suggests a deeper anxiety about the potentially precarious nature of civilization.[18]

The depiction of the first black superhero—Marvel's Black Panther—bases itself in both the stereotype and the ideology of cultural primitivism in relation to not only this black hero but also his fictional nation of Wakanda. Though writing about a much later Black Panther series, Jeffrey A. Brown, à la Edward Said, summarizes how backward-looking ideas of Africa as a treacherous "Dark Continent" permeate the Panther and his country: both are subsumed within an aura of mystery, exoticism, bizarreness, and danger that starkly differentiates them as "other."[19] These qualities pervade the Panther's introduction in *The Fantastic Four* #52–54. As the scene shifts from the Fantastic Four's New York headquarters to Wakanda, the captions describe this very foreign land as "an area wherein lies buried a mystery . . . a mystery known only to those who know of the Wakandas—and who speak the name of the Black Panther in hushed, fearful whispers . . . !" Here, Wakanda's isolation from the modern, Western world is made clear—an isolation tinged with mystery and menace not terribly dissimilar to earlier depictions of China and the "Orient." Not only is Wakanda twice associated explicitly with the "mysterious," but the captions also hint at the stereotypical danger of this realm in the fear its ruler's ancestral name conjures. The Panther's emissary's warnings to the team reinforce this lingering sense of menace, as he advises them "to remember . . . in this land, things are not always . . . as they seem!"[20]

At the same time, though, the comic disguises the stereotypical nature of Wakanda once the Fantastic Four arrive. As their plane dips below the jungle canopy, the team enters "a world of sheer wonderment—!" In the accompanying panel, which takes up roughly two-thirds of the page, the Fantastic Four's ship is eclipsed by giant technological tubes branching across the page, as well as a cornucopia of futuristic constructs. Captured here by Kirby's visuals is the exotic and bizarre nature of this technological "jungle," which the emissary's dialogue further unpacks. As he explains,

Figure 4.1. As the Fantastic Four journey to Africa, the representation of the Black Panther's Wakanda seems to present a technologically advanced nation. Such appearances are misleading, however, as the apparent "advancement" serves to disguise the ways in which the depictions of Africa and its people remain rooted in primitivist notions of the "other" that suggest difference and danger.

"The entire topography and flora are electronically-controlled mechanical apparatus! The very branches about us are composed of delicately-constructed wires . . . while the flowers which abound here are highly complex buttons and dials! Even the boulders can be heard to hum with the steady pulse of computer dynamos!"[21] Such technological wonder purports to belie the isolation and primitivism of Wakanda. Far from premodern, Wakanda appears to be on the leading edge of modern technology.

But underneath this surface wonder and mystery, Wakanda remains a jungle and thus ensconced within the primitivism its technology merely serves to mask. As the emissary's narration makes clear, Wakanda is still filled with flora and fauna, boulders, branches, and flowers, just ones now made out of wires and circuits. It remains wholly different and thus dangerous. As Mister Fantastic declares upon landing, "Stay together . . . all of you! Whoever created this electronic nightmare has kept it a secret for some deadly reason!"[22] Mister Fantastic's warning is prescient; when the Thing drinks from a seemingly harmless pool of water, it is actually a "devitalizing fluid" that robs him of his strength.[23] Thus, though Wakanda may at first appear to base itself in something other than cultural primitivism, its depiction ultimately perpetuates this ideological construction of nonwhite societies.

Perhaps unsurprisingly then, the same anxiety Achebe noted regarding the West's relationship to the "other" appears throughout this introduction. The juxtaposition of the "savage jungle" with technological wonders gives rise to a stubborn consternation. The various members of the Fantastic Four constantly wonder about what is to them clearly an incongruity. Perplexed by a high-tech ship, Ben Grimm wonders, "But how does some refugee from a Tarzan movie lay his hands on this kinda gizmo?" Reed Richards ponders similarly, "I wonder how the Black Panther . . . whoever he is . . . got possession of such a ship?" Johnny Storm is befuddled, too, at explanations of the native-built ship: "Now I know you're connin' me! How does an African chieftain latch onto a plane that flies by magnetic waves?" Sue concurs: "It's so hard to believe that a ship such as this one could have come from a land with no sign of technology . . . of industrial development—!"[24]

The second issue's flashback to the Black Panther's past is framed by these very same questions. As the team watches a ritualistic "dance of friendship" performed by the Wakandans, Reed again points to the troubling combination of "tradition" and "super-scientific wonders," ultimately concluding, "There's an incredible mystery here—and only the Black Panther himself knows all the answers!" Ben, too, seems similarly troubled: "I still don't get it! They tossed a bunch'a science-fiction gizmos at us that Doc Doom would'a been proud of usin'! And now they're actin' like they're all charged up on account'a just inventin' the wheel!"[25] These, and similar questions, reveal that very anxiety that Achebe asserted. Given how often the characters ask about Wakanda's technology, they implicitly reveal how troubled they are by this "primitive" and "savage" nation possessing such wondrous technology.

Similarly retrograde motifs occur in the Black Panther's later solo adventures. In 1973, Black Panther began headlining Marvel's *Jungle Action* title in an arc titled "Panther's Rage" by the writer Don McGregor and the artists Rick Buckler and Billy Graham. McGregor hoped to develop more fully the heretofore backgrounded Wakanda and its people, explaining, "I immediately felt that the stories had to be about Wakandans. . . . I also realized that Wakanda was a concept, but that detailing how the country worked had never been explored. . . . That meant, if the stories were situated in Wakanda, all the major characters would have to be Wakandan. And that meant all of the characters save one would be black."[26] Whatever his intentions, McGregor's representation of Wakanda still plays into other long-existing associations and stereotypes, specifically cultural primitivism's personification, the "noble savage." The noble savage, as a concrete expression of this primitivism, is an individual believed to possess a higher morality and dignity because of his or her distance from civilization.[27] "Panther's Rage" consistently bases its depiction of the Black Panther and Wakanda within this stereotypical trope.

How the story line does so, however, is via an inversion that serves as this trope's guise. Rather than showing how the Panther and Wakanda's isolation makes them superior, the feature depicts both man and country as lesser due to their infiltration and corruption by modernity. The narration as the hero, home after time abroad, carries the lifeless body of one of his tribesmen back to his village signals this idea clearly: "Once, [the Black Panther] was acutely attuned to this land . . . Once, he was part of it and it was a part of him . . . But now he is aware that there has been a subtle undefinable change . . . and he is no longer an integral part of his heritage!"[28] Not only has the Panther "changed" due to his time away from Wakanda, but, more significantly, he has lost something—his heritage, his link to the natural world—that would otherwise, "naturally," be there. In other words, modern society has corrupted what is naturally "good" about the Panther. The Wakandans themselves voice this motif. The herbalist Mendinao laments the change he observes in the Panther—noting, "There was a day when he would have kept everything in control"—and the security chief W'Kabi concludes, "Perhaps that's because he has spent so much time of late with out-worlders."[29] Later issues in the series extend this sense of corruption via contact with the outside world. The Black Panther himself connects the existence of various factions within Wakanda to this influence, telling his lover Monica Lynne, "These days the madness of the outside world affects Wakanda, Monica. They seem to fear any beliefs different than their own—as if the very existence of a belief contrary to theirs would negate or threaten their way of life."[30]

But it is the presence of modern technology—once the source of Wakanda's wonder and mystery—that stands as the clearest symbol of the country's corruption. When Monica attempts to assist a sick woman, the woman retorts, "What help could you give me? Do you come to take me back to that hos-pe-taal? I trust you no more than I do all those indoor suns."[31] In the next issue the "hos-pe-taal" appears as a "study in anachro-

Figure 4.2. Comics in the 1970s continued to rely on understandings of African primitivity. Here, the modern hospital is contrasted to the thatched huts that surround it, drawing a clear distinction between the "modern" West and "premodern" Africa.

nism," its hexagonal shape, sharp edges, and towering size contrasting the small, circular, thatched huts around it. The captions framing this panel explicate the building's incongruity to the Wakandan woman, describing it as "a demon she cannot fathom . . . a demon that arrogantly flaunts itself beside the high-ceiling, thatched roofs of the homes in central Wakanda."[32] The Black Panther expresses doubts about the technology he has brought into Wakanda. As he explains,

> It wasn't until those long hours I spent in Serpent Valley, trying to return home—that I finally realized what the real change in Wakanda was. Oh, I was always aware that the computers and machinery has affected our lifestyle . . . but never beyond the more obvious changes. . . . All the advancements I brought to our land changed our priorities. Acquiring enough food and having a roof over your head was no longer an equation for contentment. You mention sunsets and dawns . . . they're relatively unimportant now.[33]

In the Panther's monologue, the primitivist motifs introduce a further complication. The speech casts Wakanda's technology as that country's largest inheritance from the modern world of the West; that technology, further, has shifted the country away from its priorities, troped as nature (food, sunsets, and dawns). These are what is really important in Wakanda, as the distractions and temptations of technology have diminished the natural nobility of the Panther and his people. However, Wakanda had such technology prior to its alleged infiltration by the modern world as represented by the Fantastic Four's earlier arrival. So, via the Panther's speech, even though Wakanda's technological advancements are homegrown, they become something inherently foreign, and a much less advanced state thus becomes natural. Furthermore, the Panther's monologue is crucial to the story line's promulgation of the noble savage trope. The other spokespersons for this fear of corruption—Mendinao, W'Kabi, and the plotline's villain, Erik Killmonger—are all clearly and to varying extents in the wrong. In this climactic monologue, Black Panther himself expresses concern over what Wakanda's technological advancements mean for the country and its people. The series thus has its cake and eats it too, appearing to denigrate such retrograde positions via their personification in characters who are either presented as ignorant or villainous, but then valorizing them via Black Panther. The result is, on the one hand, an ideological sleight of hand, as the narrative shuns such positions before recentering them, but on the other, a further complication if not contradiction to the very nature of Wakanda's technology, which ultimately derives not from the West but from Wakanda itself.

The Black Panther's adventures are not alone in attempting to disguise such primitivism even as they promote it. The depiction of Storm also trades in similar attempts to disguise primitivist imagery, in this case initially masking it behind an otherworldly (and potentially no less problematic) exoticism. She debuts as a goddess, topless and with eyes that are "crystal blue, and older than time"; as she flies among the storm clouds, the captions describe "the glow of life shining full upon her face." Besides masking her primitivist basis, such descriptions also separate and isolate her from humankind, making her explicitly "other." But what more fully functions to disguise her perpetuation of such tropes is its basis in her mutant abilities. She has this glow as she exercises her mutant gift to control the weather by conjuring a storm. As the next caption explains, "She is happy here—only truly happy here among the elements."[34] These "elements," of course, are aspects of the natural world that have long been stereotyped as inherent to nonwhite peoples and cultures. The narration in this opening sequence further implies this connection in its claim about Storm's happiness: being "only" and "truly" happy when flying among the clouds, she prefers inhabiting a space separate from the human, modern world.

Figure 4.3. Primitivism was masked in 1970s comics in a variety of ways. Storm, for instance, occupied a natural, otherworldly space, her exoticism disguising her basis in primitive tropes. Here, she is only truly alive when using her mutant powers, preferably naked and always in tune with nature.

This ideology carries into Storm's depictions throughout the early issues of *X-Men*, most often by casting her as free (which often means naked). In issue #96, as Storm flies toward the source of a demonic invasion, the captions read, "The nightwind is a welcome caress on her bare skin as she soars high and away into the midnight sky. . . . She is free now—of houses, walls, people—of the cages mankind builds to lock himself into . . . free and happy and alive."[35] Here, in again asserting Storm's exotic and thus distanced nature, the captions echo that "noble savage" theme, specifically the idea of modern civilization and its trappings—its houses, walls, and even people!—as a corrupting cage. Later, when Storm feels similarly uncomfortable, she conjures up a "summer shower" to "refresh herself and calm her nerves" as she stands naked.[36] When the team arrives home from space in issue #109, Storm immediately goes to care for her neglected plants. She creates a shower for them and then decides to enjoy it herself. During a picnic in this same issue, she laments having to wear clothes, explaining, "It is only for the Professor's sake that I endure this land's strange taboos."[37]

A further permutation of how the series masks its stereotypical basis occurs in a story line in *Uncanny X-Men* #114–116 that stranded Storm and the majority of her team in the prehistoric Savage Land. Storm immediately finds herself at home in this primitive locale, trading her costume for a two-piece loincloth bikini, while noting, "This place reminds me of my home in Africa. I'd almost forgotten how much I missed it." Not only does this story line allow Storm to once again play into the "noble savage" motif, but it papers it over with an environmental message. After a refreshing swim, Storm thinks, "This land is so unlike New York. Here the air is clean. There—even on a good day—the sky smells to me like an open sewer. Scott says that is because of progress. Yet, how can the murder of our Mother Earth be called . . . progress . . . ?"[38] While certainly Storm—and through her, her creators—raises a worthwhile question, it also underlines her stereotypical affinity with nature and distaste for modernity.

Part and parcel of how Storm's depiction functions to disguise her basis in these stereotypes is their equation with her mutant abilities. In this, Storm joins several other similar primitivist figures whose super-heroic abilities obscure their grounding in this trope. The splash page an-nouncing the debut of Brother Voodoo, for example, emphasizes, narra-tively and visually, several patently primitivist elements: "In the jungles of Haiti, they speak his name in whispers, lest somehow they offend him— for then, 'tis said, the crops will wither—and the sun will forever cease to shine. In the shadowed back alleys of New Orleans, they speak his name in awe—for 'tis said he was old when the mountains were young—that he cannot be harmed—that he can never die! Thruout [sic] the world, they speak his name—in praise, in wonder, in reverence, in fear—but never— never—in jest! His name is: BROTHER VOODOO!"[39] Marvel's new super-natural hero is immediately connected to the jungle and nature via the imagery of withering crops and a ceasing sun, as well as comparisons to ageless mountains. Additionally, the caption conveys an exoticism and danger that is also reminiscent of Black Panther (not to mention the Yel-low Claw): his name is spoken only in whispers tinged with awe and won-der and reverence and fear. His outfit, which Adilifu Nama describes as a "barefooted island-boy getup [that] left much to be desired in terms of stylish superhero attire," adds to his primitive imagery.[40] But the prob-lematic aspects of Brother Voodoo's attire go beyond its lack of style. He stands with legs spread, arms lowered and spread, bare chested but for a diamond-patterned vest and a tooth-studded necklace. Around both fore-arms wrap sharply fanged snakes. Below a sash tied round his waist, his leggings end in dry grass. These details convey a clear primitivism about Brother Voodoo—as do the dancing and drum-playing tribesmen behind him—while a sigil burned onto his forehead and his black hair with a cen-tered, white, triangular stripe further marks his exotic and mysterious nature.

However, the ensuing depiction of Brother Voodoo masks his inherent primitivism behind standard comic book superheroics. Despite his vari-ous mystical trappings and abilities—ranging from "the power to com-mand all living things—be they human or lowly plant—the power to be heard by the loas—the spirits—in time of need—[and] the power to walk

Figure 4.4. The visual representation of Brother Voodoo communicated a sense of both primitivity and exotic mystery, both of which were also rooted in his background.

unscathed through the raging fire—through the hottest pits of hell"[41]— Brother Voodoo defaults to physical confrontation to thwart his foes. In his first appearance in *Strange Tales* #169, Brother Voodoo physically beats his enemies, only using his ability to possess others to help him continue pummeling his foes.[42] In the next issue, Brother Voodoo likewise only physically confronts his foes, battling the Council of Vaudou hand to hand before pummeling their voodoo master Damballah and his pet snake.[43] The cover and the plot of *Strange Tales* #171 also emphasize not mystical but physical prowess. On the cover, as he fights off a zombie horde, he cries, "No matter how many I smash—they keep on coming!" and his battle in the following pages would involve similar means. As Brother Voodoo fights the horde, his "powerful muscles bunch—and empty-eyed assassins are hurled through the air like so much wind-blown chaff."[44] But again, Brother Voodoo's depiction, being consistent with superheroes before and

Figure 4.5. Traditional superhero tropes provided a convenient means with which to disguise primitivism in nonwhite heroes. Here, Shaman goes to battle—as would any superhero—but does so in ways that reveal stereotypical understandings of Native Americans, in this case revealed by his choice of weapon: magical totem poles that fly through the air.

after who rely on physical strength and abilities, masks his basis in primitivist stereotypes.

Black superheroes and superheroines were not the only ones whose basis in cultural primitivism is apparent but disguised. The depiction of the modern-day Red Wolf (William Talltrees), for instance, deployed the same progressive environmental message as Storm. After he helps a woman recover her gold from a group of mobsters, he praises her intention to use it to fight pollution: "Aye! Let her help bring back the days when the wind blew clean and sweet—and when the rivers teemed with fish and the brook water was good to drink!"[45] Like Storm, Red Wolf's advocacy is based in assumed affinity with nature that is further identified as anachronistic. However, Red Wolf does not only long for a cleaner world—echoing Storm—but, unlike her, longs for an earlier one, as his dialogue explicitly invokes a time prior to modernity and its pollution. In this, Red Wolf plays on Hogue's notion of racial tradition, essentializing Native American peoples and cultures as premodern. When Red Wolf speaks of those past days, he talks about them as if he lived during them, as his comments about the wind and rivers smack more of firsthand experience than imaginative nostalgia. Thus, lurking behind his timely environmental concern is an anachronistic primitivism that has the consequence of relegating him — and what he represents — to an isolated past.

Other Native American superheroes similarly mask their primitivist basis in established superhero tropes. Michael A. Sheyahshe has identified two stereotypes about Native American superheroes. The first, the "shaman," invokes "the idea that all Indigenous people have some innate shamanistic/mystic ability," or affinity with nature. The second, the "tracker," portrays "Indigenous people as skilled trackers with supernatural sensory perception."[46] Obviously, Marvel's Shaman embodies the first of these types, and his "mysticism" is of a particularly problematic variety, for example when he attacks with magic floating totem poles![47] Both versions of Marvel's Red Wolf are likewise steeped in the figure of the "shaman." The nineteenth-century version derives his abilities from a great "wolf spirit" and routinely calls out to the "Great Spirit" or "Wakan Tanka" for strength. His modern-day descendant possesses even more mystical — and thus stereotypical — abilities. "Ancestral voices" whisper to him the danger of an impending attack. In a later issue, he describes Lobo, his wolf companion, as an "extension" of himself, "like an arm," and he gives thanks that "Pa'e," the moon, lights the path of a biker gang he pursues.[48] Importantly, these qualities' stereotypical bases are masked by making the type essential to their heroic identities. As Bogle earlier revealed, black films superficially signaled progress in black representation because of the seeming wealth of roles blacks portrayed. The same can be said here, as Native American characters like Shaman and Red Wolf appear to embody a similar progress in their very nature as superheroes. They contrast with, for example, a figure like Chief Man-of-the-Bats in that, for all the chief might have attempted to signal regarding progress, he was little more than a painted-over ersatz Batman. But the incorporation of the "shaman" figure into both of these later Native American heroes belies whatever achievement their mere existence might betoken. They, like the black film characters Bogle exposes, are the same stereotypes dressed up in only seemingly new forms.

Both versions of Red Wolf likewise played on the "tracker" trope. The nineteenth-century Red Wolf would prove himself to be the superior tracker among the other (and white) scouts stationed at Fort Rango, thus masking his repetition of this figure in a bid for equality.[49] No less impressive are the tracking abilities of the twentieth-century Red Wolf; as one caption describes, "As might his redskinned ancestors have moved along the hunting trails, so now the Wolfhead Warrior stalks his prey in the steel forest of a thousand girders."[50] Red Wolf's trading of this concrete forest for a natural one again combines surface modernity with persistent stereotype, the former similarly portraying only superficial progress that the latter betrays.

DC's Native American heroine Dawnstar provides another example of guise in the sci-fi twist her depiction attempts to give to both stereotypical roles. Her mystical affinity is not so much with nature but rather with space, though ultimately to the same ideological effect. When the raiders the team pursues escape via a "space warp," Dawnstar reveals that her tracking is undiminished. The ensuing captions speak to her quasi-mystical affinity, describing such warps as a "mysterious gateway between dimensions" and as the "one realm where instruments cannot reach—tracking devices cannot function." How space warps emanate from some mysterious dimension beyond the science of instruments and tracking devices gives them a magical quality, and thus the same quality inheres within Dawnstar's preternatural senses, allowing her to track the raiders when other technological means fail. Similarly, when they reach the raiders' lair, both Superboy and Sun Boy are befuddled by optical illusions of separate corridors—both running headfirst into a wall—while Dawnstar blithely strolls down the actual passageway between them.[51] In the end, for all the science-fictional elements surrounding her in the far-flung future of the Legion of Super-Heroes, Dawnstar incarnates the timeworn "shaman" and "tracker" figures.

Forward to Go Backward: Disguising Racialized Stereotypes

If some black and Native American ethnic heroes functioned to disguise these primitive tropes, other nonwhite heroes of the 1970s served to obscure how they promulgated particular racialized stereotypes. Amongst the African American heroes to debut in the 1970s, the stereotype of the "brutal black buck" dominated. As Bogle explains, this stereotype twinned black savagery with a menacing sexuality, codified in "blaxploitation" protagonists like Sweetback, Shaft, and Super Fly. While such films appeared to function as enticing action-adventure narratives with firmly masculine protagonists, they remained socially and politically vacant, only "giving lip service to the idea of political commitment," and thus only "play[ing] on the needs of black audiences for heroic figures without answering those needs in realistic terms."[52] Coming of age alongside these "blaxploitation" protagonists, the first black superheroes traded in the same characteristics and failings.

But the "buck" superheroes of the 1970s varied significantly at times from their filmic versions. While physical attributes are still emphasized, the rampant sexuality is tamped down, leaving black heroes who provide, at best, chaste and, at worst, neutered protagonists. They remain, however, as politically vacant as the films. If the blaxploitation film becomes a "male action fantasy" that fails to answer a black audience's real needs, then the black "buck" superhero comic enacts a kind of "liberal action fantasy" in which the dream of a greater diversity is achieved, but only in a sanitized and nonthreatening way that makes it even more vacant than its filmic comparison. And undergirding this fantasy is a reliance on guise. On the one hand, the physicality of these black heroes plays consistently within comic book tropes of enhanced strength and physical confrontation, thus obscuring how they simultaneously work within a tradition of racialized stereotypes. On the other hand, the chastening of the sexuality gestures toward a kind of progress, as the comics in this way eliminated one of the most scurrilously problematic elements of the "buck." But such progress remains only gestural, the elimination of this trait mere window dressing for what remain racially questionable representations.

All these issues crystallize in Marvel's *Hero for Hire* and its headlining hero, Luke Cage. Cage's origin trades fully on the conventions of blaxploitation films, establishing him as the outlaw and rebel so common in such tales. An inmate at Seagate Prison, Carl Lucas is also and more importantly a rebel in how he resists being controlled by any "system," be it the corrupt prison run by whites or a planned demonstration organized by the so-called militant prisoner Shades. Lucas's response to the latter establishes his individualism, as he explains to his fellow inmate, "If [my head] goes under the club, it's gonna be cause I put it there, not you!" When Shades's partner Comanche threatens Lucas, our hero swiftly punches him in the mouth, again declaring his independence: "If I need a group, Shades, I'll do the organizin'. But I don't need anybody or anything—'cept out of this hellhole! An' best chance of doin' that . . . is on my own!"[53] Here, Lucas embodies an individualist morality that cements him among his blaxploitation peers.

But the narrative rapidly walks Lucas's depiction back from the aggression and violence of the blaxploitation heroes, thus purporting him to be something different. As Lucas relates his background to Dr. Noah Burstein, a scientist newly arrived at the prison whose experiments will result in Lucas's superstrength and steel-hard skin, it becomes clear that he has been unjustly incarcerated, framed for a narcotics bust by his former friend, partner, and romantic rival, Willis Stryker. Once his powers allow him to both escape prison and fake his own death, the newly christened Luke Cage adopts a mission of personal justice, telling the grave site of his former love, Reva Connors, that he will exact revenge against Stryker.[54] The second part of Cage's origin, entitled "Vengeance is Mine," sees the culmination of Cage's quest, as Stryker's death results from his own exploding knife. Cage here again addresses Reva's memory, telling her, "It's over Reva, honey. But not quite the way I planned. Willis died by his own knife. . . . An' if you can't really call that revenge—it's sure some kind of justice."[55] Cage successfully pursues his quest for justice, if of a sanitized nature. His closing speech smooths over the rough edges of his vengeful pursuit, as the circumstances absolve him from having directly killed Stryker. Contrast this to Sweetback: "When he sees two white policemen cudgel an innocent black youth, he lays waste to them, smashing in their heads with their own handcuffs. Then he flees."[56] But even if Cage's mission culminates with a sense of justice to contrast the more naked revenge of his fictional fellows, such framing does little to contradict his basis in the same stereotype.

Whatever mollifying effect Cage's morality might have had on his replication of the "buck," it was countered by his intense physicality, a key aspect of the type. The "buck" is typically big, aggressive, savage, and violent, all qualities emphasized by the visual depiction of Cage. The splash page to his debut issue testifies to his aggressive and violent nature. He stands in the center of the page with his fists clenched and arms raised; his eyes are shut, but his mouth opens wide in a primal scream.[57] Throughout the actual comic, Cage's physicality is consistently on display. In prison, Cage's shirt is undone, exposing his chest. When Cage first gains his powers, he bursts—naked, and concealed only by a well-placed piece of wreckage—out of the containment unit. And violence is Cage's first reaction to most situations. When Comanche threatens him, Cage punches him in the face, the swiftness of his arm indicated by the motion line from the bottom of the panel to Cage's fist, and the explosiveness of the punch by the violent glow that engulfs Comanche's lower jaw. When, in a flashback, he saves his then partner Stryker from thugs, Cage attacks his assailants with a similar swiftness and ferocity. The covers to subsequent issues reinforce Cage's physicality, as he bursts through a brick wall on the cover of issue #2, savagely hammers at the rotor of a plunging helicopter—his shirt in tatters— on issue #3, and appears with fist clenched and face drawn in a snarl on issue #4.

But at the same time, these aspects of Cage's depiction were common to the comic book page, allowing them to be misperceived as some-

Figure 4.6. Comic books struggled to escape the gravity of "blaxploitation" in the 1970s. Thus, even as Luke Cage's morality seems to play against the "buck" stereotype, his visual depiction replicates much of it. The splash page to his debut did just this, presenting an angry, aggressive, violent, and hyperphysical protagonist who more than looks the stereotypical part of the "buck."

thing other than the racialized attributes they continued. The origin of his powers—being subject to a scientist's untested process that causes a painful transformation that imbues Cage with superstrength and invulnerability—combines elements of Captain America's and the Hulk's origins. Those powers themselves are likewise a staple set of abilities in comics; given the number of characters with precisely Cage's powers, his appear wholly ordinary. As well, the violence with which Luke Cage reacts was long a staple at Marvel, let alone in comics in general. But taking these traits at face value, as nothing more than commonplace aspects of superhero comics, obfuscates the ways in which they also replicate the persistent racial stereotype of the "buck."

The reduction of Cage's sexuality further hides his basis in this stereotype. As noted, this was among the most problematic aspects of the "buck," as this figure's rampant sexuality and savagery made him a threat, particularly, it was imagined, to white women. No such threat is present with Luke Cage. His relationship with Reva is not only short-lived but largely platonic. Cage later dates Dr. Claire Temple, but theirs is a relatively chaste relationship. And when Cage does encounter white women, such interactions get played for comedy, not sexual threat. When Cage helps two wealthy white sisters solve a mystery, the hero receives his reward: twin smacks on his cheeks from the beautiful siblings. Unlike the confident "buck" of the silver screen, Luke only stares bug-eyed and befuddled; in the next panel, our hero plaintively holds up his hands to the glaring Claire and stammers, "Clair [sic]—honey—don't look at me like that— I can explain—they're just young girls—a case—eh—Clair—?"[58] Cage, in this moment, appears the furthest thing from a stereotypical "buck," but that is only true regarding this one dimension. His deviations from his racialized brethren—his moral code and muted sexuality—only function to mask how embedded he remains within this stereotype.

Interestingly, DC's black Green Lantern, John Stewart, one of their earliest black superheroes, parallels Luke Cage in both his basis in the "buck" stereotype and his creators' efforts to distance themselves, if only superficially, from the same. Stewart certainly conveys the aggressive and violent nature of this figure in his debut in *Green Lantern/Green Arrow* #87. The cover to this issue features Stewart—in full Green Lantern attire—holding up the unconscious body of Hal Jordan. He thrusts his ring hand (and thus weapon) at the reader with a savage look on his face—eyes narrowed, mouth wide open—and declares, "They whipped the Green Lantern—now let 'em try me!"[59] Here, the first image of the black Green Lantern made clear his aggressive and violent nature, reminiscent

Figure 4.7. The depiction of John Stewart on the cover
of his debut issue replicated the characteristics of the
"buck"—the aggression, the anger, the physicality—as
he looms over the prostrate body of Green Lantern.

of the classic "buck." Stewart's introductory story then emphasized other
aspects of this stereotype. The replacement Lantern's disdain for authority
is his predominant character trait. He first appears when he confronts
two police officers hassling a pair of black youths gaming on the sidewalk.
When the cop asks him if he wants trouble, Stewart retorts, "I kind of
doubt you're man enough to give it—even with your nightstick!"[60] Stewart
also demonstrates this lack of respect for authority toward Hal Jordan. He
rejects the mask Jordan gives him, repeatedly refuses to follow the more
experienced Lantern's commands, and ultimately humiliates Jordan by revealing a racist conspiracy to win the presidency to which the elder hero
was oblivious.[61]

But in this climax, as well as elsewhere in the narrative, Denny O'Neil and Neal Adams give John Stewart a moral high ground akin to Cage's, particularly in how they gesture toward a more progressive representation. Stewart's humiliation of Jordan also proves Stewart right; Jordan is oblivious to the conspiracy that Stewart thwarts, making Stewart the better Lantern. Stewart captures an assassin before he guns down a police officer—the first step, as Stewart explains, toward making it look "like blacks are on a rampage" and elevating a racist senator to the presidency—while Jordan takes out a decoy assassin.[62] Stewart's moral elevation thus contrasts the ways in which his portrayal bases itself in the "buck" stereotype; thus, as was the case with Luke Cage, it serves as a guise for that foundation.

Marvel's second supernatural black hero—Blade, the vampire hunter—embodies the more traditional notion of guise, as his supernatural milieu provides but a superficial transformation of the "buck." The cover of his first appearance, like those for so many of his heroic compatriots, communicates his stereotypical nature. Wearing sunglasses and a trench coat (echoing Shaft), he brandishes wooden knives and street sass at a fleeing Dracula: "Maybe you're hot-stuff back in Transylvania, but nobody messes around with—Blade—the vampire-slayer!" His use of slang continues in his debut issue. He defends his killing of a teenage vampire, arguing, "Frankly, I don't give a flying hoot! He was a stinkin' vampire—an' better off dead!"[63] Here, Blade, like so many of his fellow "buck" superheroes, evidences his "street cred" through what his creators imagine to be a black vernacular and disrespect for authority. He has a similarly vexed relationship with the police. The Scotland Yard chief inspector Dai Thomas, for example, contrasts Blade with other vampire hunters—who, as he says, "at least . . . cooperate wi' the yard," while Blade has "to be some bloody Lone Ranger"—and their confrontation ends with Blade gut punching the chief inspector.[64]

Blade, despite his supernatural context, also remains firmly embedded in the "buck" type in his explicit (at least for comic books) sexuality. A two-page sequence in *The Tomb of Dracula* #12 depicts Blade with his lover, the stripper Saffron. He lounges on a pillowed couch; when Saffron enters carrying two glasses of wine, they kiss, but the phone rings, cutting short their romantic evening.[65] Here, Blade demonstrates the insensitivity of the "buck," not only ignoring Saffron's ministrations but also coldly leaving her to continue his mission.[66] A similarly themed sequence occurs later in the series. After Blade saves the scantily clad Saffron from a vampire attack, he holds her close and kisses her. The scene immediately shifts to

Figure 4.8. Unlike Luke Cage and John Stewart, Blade embodied more fully the explicit sexuality of the "buck." Here, the creators barely mask his romantic encounter with the stripper Saffron, depicting a chiseled, shirtless hero as well as his scantily clad lover in the aftermath of an amorous encounter.

"later that evening," when a coworker of Saffron's arrives to find Blade shirtless; Saffron wears only his shirt, making clear how the lovers have occupied themselves since surviving the vampire attack.[67] Whereas Luke Cage at least paid a kind of lip service to mitigating this objectionable aspect of this racial stereotype, Blade's depiction immerses itself in it; his supernatural context and adventures aside, Blade exemplifies an ethnic hero most firmly ensconced within the tradition of the "buck."

DC's other prominent black superhero of the 1970s, Black Lightning, provides a more provocative, if somewhat flawed, interrogation of guise. From his first appearance, Black Lightning was framed within the "buck" stereotype. On his debut cover, the hero glares as he smashes a thug into a window with his left fist, his right fist raised to deliver a second blow; behind the hero are the prone bodies of four previously thrashed hoodlums. He declares, "You pushers have wrecked the city long enough—now it's my turn to wreck you!" The interior splash page similarly depicts the hero leaping forward—teeth clenched, both fists raised—knocking back six thugs who surround him, as he tells them, "I'm here for you, killer—

Figure 4.9. Black Lightning's creators at least attempted to destabilize some of the tropes that plagued black heroes in the 1970s by revealing that much of his persona and appearance was a deliberate affectation.

and ain't nobody gonna stop me!" Here, the first images of Black Lightning capture the aggression and violence typical of blaxploitation figures. Black Lightning also deploys the stereotypically black slang of such characters, calling his assailants "turkeys" and mocking them with "fool" and "little man" as the fight continues.[68]

However, the first issue adds a twist to Black Lightning's demeanor, as that, too, is part of his disguise; in doing so, the writer Tony Isabella contested these timeworn tropes. As Black Lightning reveals himself as Jefferson Pierce—an Olympic athlete and high school teacher—he removes his mask (with attached Afro wig) and abandons his slang.[69] In this sequence, the comic and its creators destabilize this blaxploitation persona, revealing it as an affectation by which Pierce conceals his civilian identity. Furthermore, it signals the affected nature of the blaxploitation hero more generally. Pierce's masquerade as a tough, jive-talking hero subverts the very nature of the blaxploitation hero by undermining its authenticity. Rather than a representation of black identity, this blaxploitation figure and its accompanying traits constitute a mere persona, no more a part of Pierce than Black Lightning's mask and wig. In this, the creators gesture toward the emptiness, lamented by Bogle, of such heroes: just like Black Lightning's mask, wig, and speech, the blaxploitation hero stands as little more than an empty suit.

Running problematically counter to the significance of Black Lightning's affected persona, though, is the fact that he otherwise remains rooted in other aspects of the blaxploitation hero's basis in the "buck" stereotype. Black Lightning retains the physicality of the figure. The depictions of him battling his foes in his first issue establish a recurring pattern. Black Lightning's reliance on such physical means is particularly odd since, as his moniker implies, he possesses the ability to generate bolts of electricity; shockingly, he never uses these abilities in his debut issue. In the second issue, which opens with him confronting another group of thugs, he only uses his abilities to disable one, dispatching the others with punches to the chest and a swinging kick. Later in the issue, when he frees himself from the assassin Merlyn, he punches the villain, launches himself into another criminal, and, instead of using his electric powers to take out Merlyn, hurls a javelin.[70] The wrap-up to his canceled solo series in *World's Finest* (Vol. 1) #260 demonstrates the same pattern. Here, Black Lightning battles Doctor Polaris largely sans powers. In their second encounter, he delivers a right cross to the villain's face. In their final battle, he sneaks up behind Polaris to deliver another devastating right cross.[71] In these and similar scenes, Black Lightning's first—and apparently natural—instinct is to use his fists rather than his powers, rooting him in the same racialized stereotype the series elsewhere unsettled.

Black Lightning also shares a similar milieu with his blaxploitation peers, which is made clear in several ways. Like Sweetback, he is surrounded by "the trappings of the ghetto." Furthermore, such a setting was often a signal of authenticity—of "a life lived closer to one's black roots"[72]—which runs against any efforts to unsettle the blaxploitation figure as inauthentic. A flashback to Pierce's childhood and the murder of his father placed such stereotypical ghetto violence at the heart of his character.[73] The present likewise essentializes Black Lightning's connection to the ghetto, as he explains to the guest-starring Superman how his grounding in this environment—on the streets where he grew up—makes him better suited than the DC mainstay to confront its ills. "They see you coming and they just crawl right back into the gutters until you pass," he lectures the Man of Steel. "It takes someone like me to fight them; someone who fights them where they're strongest. In the gutters."[74] Completing this tableau is Black Lightning's informant, the stoolie Two-Bits Tanner, whom the comic decks out in a wide-brimmed purple hat, green trench coat, blue shirt, and orange-and-black pants.[75]

Black Lightning also possesses the individualistic, go-it-alone mentality of his blaxploitation peers. For example, when Black Lightning guest starred in *Justice League of America*, his colleagues listen to a STAR labs professor, but he goes off alone to confront the attacking Regulator. When the League offers him membership, Black Lightning spurns them, explaining, "It's not for me. I'm a loner, and I like it."[76] As a result of this and the other ways Black Lightning perpetuated the traits of blaxploitation heroes that themselves originated from the "buck" stereotype, the efforts of his creators to unsettle this persona are at best mixed.

Similar patterns remain present within comics' construction of the female counterpart to the blaxploitation "buck" hero, the "black superwoman" popularized in films such as *Cleopatra Jones* (1973) and *Foxy Brown* (1974) and by actresses such as Tamara Dobson and Pam Grier. The black superwoman was "a hybrid of stereotypes, part buck/part mammy/part mulatto" and a male fantasy: "beautiful, alluring, glamorous voluptuaries, as ready and anxious for sex and mayhem as any man." At the same time, like the "old-style mammies, they ran not simply a household but a universe unto itself. Often they were out to clean up the ghetto of drug pushers, protecting the black hearth and home from corrupt infiltrators."[77] As with Luke Cage, the latter of these traits persists in the comics version while the sexual aspect is diminished. The Teen Titans' Karen Beecher (a.k.a. Bumblebee) presents one such example. In *Teen Titans* #45 she tries to soothe her black boyfriend Mal Duncan's feelings of inequality spurred by the other Titans. She also clearly plays the role of protector. She rises to Mal's defense, declaring, "I'll show Mal—and those Titans!,"[78] before literally jumping into the fray, three issues later, with typical sass and slang. She attacks the Titans, declaring, "Sorry, sweetie—my honey-gun is canceling your gig!"[79] She further reveals her protective instinct in the next issue, not only stopping Mal from being blasted by darts but revealing that she attacked the team mistakenly, thinking they didn't care about Mal, thus further defending her home and, if not hearth, her heart.[80]

Marvel's Misty Knight presents a comic version of this black superwoman even more steeped in one side of this blaxploitation type. In her first appearance, she attacks Iron Fist, proving herself as ready and able to fight as her superpowered opponent. As well, Knight demonstrates the black superwoman's fiery temper and protective role, telling Iron Fist, whom she mistakenly suspects of both kidnapping and murder, "You're not dealing with some dumb street broad, mister. This is Misty Knight—and nobody messes with her or hers!"[81] When she reappears eight months later in *Iron Fist* #1, she makes a similar statement to the titular hero: "And when somebody leans on my partner, they've got to deal with me."[82] In this statement, Misty announces her intention to protect "home and hearth," further basing her depiction in both past and contemporaneous black female stereotypes. While Knight lacks the stereotypical sexual

Figure 4.10. The stereotyped "black superwoman" also appeared in the 1970s. Exemplified by Misty Knight, these characters typically played down their sexuality while emphasizing their physicality and love of violence as they dedicated themselves to protecting both home and hearth.

appetite, this absence does little to ameliorate the ways in which her depiction evokes other persistent racialized stereotypes.

In addition to the prevalent "buck" and "black superwoman," other tired stereotypes about blacks arrived in disguised forms within the black heroes of the 1970s. Bogle, for example, describes the stereotype of the "coon," or "the Negro as amusement object and black buffoon." He further characterizes the actions of the various "coon" forms—the "pickaninny," the pure "coon," and the "Uncle Remus"—as "pleasant and diverting" as well as "used solely for comic relief," the audience meant to be entertained by such "stumbling and stuttering idiots."[83] The "coon," of course, had been a staple of superhero popular culture since World War II (in the figure of a character like the Young Allies' Whitewash Jones, for instance), and it's hard not to see this figure being invoked, for example, when a grinning John Stewart dumps oil on the face of his racist opponent and quips, "Haven't I seen you picking cotton someplace?" When he continues grinning and flies with his palms open, falsely playing the innocent, he explains to an irate Hal Jordan, "So I maybe missed my aim with the power beam, and the senator got a little blackened!"[84] Similarly, the Forsythe sisters' kisses and Cage's resultant stumbles and stutters put him squarely in the role of "coon."[85]

Even more explicit examples of the "coon" exist. Though the Black Panther remained safe from this type during Don McGregor's *Jungle Action* run, when he later starred in his own eponymous title, scripted and drawn by Jack Kirby, his initial depiction was consistent with the "coon." In the series' first issue, he immediately appears fearful when his companion, the infamous collector Mr. Little, suggests they return an ancient brass frog to its resting place; he similarly stammers and stares in wide-eyed horror after Little destroys a pursuing ship.[86] This virulent characterization is carried forward from the initial depiction. Black Panther is cowardly when he and Little approach Africa in the latter's airship, asking, "Mister Little! Are you certain that we've got to land in this territory?" Panther also exhibits the foolishness of the "coon," as he naïvely handles a tomb's door, nearly getting electrocuted as a result, and inadvertently saves himself and his companions when he randomly presses a button that rights the runaway chariot they find themselves in.[87] Like the classic "coon," Black Panther succeeds in spite of himself.

The Falcon was similarly subject to portraying this stereotype when Gary Friedrich took over scripting duties on *Captain America and the Falcon*. Suddenly, the Falcon served as comic relief. After the duo utilize SHIELD's new high-speed underground transit system, Falcon comments, "We gotta remember this, Cap—next time we wanna spend a wild night in Newark!" When they exit the SHIELD facility via a dummy barbershop, Falcon makes a joke about trying to grow an Afro. And, finally, as the duo flee an about-to-launch rocket, Falcon directly invokes a classic "coon" figure, stating, "Now I know what Stepin Fetchit meant when he said feet do yo' stuff!"[88] As Bogle explains, Fetchit "popularized the dim-witted, tongue-tied stammer and the phenomenal slow-lazyman shuffle" to become "the best known and most successful black actor working in Hollywood" in the 1930s.[89] He thus popularized, and perfected, the classic "coon" stereotype the Falcon and other black characters later portrayed.

That such comic portrayals, quips, and sarcasm were very much a part of Marvel's overall style only disguises the behavior of the stereotypical "coon." Such quippery was very much the stock-in-trade of Spider-Man, who, for example, tosses sarcastic barbs as easily as he does the thugs he confronts.[90] Spider-Man could also play the coward.[91] Such humor could also be found in a title like *The Fantastic Four*, when, as Reed Richards warns the Thing to duck a blast from one of his experiments gone out of control, Ben Grimm sardonically replies, "I needed you to tell me that?"[92] Nor was such wit confined to the pages of Marvel Comics; DC creators, perhaps noting Marvel's success, also peppered their pages with sarcasm, such as in *Justice League of America* (Vol. 1) #81 when the Atom, while interrogating a captured Thanagarian, remarks, "Buddy, as a babbler, you're a champ—!"[93] And it is certainly plausible to take what John Stewart, Luke Cage, Black Panther, and Falcon do and say as further examples of this same trend. Certainly, the examples of the Falcon's dialogue are paired and thus juxtaposed with similar ones from Captain America.

But the ability to dismiss these racialized examples as more of the same sarcasm and humor regularly displayed in comic books is precisely what makes them such pernicious examples of how guise functions in these figures. Such humor is not only part of these companies' fare but is also steeped in a tradition of racialized humor that long predated both companies' heroes. Here the potential insidiousness of guise is exposed: it allows elements that hearken back to long-held racist stereotypes to be obscured by what comics creators had much more recently established. In a similar way to how Native American superheroes had stereotypes subsumed within their superheroic identities, so too does conventional comics humor function to obscure the racialized tradition evoked when such humor applies to black characters. What's important about the examples above from Spider-Man, the Thing, and the Atom is that they are not on the receiving end of the humor: both Spidey's and Atom's comments belittle their opponents, while the Thing's sardonic reply is directed at Reed. Such is not the case regarding Black Panther and Falcon; in both cases, they are the target of the quips they make, and thus it is they who are belittled in what amounts to something little different—once unmasked—from racialized humor of previous eras.

Asian heroes and heroines in the 1960s and 1970s were no less repackaged versions of existing stereotypes. Some—such as the Japanese Sunfire—persisted baldly in "yellow peril" imagery. The splash page of *X-Men* (Vol. 1) #64 depicts the Japanese antagonist standing on the corner of a New York rooftop, describing the city's people as "ants" that will soon learn to fear "the ominous tread of . . . Sunfire!" Even more to the point, as he leaps from the roof, Sunfire refers to the time he's wasted "reconnoitering," revealing how he has been lurking for some time within the United States, an activity all too familiar from wartime fare.[94] Similarly, Marvel's most prominent Chinese hero, Shang-Chi, the Master of Kung Fu, initially presents as an Asian threat. His first mission is to infiltrate the London home of a Dr. Petrie and assassinate him. In this instance, Shang-Chi is literally the agent of a foreign empire, having snuck into the Western metropolis to commit a nefarious deed.[95] Lady Shiva at DC appears as a lurking and deceptive presence, too, luring the hero Richard Dragon into a trap because she mistakenly believes him to be her sister's murderer.[96] In *The Avengers* #114, Mantis announces her presence with an attack from behind on a construction worker harassing the Scarlet Witch. Her subsequent arrival at Avengers Mansion is immediately met with a suspicion grounded in the "yellow peril." Captain America refuses Mantis entrance into the mansion, exclaiming, "Hold it a second! You know it's against our rules to bring unauthorized personnel into Avengers' headquarters"; at issue's end, Cap remains dubious, ruminating that Mantis's assistance in defeating their enemy "could have been a diabolically clever smokescreen to blind us to some worse trickery later!" Further ensconcing Mantis within this "yellow peril" stereotype is an editorial footnote reporting that she and the Swordsman have been "lurking through the past two issues."[97]

But the representation of these Asian heroes and heroines also attempts to mask such bald stereotyping in only slight variations of it. The comics portray, for instance, what Frank Wu casts as the "perpetual foreigner syndrome," or Asians as "non-native interlopers into American culture." As Edith Wen-Chu Chen and Grace J. Yoo explain, this stereotype implies that Asians not only are not part of US society but are unassimilable to it, and thus present a blight on the nation due to their incompatible and retrograde behaviors and beliefs.[98] Shang-Chi enacts a variation on precisely this type. His second appearance opens with him homeless, getting ready to sleep in Central Park. As he eats grass, he thinks, "The plants which grow in the soil of this befouled city contain many impurities, yet certain of them are nutritious—and I do not buy food." Clearly manifest here is Shang-Chi's contrast with the values of American society, not terribly unlike that of the X-Men's Storm. He has a strong affinity with the nature that US society has cut down and polluted; likewise, he subtly critiques a US capitalism that would require him to pay for food. The issue later strikes the same point, as Shang-Chi narrates his walking tour of the city: "I leave the grass of Central Park to walk the asphalt and cement New Yorkers think more valuable—to use the refuse, the grime, the pools of putrid liquid beneath my feet to remind me how little I understand of the world outside my father's retreat."[99]

DC's most prominent Asian hero in the 1970s, the Japanese American Karate Kid, also played to the essence of the perpetual foreigner, particularly as he traveled back in time to the twentieth century. He is shown at odds with his surroundings when the police arrive and, assuming he's part of a movie, ask for his permit—"Permit? Movie? I do not understand?"—and, when he attempts to depart via his Legion flight ring, it malfunctions, sending him careening into a building with a humiliating "Yipes" and a "KLUNK."[100] When he befriends Iris Jacobs, he tells her, "This place is as strange to me as I am to you," a point crystallized when she offers him a bus token in place of an "air-car" and he gapes at her, eyes wide and shock lines surrounding him.[101] Similar scenes occur in the series' second issue, as the Kid again finds himself at odds with the police and laments, "There are so many things about this world I don't understand!"[102] In embodying this "perpetual foreigner" type, neither Karate Kid nor Shang-Chi deviate as much from earlier racialized depictions as may seem. Their enactment of what amounts to no more than a variation on "yellow peril" imagery makes their depiction no less a mask for that origin.

If the "perpetual foreigner" represents one way in which "yellow peril" imagery was redeployed by comics, the "dragon lady" is another. Here, comics' depictions of Asian women connect back to a long history of racially derogatory representations. Robert G. Lee, for instance, enumerates the public displays of a reified and exoticized China and its people that existed in the United States throughout the late eighteenth and early nineteenth centuries. In 1784, for example, the Peale Museum, alongside weapons, utensils, and other items, included a feet-binding display that was by far the most popular part of its Chinese exhibit. By the turn of the century, exhibits by the East Indian Marine Society in Salem (1799) and a renamed Peale, now the Philadelphia Museum (1805), added clay and wax Chinese figures to these displays, making Chinese individuals a part of these curiosities. Culminating this trend was the opening (in conjunction with the Philadelphia Museum) in 1838 of the Chinese Museum by Nathan Dunn. A success early on, this latter effort eventually failed and was purchased by none other than P. T. Barnum, who had himself popularized Ah Fong Moy, a Chinese woman "always robed in resplendent silks and often seated among luxurious Chinese furnishings," at his own American Museum starting in 1834.[103] Sheng-mei Ma further details the boys' adventure comics of the 1930s—most specifically Alex Raymond's *Flash Gordon* and Milton Caniff's *Terry and the Pirates*—that traded in outworn tropes, particularly of women. Present, especially via the Dragon Lady in *Terry and the Pirates*, is a visual pattern of exotic sexuality and vicious cruelty that demonstrates the West's "dualistic impulses of fear and romance, of repulsion and attraction," toward the East and the Eastern.[104] Lee also explicates dual traits in the "deviant," a "figure of forbidden desire" that is at the same time a domestic threat.[105] Running throughout both figures, and thus the representation of Asian women, are competing valences: threat and danger as well as attraction and allure.

Marvel and DC's Asian heroines evoke every aspect of these feminized versions of the "yellow peril." Like Barnum's Ah Fong Moy, they appeared in similarly "resplendent" and "luxurious" dress and surroundings. When Mantis first appears, she wears a gold headdress and earrings, as well as a green-and-yellow dress with cutouts above the hips and a skirt slit to midthigh.[106] Lady Shiva, when she arrives in *Kung-Fu Fighter* #5, wears a tight-fitting red dress, open from neck to belly button in a diamond-shaped cutout, with a knee-length skirt featuring slits up to her hip on both sides.[107] Later, readers saw two images of her home, both of which emphasize her exotic nature and sexuality. In the first, she sits in a wicker chair in a pink dress, surrounded by various Orientalist objects, including samurai swords, a jar, and a Buddha statue.[108] In the second, she lounges seductively on a couch and pillows with a dragon pattern, the background featuring multiple swords, a jar, and Asian symbols and characters.[109]

Both heroines also evidence the cruel nature of the "dragon lady." The cover of Shiva's debut issue presents her kicking Richard Dragon's face, as does the interior splash page, where the captions announce, "And she wants only one thing—to see Dragon buried!" These intentions are enacted in her battle with Dragon, as she glares cruelly at him, punching him in the face while asking, "Will you beg . . . pig?"[110] Mantis's cruelty played out in the romantic subplot between her, the Swordsman, the Vision, and the Scarlet Witch. To start, Mantis appears cruelly oblivious to how the attention she cultivates from other heroes—Black Panther and the Fantastic Four's Thing, to name but two, besides Vision—hurts the Swordsman.[111] By the climax of the romantic quadrangle, she no longer cares: in a three-panel sequence, she rejects the Swordsman, coolly and cruelly turning her back to him, and then immediately throws herself at the Vision, pressing herself against his android body, pursing her lips, and wrapping her arm behind his head to pull him in for a kiss.[112]

Lady Shiva and especially Mantis played up the exotic sexuality of the "dragon lady" figure. Shiva's sexuality was highlighted in how her costume evolved over the series. She quickly abandons formless tunics and leggings for attire that more gratuitously accentuates her figure.[113] This sexual stereotype even more fully riddles Mantis's character. As her creator, Steve Englehart, explained: "Basically, Mantis was supposed to be a hooker who would join the Avengers and cause dissension amongst all the male members by coming on to each of them in turn. . . . She was introduced to be a slut."[114] The revelation in the comic that either Mantis or the Scarlet Witch is to be deemed the "celestial Madonna" provides further opportunities to characterize the former as promiscuous. The Scarlet Witch remarks almost immediately, "It must be me: Mantis is anything but a Madonna!"[115]

Mantis's sexuality also extends to her abilities. She defeats the villainous Lion God in *The Avengers* #114, hypnotizing him with a sensual dance: "All her movements are liquid . . . while her earlier gestures suggested water, this dance suggests glycerin! Seemingly boneless, her form subtly,

Figure 4.11. Depictions of Asian women in 1970s comics emphasized a variety of stereotyped understandings of the East that often drew from the long-held image of the "dragon lady." Lady Shiva, for instance, quickly adopted more alluring costumes that highlighted her sexuality and threatening nature.

slowly, sensuously sways in the shimmer of the Swordsman's skillful psychedelia." As well, when she initially attacks the Avengers as a ruse, she unveils her signature move—the "death-grip"—which involves her wrapping her legs around, in this case, Captain America's torso and her arms around his neck, a move she would repeat on various other male opponents.[116] Thus, though the arrival of Mantis—and Sunfire and Karate Kid and Shang-Chi and Lady Shiva—may constitute a form of progress in that a greater number of Asian heroes and heroines now populated the comic page, the nature of their representation ultimately ran counter to what their debut might otherwise be said to signify, as their depictions were but thinly veiled versions of earlier, virulent Asian stereotypes.

Figure 4.12. Mantis's first action with the Avengers saw her deploy her sexuality as a weapon, as she hypnotizes the Lion God with a sensual dance in this sequence of panels.

And, finally, there are the Latinx heroes to debut in the 1970s. Prior to this period, Latinx characters—let alone superheroes—were few and far between: The Whip in 1940 (the "first positively identified Latino 'superhero' to appear in mainstream comics") and El Gaucho in 1955 are both steeped in the tradition of the criollo/Zorro; beyond them, Latinos were relegated to sidekick or villainous roles.[117] The 1970s would add two prominent Latino adventurers—White Tiger and El Águila—who, like their nonwhite brethren of this era, disguised their stereotypical bases to varying degrees. El Águila is little more than a knockoff Zorro. He wears a similar costume, including a head-scarf mask and bolero hat, and wields not only both a sword and a bullwhip but a similar code of justice. El Águila similarly recalls the "Latin lover" stereotype popularized by Rudolph Valentino, whose seductive, dashing, magnetic, and smoldering presence "created the basis for the Latin lover as the possessor of a primal sexuality that made him capable of making a sensuous but dangerous . . . brand of love."[118]

A more interesting example of guise related to Latino stereotypes comes from Marvel's White Tiger. He, too, serves to mask the continuance of racialized stereotypes regarding Latinos but does so by modeling Spider-Man. For example, a prominent—and stereotypical—trait in White Tiger is his fiery temper. In his first appearance in *Peter Parker: The Spectacular Spider-Man* #9, he confronts a man he believes to have impersonated him in committing a crime, but his demand for answers is so heated that he strangles the man to the point he cannot talk.[119] Likewise, as White Tiger and Spider-Man battle in the next issue, the latter notes, "He's as hot-headed—and unwilling to listen to reason—as I usually am!"[120] Spidey's comment here—another instance of his trademark humor and sarcasm—draws attention to how similar White Tiger and he are, thus pulling attention away from how such hotheadedness remains a staple stereotype about Latinos. And this was hardly the only way in which connections between White Tiger and Spider-Man functioned to this end. Another canonical aspect of Spider-Man was his struggle to balance school and his superheroic adventures, not to mention freelancing at the *Daily Bugle* and caring for

Figure 4.13. Here, White Tiger's hotheadedness furthers the misunderstanding between him and Spider-Man, as he gives Spidey no chance to explain himself. The background of White Tiger's neighborhood in these panels also signals its commonality with the surroundings of other nonwhite heroes.

his Aunt May. Such struggles similarly plague White Tiger in his civilian life as Hector Ayala. However, in his case, such struggles carry more than a whiff of stereotypes about Latino laziness. A guest appearance in Marvel's *The Human Fly* #8 underlines this trait: Hector ponders, "I'm a failure at school—but I'm also the world's first Hispanic superhero—the White Tiger! . . . Mama wants me to finish, to make somethin' of myself—but the Tiger is the pride of a displaced race! Maybe I oughta just check out my future as a symbol."[121] In *Peter Parker: The Spectacular Spider-Man* #18, he skips class, preferring to toss a Frisbee, and, similarly, in issue #25, he skips studying to prowl the streets as White Tiger instead.[122] What differentiates Hector Ayala/White Tiger from Peter Parker/Spider-Man in these instances is also what reveals this pattern as a guise. Where Peter makes a wholehearted effort at fulfilling all his demands, including his education, Hector is much more—and perhaps all too—willing to ditch class and flunk out, thus perpetuating this stereotype.

Not All That Different: Common Associations between Ethnic Superheroes and Superheroines

Besides simultaneously disguising and promulgating stereotypes tied to heroes' and heroines' distinct ethnic or national origins, comic creators perceived and perpetuated their own common associations that cut across these characters and their ethnic/racial identities. In this way, comics depicting ethnic superheroes betrayed similar assumptions about all nonwhites in the nature of their environments, their assumed obligations to their communities, a common nationalism, and militancy. Such depictions, in how they transcend cultural boundaries, foster a problematic sameness and homogeneity that, like earlier stereotypes, could easily go undiscerned.

One of the most predominant associations of the black heroes that debuted in the 1970s was their urban environment. Being located in cities— and particularly New York City—is hardly unique among superheroes, of course. At DC, most heroes were associated with specific, if fictional, urban locales: Superman in Metropolis, Batman in Gotham, Wonder Woman in Gateway City, and so on. Marvel's heroes predominantly cluster around New York, whether upstate in the case of the X-Men's Westchester base of operations or in the five boroughs in the case of the Avengers, Spider-Man, and Doctor Strange. But the association with the city for nonwhite heroes becomes clearly racialized in ways that don't apply for white heroes. For

one, it is not just the city in general to which comics linked these characters, but to specific neighborhoods populated largely by blacks. Harlem is
by far the most common location. Luke Cage, for example, upon escaping
from prison, immediately establishes his base of operations in Harlem.
When Captain America first meets Sam Wilson, his soon-to-be partner
describes himself as "a big city brother from way back!" and goes on to de-
clare, "I used to have the biggest pigeon coop on any rooftop in Harlem!"[123]
After completing their initial adventure, Captain America and the Falcon
go their separate ways, the latter returning to Harlem. Further underlining
his "belonging" in this space is the crowd of exclusively black men, women,
and children that surround the two heroes as they shake hands.[124] Like
Luke Cage and the Falcon, the Black Panther eventually settles his civilian
identity in Harlem after he joins the Avengers. The X-Man Storm, though
first appearing in Kenya, eventually traces her roots back to Harlem, too;
in *Uncanny X-Men* #122, she returns to her family's former Harlem apartment.[125] Like Harlem for so many East Coast black characters, the Watts
area of Los Angeles, California, similarly serves as the childhood home
of Marvel's Black Goliath (the scientist-turned-adventurer Bill Foster),
who kicks off his five-issue solo series having resettled there.[126] The way
in which comics located, in their past and present, black characters within
racially identified urban neighborhoods fosters and naturalizes a sense of
nonwhites belonging to these spaces, thus creating a sameness about their
origins and environments that should not be dismissed as just part of the
larger pattern connecting superheroes to particular urban environments.

The visual depiction of these characters' environments further reinforces this racialized sameness, uniformly evoking an atmosphere of
urban blight, crime, and violence. The splash page of Luke Cage's debut
is awash in such imagery. Cage stands in the center of various symbols
of his city: a black youth fires a gun at a figure in the top right corner, a
police car flashes its lights and sounds its siren in the bottom middle, and
another cop stands below a woman in a low-cut dress under a sign that
reads, "DANCE"; opposite them are images of playing cards and dice, while
superimposed on the figures in block letters is "HARLEM."[127] Storm returns to a similarly blighted Harlem. Her former home is dilapidated and
derelict—cracks in the pavement, an electric call panel hanging from its
wires—as well as covered in graffiti. Storm herself remarks on "the stench"
of the building, which also lacks heat. She then finds that her former apartment has become a drug den with strung-out youths (black and white) on
filthy mattresses; newspapers, bottles, and trash are strewn on the floor,
and even more graffiti appears on the stained and cracked walls.[128] For

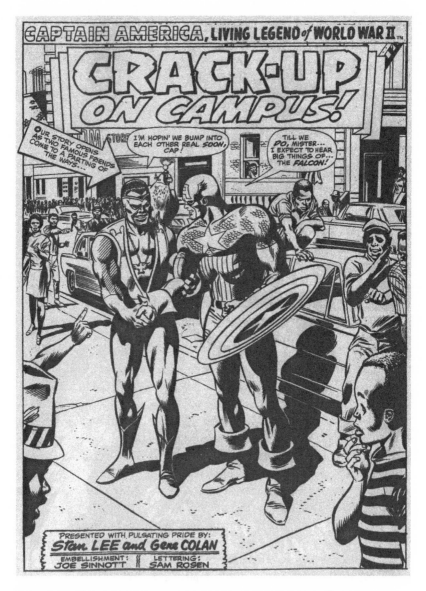

Figure 4.14. African American superheroes found themselves confined to very specific and racialized city neighborhoods in the 1970s that worked to homogenize the crusaders. In their urban locales, black superheroes found themselves surrounded—and defined in unique ways—by these imagined and racialized black spaces.

both Luke Cage and Storm, Harlem appears as a place of crime, violence, and despair.

Similar associations pervade Harlem's depiction once the Black Panther arrives there. The captions describing this urban locale convey a clear sense of its blighted condition: "Come with us to New York's Harlem, down whose mean streets blow last week's newspapers and yesterday's dreams—!" As the narrator "welcomes" readers to Harlem, the narration associates the neighborhood with violence (in its "mean streets") and a lack of opportunity (as the "dreams" of yesterday have died). Visually, the panel confirms this atmosphere, featuring boarded-up windows, a down-on-its-luck billiard hall, and two black men standing immobile against a streetlamp in the left foreground.[129]

This imagery's appearance in Black Lightning's Suicide Slum, a section of Superman's Metropolis, as well as the White Tiger's South Bronx, further exposes how these commonalities link to the characters' race. As Black Lightning explains the nature of his city to Superman, "The streets I grew up in have become infected with a vicious human cancer . . . and it's malignant as Hell! Every day that disease eats away at our city . . . at another part of our souls. They're all down there—pushers and pimps and vermin of every size and shape." As he speaks, the city appears much like Marvel's Harlem: littered streets, gray tenement buildings, and, as the moniker Suicide Slum demonstrates, little hope.[130] The same imagery appears when Black Lightning heads home in his civilian identity; he passes a row of identical brick tenement buildings on the same block that houses his "digs," the monotony only broken when a lamp comes flying out a window.[131] The White Tiger's South Bronx is depicted in similar terms. His solo backup feature in Peter Parker: The Spectacular Spider-Man opens in a garbage-strewn alley, and a flashback on the next page has Hector finding the amulets that power him in a similarly litter-filled alley. The reader glimpses the cramped conditions of his family's tenement as the flashback continues, revealing one room and one table around which the family gathers. As his investigation into his family's murder continues in the next issue, once again cinder-block housing, "Out of Order" signs, boarded-up warehouses, and "For Rent" signs define the neighborhood and the economic deprivation that permeates it.[132] In how such deprived circumstances define not only his but other ethnic heroes' locales, comics transcend racial and ethnic boundaries to homogenizing effect.

Further homogenizing are the common roles these ethnic characters have within their communities. For one, many of them take on social-service jobs. The Falcon sets himself up as a Harlem social worker in his civilian identity. Black Panther and Black Lightning share the same civilian occupation, working as high school teachers.[133] And White Tiger leaves the Spider-Man series when he and his African American girlfriend establish a "mobile college" in the South Bronx.[134]

But behind the familiar urban-social-servant roles these characters adopt exists the assumption that an obligation to work on behalf of their people motivates them. The Falcon, after being called out for his failure to fight on behalf of his people as Sam Wilson, later thinks to himself, "But, maybe it's just as important for some of us to cool things down—so we can protect the rights we been fightin' for."[135] Here, Wilson explicitly voices how he sees himself as protecting the rights of "his people" in his role as social worker. Black Lightning also fulfills a social purpose at Suicide Slum's Garfield High; as his white principal explains to him, "A teacher like you Pierce—who was once a student here himself and went on to do the things you've done—is going to be a tremendous example for these young-sters!"[136] While the Falcon and Black Lightning clearly adopt this purpose right away, Black Panther evolves toward it over a series of issues. Having joined the Avengers out of a dissatisfaction with ruling his kingdom, Black Panther finds himself still unsatisfied: "I became an Avenger . . . hoping to find fulfillment in ridding society of those who would ruthlessly destroy it! Yet, even that is not enough! I must do more."[137] He soon finds added fulfillment as an educator, teaching at a "ghetto high school" to a class of exclusively black students.[138] White Tiger feels a similar sense of calling in his identity as a college student. He tells Peter Parker during their first meeting that he has "only one place to go—back to the South Bronx . . . the university of the streets! Get a good schoolin' there—if you're into learn-ing about dope, numbers, rats and poverty. Hey hombre—I don't mean to come down on you! It's our problem—and the prof'll help our people deal with it!"[139] Not only the professor but also Hector himself serve as examples to their Hispanic brothers and sisters through their pursuit of education.

This similar, racially determined sense of obligation carries into these characters' heroic efforts. Captain America, as he searches for the Falcon, who has been framed by a gang known as the Diamond Heads, affirms his sense of the Falcon's purpose: "I know the Falcon . . . I know what makes him tick! He dedicated his life to fighting for justice . . . to help-ing his people . . . and anybody who was oppressed!"[140] Having cleared his name, the Falcon ends the issue by declaring his purpose: "So long as there's tragedy . . . and need . . . and injustice among my people . . . this is where the Falcon belongs!"[141] Black Lightning's heroic efforts derive from a similar sense of duty to his people. He tells Two-Bits Tanner, "I'll leave the world-saving to Superman and company. Suicide Slum is my turf — and it's got enough problems to keep three super-heroes busy!"[142] Black Panther similarly declares himself as fighting for his black students. He explains, for example, to the rest of the Avengers that in addition to confronting costumed villainy, "there are battles closer to home just as vital . . . battles that must be fought and won!" He goes on to describe this battle against "a creeping, insidious evil — which corrupts everything and everybody it touches! Right now, it's waging battles every day for the minds — the bodies — the very souls of kids like the ones I teach — and it must not win!" Later, Black Panther declares that "the safety of the youths I teach means more to me than the capture of costumed madmen!"[143] Further reinforcing the defense of Harlem's black youth as Black Panther's primary duty, at the end of the issue, as the remaining Avengers go off to confront other threats, the Black Panther remains at home to continue a battle that is clearly his alone.[144] White Tiger often voices a similar purpose to his heroic actions. Hector ponders, for example, during his first appearance, "Everything we won in the 60s is being taken back! It's the same old fight all over! We need a symbol — something to rally around! One of our own — to give us pride!"[145] The White Tiger, of course, becomes exactly the symbol Hector believes his people need.

The consequences of this role play into another commonality that crosses ethnic/national backgrounds: militancy and separatism. The previously mentioned schism between the Black Panther and the other Avengers over their conflicting priorities is not the first instance where the former goes it alone. Previously, when the racist Sons of the Serpent troubled New York, Black Panther quickly curtails the Avengers' efforts to deal with the threat. He avers, "Those are my people that the Serpents have been beating . . . killing! And I claim my right to take them . . . alone!"[146] In both these examples, Black Panther is not only fervently confronting the Avengers with a reality they are assumed to be ignorant of, but he is also demanding the right to deal with these black troubles without their assistance. He thus mirrors the kind of control and agency that militant movements demanded. As William Chafe explains, "Now, an increasing number of blacks concluded that white institutions and white people could not be trusted, and that their promises were simply another effort to control and define what black America was all about. In response, blacks insisted on controlling their own movement, shaping their own agenda, defining their own destiny."[147]

The Falcon serves as a microcosm of what Chafe describes as blacks' shift toward militancy, thus further demonstrating its powerful presence in these characters' representations. In his earliest appearances, the Falcon staunchly opposes militancy, as he makes clear when explaining to Captain America his motives for opposing the Diamond Heads: "They're like a black version of the Klan! All they preach is hate whitey! They're dangerous fanatics! They don't care who suffers—or who gets hurt! They can set our progress back a hundred years!"[148] Seven issues later, as the robot Bulldozer smashes the Harlem slums, it yells out, "Power to the People!" and is cheered by the black crowd. The Falcon, on the other hand, makes clear their ignorance: "The people are cheering him! They think he's helping them!"[149] The next issue ends on a similar note. Having rescued his nephew from a mob boss, the Falcon ruminates about all the other "kids who've lost faith in the law—in the world around them—and in themselves! Kids with no one to turn to—no one to trust—with nothing but bitterness and contempt—for the system!"[150] Here, the Falcon laments black youths' loss of faith in white institutions, as well as the resultant feelings of bitterness and contempt that fuel their turn to crime and their support for the black power movement's violence. Rather than responding with anger and violence, blacks, the comic repeatedly advises, need to proceed through the more conciliatory means of reason and understanding that Captain America and the Falcon both advocate.

But the Falcon would not remain such a staunch critic of militancy and black power, coming instead more and more to demand the self-control and agency underpinning the movement. This shift begins in *Captain America* #143, entitled, tellingly, "Power to the People," the words of which form a circle around an upraised fist.[151] Here, the Falcon attends a meeting of the not-so-subtly named People's Militia, where he witnesses their masked leader, "the Man," stir them into a frenzy to burn Harlem. When the crowd angrily cheers the plan—shouting, "Right on! This is the start of the black revolution!" as well as the black power slogans "Black Is Beautiful!" and "Power to the People!"—the Falcon, as Sam Wilson, again criticizes their anger, telling them, "You people aren't thinking! You're going to destroy everything you've gained!"[152] But at the end of the issue, the Falcon defends their anger to Cap, stating, "They—we—got reason to blow up!" after which he leaves to reassess his values.[153] He then ends his partnership with Captain America, telling him, "I'm gonna be proud, baby . . . proud to be black . . . and proud to be me! And it's all gonna start right now!"[154] Here, the Falcon adopts a version of black pride that was, just one issue prior, what he criticized as unthinking and bitter. And when the two are informed of drug pushers terrorizing a Harlem youth, the Falcon

Figure 4.15. This image from the splash page of Tyroc's debut immediately conveys the ways in which his character embodied a militant and separatist point of view, which would be his character's defining trait.

insists on confronting the issue alone—telling his former partner, "This is my turf . . . and this is where I start taking care of it . . . by myself!"[155]— thus demanding the same control of his destiny and that of "his people" as the Black Panther and the black power movement did.

However, it is the first black member of DC's Legion of Super-Heroes, Tyroc, who demonstrates the problematic extent to which militancy and separatism provided a common basis for nonwhite heroes in the 1970s. The cover image of his first appearance, in *Superboy and the Legion of Super-Heroes* #216, immediately establishes these themes. As four Legionnaires rapidly descend, Tyroc stands in the foreground, telling the heroes, "Stay out of our city or be slaughtered, Legionnaires! We despise everything you stand for!" Behind him, a number of black men and women stand, fists raised in solidarity with their champion. The splash page for the issue conveys a similar image, though here the Legion members fly away from Tyroc and his people, the latter of whom throw rocks at the fleeing heroes.[156] Tyroc's first appearance, in a story titled "The Hero Who Hated the Legion," establishes him and his black compatriots in complete solidarity with each other against the Legion.

In establishing Tyroc's origin, the issue's creators, the writer Cary Bates and the artist Mike Grell, continued to feature separatism as the character's predominant feature. In pursuit of a crashed satellite, the heroes journey to Tyroc's home island of Marzal, "an independent, totally self-sufficient community" that is "populated entirely by a black race that wants nothing to do with the outside world!"[157] A few pages later, Tyroc would command his people to show no friendship to the heroes, complaining that "the Legion has ignored us! Where were they when we suffered through our energy drought . . . or the terrible ion storm of last spring? Many times, we could've used their help . . . but they were always somewhere else! Is it the color of our skin that doesn't make us important enough? Racial prejudice died out centuries ago . . . but perhaps the Legion is behind the times?"[158] Here, Tyroc evidences feelings of betrayal by white institutions and "the system" that drove much of the bitterness and violence of the black power movement. By issue's end, however, Tyroc learns his lesson, the same one the Falcon advocated: that black bitterness and anger is not a solution. He asks, after the Legion intervenes to save his people, "Why did you save our city from the poisoned satellite? You went out of your way to save my life . . . even though we've shown you nothing but hatred and contempt!" The Legionnaires reply, "When it comes to race, we're color-blind! Blue skin, yellow skin, green skin . . . we're brothers and sisters . . . united in the name of justice everywhere." Tyroc can only hang his head and admit, "I guess I've been wrong . . . about a lot of things,"[159] acknowledging the limitations of separatism, militancy, and black power.

Paralleling—in both nature and effect—the militancy and separatism in black superheroes are the repeated thematic conflicts between Native Americans and whites in 1970s superhero fare. One recurring theme, particularly for male Native American heroes, stresses their need to prove their strength and ultimately their manhood. The debut of the first Thunderbird, John Proudstar, in *Giant-Size X-Men* #1 immediately sounds this note. The first images of him feature Proudstar wrestling a bison to the ground, which the captions clarify is an effort to prove his own strength as well as that of the Apache people, whom the comic clearly marks as decayed and emasculated: "John Proudstar does not like the reservation. He does not like to watch the old ones, sitting slumped against their doorsteps, dreaming dreams of glory long gone. John Proudstar is an Apache—and he is ashamed of his people. The Apache were meant to be hunters, warriors—not sad-eyed simpering squaws. They were meant to run free thru the crisp plains grasses, the wind blowing wildly thru their hair. Once nothing could stand before the Apache."[160] Here, the narrator clearly communicates how the Apache are less than they once were and are ashamed by this loss. Their existence as powerful hunters and warriors is long gone, replaced by lethargy and weakness, against which Proudstar chafes. His dialogue reinforces this motivation. As he topples the bison, he declares,

"There, horned one—do you see? There is still a man among the Apache!" And though he initially rejects Professor Xavier's offer to join his X-Men, his eventual acceptance stems from a similar desire to prove. As he tells the Professor, "I'm as good as the next guy—Hell, I'm better! You give me a chance—I'll prove it!"[161] Though the original Thunderbird's appearances were few, they established a conflict between himself and whites, as well as the need to prove himself and his people in the eyes of the latter as his primary motivation.

A second version of such native/white conflict manifests in the second Native American hero to debut in the pages of this era's *X-Men* comic: Shaman. A member of the Canadian superteam Alpha Flight, Shaman first appears in his civilian identity of "Michael Twoyoungmen, MD, staff physician at the Sarcee Reserve Hospital, outside Calgary, Alberta."[162] And it is from the nature of his civilian identity and work that Shaman's conflict arises. What insight into his character the comic provides emphasizes a conflict between his Native American and non–Native American identities. For example, he thinks to himself, "Grandpa never approved of my going to the white man's medical school, said it was a waste of time." Here, Shaman's thoughts establish a clear distinction and conflict between the ways of Native Americans and whites, as well as Shaman's having chosen to pursue the latter in his medical training, implicitly turning his back on the former. Furthermore, Shaman's thoughts cast his superheroic identity, and in particular his magic, as a perversion of those Native American ways: "[Grandpa] trained me to be a healer, a man of peace. I wonder what he'd say now if he saw how I was using the skills he taught me?"[163] Similar thoughts appear in his second appearance roughly a year and a half later. Utilizing his Native American magic to squelch a blaze, Shaman remarks on the same irony as before: "that he, Dr. Michael Twoyoungmen, who deliberately turned his back on his Sarcee heritage to become a physician, to help his people by learning the white man's medicine . . . should now use the magical skills taught him by his shaman grand-father to help red and white men both!"[164] Here, the divide between Native American and white "medicine" is drawn more sharply, as Shaman's choice to pursue one is explicitly a rejection of the other. Though the impact of both his medical and his magical practices is to help both the "white" and the "red" man, these effects are preceded by a deliberate choice of one over the other, establishing them as conflicting traditions.

This conflict between Native American and white cultures, as well as the vexed position of Native American heroes within it, receives its most significant demonstration in the exploits of Marvel's first Native Ameri-

Figure 4.16. Native American heroes in the 1970s often presented themselves as pulled between their indigenous culture and American culture. Here, the nineteenth-century Red Wolf struggles to assimilate, but in ways that suggest the superiority of American values and mores.

can hero, the Red Wolf. The origin of the Red Wolf's nineteenth-century incarnation is firmly ensconced within all aspects of this thematic pattern, beginning with that conflict between Native American and white traditions. The splash page of his first appearance immediately affirms his conflicted position, describing him as "of both the red man's world and the white man's world—and the path he walks has no turning to either side." The thin line the Red Wolf treads between the two cultures has its roots in the details of his origin. When his tribe is wiped out by white "pony soldiers," the young boy is spared and given to the care of the Wakelys, a white couple. The narrative makes clear how this change of family is a boon to the child, renamed Johnny Wakely, as "amid his new surroundings, in the North Platte River country, he grew in strength and wisdom—for now he was learning of that other world—the world of the white man and his ways." Here, his exposure to the world and ways of whites only adds to his attributes, making him stronger and wiser than he was within Native American tradition. And though he voices a preference for the new techniques he is learning, the ways of his Native American parents and culture continue to thrive within him, as a series of panels depict his quick mastery of the rifle, hatchet, and bow. The death of his adoptive parents—at the hands of a marauding Native American tribe—forces Johnny back between cultures, as his plaintive cry over their death makes clear: "Gone are all my parents! Now, which road do I follow—that of the white man, or the path of my brothers, the red men?" As the hero farms in the tradition of his adoptive parents, he continues to wrestle with this perplexing dilemma: "White men slew my Indian parents! Red men killed my white parents! Where shall I turn? Which way is mine?"[165] The young Red Wolf faces a vexed choice between Native American and white ways where he is forced to choose one and reject the other.

Johnny Wakely's further efforts to reconcile his conflict will not only lead him to the role of the Red Wolf but also establish within him that same desire to "prove" himself that Thunderbird manifests. When he journeys to Fort Rango following the burning of his farm by opportunistic whites, he not only applies to be a scout but quickly surpasses all others, including the former lead (and white) scout. As the pair fight, the fort's commanding officer initially voices Wakely's need to prove himself: "Maybe I ought to stop that fight—but that young Indian must prove he is a man to all my troops—and to himself!" And when Johnny's victory results in laughter from the surrounding white soldiers, he himself realizes, "They still think of me—as an Indian—I am not accepted as—a white man! And yet—I don't want to go back to wearing the eagle feather!" This statement, and its blatant assimilationist yearning, makes clear that Johnny, in his desire to prove himself a man, means to prove himself as good as a white man. And it is this desire that leads to his becoming Red Wolf. As he plans to warn the fort of a Native American attack—and claims, again, that doing so will "prove to all that I can walk the path of the Ta'Kai Kih—the white man"—he is shot and falls into "the burial place of the fabled Red Wolf!" As he beholds a vision of the Red Wolf, his true path appears to him, and it is the same path as Shaman's: "Neither am I white man nor red. I am a man—a brother and protector to all peoples. This is my mission—this my power!"[166] Like Shaman and Thunderbird, Red Wolf is caught between Native American and white cultures, having to prove himself and his culture worthy.

Other ethnic heroes exhibit their nationalism even more starkly. The Japanese Sunfire is perhaps the most strident example. He allies himself with the nefarious Dragon-Lord out of a nationalist zeal, proclaiming, "With your wisdom and my humble power, Japan will again find her greatness—in battle!" He is later admonished by Iron Man to "see beyond the fantasy of a national 'glory' based on physical force!"[167] And the White Tiger wears his ethnic nationalism on his sleeve—or, more accurately, his chest. In his first appearance, he wears a yellow T-shirt that declares, "LIBERTAD PARA PUERTO RICO," on the front; he would wear an orange version of the same shirt when he appeared in *The Human Fly*, suggesting his commitment to his nationalist cause.[168] As with these heroes' similar urban settings and racial obligations, these militant/nationalist sympathies demonstrate another homogenizing effect of how comics represented newly debuted ethnic heroes.

Conclusion

Given the sheer number of nonwhite heroes to debut in the late 1960s and throughout the 1970s, it is impossible to say that comics and their creators did not continue to build and further their efforts to represent a more inclusive vision of American society between their covers. Where previously the black, Native American, Asian, and Latinx presence in comics had been largely marginalized, heroes and heroines from all these backgrounds could now be found in comics, and not just as supporting or secondary characters. Creators thus accomplished a diversification of the DC and Marvel Universes that persists to this day (and not just on the comic page but also on television, computer, and movie screens).

But while nonwhite heroes occupied the comic book page in no longer insignificant numbers, their signification and thus significance remains, as with much of superhero popular culture, mixed. Though superhero comics of this time period can be—and have been—applauded for their efforts to represent not just a growing diversity but a growing *awareness* of diversity within the United States, that awareness remained mired in and thus stymied by its stereotypical and homogenizing nature. Furthermore, this era likewise demonstrates the ways in which comics worked—even if unconsciously—to disguise and so obscure these persistent issues. Just as they did in film, the trappings of this particular genre masked the ways in which depictions of ethnic characters remained tied to an exclusionary and racist imaginary; if, as scholars claim, comics have the ability to challenge and contest such attitudes (to which the myriad nonwhite heroes explicitly serve as testament), these heroes and how they were portrayed simultaneously illustrate the ways in which comics and superhero popular culture more generally assist in the continuance of them, making them more palatable by dressing them up as something different.

In this way, too, superhero popular culture of this era remained entrenched firmly in a liberal approach to race relations that—whatever its good intentions—continued to fall short of promoting a full equality. Superhero popular culture of the next decade and beyond would be hard pressed to transcend limits that seemed increasingly inescapable by the end of the 1970s. Indeed, as these, and other, newly created ethnic heroes found themselves members of various superteams, the inconsistency plaguing their representation would continue, suggesting that a nascent multiculturalism would also be handcuffed by long-extant racial attitudes.

CHAPTER 5

"Something for Everyone": The Superteam in the Age of Multiculturalism, 1975–1996

In 1975, *Giant-Size X-Men* #1 debuted a new lineup of mutants. The upstart team—now consisting of the German Nightcrawler, the Canadian Wolverine, the Irish Banshee, the African American Storm, the Japanese Sunfire, the Russian Colossus, and the Apache Thunderbird, alongside original (and white) members Cyclops and Professor X—was undeniably multicultural.[1] A full-page splash of the newly assembled team visualizes this inclusive ideal as the diverse members stand assembled before Professor X. An even more explicit invocation of inclusivity occurred in *X-Men* #99, as Nightcrawler, Colossus, Storm, and Cyclops sneak aboard a soon-to-launch space shuttle. As Geraldo Rivera reports on the launch, he tells his audience, "They're to augment Starcore's international crew—international, inter-racial, inter-sexual. Something for everyone."[2] Roughly two years later, Marvel's *The Avengers* likewise addressed issues of diversity. In issue #181, the team's abrasive government liaison Henry Peter Gyrich forces the Falcon onto the team. When the team balks at the black hero's inclusion, Gyrich explains, "If the Avengers are to be sanctioned by the government, they'll have to adhere to government policies—and that includes equal opportunities for minorities!"[3]

Comic book superhero teams, of course, had previously included nonwhite members, the Black Panther joining the Avengers being a prominent example. But what differentiates the superteams of the 1980s and beyond is how, as these examples demonstrate, the membership of the team itself became a self-conscious emblem of diversity and multiculturalism. Ramzi Fawaz, for example, celebrates the inherent "democratic" and "egalitarian" nature of such teams as the Justice League of America and the Fantastic Four that imagined forms of "international cooperation and cross-cultural alliance."[4] André M. Carrington similarly lauds the 1975 revamp of *X-Men* for replacing its formerly all-white teenage cast "to make room for a more cosmopolitan iconography" and thus incorporate racial differences and inclusion within its narratives.[5] The diversification of superteams in the 1980s thus builds on the progress inherent in the debuts of ethnic superheroes in the previous two decades. If, then, heroes from various cultural backgrounds had emerged within superhero popular culture, now they were brought further into "brotherhood" with their white peers as part of a functioning collective that even more spoke to liberal ideals concerning race.

Superteams made manifest such an ideal in various ways. One such method was the addition of a minority (and most often black) member, as exemplified by the Avengers, a quickly rearranged X-Men, and the New Warriors at Marvel, as well as the New Teen Titans, the Suicide Squad, and the Justice League at DC. As well, partnerships between white and black heroes mushroomed, pairing Richard Dragon and Ben Turner, Captain America and Falcon, Iron Man and Jim Rhodes, Power Man and Iron Fist, and Cloak and Dagger. Finally, markedly diverse teams would arrive in the form of the Detroit-era Justice League, the New Mutants, the televised Super Friends, the New Guardians, and the Blood Syndicate. These teams and titles would establish patterns for the representation of a multicultural ideal that would carry into the 1990s and beyond, in the process both reflecting and reinforcing new social understandings of race and its role in American society.

Such understandings, however, too often ignored racial problems that were hardly difficult to see in the 1980s, if Americans only *wanted* to look, as the historian William Chafe has chronicled. Ronald Reagan had arrived in office wanting to undercut the philosophies and programs of his liberal predecessors Franklin Roosevelt and Lyndon Johnson. He quickly launched efforts to attack affirmative action, and the new president further worked to reverse Great Society racial programs by packing the Civil Rights Commission and the Equal Employment Opportunity Commission with administrators hostile to their core missions. While the economy recovered from an early recession after 1982, the ensuing economic gains were not evenly shared; instead, African American income suffered in relative terms. If African Americans—as Chafe bluntly explains—"were not Reagan's top priority," they faced problems inside the Democratic Party as well, where some working-class voters chafed at what they viewed as their party's "inordinate sensitivity to blacks and Chicanos." The end result was the sharpened development of a "two-tiered society" in which increasing proportions of blacks as well as Latinos lived in poverty (with more than one-third of both groups experiencing such conditions).[6]

Within this context, the diversified superteams of this era offered a contrasting but ultimately superficial picture of continued racial progress and amity. Popularly understood as "multiculturalism," this ideology did not suddenly appear, however, in the last quarter of the twentieth century. It stemmed instead from the first quarter of that century and from Horace Kallen's "cultural pluralism," which eventually generated metaphors for US society like the earlier-referenced "orchestra" or "salad."[7] As noted in chapter 2, World War II encouraged Americans to craft a kind of pluralist national unity—embodied by the phrase "Americans All"—that allowed for ethnic identification so long as the different parts of the whole worked harmoniously to defeat the Axis.[8] Multiculturalism proper emerged from these predecessors in the final quarter of the century, the result of black frustration, white backlash, increased Asian and Latin American immigration, and skepticism about the Vietnam War. This multiculturalism, as David Hollinger has shown, flourished in the 1980s and early 1990s, in part by "directing itself in simple terms against an evil widely resented[:] the narrowness of the prevailing culture of the United States." It also thrived in part on its vagueness, speaking to contemporary concerns but failing to address the problems of the day because of "the generalities of [its] commitments."[9]

Whatever its good intentions, multiculturalism had clear flaws. Efforts under its auspices often reinforced, rather than unsettled, racialized boundaries and divisions. Hollinger sums up the double-edged sword of multiculturalism, noting that in recognizing diversity, it could also reinforce rigid cultural boundaries. For instance, the ethno-racial pentagon organized cultural diversity on a racial rubric based—despite its use in antiracist efforts to build a more equitable society—on "old, racist materials."[10] Werner Sollors, in *Beyond Ethnicity*, agrees and reproaches such attitudes that presume an inseparable gap between whites and nonwhites too often replicated in multicultural efforts.[11] A common theme within these critiques is that multiculturalism, in its desire to recognize racial, ethnic, and cultural diversity, can function contradictorily to reinscribe the boundaries and divisions not only between nonwhite cultures but between these and white culture.

Multiculturalism also contradicts itself in the way in which it reduces or flattens racialized persons. Both Sollors and Hollinger lament how the strictly bounded definitions of ethnicity preclude the inclusion—and thus foster the erasure—of persons of mixed racial heritage or identification.[12] Additionally, bell hooks points out the deleterious effects of those rigid categories on the individuals classified within them. According to hooks, nonwhite bodies get commodified as "exotic," offering a tempting field for whites to indulge themselves in while remaining unchanged both in their nature and in their dominance.[13] Scholars have devised apt metaphors to capture this effect, Anthony Appiah, for one, likening it in both its inflexibility and inauthenticity to organizing library books by size and shape; doing so, according to Hollinger, reduces nonwhite persons to only a miniscule part of their identity.[14] Stacy Alaimo likens the effects of multiculturalism to the It's a Small World ride at Disneyland, where whites remain secure in their identities as they pass through a world of colorful and entertaining cultures, while the persons making up those cultures are static and caricatured.[15] Such comparisons capture not only the essentialization and flattening of racialized personhood for white consumption but also the distancing effect that results from the maintenance of these boundaries. Effectively erased are the persons within these categories, as they remain perceived via static and commodified forms.

The comic book superteams of the 1980s replicated and reinforced the contradictions and limitations of multiculturalism. While including nonwhite heroes among their memberships, these teams and partnerships simultaneously maintained a distance between these heroes and their white compatriots, while also reductively representing nonwhite individuals and persons. As well, the superficial celebration of multiculturalism that took root in this era actually encouraged Americans to feel proud of their accomplishments in pursuing racial equality, allowing them to overlook continuing problems in American society. In their own way, these multicultural superteams did the same, painting over deeply rooted and persistent problems related to racial equality with harmoniously utopian representations that belied those issues. In doing so, comic books reflected all too accurately American struggles to come to terms with diversity in the 1980s and beyond.

Token Efforts: The Birth of Multiculturalism in Superhero Popular Culture

Going into and throughout the 1980s, several superteam comics strived to represent diversity through the addition of a "token" nonwhite—and most often black—hero to an otherwise white roster. Interestingly enough, the Falcon explicitly acknowledged his possession of this status, telling Captain America, come to pitch him on accepting membership in the Avengers, "Oh, well then maybe I oughta change my name to 'The Token,'

Figure 5.1. African American heroes like the Falcon joined superteams, but their token status undermined the multiculturalism that promoted their membership. Here, as usual, the Falcon takes a back seat to his compatriots, apparently an afterthought in terms of team unity and action.

huh?"[16] Here, the black hero—and through him his creators—gestures toward an explicit critique of such tokenism. But despite this apparent critique of such middling efforts, the token structure was near ubiquitous in the 1980s. Additionally, these lone nonwhite members very often possessed a secondary status on these teams and were depicted, both visually and narratively, as distant or separated from the rest of the team. Though part of these groups, and sometimes even leaders, the nonwhite members of several teams suffer from a variety of implicit and explicit constrictions that grate against the putative multicultural aims of these comics.

One only has to examine further the Falcon's short-lived stint with the Avengers to perceive these problems. For one, he participates very little in the team's adventures. Though listed as part of the roster in issue #181, he actually appears three issues later, arriving during a fight with the Absorbing Man but contributing nothing to the Avengers' victory. Falcon's first active contribution to the team would not come until issue #187, when he has to rescue Captain America from the team's crashing Quinjet. Though he would participate more fully in subsequent battles, the Falcon, given his departure from the team in issue #194, spent nearly half his time as an Avenger not actually participating in their adventures.[17]

The Falcon's marginalized position is reinforced visually throughout his brief tenure. He did not appear on a cover until issue #186. In this same issue, as the team sits at dinner, Falcon leans back in his chair with his arms crossed and head down, his posture indicating his withdrawal from the conversation. But for one bit of dialogue, he remains silent; and when the team assembles, the seven panels depict every member of the team except Falcon. Most evoking his secondary status, though, was how often Falcon was placed behind the rest of the Avengers. In issue #187, when the team join hands against the eldritch demon Chthon, the rest of the members are positioned alongside the central figure of Quicksilver, while Falcon reaches in from behind his teammates. In the next issue, when the team rushes to confront the villainous Vanadium, the Falcon again takes up the rearmost position. When the team first battles the Grey Gargoyle, the Falcon lags behind and is the only member who does not directly attack him. Again, when the Avengers battle Inferno in #193, the Falcon is repeatedly depicted in the rear.[18]

Adding to this visual marginalization, narrative patterns inscribe the Falcon within a secondary position on the team. He often plays the inexperienced rookie, despite having debuted (in real time) almost a decade earlier. For instance, during an attack from Modred, Ms. Marvel chides the Falcon, who thinks, "Swell. For a minute there, I forgot I was the new kid on the block." As a rookie, the Falcon also needs to prove himself as an Avenger. Almost immediately after Ms. Marvel's admonishment, the Falcon attacks, thinking, "But maybe I can make an impression on these high-and-mighty Avengers—by layin' in the first punch!"[19] Perhaps not surprisingly, the Falcon doubts his place among "Earth's Mightiest Heroes," asking himself during battle, "What am I doin' with the Avengers anyway?"[20] Not only do events in the comic gesture toward his secondary status on the team, but his own thoughts reinforce his status and perhaps even his illegitimacy as an Avenger. All of this falls far short of the multicultural ideal the Falcon's inclusion supposedly embodied.

Even more pernicious is how the blame for this failure falls on the Falcon. Echoing the brotherhood comics of previous decades, the onus for remedying the situation falls on him: the Falcon needs to change in order to resolve the tension within the team. Captain America scolds him, "If we're going to make this partnership work, you're going to have to accept a lot of things—starting now."[21] Cap's "we" notwithstanding, only the Falcon explicitly has to change. And the Falcon ultimately takes responsibility for the team's lack of cohesion when he quits, explaining, "Maybe that'll ease some of the tension I seem to have brought in with me."[22] By the end of the Falcon's brief stint as an Avenger, the team's—and title's—multicultural experiment has failed. But the blame for this failure should fall—whatever the creators would have the reader believe—on the patterns of representation that from the start precluded his full equality with the team's white members.

The patterns of exclusion and distance that appear in the Falcon's representation recurred in DC's launch of *The New Teen Titans* in 1980. Alongside previous Titans Robin, Kid Flash, Wonder Girl, and Changeling (originally Beast Boy), and new members Starfire and Raven, the team included one black member, Victor Stone, a.k.a. Cyborg. Like the Falcon, Cyborg often appears distanced or separated from the team, sometimes literally. In the second issue, the rest of the team hangs out poolside while Cyborg works elsewhere with his estranged father.[23] Similarly, Cyborg is absent in the next issue when the team hangs out at Wonder Girl and Starfire's new apartment.[24] In each of these cases, the team gathers without Cyborg, distancing and excluding him from their activities.

Cyborg is also socioeconomically (and geographically) separate from the team. The bulk of the team ranges from middle class (such as Kid Flash, who hails from a small midwestern town), to upper middle class (Donna Troy [Wonder Girl] working as a fashion photographer and Starfire, who becomes a model), to the exorbitantly wealthy (Robin, being the ward of the "millionaire playboy" Bruce Wayne, and Changeling). Cyborg, however, comes from someplace very different. In issue #3, the scene shifts to Cyborg's New York home, which a caption negatively compares to the alien Starfire's home planet: "If Tamaran was paradise, then this dark, seamy side street is most definitely hell."[25] A day-in-the-life issue five months later cast Cyborg's home as "a dirty, filthy reminder that riches and squalor exist side-by-side even in the greatest metropolis." Outside Cyborg's apartment, the pavement is cracked and garbage piles up near a stoop, while papers and other refuse litter the street. Two black men attempt to steal the visiting Changeling's car.[26] Cyborg is thus both physically and socioeconomically separate.

Cyborg's characterization further distinguished him from his teammates. Cyborg is the only Titan not accepted as human. He tells them, as he arrives at Changeling's mansion, "Try askin' directions in this town when you look like me!"[27] The orange-skinned Starfire and green-skinned Changeling, however, do not appear to suffer the same lack of acceptance. Cyborg likewise occupies the role of the rookie member despite Starfire's and Raven's similar lack of experience. When the team faces the demonic Trigon, Cyborg hangs back alone, explaining to his teammates, "You're used to things on a cosmic level. I'm not. . . . Till I met you birds, I wasn't any big-shot super-hero."[28] But what Cyborg describes is true of the other new members as well: Starfire and Raven were not heroes prior to joining

Figure 5.2. In addition to being physically different—and thus separate—from his comrades, Cyborg is also isolated by his explosive anger, which relies on long-held stereotypes of the African American "buck." This kind of anger echoed across a range of black superheroes in the 1980s.

the Titans, the former being an alien princess who escaped slavery when joining the team, and the latter, a demonic mystic with no prior superhero-ing experience. Yet only Cyborg, the team's lone black member, plays the part of inexperienced rookie.

Cyborg's anger most separates him from his teammates. His volcanic temper is on display from the team's introduction, where he attacks a protoplasmic foe, shouting, "I'm gonna show this hunk 'a gunk what it's like to face a guy who'se half man, half robot—an' mad as all get out!"[29] Nor is Cyborg's wrath reserved for his enemies. Over the course of the team's debut, Cyborg yells at his father, blaming him for his disfigurement and declaring he never wants to see him again; tells Changeling, "You should've called yourself the jerk! It fits you better"; and retorts to Robin, "What's with you, Batboy? Your shorts too tight or something?"[30] In later issues, he generally serves as a source of tension within the team. Conse-quently, Cyborg mirrors the Falcon in creating a distance between himself and the rest of his team, a distance that again belies what ideological pur-pose his inclusion seems meant to serve.

Such anger, and its problematic effects, persists late in the decade and into the 1990s with Night Thrasher (Dwayne Turner) in Marvel's *The New Warriors*. The splash page of the series' first issue introduces this new hero.

He wears a black bodysuit, with a red face mask, a red belt, and a red cloth tied around his right thigh. A blade protrudes from his cocked right hand as he dangles a young man off a rooftop, holding him by his throat. On the next page, he drops the youngster—Richard Rider, formerly the hero Nova—causing Rider's dormant powers to kick in.[31] In this sequence, readers are made immediately aware of Night Thrasher's hard-nosed, by-any-means-necessary attitude that differentiates him not only from his teammates but from traditional superheroes as well.

Further separating Night Thrasher as a kind of antihero in comparison to his more traditionally heroic partners is his professed willingness to kill, although he never actually kills anyone in the series. When the team confronts the Juggernaut, Night Thrasher announces his own take-no-prisoners attitude, ordering Firestar to microwave his heart. In the series' second issue, Night Thrasher stands over his vanquished opponent and former friend Midnight's Fire, blade to his face, preparing to kill him; only the team's urging stops him from doing more than slashing his left cheek. In the final panel of the issue, Night Thrasher walks in the foreground, his back and head turned from the rest of the team, reinforcing how he stands apart from them, both physically and morally.[32]

Night Thrasher's anger would only grow. He explodes when the Juggernaut turns away from his futile attack, and the next panel provides a close-up on his face, his pupils no more than pinpoints within the whites of his eyes.[33] He similarly loses control when thrown across a room by the Mad Thinker's android Primus, and when caught in Asylum's dark energy, he devolves into animalistic snarls.[34] Not unpredictably, Night Thrasher's rage makes him a disruptive force that must be contained by his white teammates.[35] In these ways, Night Thrasher functions more like an opponent of his teammates than their ally.

Proving a similarly disruptive force and marginalized presence is Rage, who arrived in *The Avengers* not long after Night Thrasher's debut. When he first appears—wearing a ski mask, black leather vest, pants, and gloves, with studded leather bracers on his wrists and studded belts draped around his waist—Rage is all attitude and swagger. He bursts into the mansion, directly challenges Captain America—demanding, "How come you don't have any righteous African Americans in this chicken outfit?"—and mocks the former members Black Panther and the Falcon.[36] Rage immediately functions as a source of disruption, a walking, talking challenge to the Avengers' status quo that again only marginalizes him. Rage further embodies token marginalization when the Avengers create primary and reserve teams. All the nonwhite members—the Falcon, the second Captain

Figure 5.3. The ways in which over-the-top anger could dehumanize black superheroes are embodied by the New Warriors' Night Thrasher. Such anger marked African American heroes as different and often presented them as disruptive forces to the teams they joined. Here, Night Thrasher seems as much animal as human when trapped in dark energy.

Marvel (Monica Rambeau), and, as a probationary member, Rage—are on the reserve team. The way in which Rage's membership in particular is qualified as a probationary reserve substitute reinforces how "token" black members of superteams would often possess secondary status within the established teams they were meant to otherwise diversify.

A similar pattern of secondary or qualified membership plagues multiple teams from this era. The cover of DC's relaunched *Justice League* presents the 1987 lineup, which includes the second Doctor Light (Dr. Kimiyo Hoshi) alongside the otherwise wholly white membership (except for the alien Martian Manhunter). However, she is never an official member of the team. Throughout the series' first three-issue story line, Doctor Light only appears in civilian attire, even when she assists the team in battle. She does possess a Justice League signal device, but it is given to her by the industrialist Maxwell Lord, who at this point in the series has no official standing with the League. Only in issue #4 does the team attempt to address her membership—while, like Rage, she waits in a hallway outside—but she storms out of their headquarters, declaring that she is quitting a team that, in fact, she was never actually a member of.[37]

Figure 5.4. Much like African American superteam members, Latina heroes like Firebird found their membership compromised and limited, distanced from their comrades-in-arms and deprived of any meaningful sort of agency. The illustration here baldly depicts Firebird's isolation.

Marvel's Latina superhero Firebird suffers from a similar marginalization within the two different teams she "joins." In her first appearance in *The Incredible Hulk* #265, she is a member of the southwestern-based Rangers. But, as Frederick Luis Aldama explains, she and fellow member Red Wolf "are outwitted and outperformed when the Anglo superheroes Night Rider, Texas Twister, and Shooting Star arrive on the scene," and both "are asked to stand aside while Night Rider and the others rescue their Anglo team members."[38] Firebird would similarly achieve only "hanger-on" status when she appeared in the early issues of Marvel's ongoing *The West Coast Avengers* series. A plotline relating to the team's search for its final member pits Firebird against the former Fantastic Four member the Thing. Firebird, despite wanting the position that the Thing repeatedly turns down, is never considered until she finally gives up and departs in issue #10.[39]

The series also visually underlines her nonstatus within the team. In issue #6, she stands outside of the team's circle, her back turned; the same occurs in issue #8, as a backgrounded Firebird turns sadly away from the rest of the team.[40] Issue #9 ends and #10 begins with yet another instance of this motif: the gathered West Coast Avengers surround the Thing, who has finally accepted the offer of membership, while Firebird again dejectedly stands outside the circle.[41] She never achieves equal status, always relegated to a marginal position.

Some of these "token" members—specifically DC's Bronze Tiger and Marvel's Storm and the second Captain Marvel (Monica Rambeau)—

ascended to leadership of their respective teams, a move that represents a clear reversal of the pervasive marginalized status of such figures in general. However, their elevation proves ambiguous in effect. These ostensible leaders find those roles limited or undermined. For example, Bronze Tiger (Ben Turner) first appeared in a secondary role on the Suicide Squad, playing the heavy for Colonel Rick Flag, the team's field leader, when they recruit the convict Deadshot. He stands behind him, unnamed and unidentified, only referenced when Flag explains that Turner will rip off the villain's legs and beat him to death with them if he gets out of line. When the team later confronts the monstrous Brimstone, Bronze Tiger does not take an active role in the fight, simply staying next to the Enchantress and, when she transforms into her evil persona, knocking her out.[42] In both instances, Bronze Tiger reins in the villainous members of the team. He's not there to fight alongside the members of the team; he's there to control the other members, if necessary.

Bronze Tiger's role on the "team" remains similarly compromised in the ongoing *Suicide Squad* series. When he does get the chance to lead, he is undermined. He himself possesses doubts, confessing to the demoted Flag, "This is my first solo field command and I don't mind saying I'm a little nervous." Bronze Tiger is likewise left in the dark about the team's true mission, as it is heavily implied that only Flag knows the team cannot escape the blast radius of a bomb they've been sent to plant.[43] Too, Bronze Tiger is quickly taken out of the fight when a Manhunter breaks his leg and renders him unconscious. Not only is Flag reinstated as leader by the next issue, but when Flag is unavailable for the team's next mission, Nightshade is put in charge without any explanation as to Bronze Tiger's demotion.[44]

Other ethnic characters served much lengthier tenures in leadership positions, thus more firmly following through on the symbolism of occupying this role. Storm, the sole nonwhite member of the X-Men after the rapid departures of Sunfire and Thunderbird, ascends to team leader when Cyclops departs following the "Dark Phoenix Saga" and would remain ensconced in this position for several decades. But Storm finds her initial stint as leader of the team repeatedly undermined, and she has doubts about her ability to lead. In *X-Men Annual* #4, for example, she expresses her sense of futility after the apparent death of Nightcrawler, lamenting, "Some leader of the X-Men I am turning out to be." In issue #142, Storm's thoughts again turn to her inadequacy as leader: "I'm certainly 'justifying' Xavier's faith in naming me team leader. My debut is rapidly turning into a debacle."[45] In both examples, Storm herself points out her own limitations as leader, from the start undermining a status that might otherwise serve as a contrast to how such "token" members are usually positioned.

Adding to these limitations, Storm's leadership of the team remains secondary to that of Cyclops. Whenever Cyclops returns to the team, Storm defers to him. In *Annual* #5, Professor Xavier turns to Cyclops for leadership, asking for his assessment of their situation and, later, having him put teams together as the X-Men split up. Throughout, Storm remains silent. In issue #155, Professor X again turns to Cyclops for his thoughts first, only asking for Storm's second.[46] And though Storm eventually asserts her position as leader, her defense — "If you wish to reclaim that position, Cyclops, all you need do — is ask for it!" — is hardly the most vociferous.[47] In fact, it would not be until issue #201, six years and over sixty issues after assuming leadership, that Storm would actively defend her right to lead the X-Men, defeating Cyclops in a Danger Room duel.[48]

From this point on, however, Storm embodies much more fully the role of leader. She asserts her authority over Wolverine, for instance, when he acts alone, telling him he must either obey her or leave the team; similarly, when the rest of the team reacts emotionally to an attack, it is Storm who remains calm, ordering the wounded cared for and leading the survivors on a rescue mission.[49] Later, she would assert her command over Wolverine again, naming him leader in her absence; unlike her exchanges of power with Cyclops, though, this one leaves no doubt that Storm retains the ultimate leadership role on the team.[50] Even when reduced to the physical stature of a child for a time, Storm retains her confidence that previously could be shaken. She, for example, equals an adult Jean Grey during a training session and brokers peace between the established X-Men and the newly arrived Cable — all of this just prior to leading the team during its final confrontation with the mutant-enslaving nation of Genosha. Restored to her adult form at the story line's end,[51] Storm would continue unquestioned in this role, largely to the present day, a clear sign that whatever the ambivalence around her initial ascendance to this role, Storm came to possess and still possesses a central role on the team.

Another seemingly "token" member of a superteam also embodies the inclusion and equality that all such heroes were an effort to achieve. The second Captain Marvel (Monica Rambeau), a mainstay of the Avengers in the 1980s, transcended the problems endemic to token heroes, at least while written by her creator, Roger Stern. Much of her significance stems from how her depictions invoke stubborn stereotypes and patterns — not only of such heroes but of black women in particular — only to transcend and thus contest them. In her debut, for instance, she fits the part of the

1970s black superwoman. She walks confidently in a green pantsuit and orange blouse under a jacket, sporting a large Afro and thus looking every bit a Foxy Brown or Cleopatra Jones. She demonstrates a similar toughness when accosted by two men who steal her purse. She flips the first over her back when he attacks her from behind and, when he subsequently draws a knife, subdues him by grabbing his neck, stunning him with her speed.[52] She, also like her 1970s predecessors, does not play by the rules, being, for example, chastised by her boss after he passes her over for promotion due to her "unorthodox" methods. She likewise plays into the sexualized nature of these women when she gains access to the oil rig serving as a villain's headquarters by disrobing to display a tiny string bikini.[53]

Besides initially replicating the traits of the "black superwoman" from the 1970s, Captain Marvel likewise at first appears relegated to the same secondary status other, similarly "token" members occupy. Though invited to join the team, it is as "an Avenger-in-training" until she learns how to better utilize her powers. This occurs despite the fact that the Avengers had accepted other such neophyte members—including, only five issues prior, She-Hulk—without such qualified status. Over the next handful of issues, the series reinforces her subordinate status, repeatedly referencing her need for training.

Captain Marvel, however, ultimately overcomes these forms of stereotyping and marginalization. For one, in *The Avengers*, gone is the black superwoman characterization. She instead plays the rookie/newcomer role, at times remarking in wonder upon what she experiences. However, Captain Marvel becomes not only a full-fledged member of the team but eventually a mainstay, growing organically into a more prominent role, not unlike Storm. Over the course of Stern's sixty-plus issue run, only three members maintained an almost constant presence on the team: Captain America, the Wasp, and Captain Marvel. She also gradually rises to leadership. When both of the other mainstays are incommunicado, Captain Marvel takes charge, laying the groundwork for her eventually becoming the team leader a little more than a year later. Though her tenure as Avengers chairperson would be short-lived, Captain Marvel distinguishes herself from many of her fellow "token" heroes, overcoming the limitations that pervade those other characters' positions and thus, for her part, advancing the multicultural ideal that was part and parcel of all such heroes' inclusion.[54]

But what further differentiates Captain Marvel from the other "token" heroes is that her characterization was not based in her racial/ethnic identity. Her specific character plots range from testing the limits of her power,

Figure 5.5. Among the various "token" members of 1980s superteams, the second Captain Marvel (Monica Rambeau) stands out, as she became a mainstay of the Avengers over the bulk of the decade and one of the team's most powerful members.

to a long-percolating subplot of opening her own business, to revealing her secret identity not only to her parents but to other members of the team. Her enemies, as well, are not based in her race and thus do not segment her in the same way Night Thrasher, for example, was the sole means by which the team confronted nonwhite characters and their situations. Her earliest specific nemesis was the mentally unstable Blackout, who contrasted her light-based powers with his manipulation of the "darkforce." Similarly, she confronts the villainous Nebula, granddaughter of Thanos, and her gang of space-faring henchmen before the rest of the Avengers can because her powers allow her to be sent on a deep-space mission.[55] In such conflicts, Stern's depiction of Captain Marvel avoided essentializing her race, putting her in situations and pairing her with antagonists based on her powers rather than her identity. As a result, the Monica Rambeau version of Captain Marvel achieves the kind of inclusion that most "token" members in the 1980s, to one extent or another, approximated.

"Super Buddies": Interracial Team-Ups and Partnerships

Superhero popular culture in the 1980s also latched onto partnerships between white and nonwhite superheroes to represent positive racial relations. Such interracial team-ups fall into the pattern of what Donald Bogle calls "interracial buddy pictures," exemplified by Rocky and Apollo Creed in the *Rocky* films, Han Solo and Lando Calrissian in *The Empire Strikes Back* (1980) and *Return of the Jedi* (1983), and Martin Riggs and Roger Murtaugh in *Lethal Weapon* (1987). These films served a particular white desire, presenting utopic partnerships between blacks and whites that erased racial tension that whites longed to disappear in reality. Adilifu Nama identifies a similar pattern on television, where African Americans played a complementary second fiddle to white partners, lending them the cachet of their "cool" and hip nature.[56] All sought to represent a simplified world of racial partnership, balance, and equality designed to satisfy white audiences.

Superhero popular culture in and around the 1980s was replete with such seemingly harmonic pairings. As Ramzi Fawaz notes, the "cross-racial male bonding" in these pairings served an inherently liberal purpose.[57] Marvel Comics paired mainstays Captain America and Iron Man with the Falcon and Jim Rhodes, respectively, while also joining up Power Man and Iron Fist, as well as introducing Cloak and Dagger. DC Comics presented an early version of these pairings when Richard Dragon worked alongside Ben Turner (later Bronze Tiger of the Suicide Squad). *The All-New Super Friends Hour*, which ran for two seasons in 1977 and 1978, paired DC's classic white heroes with a variety of new ethnic superheroes, including Black Vulcan, Apache Chief, Samurai, and Rima the Jungle Girl. Although offering a seeming multicultural image of equality, these partnerships ultimately contradicted that representation. The putative equality these less-than-dynamic duos proffer grates against the inequality and distance that inheres within them. Multicultural egalitarianism remained a long way off in comics, just like in American society, despite the best efforts of a superficial multiculturalism to disguise this reality.

The earliest of these superhero partnerships maintained the dominance of the white hero. With both Richard Dragon and Ben Turner as well as Tony Stark and Jim Rhodes, the sidekicks (and the subordinate roles) are clear. Rhodes is literally Stark's employee. He first appears as a helicopter pilot for his boss. Later, Rhodes waits around the office until he gets an alert that Stark is in trouble, to which he responds immediately.[58] In both instances, Rhodes literally waits on Stark, hardly an equal partnership. A similar dynamic exists between Dragon and Turner, which is especially ironic given that both are trainees, and that the latter's training predates the former's. Nonetheless, Turner defers to Dragon. In their first mission together, Turner exclaims, "Lead on, Rich!" as he plays second fiddle to his white partner. In issue #3, he becomes something like Dragon's butler in delivering a letter; more to the point, he cannot understand the missive — "To me, it makes no sense!" — which his white partner easily comprehends. He later, like Rhodes, serves as Dragon's driver.[59] All the while, Turner defers to his partner's racism. When they first meet, Dragon refers to Turner as "a refugee from a minstrel show" and declines his offer of tea, saying he "won't accept anything from an ape!" Turner responds only with a wide, white-toothed grin.[60] A clear hierarchy positions the white partner above the black one in both pairs.

The lengthy partnership between Captain America and the Falcon likewise positions the Falcon as subordinate and even inferior. To begin, Captain America decides on his partner, a fact the Falcon learns when Cap teams up with an apparently resurrected Bucky; all Falcon can do is bemoan his disappointment to his falcon, Redwing. And once the two officially team up, the Falcon remains unconvinced of his equality. He calls himself a "lightweight" compared to Cap and sets out to prove his worth by capturing Spider-Man, mistaking him for a menace. Not only does Falcon fail but he gets himself captured, requiring both Cap and Spidey to rescue him.[61] From its earliest days, then, the partnership between Captain America and the Falcon consistently put the latter in a lesser position relative to the former.

A later story line, in which the Falcon gets his now familiar wings, similarly highlights the black hero's inferiority. When Cap gains superstrength, his enhancement stirs up the Falcon's feelings of inadequacy. As the Falcon complains, "I was glad for him, Redwing — really proud that my partner snapped up some super-strength. But I don't know — something happened when he did all those dudes in! I felt . . . Okay, I felt inferior — and that's not the way this man wants to feel!"[62] These feelings prompt the sidekick to get a flight-capable costume, an effort to assuage what he and his creators, apparently, perceive that he lacks.

Marvel featured two other interracial partnerships that began in the 1980s, pairing Luke Cage and Danny Rand as Power Man and Iron Fist, as well as the teenagers Tyrone Johnson and Tandy Bowen, who would become Cloak and Dagger. Both pairings again attempted to symbolize US society's greater equality. Adilifu Nama praises both, arguing that the first pairing signified real racial progress. He also credits Cloak and Dagger as "symbols of the interconnected nature of black and white folk."[63] But

Figure 5.6. The arrival of *Power Man and Iron Fist* seemed to suggest much in the way of interracial progress. Luke Cage not only got top billing (over his white partner) but takes the lead in a cover illustration that also paid homage to Cage's history. Beneath this veneer of equality, however, inequality continued to lurk.

much within both partnerships also runs counter to the equality and connectedness between races they appear to symbolize.

The very title of *Power Man and Iron Fist* seemingly suggested such progress. For, unlike Ben Turner and Jim Rhodes, Power Man, the black hero, receives top billing, Also, the numbering of the series, which starts with issue #50, carries on from Luke Cage's solo title, not Iron Fist's. Furthermore, the cover of *Power Man and Iron Fist* #50 privileges Luke Cage. Though both heroes appear running toward the reader, Cage is in front with Fist trailing. Most of the various background images—a cinderblock tenement building, playing cards, dice, coins, images of the villains Stiletto and Discus, a cabaret sign, and an exploding police van—recall the background images from the cover and opening splash page of *Luke Cage, Hero for Hire* #1, presenting an homage to Cage's history.

The cover of *Power Man and Iron Fist*, though, belies the less laudatory dynamics between the two heroes. The two-part story line in Cage's title that led to the renamed series opens with Power Man in the role of antagonist/villain. The opening splash page of #48 depicts Cage bursting through the wall of Danny Rand's town house; he then battles, over the course of the issue, Misty Knight, Colleen Wing, and Iron Fist, barely stopping himself from strangling the latter to death. The next issue depicts him as helpless and needing the others' aid to rescue the kidnapped Claire Temple and Noah Burstein, as well as to clear his name for the crimes that put him in jail in the past.[64] Thus, in the initial stages of this team-up, Luke Cage goes from antagonist to victim, unable to fix things without help.

Nor would this situation be the end of Cage's need for help. Though in possession of the evidence necessary to clear his name, Cage alone cannot secure his innocence; that requires the efforts of Rand's lawyer, Jeryn Hogarth, who continues to assist Cage even after his case is closed. A montage depicts Cage's tutelage at the hands of the lawyer. Over a series of weeks, Hogarth instructs Cage in the proper running of his business. As a result of this mentorship, Cage "begins to feel an inner satisfaction as his natural shrewdness is augmented by the beginnings of business acumen. . . . He is mildly astonished that it is not, as he might have once supposed, the least bit beyond him." The accompanying images depict Cage in the role of pupil, looking over Hogarth's shoulder as the lawyer explains a document or sitting with his fist under his chin as Hogarth signs forms.[65] This series of images and descriptions subordinates Cage to a man subordinate to his partner, hardly the image of equality their nascent partnership hopes to embody. The contrast between his "natural" qualities and this business education also plays, of course, to racialized understandings.

Iron Fist plays the role of Cage's instructor to similar effect. The white hero teaches Cage to fight. He throws Cage to the ground repeatedly and chides him: "Come on, you can do better than that! We've practiced that throw enough for you to know it by now!" As with business, then, Cage is not fulfilling his potential in combat training. In the end, Iron Fist success-fully unleashes Cage's physical potential in much the same way Hogarth does his intellect. As Cage notes, "Man, with my strength and your moves, I'm gonna be the baddest dude this side a' Sonny Chiba!"[66] Here again, though, Cage is more Iron Fist's project than partner.

The series also undermines the pairing's putative symbolic potential by repeatedly reinforcing the socioeconomic and even ontological differences between the heroes. The banner across the top of each issue's opening splash page immediately hits this note: "Luke Cage: a child of the streets . . . Daniel Rand: a son of the mystic city of K'un-Lun . . . Two men from different worlds—both reborn with a strength and power beyond belief! And together, no one can stop them!"[67] And though this banner ends by emphasizing the pair's coming together, a recurrent theme in the series is what differentiates them. Issue #51 opens in Harlem, as Cage gives Rand a tour of his old neighborhood, where Iron Fist is out of his depth. He gets clocked from behind by a man wielding a chair, and Cage clearly knows the "turf" better. Though this sequence reverses their hierarchy—Cage now knowledgeable and Fist ignorant—it is based in another clear divide: Cage comes from and thus understands a very different world than Iron Fist. The point is reinforced when the scene shifts to Rand's estate, the narra-tor describing "a journey . . . from the bottom of the socio-economic lad-der . . . to very near the top," from buildings likened to "tombstones" to "an officially recognized landmark." The next panel's caption makes clear that though Cage has been staying with Rand for some time, "he's still not used to the place."[68] Cage is as much a fish out of water in the wealthy so-cial sphere of his partner as Iron Fist is in the impoverished urban ghetto that Cage calls home.

Indeed, Cage's discomfort in Rand's economic sphere proves a con-tinued source of tension. For example, Cage is displeased with the Park Avenue locale of their business, telling his partner it's "too rich" for him.[69] The pair similarly differ on their ideas of potential clients, eventually oc-cupying different locales, Cage in his former haunt, the Gem Theater, and Iron Fist in their more opulent digs. Underlining their inherent differ-ences, a caption points out the incongruity of Iron Fist linking "his for-tunes to the gritty reality of Times Square . . . and particularly to a certain resident of Forty-Second Street's Gem Theatre."[70] This oddity is particu-

Figure 5.7. Much like Power Man and Iron Fist, Cloak and Dagger debuted suggesting a deep sense of equality between the black and white heroes. The comic drove the point home visually over the three panels depicted here. Such egalitarian aspirations, however, were too often undermined by the stories and illustrations that followed.

larly one-sided, as it is only strange that a man like Iron Fist—wealthy and white—would team up with Cage. As much, then, as the series' linking of these two heroes on the surface suggests equality, the deeper characterizations of Power Man and Iron Fist reveal a persistent inequality.

Like Power Man and Iron Fist, Cloak and Dagger, Marvel's second prominent black-and-white duo of the 1980s, intended to represent an equality between nonwhites and whites. Both Cloak—Tyrone Johnson, "a poor black boy from South Boston"—and Dagger—Tandy Bowen, who "grew up in . . . a wealthy suburb of Cleveland"[71]—are teenage runaways in New York who were captured and given experimental drugs. Managing to escape, the two find themselves transformed, Tyrone becoming Cloak and able to transport himself and Dagger, as well as engulf enemies, in the billowing folds of his eponymous garment, and Tandy able to project daggers of light from which she draws her costumed identity.

Cloak and Dagger's early appearances signaled equality. The pair debuted in a trio of symmetrical panels: equal-sized close-ups on Cloak and Dagger frame a middle panel in which the two race into action. Their dialogue is similarly complementary. Cloak warns their prey, "We have come for you, Simon Marshall," to which Dagger adds, "You have so much to pay for."[72] They continue this pattern as they confront not only Marshall but Spider-Man, Dagger killing the former while Cloak distracts and contains the latter; the two function again in perfect tandem to escape Spider-Man,

Dagger using her light-knives to drive the hero into the folds of Cloak.[73] A full-page sequence in *Marvel Team-Up Annual* #6 serves much the same symbolic function. At the top, a horizontal panel shows the pair about to confront a group of thugs. This panel is followed by two columns of four equal-sized panels, the column on the left depicting Dagger's attack while that on the right presents Cloak's. In both columns, the last panel is a close-up on each hero's eyes, before a final horizontal panel shifts to the observing Spider-Man and his reaction.[74] The ways in which the duo's efforts are matched visually and thematically convey a theme of balance and equality: what one does the other matches and completes.

However, the seeming equality of the interracial pair is ultimately undermined. Morally, for example, Cloak is the lesser of the two. He remains steadfast in their mission of vengeance, while Dagger quickly wavers, eventually wishing to give up their quest.[75] More to the point, Dagger comes to express mercy for their targets, while Cloak remains all too willing—if not eager—to kill. In the first issue of their original series, Cloak urges his partner to destroy an attacking gang member, but Dagger balks.[76] Though the pair originally equally thirsted for vengeance, Dagger comes to question their actions; no such moral qualms plague Cloak.

Cloak is also the less human. His physical form decays over the course of their appearances. At first, he possesses a normal human form and features. His muscular body appears fully beneath the folds of his cloak; his face is rounded and contoured, though his eyes are wholly black.[77] Such is no longer the case in the first limited series, where the lower third of his face becomes much more angular, his skin more weathered, and his frame emaciated. This decay is even more pronounced in the duo's second series. Here, a close-up depicts Cloak's now demonic face. His eyes, glowing red, are but slits in his otherwise wrinkled, craggy visage.[78] Other aspects of Cloak's character add to his dehumanization, particularly in contrast to the more human Dagger. As the pair take sanctuary at Holy Ghost Church, only Dagger finds solace. She showers and eats; Cloak does not partake of either comfort.[79] Similarly, when the pair travel to Long Island, Dagger dresses in civilian clothes while Cloak remains, as ever, clad in his voluminous costume.[80] Dagger possesses the ability—or, perhaps, privilege—to appear, to use the duo's own term, "normal," an appearance, and thus a humanity, forever denied her putative equal.

Cloak's physical decay results from his eldritch abilities, the starkest evidence of persistent inequalities in the pair. There is a clear difference in the toll the drug-awakened abilities take on them. Cloak's powers create in him a dependency and craving consonant with drug addiction. As he explains to Spider-Man, Cloak feeds on "light and warmth," a need that Dagger appeases.[81] A full-page splash in issue #2 of their original series conveys the same sense of unrelenting need: an emaciated Cloak crouches in pain and hunger; the narrator asks, "Have you ever known hunger . . . real hunger . . . a gnawing in your gut that means your body's feeding on itself? Then imagine the hunger of the man called Cloak, a being of darkness . . . who must feed on the light and life of others to satisfy the cravings of his soul."[82] In contrast, Dagger suffers no parallel addiction or curse from her powers. Though Nama credits the series for how "Cloak's addiction to light and Dagger's compulsion to supply his craving made Cloak and Dagger the first comic to overtly deal with the strange dynamic of pathological co-dependency,"[83] Dagger's use of her abilities to satisfy Cloak does not merit the label of "compulsion," certainly not to the extent of Cloak's hunger. Rather, she chooses to feed his darkness.[84] Though Dagger certainly plays a role in supporting Cloak's hunger for light/life, her actions are cast as a choice rather than a parallel and equal compulsion.

Cloak and Dagger's creators attempted to redress this discrepancy in the graphic novel *Predator and Prey*, in which Dagger appears to suffer from debilitating effects of her own powers: "She is . . . plagued by internal turmoil similar to Cloak. Dagger's brilliant light fills her with a burning sensation that only Cloak's power of darkness can cool."[85] This effect—Dagger's excess of light—would subsequently pop up sporadically in their story lines. As she and others travel through Cloak, she feels his darkness, noting the "cooling" effect it has on her "fires."[86] An appearance in *Marvel Fanfare* was built around Dagger's "curse," as her exhaustion with their mission leads her to escape into a dance club where her powers threaten to run amok. Cloak, in a reversal of their more prevalent pattern, arrives and voices what this plot seems meant to show: that Dagger suffers her own powerful and threatening curse.[87] Dagger would come to a similar revelation in their feature in *Strange Tales*: "When I'm too full of light, I forget about . . . everything! I become cold—aloof—almost . . . cruel! Only Cloak's siphoning off my excess light—keeps me . . . human!"[88] Here, Dagger even more fully parallels her dark partner, as she becomes less human (though no less beautiful), and Cloak serves as the means by which this transformation is abated.

But important differences remain, despite this effort to better match the heroes' respective suffering. Dagger's curse is sporadic, multiple years passing between appearances, while Cloak's is constant and overwhelming. Furthermore, Dagger can expel her light, thus freeing herself from its curse.[89] No such safety valve exists for Cloak; his only recourse in the event of Dagger's absence being to suck the light—and life—out of others. Thus, this effort to equalize Cloak and Dagger remains riven by differences that undermine the partnership through which black-and-white tandems like Cloak and Dagger—as well as Power Man and Iron Fist, the Falcon and Captain America, Jim Rhodes and Iron Man, Ben Turner and Richard Dragon—allegedly embodied racial balance and harmony.

But comics were not the only place in superhero popular culture where such interracial duos and their limitations manifested in the late 1970s and early 1980s. The Saturday morning cartoon show *The All-New Super Friends Hour* featured one segment per episode that paired an established (and white) Super Friend with a guest star, among which were several new ethnic superheroes: Black Vulcan, Apache Chief, Samurai, and Rima the Jungle Girl. In Black Vulcan's team-ups—first with Aquaman and then with Batman and Robin—he appears relatively equal to his partners. In "The Whirlpool," when he and Aquaman rescue a supertanker, Black Vulcan uses a lightning bolt to seal a leak and also frees both himself and Aquaman from a cargo net dropped on them by the ship's captain. Similarly, in "The Day of the Rats," Black Vulcan pens up a swarm of rats with a "lightning fence" and uses his abilities to short out the device that maddens the vermin.[90] In both appearances, Black Vulcan is a capable hero and partner. He of course emulates so many other of his 1970s black brethren—like the Black Panther, Black Goliath, and Black Lightning—in having his race be a part of his superhero identity, but otherwise he is as generic a personality as any of the other Super Friends in the series.

The same progress, however, cannot be assigned to the other ethnic superheroes. Apache Chief, Samurai, and Rima play secondary or subordinate roles in their various team-ups. Apache Chief distracts a panther and a pair of boars, allowing Wonder Woman to locate the heroes' goal, a giant king cobra.[91] And though he joins Batman and Robin to track a snow creature, the size of the giant snowman's footprints make his skills superfluous.[92] Rima's purpose is also subordinate: she uses her power over nature—for example, summoning a bear to topple two trees over a ravine as a makeshift bridge—to allow Batman and Robin to save a group stranded by a fire, a rescue in which she plays no active role.[93] Samurai also provides support to Superman in saving an alien ship: his actions allow Superman to lift the ship out of a volatile volcano. As with Rima, Samurai's job is only to provide the means by which his white partner can accomplish their goal. And Black Vulcan's depiction in later episodes would be just as problematic. In "Bazarowurld," Black Vulcan and Superman find themselves trapped by Bizarro on his home planet; Superman defeats his twisted counterpart—despite having lost his powers from red kryptonite—while Black Vulcan cannot free himself from a hall of mirrors.[94]

In these ethnic guest appearances, *Super Friends* replicated the problems of interracial comic book partnerships. Nonwhites—as was the case with their comic book compatriots—remain subordinate, contradicting the equality and connection superficially portrayed in these team-ups. But the ethnic Super Friends were not done appearing on Saturday mornings, as they and other ethnic heroes would continue to appear, not just as guest stars, but as full-fledged members of superteams that would also develop over this period.

More (and Less) Multicultural Superteams

Building on efforts that employed tokens and team-ups to allegedly promote diversity, other creators ostensibly celebrated (but also reflected the problems of) multiculturalism through the creation (or re-creation) of more profoundly diverse teams. As mentioned earlier, *X-Men* was relaunched with an ethnically diverse lineup, a pattern that would be repeated in its first spin-off title, *The New Mutants*. At DC, *Justice League of America* was similarly revamped, adding two nonwhite neophytes—Vixen and Vibe—to its more established members. Two new titles launched later at DC and featured truly multicultural lineups: *The New Guardians* and, as part of Milestone Comics, *Blood Syndicate*. And of course *Super Friends*, throughout the 1980s, continued featuring Black Vulcan, Samurai, Apache Chief, and Rima.

But although such teams symbolized a broader conception of diversity in the United States, their efforts foundered. Similar to the partnerships and teams with token members, though putatively colleagues, there remained clear differences and divisions between the white and nonwhite members of these teams that grate against the tolerance and harmony multiculturalism strives to promote. Additionally, the depictions of these nonwhite characters commodify their ethnic identities as exotic, as "spice," to use bell hooks's term for what she criticizes of contemporary mass/popular culture in general. What then may mistakenly seem like a genuine interest in the "other" instead maintains that hierarchical and distanced status quo, as nonwhites remain exploitable for patriarchal and imperialist fantasies.[95] In the comics, this commodification appears not only in a continued reduction of racialized individuals to stereotypes but also in an entrenched sexualization that is likewise inconsistent with these creators' lofty intentions.

The standard-bearer for comics' efforts to promote multiculturalism, Marvel's 1975 relaunch of *X-Men*, succumbs to the limits of these efforts. *Giant-Size X-Men* #1, in this way, introduces the multicultural Night-crawler, Wolverine, Banshee, Storm, Sunfire, Colossus, and Thunderbird, but at the same time marginalizes them. In the story, the previous (and white) X-Men—Cyclops, Jean Grey, Angel, Iceman, Havok, and Polaris—respond to the detection of a powerful mutant on the South Pacific island of Krakoa; almost immediately upon arrival, the team is attacked and, with the exception of Cyclops, captured by that mutant—the island itself—which feeds off mutants' powers. Cyclops returns to Professor X, who then assembles the new team, which embarks to rescue the captured members.

Victory comes, however, not at the hands of the new team but via its previous members. Storm uses her abilities to recharge Polaris's magnetism, but this stratagem counterproductively makes Krakoa stronger. Only when the brothers Cyclops and Havok provide power to Polaris is the island defeated. As well, the team's escape from the whirlpool created by Krakoa's removal is accomplished by Iceman, who creates a vessel to protect the team, and Havok and Cyclops, who provide propulsion.[96] The new multicultural members play, at best, an assistive role, freeing the captured members so that they can achieve victory while the new members futilely strike against their island opponent. Though all are X-Men, some X-Men—specifically, the white American X-Men—are more central to the plot than others.

Further undermining the story's aims are its assimilationist elements. Once the new members are gathered, Xavier gives the non-English-speaking members a "telepathic crash course in the English language" to close "the communication gap." Their new identities are likewise imposed, Cyclops telling the objecting Thunderbird, "The professor has given you all code-names, group! You might as well start getting used to them!"[97] In other words, the various new members of the X-Men have to assimilate to new clothes, new names, and even the English language, an assimilation imposed by the two remaining white team members, Cyclops and Professor X.

The new team's lack of cohesion further contradicts its multicultural ideal. Here, *X-Men* demonstrates the way in which the cultural or racial distinctions multiculturalism accepts divide cultures, thus frustrating the unity for which this ideology strives. The "all-new, all-different" *X-Men* is replete with tension, most often involving Sunfire and Thunderbird, two of the three nonwhite members. Sunfire initially refuses to participate in the rescue mission, due to his dislike of other mutants. Thunderbird echoes this sentiment as he tells Storm, likewise possessed of her own doubts about her newfound fellowship, "This group ain't exactly a mutual admiration society! . . . We're all involved in this fiasco for our own reasons, girly—an' patting each other on the back ain't one of [them]." Reinforcing Thunderbird's point are his references to Storm with "girly" and, more pointedly, to Sunfire as "the Jap!"[98] Most significant, and troubling, this subplot resolves only after Sunfire departs the team and Thunderbird is killed.[99] From that point on, the team achieves a greater coherence. Thus, not only did this subplot replicate divisions lingering within the multicultural ideal, but it implicitly associated that tension—its cause and its solution—with nonwhite members of the team.

Further undermining the comic's intent is its representation of ethnic/cultural identity. *X-Men* falls prey to what hooks critiques about mass culture's commodification of race and ethnicity: "Within commodity culture, ethnicity becomes spice, seasoning that can liven up the dull dish that is mainstream white culture," a solution based in the assumption that nonwhites are "more worldly, sensual, and sexual because they were different."[100] The entire premise of the new *X-Men* can be read as an example of the assumptions hooks explicates. The "dull dish" that was the original *X-Men* is "livened up" by an infusion of ethnicity. Prior to *Giant-Size X-Men* #1, sales of *X-Men* had deteriorated to the point that the series had been in reprints from 1970 until 1975; it took the rebirth of the team in this multicultural form to turn the series into a sales juggernaut.

Examples of how race and ethnicity serve as "spice" riddle the series. The characters' dialogue clearly marks their racial/ethnic backgrounds. Banshee's Irish brogue is apparent in such dialect as "begorra!" and "'tis" and "ye" and "foine" (fine).[101] Nightcrawler's dialogue is similarly peppered with German: "Herr," "mein Gott," and "der Jahrmarkt;" he similarly refers to his opponent, the frog-like Croaker, as "Herr Frosch."[102] Colossus's dialogue draws on similar ethnic epithets—most commonly "tovarisch"[103]—and at times his Russian dialogue also appears in a Cyrillic font, for instance when the X-Men's jet is shot down, and again as the team confronts a belligerent squad of American soldiers.[104]

X-Men commodifies both Sunfire's and Thunderbird's cultures to an even greater extent. Both wear costumes emblematic of their racial/cultural background. Sunfire's dress features a stylized rising sun image, with the orb of that sun serving as a buckle around his midsection, and red and white "rays" emanating from it. Thunderbird's appearance is perhaps even more problematic. His costume is replete with elements stereotypical of Native Americans: fringe at his shoulders and boot tops, a stylized eagle emblem, and a headband with two feathers. Regarding the feathers, Michael A. Sheyahshe points out that the Apache, with whom Thunderbird is identified, "do not wear feathers in this manner," and thus "this choice aligns the characters with an iconic stereotype of all Indians dressing similarly."[105] Adding to the problematic stereotypes fused into Thunderbird's appearance is his skin; while Sunfire is colored with the same hue as the Caucasian Professor X and Colossus, Thunderbird's skin is given a noticeably red hue.

However, it is Storm's depiction—and especially her exotic nature and sexuality—that most fully commodifies ethnicity. Storm's otherworldly nature and sensuality, on display from her very first appearance in 1975, continue throughout the 1980s. When captured by Doctor Doom, Storm—though trapped as a chrome statue—somehow trades her usual costume for no more than a white scarf around her neck that swoops to cover her breasts and a skimpy white skirt.[106] Her penchant for nudity likewise remains prominent. She conjures up a rainstorm after a team workout (her naked body covered only by strategically placed hair and wind) and later, after waking up in the demon Belasco's Limbo, refreshes herself with a naked swim.[107] Her otherworldly connection to nature likewise persists. In space battling the alien Brood, Storm laments the loss of control over her powers in grounding her connection to nature: "My mutant powers—and more importantly my very soul—are bound to the primal force of a living world, our earth. . . . My spirit is wasting away, and the longer I am separated from my home the more I will lose."[108] The lingering effects of losing her mutant powers cause Storm, in issue #173, to radically alter her look but not its effect. She cuts her hair into a daring Mohawk and dons black leather boots, pants, and vest over a white half blouse, a look that is no less exotic for its extremity. When she temporarily loses her powers, Storm not only returns to Africa but also suddenly embodies a heightened mysticism, seeing an apparition of mountains and then her mother as she crosses the Atlantic.[109] Though Storm's powers would change over these years of plots, the commodification of her race and culture as exotic remained consistent.

X-Men's first spin-off title, *The New Mutants*, would likewise continue an unsuccessful commitment to diversity. Though Fawaz celebrates the series for its depiction of "mutant solidarity" as a response to the failure of postwar liberal ideologies, such solidarity—coming from the pens of white creators—hinges upon, at least in part, these characters' representation as "other."[110] For one, the dialogue is "spiced" with dialects and non-English vocabulary and phrases. The Kentuckian Cannonball, for example, speaks with a Southern accent, most often demonstrated by dropping the end letter of words such as "copin'" (coping) and "knowin'" (knowing).[111] The Scottish Wolfsbane likewise demonstrates her ancestry in her dialogue:

"I could na' help myself" and "Och! What're those spaleen doin' to him, the poor man?"[112] Karma, too, makes explicit her French/Vietnamese roots, responding to Xavier with "Oui, m'sieu," and exclaiming, "Voilà."[113] Portuguese similarly peppers Sunspot's speech; he calls Cannonball "senhor" and a hostile student "hombre," as well as exclaims, "Dio!" when facing a mutant-hunting Sentinel.[114]

Adding to the team's "spice" was also the nonwhite members' stereotypical traits. The Brazilian Sunspot, for example, is hotheaded; in his first appearance, he loses his temper during a soccer match, tackling another player and, when his mutant strength subsequently activates, throwing him across the pitch.[115] Sunspot is similarly belligerent toward El Lobo, the Latino member of Team America, slamming him against a wall.[116] Sunspot at other times plays the role of a Latino lothario. At the end of the graphic novel, he flirts with Wolfsbane, telling her, "I could never refuse a beautiful girl anything"; in the series' first issue, he flirts with her again, kissing the naïve Rahne Sinclair's hand.[117]

Multiple stereotypes and problematic associations similarly "spice" the depiction of Karma. She continues the assimilationist trope of the X-Men. After being washed and having her hair cut, Karma is told that she has transformed from "an ugly duckling" to a "swan,"[118] comments that evoke a process in which immigrants had to be cleaned and refashioned to enter and assimilate into America. Karma's representation also replicates the model-minority stereotype; Xavier offers her a job at his school, telling her she is "bright, well-educated, articulate, multilingual—a perfect choice."[119] Furthermore, Karma evokes aspects of what Robert G. Lee calls the "gook" stereotype, where Asian Americans, after the Vietnam War, appear as "the invisible enemy and the embodiment of inauthentic racial and national identities."[120] The very nature of her mutant ability plays into this insidious stereotype. As Karma, she has the ability to psychically possess others, controlling a Brazilian policeman at one point and forcing a government official to confess to another.[121] She literally acts as an "invisible enemy," taking over the minds of others and making them do her bidding unbeknownst to anyone else; a twist, yes, but still a version of this Asian—and specifically Vietnamese—stereotype.

Finally, the depiction of Dani Moonstar, the Cheyenne member of the team, relies on the common Native American stereotype of a connection to nature that is a first step in her exoticization. In her first panel, she "sits in silent harmony with the world, as it spins toward another dawn. She treasures these idyllic interludes—when she is at peace with herself and truly happy."[122] This connection reappears when she finds her way into

THE *MEDICINE BOW MOUNTAINS,* NEAR THE TOWN OF SUNDANCE, COLORADO...

SHE SITS IN SILENT HARMONY WITH THE WORLD, AS IT SPINS TOWARD ANOTHER DAWN.

SHE TREASURES THESE IDYLLIC INTERLUDES--WHEN SHE IS AT PEACE WITH HERSELF AND TRULY HAPPY. HER SECRET TERROR IS THAT, OF LATE, THEY ARE BECOMING IN-CREASINGLY RARE.

Figure 5.8. Like her fellow New Mutants, the Cheyenne Dani Moonstar cannot escape racialized and stereotypical assumptions. In her earliest appearances, for instance, she exhibits a close connection to nature and mysticism, as well as, in future issues, an exotic sexuality.

the X-Men's attic and cares for Storm's neglected plants.[123] Her rapport with nature is likewise demonstrated by her ability to psychically communicate with animals, and particularly with Wolfsbane in her wolf form; the description of this connection with Wolfsbane—that it is part of the "psionic rapport her Cheyenne teammate shares with all animals"[124]— explicitly ties it to her Cheyenne identity. Moonstar's confrontation with the Demon Bear that killed her family ratchets up this intrinsic connection to an exotic mysticism that more and more surrounds her, an image of this bear first appearing to her during a prophetic nightmare.[125]

Concomitant with this mysticism is an uninhibited and growing sexuality that further exoticizes her. It first manifests during the team's Rio sojourn; whereas Rahne is scandalized by the forwardness of the Brazilians during Carnival, Dani seems tantalized: "I dunno, Rahne, it looks like fun t'me." When the pair join in, Dani dons a barely there bikini-style dress that she describes as "a trifle more modest than I had in mind." Dani similarly contrasts the later member Amara Aquilla, a.k.a. Magma. On the beach, Dani wears a two-piece bikini, while Amara finds her rather staid red one-piece suit "incredible," "slippery," "snug," and "very daring," comments suggestive about Dani's much more revealing attire. Finally, a mental alert from Professor X wakes Cannonball, who finds Dani dressing, revealing her predilection for nudity.[126] As much, then, as not only *The New Mutants* but Marvel's mutant family have been celebrated as purveyors of color-blind tolerance and inclusion, these titles also betray such lofty goals in their commodified and exoticized treatments of race and ethnicity.

Efforts to promote multiculturalism via DC's properties were similarly compromised. Like the relaunched *X-Men*, the continuing adventures of the Super Friends undercut their inclusive aims by persistently marginalizing ethnic heroes. *Challenge of the Super Friends* (1978) appeared to include Black Vulcan, Samurai, and Apache Chief as more than just ethnic guest stars. In the opening credits, these three heroes appear in line with the rest of the team. They each likewise get their own feature moment in the credits, Apache Chief pursuing the villainous Giganta, and Samurai and Black Vulcan flying next to each other before a starry background. And the series' plots sometimes seemed to strive for a similar level of inclusion. For example, "Invasion of the Fearians" included Samurai amongst the heroes as an alert came in and later showed him using his powers to disperse the earth's increased humidity. In the same episode, Black Vulcan uses his abilities to block a blast from the Fearians' neutron eraser and helps to capture Gorilla Grodd, while Apache Chief uses his size-changing powers to stop a flood.[127] Similarly, in "The Time Trap," Apache Chief and Aquaman work together to combat Black Manta, and Samurai joins Green Lantern, Batman, and Robin to thwart Sinestro and Captain Cold.[128] The three were also occasionally important to an episode's climax. In "Super Friends: Rest in Peace," Apache Chief disposes of the noxium crystal that threatens the team and turns the Legion of Doom's "mental matter ray" against them; similarly, Black Vulcan takes out Captain Cold and rescues Hawkman when he's transported into the pages of *Jack and the Beanstalk*.[129] In adventures such as these, *Challenge of the Super Friends* seemed to no longer put the new ethnic heroes in a secondary status.

However, the series struggled to maintain this level of inclusion. When various members of the team are stranded in the past, Black Vulcan, though among the assembled heroes, plays no role in rescuing them. Flash shows up and apologizes for being late, Superman explains the situation, and both Flash and Hawkman use the computer to work on a solution; Black Vulcan says and does nothing. Similar moments occur in "Wanted: The Super Friends." When the entire team assembles, only the white members have any dialogue; similarly, though Samurai appears along with Green Lantern, Wonder Woman, Batman, and Superman in a trap, he is silent while the others figure out a means of escape. In "Secret Origins of the Super Friends," the trio are literally marginalized, as all three stand together, separate from their teammates. And in "Swamp of the Living Dead," Apache Chief, Black Vulcan, and Samurai are not only the first

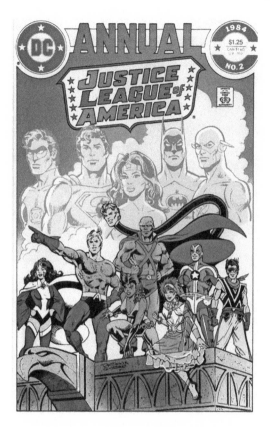

Figure 5.9. The "Detroit Era" Justice League presented a multicultural team to readers. Based in the city—with all of its ethnic connotations and meanings—the team featured Vibe and Vixen. While the inclusion of nonwhite characters surely was meant to gesture toward egalitarianism, the stereotypical presentation of both characters instead continued to commodify ethnicity.

Super Friends to be captured but they also do not speak.[130] Thus, the results of this iteration of Super Friends are, at best, mixed; the story lines and visuals as much marginalize the ethnic heroes as include them.

Super Friends, however, was not the only DC superteam to attempt to foster multicultural understanding via the inclusion of nonwhite members. *Justice League of America* undertook modest efforts in this vein. The so-called Detroit Era Justice League featured the established members Aquaman, Zatanna, Elongated Man, Martian Manhunter, and (later) Batman alongside four new members: Steel (Hank Heywood), Gypsy, and two nonwhite characters, Vibe (Paco Ramone) and Vixen (Mari McCabe). The team's relocation to a secret base in Detroit added to this multicultural attempt, a move that placed them within an urban — and multicultural — community. However, such attempts remained problematic, as Vibe and Vixen continued the commodification of ethnicity as a result of their flattened, stereotypical nature.

Vibe, as Aldama summarizes, "is dressed to the nines in break-dancing regalia: baggy yellow pants, a *V* lettered vest top, a red bandana around his neck, green gloves, and yellow wraparound sunglasses. For that finishing ethnic touch, he sports a 'soul patch' and is colored a slight shade of brown."[131] Vibe is "all spice" — the brightly colored costume, the break dancing, the ethnic "touches" of soul patch and brown skin. Vibe's reification is further burdened by a conglomeration of Latino stereotypes. In his early appearances, he plays the role of both the lothario and the macho. Demonstrating the former, he immediately flirts with Vixen, asking her, "And where have you been all my life anyway, beauty?"[132] In the same issue, he inserts himself into his new friend Steel's innocent attraction to Vibe's sister, Rosita, telling him, "Back off 'amigo.' You want to talk to my sister, first you talk to me, understand."[133] Later, Vibe will utter a similar warning — "I know what chu really want, and if chu take even one step toward my sister, I break both chu're arms!"[134] — again playing the stereotypically patriarchal and macho Latino. Furthermore, as the last example demonstrates, Vibe's dialogue is "spiced," as he effects a stilted English.

Though not as multifaceted, for lack of a better term, as Vibe's, the depiction of the African Vixen, too, relied on flattening stereotypes. She is ethnically mysterious, as, the narrator notes, "even now, a member of the League, her origins remain mysterious, her past elusive." She likewise demonstrates a familiar affinity with nature, feeling at once reborn and at home when in nature: "She feels alive for the first time in weeks. Alive and in her element."[135] Vixen is also profoundly sensual. She flirts with Martian Manhunter as well as Dale Gunn, standing, for example, behind them in the team's jet, her right arm across the Martian's left shoulder and her left arm and leg perched on Gunn's chair. Vixen's rampant sexuality irks Zatanna, who remarks, "She certainly lets you know she's interested . . . and it seems like she's interested all the time."[136] Clearly, Vixen lives up to her name in a way that again equates racial and cultural difference with unbridled sexuality.

These modest efforts in the mid-1980s would be followed by broader efforts at DC to represent multiculturalism. The first of these, *The New Guardians*, represents the absolute nadir of superteams' multicultural

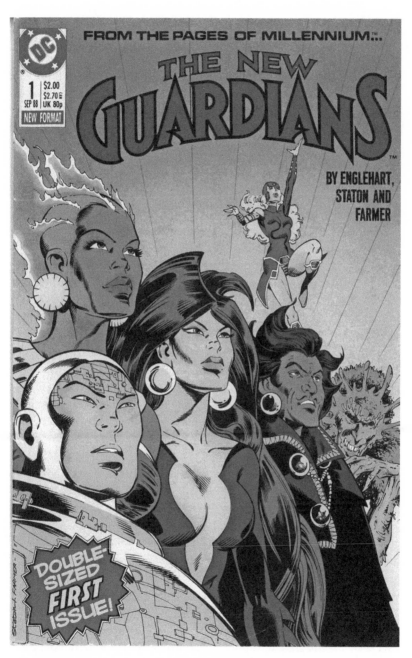

Figure 5.10. The apotheosis of the failures of multicultural superteams appeared in the pages of *The New Guardians* in 1988. Here, flatly stereotyped characters banded together to guide the next evolution of humanity. Despite its good intentions, the series presented sexualized and racialized characters that reveal the limits of superficial multiculturalism.

efforts. The series, beginning in 1988, spun out of DC's multititle cross-over *Millennium*, which ended with a group of individuals being chosen as the next evolution of humanity. Six of these Chosen—Gloss, "from China"; Ram, "from Japan"; Floro, "from that other dimension"; Extraño, "from Peru"; Jet, "from the U.K. via Jamaica"; and Harbinger, "raised on a UFO!"[137]—would form the New Guardians, with a seventh, Tom Kalmaku (Green Lantern's former sidekick), initially choosing to stay with his family and the eighth, the racist South African Janwillem Kroef, refusing to join. The comic is steeped in the cultural issues of its times: race, homosexuality, the AIDS crisis, South African apartheid, the "war on drugs," and the Cold War, to name but a few. The series is likewise steeped in a deeply flawed representation of a superficial multiculturalism.

The representation of the nonwhite members is steeped in a commodification of ethnicity and sexuality. Gloss, for example, wears an overtly sexualized costume, which consists of a green leotard with a telescoping opening that runs from her shoulders, narrowing just below her hips. Her flowing red hair drapes the entire length of her body, and her left leg bears a full-length flame tattoo. Extraño is even more scurrilously typed; he is "presented as a limp-wristed Latino who speaks in truncated half sentences, refers to his team members as 'Honey,' and is more concerned with color coordination than with using his superpower—illusionism—to fight Western imperialism."[138] One might also add how Extraño's referring to himself as "auntie" leaves much to be desired about homosexuality's representation.

But beyond these discrete instances of commodification, the series bases its very premise in the assumptions about ethnicity and race that bell hooks laments. The team's entire purpose is to foster the next generation of humanity, which immediately prompts Ram to boast about his sexual experience and, in a later scene, Gloss and Jet to go to a nightclub in order to pass on their DNA, "or at least," as Gloss suggestively declares, "perfect the technique!" Here, the series explicitly links sexuality and ethnic/racial identity. In contrast, the blonde, blue-eyed, and white Harbinger is utterly naïve about sex. She explains, "I want to do what real earthwomen do, and that includes falling in love and . . . everything . . . but I'm . . . inexperienced"; Harbinger's naïveté even goes so far as to cause her to mistake a hug from Extraño for sex.[139] Here, the white Harbinger is cast as a sexual blank slate or innocent in contrast to the more rampant and worldly sexuality of her racialized peers. Such a contrast presents a textbook version of what hooks decries: mass culture's promulgation of ethnic sexuality as compensatory to white innocence.

The series' treatment of AIDS similarly grounds itself in this binary opposition. In the first issue, the Hemo-Goblin, a vampiric creature infected with HIV, scratches both Jet and Extraño, who are later confirmed to be HIV positive. Harbinger is also HIV positive, due to a psychic link she shares with Jet. However, after Jet's death, Harbinger is no longer infected.[140] The unfortunate subtext of this subplot suggests that Harbinger is healthy except when in contact—psychic or otherwise—with the nonwhite Jet, a problematic notion reaffirmed by the editors. In their response to a letter complaining about Harbinger's cure, the editors curtly reply, "Harbinger's disease was Jet's disease, not her own. With Jet's death, their link broken, Harbinger no longer had the disease."[141] Here, again, Harbinger's innocence—or perhaps better, purity—contrasts with Jet. The treatment of Extraño's HIV status likewise reinforces these problematic assumptions. Though Hemo-Goblin initially appears to be the source of Extraño's infection, the series ultimately points elsewhere. Extraño repeatedly mentions his familiarity with the disease, and he visits the graves of friends he has lost "to this vile scourge"; when he reunites with his gay friend Paco, their first words—spiced in Spanish—are questions about each other's HIV status.[142] The sum of these references is to attribute HIV and AIDs to homosexuality and otherness: Extraño has it, his gay friends died of it, and it is the immediate concern of all gay men. Again, the series editors reinforced this message. When readers raised questions about the source of Extraño's infection, the editors initially played coy; only in issue #11 would they confirm that Extraño was infected via a prior sexual encounter.[143] As did Jet, the unfortunate subtext of Extraño's depiction serves to commodify racial/ethnic identity in sexualized and exoticized terms that contrast with white innocence and purity.

How *The New Guardians* represents diversity in its climax puts the final nail in the coffin of its multicultural aims. In the climactic battle with Kroef, his monstrous creations, the "neo-hybirds," are revealed as the true next evolution of the human race when they transform into disembodied light-shapes, floating into the sky as blue and white lights.[144] As a symbol of a multicultural "future," this imagery is empty, promoting a fantasized version of tolerance and color blindness rather than grounding such concepts within real-world ideas of race, ethnicity, and sexuality. To echo Marc Singer, *The New Guardians* "erases all racial and sexual differences with the very same characters that it claims analogize our worlds' diversity."[145] In fact, the characters who have represented a diverse future for twelve issues—and at least represent real-world forms of racial, cultural, sexual, and gender diversity—are, in the end, not the harbingers of a multicultural future at all; that future is only an empty metaphor of disembodied light.

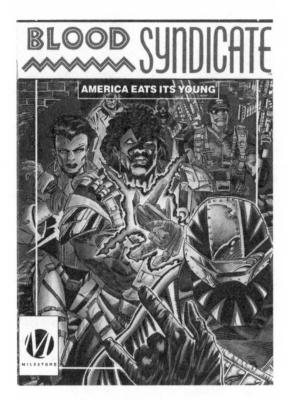

Figure 5.11. Clearly intended to promulgate multiculturalism and tolerance, Blood Syndicate's diverse lineup—shown here on the cover to the series' first issue—grated at times against how those racial groups often fell into stereotypes and other problematic representations.

If *The New Guardians* and its white creators fell short of its aims, Milestone Comics, run by minority creators, and in particular its superhero team title *Blood Syndicate*, might be expected to better symbolize and promote multiculturalism. The team comprises members of various previously opposed Paris Island gangs, all of whom possess powers after the "Big Bang," in which they were exposed to a mutagenic gas. Populating the Blood Syndicate are numerous Latinos, including the Puerto Ricans Tech-9, Fade, Flashback, and Brickhouse (and later Aquamaria and Oro); the black Muslim Wise Son; the Korean Third Rail; the African Americans Holocaust and Masquerade; and Kwai, a reincarnated Chinese warrior. (The only white member is Boogieman, and he keeps his ethnic identity a secret from the rest of the team for much of the series.) The creators made clear their intent, stating, "The variety of cultures and experiences Out There make for better comics In Here. When people get excited about the diversity In Here, they'll get just as excited about the diversity Out There."[146] However, the representation of such multiculturalism in *Blood Syndicate* is not as clear-cut in its effects as the Milestone editors hoped.

Hearkening back to the new *X-Men*, *Blood Syndicate* similarly depicts its membership as divided and in tension. Aldama writes how "enemies materialize in the form of crack addiction, greed, religious fundamentalism, sexism, racism, and so on";[147] however, these "enemies" all function within the team. Flashback hides her crack addiction. Masquerade greedily double-crosses the team. The Wise Son, a fundamentalist Muslim, is sexist. And the entire team turns against Boogieman when they learn his true ethnic identity. Too, members spend as much time fighting each other as they do their enemies. The first issue, for instance, ends with Tech-9 and Holocaust squaring off for the right to lead the team. Roberta "Rob" Chaplick, the white reporter who observes the team over its first four issues, even notes that the various members only "trust each other when they rally against" someone or something else.[148] Such internal strife hardly conveys the wholly positive and "exciting" image of diversity motivating not only *Blood Syndicate* but Milestone as a whole.

In its own way, *Blood Syndicate* also perpetuates the exoticized treatment of ethnicity decried by hooks. The difference between the team's Paris Island neighborhood and the rest of the fictional city of Dakota gets spatialized in the fact that the bridge between the two lies in ruins, making the journey to Paris Island like "a trip to another world."[149] And Chaplick's sojourn with the team has the same transformative effect that hooks critiques throughout mass culture. She thinks, as she departs from the team, "They do have a lasting effect on me, though. I'm sure that I'll never stop thinking about them again."[150] Here, Rob testifies to the effect her exposure to Blood Syndicate has had on her, claiming it has altered her, changed her into something other, something more, than what she was. But this is as far as the evidence of her transformation goes; Rob's return to Dakota proper is also her departure from the comic, and so readers never see whether this experience has enacted a substantive change in her. As a result, it can just as easily be read as another example, à la hooks, of the ways in which whites claim profound transformation from interacting with "dangerous," "fascinating," and "exotic" minorities but remain, in fact, little changed.

Another means by which the series promulgates such attitudes is its graphic depiction of violence. During an attack on a crack house, Tech-9 shoots the hands of his opponents, their remaining stumps depicted in grisly detail; Masquerade turns into a lion to deal with his attackers, and the last panel of this sequence shows him back in his human form standing over them, his eyes glowing red slits and with a long trail of blood dripping from his smeared mouth.[151] A similarly grisly scene serves as the denouement to the title's opening arc. At the end of issue #4, Tech-9 literally melts into a pile of blood-soaked gore.[152] On the one hand, the series' violence can be seen as an effort to portray a grittier, tougher reality than commonly seen in comics. However, it has the side effect of continuing to exoticize minorities and their environments as "different," "strange," and yet also "fascinating." The editor Matt Wayne, regarding the series' cancellation, stated, "Our sense of Dakota as a place where many voices can be heard has been diminished."[153] However, there are ways in which the series itself functioned to diminish the "voices" and diversity that this team, like so many others in the final quarter of the twentieth century, was meant to promote.

Conclusion

These patterns—both problematic and positive—of racial/ethnic inclusion in the comic book superteams established by the early 1990s would continue to appear in other titles through the turn of the century. Following Chris Claremont's departure from the series, two titles—*Uncanny X-Men* and *X-Men*—featured two teams, each with a single "token" ethnic member. Storm led the "gold" team comprising Jean Grey, Colossus, Iceman, and Archangel, while Cyclops captained a team that included the recently transformed-to-Japanese Psylocke within its otherwise white membership. Jim Lee, the artist on *X-Men*, would soon depart to create his own series at the newly founded Image, but his headlining title, *WildC.A.T.s*, hardly tread new ground with Voodoo, who debuted as a black female stripper before joining the team. Marvel's 1997 release *Thunderbolts*, in which the disguised Masters of Evil sought to replace the absent Avengers, included the Japanese American novice Jolt (Hallie Takahama), but distinguished her from the rest of the team not only via her age but her ignorance to her teammates' true identities. The relaunch of *The Avengers* the following year introduced the African American hero Triathlon, who would join an otherwise white lineup; however, creators Kurt Busiek and George Pérez found ways to acknowledge and thus trouble this persistent "tokenization."[154] Even the celebrated cartoon series *Justice League* found itself treading familiar racial ground in its run starting in 2001. Its first lineup featured Green Lantern John Stewart as the single nonwhite member and in the multipart episode "Star-Crossed" cast Hispanic voice actors to portray the roles of the invading alien Thanagarians, playing once again on an equivalence between "ethnic" and "alien" as well as, implicitly, anti-immigrant anxieties.

On the other hand, there are teams that at least made some effort to bend if not break out of these molds. Despite the early missteps of the animated *Justice League*, when it relaunched as *Justice League Unlimited* (2004), the cast grew to include, alongside Green Lantern, animated versions of black characters like Steel, Mister Terrific, Static, and Vixen, as well as Latinx characters like El Diablo and Fire. *The New Warriors* would similarly expand beyond Night Thrasher as its "token" member, adding Silhouette and Rage (both black), as well as an Asian American version of Turbo. When DC's *Legion of Super-Heroes* rebooted in 1994, it provided an opportunity to diversify its lineup in the form of black characters like the speedster XS and both Kid Quantums. And a new team of young mutants—*Generation X*—also debuted in 1994 and featured a cast at least as diverse and less stereotyped as the 1975 "all-new, all-different" *X-Men*: the Chinese American Jubilee, the Muslim character M/Monet St. Croix, the Samoan Mondo, the Latino Skin, and the African American Synch. These ultimately mixed results in the 1980s and beyond set the stage for future efforts to address issues of race and multiculturalism, suggesting the possibility for more probing examinations but also establishing limits that would continue to hem in comic book creators as a new century dawned.

CHAPTER 6

Replacement Heroes and the Quest for Inclusion, 1985–2011

On May 1, 1992, Rodney King stepped to a bank of microphones. Around him, Los Angeles burned, the City of Angels experiencing the third of four bloody days of race riots. His beating at the hands of white police officers had occurred more than a year prior, but emotions, little calmed by the passage of time, exploded when his assailants were acquitted. Still suffering from his brutal beating, King now asked, "People, I just want to say, you know, can we all get along? Can we get along?"[1] King's plaintive plea made clear that the "race problem" had hardly been conquered. Despite the hard-won gains of a broadly defined civil rights movement that had grown out of World War II and seeded 1980s multiculturalism, race remained a divisive and even explosive issue.

While the Rodney King incident rang "like a fire bell in the night"—to use Ronald Takaki's apt phrase that echoed Thomas Jefferson's fears about slavery in 1820—one needn't look far to find other instances of crisis leading into the 1990s. Takaki himself lists any number, including the racially motivated beating that killed Vincent Chin (a Chinese American mistaken for Japanese in Detroit) in 1982 and George H. W. Bush's Willie Horton campaign commercials in 1988.[2] And George Sanchez reveals how the violence of the Los Angeles riots following the acquittal of King's assailants was based in a growing nativism in late twentieth-century America that transcended issues of just black and white. As he notes, the well-known attack on the white truck driver Reginald Denny was preceded by several less well-known attacks on immigrants.[3] Clearly, Americans were struggling to come to grips with broad sociocultural changes that, sadly if unsurprisingly, often provoked defensive responses that underlay such violence.

Multicultural teams of the previous decade had attempted to imagine a more cooperative future, but they stood in stark contrast to this reality at the end of the twentieth century, and comic book writers and artists returned to the drawing board to wrestle anew with this vexed situation. Their resulting attempts to promote multiculturalism often deployed a common strategy: ethnic replacement superheroes, which introduced non-white versions of white heroes or transformed white characters into ethnic ones. Such replacements had been seen before, but in the 1990s this pattern became more prevalent, achieving a kind of critical mass in terms of ethnic representation. Seemingly a ready-made solution for diversity, playing with established characters in this way actually (and perhaps not surprisingly) proved problematic. The writer Geoff Johns acknowledged such difficulties in the adventures of the Justice Society of America. In a 2002 issue, Sand, the protégé of the original Sandman, talks to Hawkgirl about the difficulties of following in another hero's path. "Legacies are difficult that way," Sand explains. "You have to carve out your own niche in them."[4]

Carving out authentic and individual niches for these ethnic replacements proved a daunting task for writers and artists. Nonetheless, these replacement crusaders, overall, suggested a maturing national conversation about race. Several, to be sure, remained wholly steeped in stereotypical and racist tropes, but others began to take at least some steps away from this basis. The most successful replacement narratives of this era achieved such progress by presenting coming-of-age stories that even casual readers recognized as the journey of Peter Parker into Spider-Man. But where such connections before subordinated the ethnic hero (such as in the case of White Tiger), these tales now grounded ethnic characters in larger tropes closely connected to the mainstream superhero tale. Assuming their new roles without any experience, the replacement heroes often underwent an apprentice-to-master story arc that revealed them as agents firmly in control of not only their new powers but also their destinies. In addition, newfound abilities often brought crises of conscience as the replacements now decided how best to use their powers. Such strategies, when deployed effectively by creators, allowed these oft-racialized comic book characters to move beyond the stereotyped expectations of race to a more human and empathetic realm.

Transformed Heroes, Transforming Problems

Several of these ethnic replacement heroes were not replacements at all; they were literal transformations of existing white heroes into one ethnicity or another. Though, to varying extents, built on good intentions,

Figure 6.1. *The Punisher* referenced the Rodney King beating when Frank Castle was temporarily transformed into a black man. While the comic here pointed to structural issues that promoted racism, the ensuing story line struggled to maintain a consistent position, muddying what was clearly intended as a sympathetic portrayal of the African American experience at the turn of the century.

such figures (perhaps unsurprisingly) found themselves trapped in limiting characteristics grounded in largely negative understandings of nonwhites. Perhaps no title better illustrates both sides of this point than a short-lived story line from 1992 in *The Punisher* that saw its titular white character temporarily transformed into a black man. On the one hand, the writers Mike Baron and Marcus McLaurin, working in conjunction with the penciller Val Mayerik, attempted to highlight some realities of black life in America, such as police harassment. As the now-black Frank Castle arrives in Chicago, exhausted from a nineteen-hour drive, he is pulled over by the local police. A pudgy white cop orders him out of the car, and Castle complies, but racial abuse follows anyway, one cop asking, "What you doing in this fine car, boy?" Another declares, "Maybe the coon's got his tongue!" Castle, thinking about how he "had no patience for bigots when I was white," lashes back, slugging one cop before the others surround our hero and beat him into submission, continuing to swing away with billy clubs after the bloodied Castle hits the ground. At this point, Luke Cage fortuitously arrives, whipping the cops and then driving Castle to safety.[5] The Punisher's welcome to the Windy City, echoing the Rodney King attack, clearly suggested the kinds of institutional racism and oppression blacks continued to face.

Despite their good intentions, however, the creators quickly and unfortunately succumbed to old portrayals of the inner city. As Cage and Castle arrive to Chicago's South Side, which Cage refers to as "home sweet home," *The Punisher* presents a stereotypical view of the city: litter-filled streets and buildings on the verge of collapse. The Royal Tuck Hotel—where Castle has stashed some weapons for just this kind of emergency—is located in a neighborhood that looks even worse, the trash-strewn streets featuring junked cars and the dilapidated hotel. Seeing the interior, covered in graffiti and home to dirty, drunken bums, Castle reminisces that "this used to be a fine hotel."[6] This all-too-predictable comic book ghetto similarly hosts (and defines) its all-too-predictably stereotyped inhabitants. As they move through the city, the heroes confront gangbangers like those on the front steps of the hotel, dressed menacingly and always looking for a fight. In another instance, a black kid tries to sell "some righteous coke, bro!"[7] As was the case in previous decades, *The Punisher*'s creators located—and defined—blacks within a blighted urban milieu and stereotypical roles.

Further undermining the intentions behind this story line is a somewhat muddled moral struggle that ensnares Castle. As the story advances, Castle tries to live by the higher moral code of the black Cage. Cage insists that Castle not kill, an idea antithetical to his very existence as the Punisher, but also one that, far from earlier representations of such dyads, morally elevates the black character. As well, their argument about the root causes of inner-city problems serves to assert a concept of black personhood. When Castle angrily asserts, "Why don't you wake up, Cage? This ain't about race," Cage explains, "Movies and T.V. still hype brothers as the street thug, the hood, the man to fear. You know that look in the eyes of strangers. That feeling . . . It ain't about race, no—it's about image, and knowin' who you are, when no one else does." Castle is skeptical, asking, "Oh, and you know that because you're black?" Cage replies bluntly, "I know 'cause I was one of them—a hood. I'm proof there's a way out. And nobody has to die." The conversation leaves Castle to ponder his place in the world, thinking, "For him, it's about self-respect. For me it's simpler. Life and death."[8] Castle's realization here regarding not only Cage but black men in general and the ways in which society and media have served to denigrate black personhood again gestures toward a kind of nuance the series' creators sought to achieve.

Unfortunately, the upshot of this moral struggle falls prey once again to assumptions about the experience of ethnicity. For as much as the conversation above emphasizes black personhood and individuality, the full-est impact of this experience falls, as it did before in *Green Lantern/Green Arrow*, on a white hero: Castle. Castle continues his moral questioning, noting that he's different from Cage: "I know that any scum I let live to fight another day may kill more innocents—or shoot me in the back." Thus, as Cage tries to convince local kids that crime doesn't pay, Castle finds this all too preachy, and he hands a pistol to one local woman so she can defend herself when the need arises. Nonetheless, Castle slowly adapts to Cage's moral code as the story progresses. He begins to go on missions unarmed, demonstrating a real commitment to his new way of life.[9] Thus, Castle's dabbling in the black ghetto enacts a transformation in the anti-hero that reinscribes black identity and experience within those tropes of transformative "otherness" explicated by bell hooks: it assumes black experience solely exists to alter the white conscience and consciousness. This limited commitment to a representation of black experience that goes beyond the superficial and the stereotypical was ultimately paralleled in Marvel's truncation of this plot. Although the Punisher was transformed in issue #59, the cover of issue #62—with the once again white Punisher jumping down from above, almost upon the viewer, blasting away as the text reads simply, "He's back!"—demonstrated that any changes (either cosmetic or moral) in the Punisher would be short-lived.

Other white-to-nonwhite transitions did even less well. The arrival of the Japanese version of Betsy Braddock (a.k.a. Psylocke) in the pages of *Uncanny X-Men*, for instance, suggested a much less positive take on the matter, the hypersexualized nature of the replacement hero reducing her to little more than another objectified "Oriental" stereotype. While Psy-locke seemed to be empowered by her racial transformation—her psy-chic powers were amplified and she became a more effective fighter—her appearance undermined any sense of improvement, as race and gender worked together to flatten the character into an all too easily understood trope. Psylocke certainly achieves at a high level as a superhero, but she never escapes racialized understandings of Japanese and other Asian women.

In particular, understandings that intertwined sexuality and violence were explicitly on display from the start of her transformation. After a trip through the Siege Perilous, an extradimensional teleportation device, Betsy washes ashore without any memories of her past on an island near China and is found by Matsuo Tsurayaba, who places her mind into the brain-dead body of his Japanese lover, Kwannon, and then brainwashes her into becoming an assassin for the Hand.[10] Suddenly Japanese in ap-

Figure 6.2. The British-to-Japanese transformation of Psylocke fell victim from the start to stereotyped understandings of Asians in regard to both gender and violence. Here, in confronting her erstwhile teammate Colossus, Psylocke exhibits newfound hypersexuality emphasized by her petite size and revealing new outfit.

pearance, Psylocke showcases a similarly sudden hypersexuality, a pernicious assumption about Asian women earlier reflected in characters like the Avengers' Mantis. As we watch her "grow up" again during the brainwashing process, Betsy emerges into adulthood as a sexpot, her jumpsuit open to her navel, her long hair blowing in the breeze as she arches her back and purses her lips.[11] Alongside her newfound sexuality is a predilection for violence that is, again, based in racialized assumptions. She, for example, has to defeat—and kill—each of her teammates (in her mind) to finish her reprogramming, and she does so ruthlessly. Her showdown with Piotr Rasputin (a.k.a. Colossus) is especially revealing of what defines the reborn Psylocke. As she confronts her former teammate, the shirtless Piotr stands facing the reader, who sees Psylocke only from the back in her new skimpy getup. She is dwarfed by his size, emphasizing her petite figure. By issue's end, seemingly reprogrammed, Psylocke bows down obediently to the Mandarin, her "rightful lord and master." As Matsuo and the Mandarin gloat, the now-Asian Psylocke, face deeply shadowed, looks absolutely malevolent.[12]

As the story moves forward, the new Psylocke continues to embrace violence alongside her sexuality, further and inextricably meshing these two stereotypes. Assuming the role of Lady Mandarin, she demands fealty to Mandarin from local gang lords. When they refuse to comply, she cuts through the thugs ruthlessly. In the aftermath of battle, Lady Mandarin, Hong Kong stretched out behind her, revels in her power and gloats, "For all their vaunted power, how easily I broke them to my master's will! How glorious the triumph feels!"[13] The connection between her love of violence and her overplayed sexuality continues as the scene cuts to Matsuo's base, where Psylocke trains, taking on Hand ninjas. Fighting in her new uniform, a dark-blue, skintight tunic, Psylocke embraces a gratuitous sexuality. She easily defeats highly trained ninjas, using both martial arts and a willingness to trick her enemy (pretending to be injured, for example, to lure one ninja to his defeat). After the training session, Psylocke takes a bath, her head rolled back in the tub, breasts covered (barely) by the hot steam from the tub, a wet thigh poking above the water's surface. As she bathes, Matsuo stands in the background, observing the naked hero, who responds to his orders submissively. As she exits the bath and walks toward Matsuo, still naked, her body is almost totally exposed. In the final panel, Matsuo strokes her face, and Psylocke looks down again as she is forced to quietly admit that she serves the Hand "with all my heart."[14] By the end of this scene, the ruthless and sexualized Psylocke now additionally mimics the submissiveness often assumed to be present in Asian women.

Even after being freed from Matsuo's control, Psylocke's ensuing adventures continued to highlight this demeaning connection between her physical empowerment, her violence, and her sexuality. As she and Wolverine battle Matsuo and the Mandarin, Jim Lee draws Psylocke—as quickly became the norm—from behind and below, her fearsome fighting prowess always showcased hand in hand with her exotic, over-the-top sexuality.[15] When Psylocke, Wolverine, and Jubilee move on to their next adventure, Betsy's sexuality remains emphasized. When the trio go out to get some grub, Psylocke comes along but keeps her distance, sitting at another table in an absolutely ridiculous dress, the long, flowing skirt cut practically to her waist and the top of the dress cut to her navel, her breasts somehow impossibly covered as she leans back in her chair. After Wolverine is captured, the remaining duo go to battle, Psylocke shot from above, crouching in her thong and waiting to spring into action. As usual, she fights exceedingly well, but always framed by her sexuality.[16]

And as Psylocke moved into the new and massively popular *X-Men* title in the early 1990s, she continued to exist primarily as a Japanese sex object, if an incredibly lethal one. For example, when an emergency alarm summons her from her laps in the pool, Betsy arrives wearing a very revealing bikini. She then poses, as always, like a swimsuit model, hips thrust back, chest thrust forward. Her hypersexuality also results in an extended flirtation with Scott Summers (a.k.a. Cyclops), even though he is in a relationship with Jean Grey at this time. In one instance, while the X-Men enjoy a day off at the lake, Betsy interrupts a conversation between Jean and Scott, emerging from the lake, her one-piece suit clinging to her suggestively. Accentuating her figure, Betsy reaches behind her head to play with her hair, adopting yet another very seductive pose.[17] What progress Psylocke's transformation into a Japanese woman might have signaled, her violent, sexualized, and otherwise-stereotyped representation contradicted.

At least one such transformation of a white hero managed to dodge the worst pitfalls of this troubling trope, even if problems still surfaced. In Marvel's *Thunderbolts*, Abe Jenkins (a.k.a. Mach-2) was altered to appear as a black man to hide from the authorities. This change was only used in a very limited way to address—not unproblematically—white racism. When Jenkins reveals his new visage, his then girlfriend Songbird faints, setting up a subplot of her coming to terms with his dark skin.[18] Roughly a year later, this subplot would resolve when the two passionately kiss and Songbird offers the following admission about coming to terms with his appearance: "To tell you the honest truth, I don't know if I really ever will be—but I sure am okay with the whole heart thing . . . and when you come right down to it . . . that makes everything else not matter much at all!"[19] Here, Songbird's confession echoes those paeans of the white liberal conscience that pervaded series like *Green Lantern/Green Arrow* in the 1970s; she ultimately excuses her aversion toward his racialized appearance by dismissing it as irrelevant to what's inside and thus behind that surface.

Jenkins's transformation would be deployed similarly in addressing more obvious discrimination. The issue following the reveal of his new look sees him attempt to buy a new computer chip at an electronics store; the store's owner balks at the idea, assuming it is beyond what he can afford solely based on his appearance.[20] Months later, Jenkins returns to this same store, now responding to a "Help Wanted" sign. Recognizing Jenkins from their earlier encounter, the owner strives to redeem himself, describing his regret for his previous assumption, which he describes now as "a dumb, rude thing to do." Somewhat detracting from this lesson is the fact that prior to the owner's retraction, Jenkins proves his tech savvy by upgrading a computer chip, thus hearkening back to ways in which blacks, to foster such "brotherhood" as the owner now embodies, had to first prove themselves.[21]

Such literal transformations, given their troubling nature, were more the exception than the rule, however; much more common at Marvel and DC was the actual substitution of a nonwhite character for a historically white one. Such swapping of the characters behind a hero's mask was not new. Twice, for example, Tony Stark stepped away from being Iron Man and was replaced in the role, first by the former boxer Eddie March and later, and for much longer, by Jim Rhodes.[22] Monica Rambeau's adoption of the Captain Marvel identity is another early example at Marvel. And built into the mythos of DC's Green Lantern was the idea of such substitutions, precipitating the debut of John Stewart in the role. In the late 1980s and early 1990s, however, substituting established heroes became a definite trend. At Marvel, both the original Thor and Captain America had newcomers in these roles. DC's substitutions were even more prevalent, as practically all of their major heroes—Superman, Batman, Wonder Woman, Green Lantern, and Green Arrow, to name a few—were replaced by alternate versions at one time or another. Within this context, the substitution of ethnic characters for traditionally white heroes established itself as another method by which comics and superhero popular culture more generally sought to foster diversity.

James Rhodes's second stint, beginning in 1992, as an Armored Avenger, escaped the problematic racialized tropes of the temporarily black Punisher, but found others. Dubbing himself War Machine and donning a unique black-and-white armored suit, Rhodes in this second go-around appeared poised to become an independent and thus forward-looking character. Instead, Rhodes struggled to escape other old stereotypes, trapped by long-standing but hardly empowering images of anger, objectification, and subordination that hardly constituted a uniquely realized individual. Instead, Rhodes remained trapped by racialized understandings of his community that did not permit him to be seen as a singular individual.

Rhodes indeed comes off as a stereotypically rage-filled and inarticulate African American throughout the story arc. When he learns of his close friend's death, Rhodes explodes at televised news coverage; "Bull!" he shouts as he smashes the TV into silence with a lamp and curses everyone he can think of to blame: "%$#& the doctors," "and %$#& you, too, Tony—for dyin' on me."[23] When not cursing, Rhodes seems barely articulate, haltingly expressing himself with words. Rhodes's eulogy for his friend and boss who has just promoted him to run the massive company consists of two bland sentences and, "Goodbye, m'man. We're gonna miss you." His first meeting with the board of directors as CEO of Stark Enterprises lasts less than ten sentences, his main point being that he will try to stay out of their way as they run the company, thus disempowering himself almost immediately, and not only linguistically. Unfortunately, when he does speak, Rhodes is apt to slip into a stereotypical patois, dropping phrases like "Yo momma" or "My momma said there'd be days like this."[24]

Additionally, the War Machine story arc presented Rhodes as an objectified body. Most prominently, this occurred in his relationship with Rae LaCoste, who is white. When dinner quickly leads to something considerably more romantic, the scene cuts to Jim and Rae in a bedroom, Rae, wrapped only in a sheet, sitting on a bed and Jim, shirtless and muscled, in pajama pants, looking pensive. When she asks what is bothering him, Jim explains, "I just hope you know what you're getting into." Rae seems to not understand, and Jim adds, "This complexion doesn't come from Coppertone. There folks that'd say—." But Rae interrupts to condemn such bigots, arguing, "There are people who think the earth is flat. I don't pay much attention to them, either. Besides, I like your complexion." Jim abandons his objections at this point, but their romantic moment remains plagued by the emphasis on—and thus objectification of—Rhodes's body.[25]

Finally, Rhodes struggles throughout the story arc to assert any real sense of control over his future. He remains subordinated at the company. As Stark has explained in his last will and testament, the company has plenty of people who can run the business; he wants the apparently not-ready-to-run-a-business-yet Rhodes around to act as a vaguely defined "moral rudder." Such subordinate positioning persists even after Stark's inevitable return. After discovering that Stark is still alive, Rhodes is furious, finally noting angrily that he is sick and tired "of bein' [Stark's] sidekick." However, such statements at best only paid lip service to Rhodes achieving any kind of independence and agency. Acknowledging that Rhodes is indeed leaving, Stark urges him to take the War Machine armor. Rhodes protests that he doesn't want it, but Stark knows better. "We both know that's not true," Stark tells the angry Rhodes. "Take it. Use it [and] be better than me." Rhodes remains resistant, saying simply, "@&$% you," as he stalks off. He realizes that Stark is right, however, and eventually takes the War Machine armor, thus acquiescing to the idea that Stark knows him better than he does himself. If his subsequent decision to contact and briefly join the West Coast Avengers shows a glimpse of agency, his life remains largely directed by Stark, as further evidenced by his departure from the team when Iron Man/Stark returns.[26]

Such blinkered replacements would persist into the new century, and, perhaps tellingly, in much lower-tier heroes than before. Debuting in 2007, the Sonia Sato version of Judomaster at DC offered little beyond common stereotypes and racialized humor. When going into battle, for example, she wisely advises her Justice Society of America teammates, "He who is prudent and lies in wait for an enemy who is not will be victorious." When asked if the quote comes from *The Art of War*, she replies, "Fortune cookie." Otherwise, Judomaster is most noted for her struggles with the English language, sometimes speaking to her teammates in Japanese.[27] When she has to deliver a eulogy for Damage, a fallen teammate, Judomaster focuses her eulogy around her ineloquence, apologizing haltingly, "My English is not very good." Although she promises to remember her fallen comrade with her actions (given her struggles with words), living to honor Damage does not come naturally to Judomaster, who, in a fairly stereotypical way, grieves initially by seeking revenge.[28]

Another replacement superhero emerged in 2006 when DC's venerable Uncle Sam—the embodiment of America—recruited a new team of Freedom Fighters. The new supersquad included the Native American John Trujillo, who replaced the original Black Condor but struggled to establish himself as a unique individual under the weight of stereotyped understandings of indigenous communities. His origin story, for instance, is steeped in reductive tropes of Native Americans that, while seemingly more positive than in the past, hardly humanized Trujillo. Indeed, the tale is grounded in the history of the Old West, a sepia tint to the artwork driving the point home, as well as a primitivist depiction of Native American culture. During the Civil War, the narrator notes, "legendary 'Indian fighter' Colonel Kit Carson led a brutal campaign against the Navajo of the Southwest" that resulted in their being confined to the brutalities of reservation life. When the Navajo eventually returned home to rebuild their way of life, they found themselves menaced by cattlemen wanting to steal their land. Faced with this threat, a Navajo youngster, wanting to aid his people, was transformed by "Tocotl, the mystical Spider Woman," into the Black Condor. Given this last bit of detail, it is perhaps no surprise that the modern-day version of the Black Condor also feeds into assumptions about Native American mysticism. In the present, Trujillo reenacts the same ritual, as the time has arrived, again, for someone to "seek the power of the Black Condor to defend the land and her people."[29]

Figure 6.3. The arrival of a race-swapped Black Condor communicated a host of stereotyped understandings of Native Americans. The hero's imposing physique, glowering red eyes, and face paint suggested his proclivity for violence. His explanations of his powers, meanwhile, grounded him in a stereotyped Native American affinity for nature. Finally, his penchant to threaten played to long-held attitudes about Native American savagery.

After joining up with the Freedom Fighters, Black Condor played to another Native American stereotype, that of the savage rooted in nature. The Black Condor looks very "native": eyes and lower jaw painted black, hair cut into a Mohawk, a thunderbird painted on his chest. As the hero arrives to his team for the first time, the reader looks up at a menacing Black Condor, wings out, all muscles and attitude, his eyes glowing red from behind his stereotypical face paint. Black Condor routs the enemy, declaring, "I am the Black Condor. . . . I draw my strength from the earth below me and the sky above. Collect your men and leave or worse things will happen to you." Having again established the assumed connection between Native Americans and the earth or nature, the Black Condor's threat to the fleeing villains—"I will paint my face with the blood of my enemies"—then plays on the trope of Native American savagery.[30] An ensuing showdown then links these stereotypes that continue to define him as something less than an individual. As he takes on one enemy, he, in response to his godlike opponents, describes himself as a "god killer"; in the final showdown, he boasts, "Your numbers are meaningless. The wind knows no opposition."[31] Here, his connections to nature and to "native savagery" work together to flatten him into a recognizable type.

The arrival of Black Condor among the Freedom Fighters also generates various problematic tensions within the team, not unlike John Proudstar did among the X-Men almost two decades earlier. When Uncle Sam introduces Black Condor to the team, Trujillo is unimpressed, standing with his muscular arms folded across his chest and glowering at them.[32] Trujillo also sparks sexual tensions. Phantom Lady, though unimpressed with Trujillo's tact, cannot help admiring his body, noting that "he's definitely got the raw sexuality working for him." Later, Black Condor seeks out Phantom Lady. When the ensuing conversation grows heated, Phantom Lady lunges forward and kisses Black Condor. He rebuffs her, delivering instead a lecture on her childishness and selfishness.[33] In these encounters, Black Condor both initiates conflict and appears as another objectified and sexualized ethnic body, thus remaining as counterproductive as many other such replacement heroes.

If these examples of replacement heroes in the late twentieth and early twenty-first centuries establish the shortcomings inherent in this pattern, there are also those who, it is important to note, managed to overcome at least some of them. While hardly untrammeled beacons of racial equality, such characters stand as signposts along the way to changing representations of race that reflected a maturing national conversation.

While avoiding the objectification that hemmed in Psylocke, the second Doctor Light's origin story seemed poised to compromise her representation of Asian identity in other ways. From the start, Dr. Kimiyo Hoshi (a.k.a. Doctor Light), first appearing in DC's *Crisis on Infinite Earths*, is a stereotypically cold and angry Asian woman, even if well accomplished in the professional world. When a male colleague panics as the end of the world looms, Hoshi chastises him. She brooks no dissent, going on to say, "Silence, you miserable toad. We were given the assignment of charting this phenomenon . . . not of giving in to your baser instincts." Nor was such emotion (or lack thereof) restricted to her work. While her father expresses disappointment in a daughter he "did not raise . . . to be so cold," Hoshi is unmoved, describing her father as being "as weak as [the other scientists]. No wonder mother left you. All right, go! Run to your loved ones—leave me alone! If I am to perish, I do not want to die in the midst of cowards."[34] Such a cold if not outright cruel attitude puts Hoshi/Doctor Light in a line of descent of such similar Asian figures as the Dragon Lady.

Embarking on her new career as a hero does little at first to mellow

Hoshi and thus ameliorate these issues. After being transformed into the new Doctor Light, our hero arrives to save the DC Universe. She shows up, of course, belligerent. As some heroes mistakenly attack, she yells (in Japanese): "No! You stupid cretins—you don't realize what you are doing." When the heroes, not understanding Japanese, don't respond appropriately, she screams, "You fools will just have to learn what the new Doctor Light can do!" Superman can understand her, but that hardly changes her demeanor. Instead, she lectures the Man of Steel: "Cannot any of you think, man? I tell you, this world is populated by morons."[35] Even when saved by another hero, Doctor Light remains ungratefully angry, yelling, "Unhand me, dolt. No one touches Dr. Light! I am capable of saving myself!" When mobs of people start to walk to their doom under the Psycho-Pirate's control, Doctor Light is contemptuous of them even as she saves them: "Instead of creating a wall of light blocking the fray, I should let them die."[36]

Crisis on Infinite Earths ultimately allowed Doctor Light some redemption from this stereotyped start. A key turning point in her ascension to selfless hero arrives when she flies off with a squadron of heroes to battle the Anti-Monitor. As she watches Supergirl sacrifice her life to save Superman and destroy the Anti-Monitor's machinery, Doctor Light observes, "Sh-she is a hero . . . totally selfless and concerned only with others. While I have wasted away my life with selfishness." Supergirl, she adds, has "shown me the truth!" And in the end, Doctor Light plays a significant role in defeating the Anti-Monitor, becoming a real hero.[37] Though perhaps something of a middling gesture, Doctor Light's final redemption and heroism at least shifts a significant aspect of her character away from stereotypes in which she was initially grounded.

Another replacement hero to debut not long after Doctor Light traces a similar narrative trajectory. Yolanda Montez arrived as the white-to-Latina legacy hero Wildcat in Infinity, Inc., a team comprising various descendants of the original Justice Society of America. Readers meet the new Wildcat in her civilian identity when she sneaks into a wedding reception. Without an invitation and facing a twelve-foot wall, the immediately sexualized Montez gracefully somersaults over the barrier, all the more impressively while wearing an impossibly revealing outfit: a leopard-print top barely held together by strings running across her large breasts and a long, flowing skirt that rides high up her thighs.[38] Such objectification was not limited to her civilian attire, as she sported a skintight bodysuit as Wildcat that, as Frederick Luis Aldama explains, emphasized her physical appearance over whatever agency she might have possessed.[39]

Figure 6.4. The white-to-Latina replacement hero Wildcat debuted to myriad stereotypes—hypersexuality, impetuousness, and bravado, among them—and her code-switching served to remind readers of her "difference." While later stories helped to humanize the new Wildcat, at least a bit, Yolanda Montez suggests the vexed understandings of race in the turn-of-the-century United States.

In addition to being defined by her appearance, Montez's impetuousness and bravado comport with traditional Latinx stereotypes. When the Infinitors investigate shark attacks, the new Wildcat sneaks along, even though she is not officially part of the team yet. When Nuklon, another member, is upset, she replies, "Chill out, amigo! I'm practically one of the team, right?" When he promises not to "snitch" on her, Yolanda tells Nuklon, "You're puro corazón . . . all heart!"[40] As these examples also demonstrate, Wildcat code-switches frequently between English and Spanish, a clear and ever-present signal of her difference. When the heroes at the wedding are whisked away by Harbinger as part of the *Crisis* story line, Montez says, "¡Parece mentira! [It seems incredible!]" Later, when battling vicious, gigantic sharks, Wildcat is in deep trouble, screaming, "¡Ay de mí!" As she swims for her life, she thinks, "Andalé [hurry], Yolanda!" And, finally, as more sharks surround her, Yolanda thinks, "Ahora estoy a las puertas de la muerte de seguro! [Now I'm at death's door for sure!]" This code-switching is so identifiable and thus defining that her godfather (and the original Wildcat), Ted Grant, recognizes Montez in her costume after hearing her speak in Spanish.[41]

Like Doctor Light, Montez/Wildcat enacts a redemptive narrative arc that more fully humanizes her. Montez, in contrast to her cocksure bravado, comes to understand that she must—as her forebears in the 1970s and 1980s comics books had done—prove herself to her teammates. As she first arrives on the scene in *Crisis on Infinite Earths*, Wildcat watches members of the All-Star Squadron from afar. As she prepares to introduce herself, she says, "I am un poco asustada, scared they won't accept me." Watching Green Arrow, Atom, and Liberty Belle—all "legends," she thinks—Montez expresses a lack of confidence: "And I . . . I am a cambio . . . a . . . replacement for one of them." She overhears the Atom complaining, feeling his age and upset by the original Wildcat's catastrophic injuries. "There will never be another like him," he says. "Wildcat is gone." In response, Montez thinks, "Not gone, Atom . . . I'm here, but that isn't good enough, and I know that now." As she climbs away, into the darkness, she thinks, "I'll prove myself worthy of the name Wildcat. And when I do . . . I'll come forth. And if I don't . . . I can't . . . you'll never see Yolanda Montez again."[42] But readers did, of course, see Montez as Wildcat in the future, as she proved her worth in the *Crisis* story line, standing "ready to prove herself and fight."[43] Likewise, her development proved her to be at least a little more than a Latina stereotype.

The arrival in 2006 of Ryan Choi as DC's new Atom even more thoroughly suggested the possibilities in legacy heroes, although his creators stumbled at times in reducing Choi to the model-minority stereotype. An idea that gained increasing popularity in the 1970s and afterward, the model-minority stereotype was first popularized by William Petersen in a 1966 *New York Times Magazine* article that highlighted Japanese American upward mobility; here, he pointed out, was a group that had faced the zenith of racism—they had been locked away by the government during World War II, after all—but had succeeded nonetheless, rising to economic and academic success after the war. Such praise, however, was mustered mainly to attack other nonwhite groups that had not similarly risen. Reacting against student radicalism and what he took to be eroding American standards, Petersen promoted a racist view of society and especially African Americans. It is worth pointing out, too, that Petersen's argument shortchanged Asian Americans, ignoring, of course, those within the so-called model minority who did not make it (as well as the success of those African Americans who did).[44] Ultimately failing to see such individuals as individuals—as opposed to relatively similar actors defined by their group—would prove a recurring problem for Americans, even as they moved into the twenty-first century.

Thus, when readers initially meet Choi as a child in Hong Kong, he is a classic model-minority overachiever, taking kung fu classes and excelling academically as a very bright goody two-shoes. He worries about respecting his teacher while other students don't. When his classmates list their heroes—Bruce Lee and Jackie Chan—Ryan picks Feng Jishen, who, he must explain to his befuddled pals, is the guy who invented the rocket more than a millennium earlier. Flashing forward fourteen years, the story shows Dr. Ryan Choi arriving in Ivy Town, where his boss, Dean Mayland, reinforces the overachievement stereotype associated with the model minority, observing how young the newly arrived professor looks, praising how well he speaks English, and complaining that Choi is "so accomplished at less than half my age."[45]

The model-minority motif created problems that were only somewhat counterbalanced by the coming-of-age story that simultaneously functioned in the new Atom's adventures. A nerd with seemingly no friends, Choi is bullied in high school, living the stereotypical experience of the teenager. His refusal to do as he's told earns Ryan two beatings a day until he finally gives in and does the bullies' homework. When Ryan attends a school dance and sees his dream girl, he is too nervous to speak intelligibly. Bullied and unable to speak to girls, Ryan represents a universal story of teenagers. As readers relive Ryan's ensuing beating at the hands of his three tormentors in a heavy rainstorm at the dance, the hero narrates: "Just a little fellow, really, against three bigger, older, crueler guys. This scene has happened in every country in the world. That gave me no solace."[46]

The creators of the new Atom, in working to expose prejudice, also occasionally fell into long-standing stereotypical tropes. For example, Choi, not unlike Jim Rhodes and Psylocke, finds himself repeatedly objectified. Even as college coeds and his colleagues admire his body in seemingly flattering ways, such attention threatened to reduce the Asian American from agent to object. The female students on campus are smitten by the handsome new professor, one describing him as a "hottie." Later, in the aftermath of Choi's first battle as Atom (versus a hungry rat), he grows to normal size at an awkward moment, suddenly appearing naked. He is embarrassed as two female students walk by outside the window, one singing out, "Hope to see even more of you on campus!" While fending off the advances of students, Choi also must deal with the aggressive Professor Zuel, who demands that they go to the drive-in to see a horror double feature that night. There, Zuel jumps on top of him, although her sexual aggression is momentarily derailed when—possessed by M'Nagalah—she suddenly grows to an enormous height of thirty feet, puts Choi in a plastic bubble, and swallows him![47]

At other points in the series, however, the creators address racism directly and more thoughtfully. The series at times, for instance, invoked

Figure 6.5. Whereas the arrival of Ryan Choi as the new Atom suggested that race-swapped superheroes might address issues of race more thoughtfully, the series stumbled at times. Here, as female students gawk at and catcall the naked hero, Choi is reduced from agent to object, a fate that also befell replacement heroes like Psylocke and War Machine.

earlier forms of racism in order to critique and/or interrogate them. One such explicit example is when our hero's archenemy, Dwarfstar, plots revenge on Choi, whom he calls a "little Chinese monkey." Such racist attitudes and the exploitation that resulted are also tied to American history in one convoluted story involving time travel. As he battles three cowboys from the past, still not understanding why they are after him, the Atom thinks, "My people . . . they built the railroads that helped make this country"; but, he observes, despite the contributions of Chinese Americans to the building of the United States, "in the cowboy shows, we're always the cook."[48]

The series likewise implicitly challenges the "perpetual foreigner" trope that was so much a part of previous Asian heroes, such as Marvel's Shang-Chi and DC's Karate Kid. Aided by the obvious diversity of his surroundings—illustrations of Ivy Town's streets and its university's classrooms typically include multiethnic tableaux—Choi adjusts to life in America, though not without difficulty. The English language and American customs prove difficult to master. Ryan is mystified by backslapping and wonders about the term "sweetcheeks": "Of all the American sexy compliments, . . . the one that's the most baffling to me. . . . Even with a lifetime of American TV, I'm not sure how to respond . . . Ignore her? Call her sweetcheeks back?" When confronted by the cowboys from the past, Ryan realizes, "Holy Pete. My mom was right. America still is like *Bonanza*!" But the Wild West experience also convinces Choi of the need to expand his vocabulary: "I've got to learn some good English curse words!"[49]

Despite the many obstacles to his adjustment, Choi quickly feels at home in the United States, overcoming any distance that exists as represented by how he comes to embrace his superheroic role. Choi's success in adapting to life in America and especially as the new Atom occurs in part because of the Lighter Than Air Society, a diverse group of Ivy University scientists who agree to become Ryan's support team. Although Choi comes to rely on his colleagues to solve a host of problems, he does so in ways that do not diminish his stature as a hero; while he needs their help, the Lighter Than Air Society clearly serves a subordinate role to Choi. The scientists themselves acknowledge Choi as their leader, working on his ideas and at his direction. As a society member explains, expressing great respect for Ryan, "We couldn't hold him back . . . That young man was built for . . . investigating great things."[50] Choi is ultimately a hero in control of his destiny; though initially anchored in part by "model minority" and "perpetual foreigner" tropes, he ultimately transcends them, and so is defined not by his ethnic association but by his individualism.

A "Different Mirror": Replacement Heroes and the "Peter Parker" Trope

As the 1990s arrived, Americans faced looming demographic changes with more than a little anxiety. A cover story in *Time*, for example, noted that within half a century or so whites might very well no longer constitute a majority of Americans; such a transformation, some feared, would create a "minority majority," with potentially ominous consequences for white Americans and "their" country. Foundational to such concerns, issues of identity confounded Americans. As *Time* suggested, such a demographic shift raised basic questions about a national identity rooted in the American psyche, as well as individual perceptions of the nation that were ineluctably bound up in "their idea of what it is to be an American."[51]

Scholars weighed in. In the context of what came to be known as the "browning" of America, some expressed deep concerns about the future. Arthur M. Schlesinger Jr.'s 1992 book, *The Disuniting of America*, presented the looming demographic change as part of an even larger threat, warning in loaded language of an all-out assault by "the cult of ethnicity" on American identity. Somewhat defensively, Schlesinger argued that the essential process of assimilation—which created a shared language, institutions, ideals, and thus unity—was threatened by encroaching ethnic separatists who wanted to deny the United States' European roots. "It may be too bad that dead white European males have played so large a role in shaping our culture," Schlesinger wrote. "But that's the way it is. One cannot erase history." Although Schlesinger concluded his book a bit more optimistically by noting that Americanization had not lost its power and might yet defeat what he perceived as the ethnic forces working to undermine the melting-pot ideal, *The Disuniting of America* cast a suspicious eye on the growing diversity of the United States.[52]

In *A Different Mirror*, published one year after Schlesinger's book, Ronald Takaki saw opportunity where Schlesinger perceived threat. Arguing that changing demographics should lead historians to see the past differently, Takaki took on Schlesinger as well as similarly leaning scholars, such as Allan Bloom and E. D. Hirsch. Takaki adopted a comparative approach to capture more fully and meaningfully the history of "the mosaic called America." By listening to and thus better understanding the stories of a wide range of ethnic groups that helped to build the United States, he averred, Americans could better understand their multicultural present and future. Doing so, Takaki contended, was essential if Americans hoped to navigate the clear tensions generated by demography in turn-of-the-century America. History could be a springboard to a broader social justice, he suggested, if the histories of minority groups were better understood as the history of America and, thus, if minorities were—finally—granted some degree of agency in their own lives and in American history. Moving in this direction, he concluded, offered Americans a chance to see themselves anew and thus to eschew Schlesinger's more fearful vision.[53]

Takaki's more hopeful vision of multicultural amity was reflected in another group of replacement heroes, who often employed a well-known comic book trope—Peter Parker's fraught journey to heroism—to present replacement heroes as authentic individuals and heroes. Peter's character arc needed little explaining to comic book readers, nor likely to most Americans, who had at least some inkling of the cultural icon's origins. When Peter receives his powers from a radioactive spider's bite, his first instincts are selfish; he uses them to make money and to better his own life. When his self-absorption leads him to let a fleeing criminal escape, he thinks little of it. When the very same criminal later kills his Uncle Ben, however, Peter belatedly realizes the larger lesson: "With great power

Figure 6.6. The arrival of Steel as a replacement Superman at first suggested little change. As he emerges from the rubble of the inner city, the hero is shadowed, muscular, and snarling. While the initial impression thus cast back to the 1970s and to figures like Luke Cage, the new hero's journey to heroism ultimately created a humanized individual who was not defined only by his race.

there must also come—great responsibility!"[54] While he does not emerge a perfect hero thereafter and instead often barely manages to juggle a range of problems—school, jobs, girls, and whatnot—readers gravitated toward his coming-of-age arc. Parker's story, perhaps at times inadvertently, provided creators with a mirror by which readers might see ethnic heroes differently, creating a narrative guise of sorts that—unlike the dehumanizing guises noted in earlier chapters—actually included newcomers as valuable and human parts of the superhero community.

The "Death of Superman" story line, for example, offered its creators an opportunity to introduce Steel, an African American legacy hero for the Man of Steel, who borrowed mightily from the Peter Parker model. Here, the Metropolis high-steel worker John Henry Irons serves as a black replacement, inspired to take on this new role after having been saved by Superman.[55] While the adventures of Steel at times struggled to escape old tropes of the black superhero, the use of the traditional Peter Parker

arc (especially in tracing a hero's coming to grips with the moral requirements of his newly acquired powers) distinguished Steel from many of his
African American forebears.

The arrival of John Henry Irons at first hardly seemed progressive. Instead, Irons appeared in familiar dehumanized forms. As the police arrive
at the aftermath of Superman's fatal battle, sirens wailing, a black hand
arises from the rubble. Successive panels depict, first, ominous eyes in a
completely shadowed face glaring out of the debris; next, a muscular upper
torso, still deeply shadowed; and finally, a full-page splash revealing the
new hero, a hypermuscular black man in shredded overalls. As he snarls
over his shoulder, the first images of Irons evoked earlier portrayals of
Luke Cage, a barely articulate and hypermasculine black figure standing,
barely clothed, in the rubble of the inner city.[56] Such objectification would
continue, as Steel becomes an object of the feminine gaze throughout his
adventures. Early on, women ogle our hero as he walks the mean streets
of the city. Later, his impressive physique is emphasized when he flies into
town, unknowingly observed by the police lieutenant Shauna Beryl, whom
he works with from time to time, and her friend. Both women gaze admir-
ingly at Steel, the friend wondering, "He as big and strong as he looks?"[57]

In addition to this objectification, Steel remained clearly connected
to the stereotypical comic book "ghetto" that black heroes have occupied
since the 1960s. As the planet faces obliteration and Coast City is literally
wiped off the face of the map, Steel takes on some local drug kingpins before only belatedly heading to Coast City to see what he might do there.[58]
In the aftermath of Superman's return, Steel returns to the inner city, this
time in Washington, DC, a city that, he observes, "still feels like—and
smells like—home."[59] Furthermore, the first issue of his series contrasts
Irons's neighborhood with the rest of Washington. Images present the
Capitol building, a bright sun behind it, and white politicians and tourists
in a pristine city. The book then juxtaposes this picture to streets full of
litter and impoverished people, both black and white, as the narrator describes what life looks like "in the shadow of power—the hood of [Wash-
ington, DC, which] boils in poverty, despair and anger."[60] Five issues into
his own series, Steel remained anchored to the stereotypical urban milieu,
thinking, "My job is on the streets. To . . . stop the madness that's destroying so many lives."[61] These streets are likewise populated by flatly stereotypical characters. Most often and obviously, undeveloped gang members
and drug dealers reinforce long-held images of the city, populating an area
where "the fast money of easy street doesn't trickle down," leaving only
"alleys shadowed by the bombed-out shells of ancient tenements." Amidst

the destitution, a shirtless, animalistic gangbanger with shoulder-length hair grimaces as he interrupts a friend, his voice dripping with a ghetto-inspired fright: "We been stalking the Man o' Steel for a week now! . . . . It's time to get on wit' da action."[62]

Despite these fraught beginnings, Steel ultimately rises above such stereotyped understandings. Of the four competing replacements for Superman, Steel is the one most evocative of Clark Kent's heroic spirit and selfless morality. In this, Steel's creators employed a coming-of-age arc focused on the moral dimensions of the hero that embedded Steel in the larger community of superheroes. Irons, for example, gains complexity as readers learn that he, like Spider-Man, is motivated largely by guilt owing to the results of his earlier work as a weapons engineer. In scenes almost too numerous to count, Steel laments his professional accomplishments, blaming himself for "so many killed" and expressing anger that "the weapons that I helped create are killing kids in my home town!" He openly admits to his complicity in these atrocities, regretfully thinking, "I hadn't really understood what I was doing [as a weapons developer]. Maybe I didn't want to understand. I made too good a living." Having seen the damage caused by his weapons to innocents, Steel makes clear his altruistic mission: eradicating these weapons from the streets.[63]

Irons's overwhelming sense of guilt suggests and helps to elucidate another quality that makes him more like his fellow heroes: his deeply held sense of morality. Steel's interaction with a more violent Superman replacement highlights his morality, as he argues against unnecessarily killing bad guys. As he explains, "The real Superman wouldn't have killed that punk! He never countered the threat of violence with unnecessary force. You may look the part, but you're just a cold-blooded fraud!" Steel's morality also leads him to risk his own life to save the lives of others, and he willingly takes on what he assumes to be a suicide mission, again likening himself to the original John Henry as he flies into a giant machine to save the earth.[64] In this way, Steel comes to understand his role as protecting a "family [that] encompasses all of humanity."[65]

Irons's intelligence further distanced him from reductive understandings of black personhood. During the "Return of Superman" story arc, for example, Steel reasons out the machinations of the evil Superman replacement. He also devises thoughtful plans and again echoes Spidey in deploying the age-old strategy of angering the villain and thus provoking him to inadvertently reveal his plans.[66] This intelligence was encouraged from the beginning of Irons's life, when his grandfather tells him the story of John Henry and explains that the family hopes Irons will use his intelligence "to become the machine's master."[67] Here, in basing Steel's portrayal in this common comic book trope, his creators further ensconced him within the tradition of the classic superhero.

Steel becomes even further removed from the reifying stereotypes that preceded him as he struggles with crises of conscience. Unlike the classic Superman, Steel explains, "I'll fight for truth and justice . . . but my fight may have to be outside the law."[68] As his family is attacked, Steel drifts from the Superman ideal, thinking about killing his nemesis, Colonel Weston.[69] When he catches Weston, Steel threatens to kill him by dropping him from the sky if the colonel doesn't spill the beans on his operations. Steel then drops him, but catches Weston before impact (after the colonel has provided the information Steel wants). While Lieutenant Beryl is pleased to see that Steel is indeed "one of the good guys," Steel replies, "It was touch and go there for a while."[70] In flirting with illegality, Steel brings not only an edginess to his heroism but also a complexity to his character, for example when he notes, in future adventures, the need to avoid legal constraints and later again flies a criminal into the air to extort information.[71] Steel's adventures thus portray him as neither a staunch, law-abiding superhero, nor an over-the-top violent vigilante; instead, he is someone trying to navigate between such extremes and thus to stake out his own morality.

The complexity of Steel's character was matched by the African American Firestorm, who took over for the white Ronnie Raymond in 2004. As with Steel and other replacement heroes, Firestorm's creators were self-conscious in their efforts to address race. For instance, a 2006 story line brought the new Firestorm, Jason Rusch, to Capitol Hill. As his white ally, Senator Lorraine Reilly, makes a speech, our hero sits to the side, looking disheveled after a recent battle. After her talk, three older, white colleagues speculate about her relationship with the black youth. One suggests that Jason's presence must be part of "some kind of Big Brother thing." Jason, aware of this unwelcome attention, notes that Lorraine's fellow senators don't seem to like him. Lorraine replies, "They're good people. But as tolerant and liberal as they are—sometimes they're just not used to dealing with real, live examples of the citizens they claim to represent."[72] Here, the comic intentionally exposes the kinds of limitations dogging liberalism since World War II.

Firestorm's origins take place in a familiar urban ghetto—in this instance an economically devastated Detroit—but the setting hardly defines the hero.[73] Indeed, if the ghetto is expected, the black kid living in it—Jason Rusch—is not, being immediately established as more than just the stereotypical thug. Instead, in tying Rusch to a coming-of-age story arc, the creators make Jason more than just a typed black character. Thus, readers meet the hero as an inner-city youth working hard, in classic Peter Parker style, to scrape together enough savings to start college. For example, Jason's sense of success in finding a job, which an amused friend describes as transforming him into a "celebrity" while also "makin' some respectable bank," is quickly extinguished by the image of Jason dressed as a giant chicken, advertising Ho-Ho Charlie's Chicken Shack in the muggy heat of a Michigan summer. Like Parker, Jason here exhibits a similar hard luck. Furthermore, Jason, again like Parker, cannot talk to his crush at work, coming off even more relatably.[74]

Too, Jason's problems cut as deeply as Peter Parker's. While Peter has tragically lost both his parents, Jason is missing his mother, who left some time ago, leaving him with his father, an abusive man who beats and bullies him. In one particularly jarring scene, Jason comes home to his father, who berates his son for not paying his rent. Jason's timid explanations don't mollify his father, who just grows angrier, eventually shoving his son to the floor. Jason, clearly affected by years of abuse, meekly cleans up and offers to make dinner for his father.[75] Even more unfortunately, while Peter Parker can turn to the miserly J. Jonah Jameson for a (legitimate) job, Jason Rusch, desperate for money, seeks extra income by going to work for a local thug, Stevie Golek.[76]

This coming-of-age narrative similarly structures Jason's heroic adventures. When an unexplained, blinding flash of light brings him the powers of Firestorm, he embraces—but struggles to master—his new powers. As survivors flee, Firestorm appears for the first time, standing defiantly in a full-page splash, one fist raised threateningly, the reader looking up at an imposing Firestorm. His projected confidence belies his limited mastery of his new powers, however, as he quickly realizes he does not understand or know how to control them. The new hero gradually masters his powers, figuring out how to merge with another person to become Firestorm (as he cannot become the hero without making eye contact with someone else), how to "see inside" the molecular structures of objects, and how to return to his normal state.[77] At each step, Jason demonstrates not only this common story but, even more significantly, the common and thus human desire and willingness to shape his own future.

As he seizes control of his destiny, Rusch, like Steel, suffers a humanizing crisis of conscience as he tries to figure out how best to use his new power. Angered by the thought that his friend Mick pities him, Jason pulls Mick into his Firestorm persona and storms off on an adventure that sug-

Figure 6.7. Much like Steel, the new Firestorm's initial appearance seemed to suggest that old stereotypes of the angry black "buck" still predominated. Here, the new Firestorm embodies rage and physical threat, the reader looking up at the glowering Firestorm, his raised fist driving home the threat he poses. The series that followed, however, used the Spider-Man trope to humanize and complicate Jason Rusch and his alter ego.

gests how Jason might become corrupted by his powers, clearly playing on issues of power and responsibility also endemic to the Peter Parker/ Spider-Man model. Firestorm visits a porn shoot on a rooftop and then seeks out a racist cop, threatening him to quit his job or else.[78] Firestorm doesn't continue such actions, surviving his crisis of conscience with the superhero's morality and sense of responsibility intact.

Still, Jason's outbursts of immaturity often result in paternalistic lectures from white characters that, despite perhaps appearing problematic, continue his growth. When a cop whom he has pulled into the Firestorm matrix worries about him becoming addicted to his powers, Jason is nonplussed: "I've got this under control. [I'm a] good guy." When he later works with Lorraine in her superhero identity of Firehawk, he asserts himself, interrupting her orders to say, "Just—just listen to me, okay? Stop treating me like I'm a kid!" Lorraine quickly apologizes. While a scathing lecture from Batman later takes on the form of a parent lecturing a child—"Do I make myself clear?" asks the Dark Knight—Jason takes it in stride, noting that the less powerful Batman "got me shaking" and adding, "That's what I want to be."[79] Like Steel, then, the Jason Rusch Firestorm is inspired by—but not limited by—established forms of heroism, further cementing the complexity inherent in the character. As well, such conversations as these continue to enact the Peter Parker trope, as each of these "mentors" plays the role of Parker's Uncle Ben to the young Jason.

DC Comics also brought a black-from-white replacement hero into the Justice Society of America (JSA) in the early twenty-first century. Here, Michael Holt became the new Mister Terrific, an impressively well-rounded hero. He boasts a most impressive intelligence, immodestly explaining that he had mastered the possibilities of time travel "while other children struggled with Sesame Street." Holt effectively applies his mental brilliance to battle as well, for example when he outwits Kobra and then, after throwing the villain to the floor, jokes that he is more than skilled enough "to charm your particular member of the Elapidae family back into the basket!" Holt's seemingly unlimited knowledge is also displayed after Sentinel suffers potentially fatal injuries in battle. Mister Terrific rushes him to the hospital, where he barks out orders while diagnosing "a hundred percent pneumothorax on the right side."[80] Such intelligence makes him a natural leader. In the field, even with putative leader Sand with him, Mister Terrific takes charge of the team, telling Sand what to do. When the Injustice Society rears its ugly head, Mister Terrific again assumes control, piecing together a mystery to thwart them. The return of Hawkman later presents the JSA with a leadership crisis—who should lead, Sand or Hawkman? The team wisely elects Mister Terrific, much to his self-effacing surprise.[81]

In presenting such a character, DC ran a parallel risk of highlighting a flawless hero so far removed from imperfection that he could not possibly seem real. JSA creators, however, worked in later stories to build a more relatable character. Throughout, Holt humbly acknowledges the burden of the legacy he carries, noting that his Golden Age namesake is "a hard act to follow."[82] He also suffers an existential crisis of sorts in "The Return of Hawkman," the idea of reincarnation knocking him for a loop. As he explains to the Flash, "I don't believe in souls." His explanation for this finally makes Holt seem like a real human being: "I've always excelled at everything I tried to do. Athletics. Academics. And I was a good husband, dammit. But when my wife, Paula, was killed in a car accident . . . she was gone. I didn't feel her 'soul' around me. I didn't feel anything." Holt's loss, and the trauma it inflicts, underlines the humanity his otherwise near perfection threatens to eclipse.[83]

Not to be outdone by its competitor, Marvel Comics also produced black-from-white replacement heroes in the 1990s and beyond that used the coming-of-age arc to similar effect. The cyborg Deathlok, reborn in 1990 as a black man, showcased the talents of the writer Dwayne McDuffie and presented a subtle approach to race. Here, the African American hero quietly subverted a wide range of long-dominant black stereotypes. The protagonist, Michael Collins, has a sharp intellect, working as a software designer for high-tech artificial limbs; a gorgeous wife, Tracy, who is also working on her PhD; and a well-adjusted son, Nick. No longer tied to the city, Collins and his family live in a comfortable suburban home. In addition to defying the expectations of a brash, loud, and streetwise black hero, McDuffie also presented Collins as a profoundly moral man. When Collins sees his son playing a video game and arming his character with the biggest weapon possible, he advises, "Being a hero isn't about looking tough. It's about making tough choices. It's about sacrifice." He concludes the lesson by teaching Nick, "You have to do what's right, boy. Not what's easiest."[84]

Collins's morality drives the story forward when he discovers that Roxxon Oil, which runs a wide range of companies, including the operation Collins works for, has unbeknownst to him been using his work to build Deathlok, a half-human/half-computer killing machine designed for military deployments. Collins is outraged, prompting a moral crisis. That evening Michael asks Tracy, "How would you feel if I had to give up my job . . . on moral grounds?" When Collins subsequently confronts his corrupt boss, Harlan Ryker, Ryker shoots him with a tranquilizer dart and has Collins's brain placed into Deathlok, which is shipped off to the Federative Republic of Estrella to take out a band of rebels who are delaying work on a dam.[85]

Here, Deathlok's creators again invoke the apprentice/mastery narrative that successfully elevated other nonwhite heroes of this era. Deathlok operates with ruthless efficiency in Estrella, gunning down rebels, the computer doing all of the thinking (as revealed by the narrative boxes, colored blue). But midmission, a yellow narrative box clicks online, and Collins's consciousness begins to assert itself, a replacement hero struggling to master his new powers. As Deathlok continues his reign of violence, Collins likewise continues to piece things together, eventually realizing, "I'm responsible for this. I've got to stop it!" Having realized that his brain is inside Deathlok, Collins works to reprogram the cyborg, and he succeeds; Deathlok refuses to kill a lone surviving girl, despite Ryker's command to do so. When Ryker tries to reprogram Deathlok to ensure that the computer and not Collins is in charge, Collins once again resists the programming and breaks free, becoming his own man.[86]

Deathlok's final transformation into a superhero stems from another crisis of conscience. Now powerful but grotesquely unrecognizable, Deathlok cannot return to his former life, and having decided to destroy himself so that this technology can never be used again, Collins patches himself into the video game that his son is playing to say goodbye. When his son wants to kill some prisoners in the game, Collins tells him, "A hero would find a better way than the way you're playing this game." His son replies that the other way is harder, but Collins insists, "You have to do what's right, boy." This talk pulls Collins back from the brink, as he realizes he needs to learn to be a hero as well.[87] In essence, Collins as Deathlok here fulfills the apprentice/master narrative in classic fashion; like Peter Parker, he has learned his own version of power and responsibility.

Deathlok's conscience remains his guide, placing him further within the classic superhero tradition. Having decided to be a hero, Deathlok finds himself in Coney Island, seemingly depicted as the standard comic book interpretation of the ghetto, a full-page splash showcasing a trash-can fire burning amidst the debris of a crumbling city block. When Collins prevents a random mugging, however, the victim, Jesus, returns the favor by taking Deathlok to his apartment to hide, moving past the stereotypes suggested by the urban milieu. Jesus wonders why our hero helped him out; the morally driven Collins explains, "I help people because it's the right thing to do."[88] Similarly, Collins eventually realizes he must return to Estrella, a trip that will complete his redemption. Once there, Deathlok wins the trust of the rebels he once slaughtered and helps them destroy a dam, which, as a rebel commander explains, "will be completed soon. When it is, our way of life ends forever. Our homes and lives will be destroyed." Although the story doesn't have a completely happy ending—the government has collapsed, but who knows what will fill its place?—the rebel commander says, "I don't know what the future will bring for my people, but I do know that for the first time they will have a say in that future."[89]

The same is true of Deathlok, who, much like the rebels of Estrella, also asserts his control over his destiny when he returns to the United States to confront Ryker. He faces his ultimate crisis of conscience as Deathlok, in a full-page illustration, grimly stares down the reader as he levels his gun, saying, "I'm going to blow your brains out." In a complicated series of twists, Ryker stops the assassination by revealing that he still has Collins's body and that he can restore his brain to it. Although Collins struggles with this offer, our hero ultimately realizes a higher moral calling and refuses Ryker, telling him, "If I'd've sunk to your level—human body or not—then I'd be a monster."[90] Recognizable in this declaration and, in fact, this entire arc of Deathlok, is the ethnic replacement's ability to surpass what might seem an otherwise facile means of achieving diversity.

The coming-of-age arc worked well for representatives of other racialized groups as well. DC found some success applying the arc to its own white-to-Latino hero, Blue Beetle, who arrived in 2006. Readers first met Jaime Reyes as a Peter Parker–like teen living in El Paso. A jocular free spirit, Jaime doesn't seem to take anything—even the potential end of the world—too seriously. After accidentally discovering a mystical scarab and becoming the Blue Beetle, Jaime suddenly becomes an important player in the very survival of the earth. He finds himself face to face with the pantheon of DC's greatest superheroes. Jaime is disbelieving about his new powers, even as he visits the Batcave and is introduced as the Blue Beetle. "The what?" Jaime asks. "I'm not the new Blue Beetle. I'm not anything."[91]

Suddenly a superhero, Reyes must work to master his new powers quickly. Indeed, he finds himself having to pilot a spaceship filled with well-known crusaders, although he obviously feels overwhelmed and uncertain. Booster Gold's sarcasm and seeming calm disturb Jaime, who asks, "How can you act like all of this is normal?" The Dark Knight somewhat condescendingly describes the new Blue Beetle as a kid, and this actually fits Jaime's role in this epic adventure. He is clearly in over his head, pointing out as things get hairy, "I don't even know how the hell I got here." When the scarab provides the heroes with the location of the enemy's satellite, Jaime again emphasizes that he doesn't know how it is that he does this.[92] Thus, the comic presents an interesting juxtaposition: Jaime's role is absolutely essential for the mission's success, but he really only carries the scarab, which does all the work. Nonetheless, the situation feels authentic, capturing the awe and wonder of a high school student suddenly thrown into an end-of-the-universe crisis.

In the pages of a new, ongoing *Blue Beetle* title, the writers Keith Giffen and John Rogers introduced readers to a very human, and familiar, youngster. His friends Brenda and Paco bicker constantly, nicely capturing the angst of youth, and his working-class family is unique yet believable, his mother working as a nurse and his father as the almost-too-understanding boss at his auto garage. While constantly squabbling with his sister, Milagro, Jaime tries to find his way in a world that offers limited options. Seeing his dad struggle to keep the garage running, Jaime offers to help out, but his father pushes Jaime to finish his schoolwork—a path to a

Figure 6.8. An oft-repeated part of the coming-of-age trope at the turn of the century had new heroes struggling to command their newfound powers. As Jaime Reyes struggles for control of the Blue Beetle armor, he also struggles to assert agency in his own life. As Reyes and others came to master their powers, they simultaneously appeared more human and recognizable to comics readers.

better life—instead.[93] Reyes also continues to struggle with mastering his powers, at first having virtually no control over them. Backgrounded by El Paso, Jaime fights for control of the Blue Beetle armor, and by issue #3 our hero has begun to successfully take control of both his new powers and his life. He begins, for example, to ask questions of his armor (which talks to him throughout the stories, although the reader cannot understand the symbols used to depict the armor's "voice"). When he asks the scarab/ armor to show what it can do, he is overloaded by its possibilities but quickly asserts his control, ordering, "Whoa! Tone it down!" He then decides which powers to practice as he begins to master his new potential.[94]

Further signaling his growth is how Reyes becomes more assertive when meeting other superheroes. (One wonders if Batman would even recognize the Blue Beetle he met not all that long ago.) For example, when Oracle and her Birds of Prey team contact Reyes to provide help, he asserts his independence by pointing out the stupidity of the name Birds of Prey and mocking Oracle. Jaime angrily accuses the heroes of recruiting him to win their battle and then abandoning him, concluding emphatically, "You and your super pals or your Justice Squad can go to hell!!" Oracle is frustrated at failing to win Jaime over, especially when the Black Canary points out that "the shadowy genius mastermind behind the world's greatest heroes just fail[ed] to recruit a sixteen-year-old boy." Oracle can only weakly reply, "Shut up." Black Canary's response captures what the reader must have felt: "I like him."[95]

Reyes also becomes more assertive in facing down bad guys, as seen in his battle against La Dama, the criminal mastermind behind his first adventure. Battling one of her operatives, who makes trees become sentient and attack, our hero wrestles with his armor, which initially doesn't respond as ordered. He finally seizes control, yelling at the scarab, "I'm sick of this! You're not in charge! This is my life! My life!" In the aftermath of the attack, Jaime declares his independence: "I'm sick of fitting into everybody else's plans. Sick of everybody knowing more than me. Sick of nutjobs and trees taking swings at me and I have no idea why." When Brenda asks if there is someone he can call, Jaime exhibits his distrust of authority and other heroes: "And get spoon-fed whatever they feel like telling me? No. We do things on our own." Later, the armor wants to kill a bad guy, but Jaime asserts his control, forcing the armor to stop zapping his opponent.[96]

But it is the 2011 arrival of Miles Morales in *Ultimate Comics: Spider-Man* that most suggested some hope for white-to-nonwhite and other replacement heroes via the coming-of-age trope popularized by his namesake.[97] A well-developed character, Morales lives in the city but is not flatly defined by it, as readers familiar with comics past might expect; as well, Morales's environment is an intentionally multicultural one.[98] The series introduces Morales and his parents as they attend a charter-school lottery in Brooklyn. His nervous parents see Brooklyn Visions Academy as a ticket to a better life, and, somewhat dramatically, Miles's name is the last one drawn, making him one of the lucky forty (out of seven hundred applicants) to get in. As his parents celebrate, Miles looks quiet and thoughtful, the artwork highlighting one girl and one boy whose names were not drawn, emphasizing Miles's good luck as well as his empathy for others.

After gaining his powers, Morales must deal with significant changes in his life while living in the inner city. Here, the writer Brian Michael Bendis and the artist Sara Pichelli again present a fairly nuanced tableau. The city itself, as illustrated by Pichelli, is diverse and active, not the typical slums presented in earlier comics. Just as importantly, it is populated by more complex characters than comics had often presented. For example, Miles's

Figure 6.9. Readers met Miles Morales, the Ultimate Universe's Spider-Man, as a complex and well-developed character who inhabited the urban landscape but was hardly defined by it. As a result, the new Spider-Man was a human and empathetic character.

dad finally comes clean with his son, admitting that his desire to sepa-rate Miles from his Uncle Aaron is grounded in a previously hidden family history: his uncle is a thief, and both his uncle and his dad have done prison time. But, his dad says, he came to see that he could have a better life, while Aaron never was able to see this. Miles and the reader, how-ever, don't get any easy answers about success from his father, who knows better. As he explains, "Anyone can be bad, anyone. It's easy. It's the easi-est thing. But to stay focused. To live a good life . . . it's the hardest damn thing. Do you understand?"

As Morales must come to grips with his powers, he begins the classic apprentice-to-master motif. Miles talks to his one good friend, Ganke Lee, an Asian American genius who also attends the Brooklyn Visions Academy. Wrestling with his newfound powers and what they might mean for his life, Miles gets a late-night text from Ganke, who has come to an interest-ing conclusion: Miles might be Spider-Man. To test the theory, Miles scales the walls and ceilings of his room. Ganke is thrilled at this turn of events, but Miles isn't, saying, "I don't want to be Spider-Man." His friend can see the upside and pushes Morales to act when they come across a burning apartment building. After saving two lives, Miles still struggles with the changes in his life, telling Ganke, "I didn't ask for them and I don't want them!"

The death of this universe's Peter Parker, however, provokes the by-now-expected crisis of conscience for Morales, who sneaks out of school and arrives just in time to watch the original Spider-Man die. As he returns to his dorm room, racked with guilt, Miles slumps against the wall as he explains to Ganke, "You know I could have helped stop this." Although the logic is a bit convoluted, Miles argues that if he had started using his powers as soon as he got them—instead of "hiding in this room"—he would have met Spider-Man, would have been in the know about what was going on, and "would have been the extra something that stopped this from happening." Ganke tries to comfort Miles by suggesting another possibility: maybe Miles was given these powers so he could replace Spider-Man.

If Miles has any doubts about his future, they are pushed aside when he meets Gwen Stacy at Parker's funeral and asks her, "Why did he do it? Why did he become Spider-Man?" Gwen stares at Miles over her shoulder and walks silently into the church before returning to talk with him, explaining, "Because his uncle, the guy who raised him, died. Peter thought he died because even though he had these powers he didn't do anything to help. 'Least that's the way Peter saw it. And his uncle told him these words, words to live by: That with great power comes great responsibility. Okay?" Here, Miles fully inherits the Spider-Man legacy.

Bendis further humanizes Miles through the use of humor. Thus, when Miles first heads out to patrol the city streets, he dresses in the plump Ganke's ill-fitting old Spider-Man Halloween costume. While carrying all the hallmarks of the classic Spidey look, the boots and gloves are too large, sagging comically on the slender Morales. The overall effect makes Miles look quite young and ill-prepared. As he goes to battle against his first bad guy, the nondescript Kangaroo, Miles exhibits Peter's gift of gab, confronting the baddie with a simple, "Wow. That ain't nice at all." The new Spider-Man then crouches on a car and taunts Kangaroo, "I think an apology of some sort is due. To all of us really. We'll wait." Here, Miles's demonstration of the Parker-style wit puts him, via such humor, on par with the original hero. Unlike such humor prevalent in earlier decades that made characters like the Falcon its object, Miles subjects others to his barbs.

The first new Spider-Man story arc climaxed with the return of Uncle Aaron, who discovers that Miles is Spider-Man and forces him through another crisis of conscience. Now revealed as the Prowler, Aaron blackmails Miles into helping him take down the Scorpion, a competing baddie. Miles is torn, but ultimately confronts the Prowler. When Miles later meets Peter Parker's Aunt May, she advises him, "Do what your heart tells you." She also gives him Peter's web shooters and offers the following advice: "Don't do what Peter would do. Do what Miles Morales would do."

Now fully established as the new Spider-Man, Miles controls his destiny, and when he later joins the Ultimates—the biggest heroes in this universe—he completes his ascendance as a fully individualized hero.

Conclusion

In 2004, *Truth: Red, White & Black* called for an accounting of America's racist past. The tale introduced three potential black Captain Americas by traveling back to the pre–World War II days of American history, using them to expose readers to a variety of perspectives on racism, both then and now.[99] Drawing on African American history much like Steel employed African American folklore, the creators Robert Morales and Kyle Baker introduce the first hero, Isaiah Bradley, with his wife, Faith, at the 1939 world's fair. Visiting during Negro Week, the politically aware couple joke about W. E. B. Du Bois; the creators here juxtapose the black scholar's insistence on African Americans standing up for themselves against the "Amusements Area of the Fair," a section of the exposition that, according to Isaiah, "wasn't so high-minded." The couple are refused entrance at a tent advertising "a bevy of international beauties," the barker noting that the girls would be "upset" if he let them in: "They don't like being looked at like they're animals . . . you know how they are." Isaiah clenches his fist at this racism, but Faith, looking just as unhappy, restrains him from fighting back. Thus, immediately, Morales and Baker confront their readers with the stark racial discrimination of the American past.

But they also examine racism through an economic lens as the scene shifts to introduce Maurice Canfield, a radical labor activist, who arrives to visit his parents in their expensive Philadelphia home after a bruising fight. He explains to his upset parents that he was beaten up while working to organize stevedores in Newark. Canfield notes that he was working with Jules Edelman and that the upset workers did not want to listen to "a Negro and a Jew giv[ing] them counsel about their economic survival— let alone their social responsibilities." While his mom complains about such danger in his life, her son—driven by an inherent morality—insists, "I don't want a fortune based on Negroes that are compelled to lighten their skins and straighten their hair. Especially when they turn around and take their self-hatred out on me."

Adding an institutional angle to their presentation of prewar racism, Morales and Baker finally introduce Luke Evans, an African American in the US Army, whose old nickname, Black Cap, doesn't fit anymore (since he has been demoted to sergeant after standing up for a black soldier killed by white comrades). As he shoots pool in a seedy bar in Cleveland with a friend recently released from jail, Evans leans over the table and prepares to strike the cue ball, remarking, "This is the only place I get to shove ol' whitey around." Here, Evans voices his awareness of structural racism and discrimination, which render him powerless. This army is far from the utopian organization promulgated in films of and about this era.

The racial tensions introduced in *Truth*'s prologue are then highlighted as the three unique protagonists come together at Camp Cathcart in Mississippi in May 1942. Following the Japanese attack on Pearl Harbor, Evans is ready to fight, while Bradley and Canfield are forced into military service. At the camp, the commanding officer is blatantly racist, and white soldiers complain about the stench of the black soldiers. Not surprisingly, the radical Maurice chafes at such treatment, gets in fights with white soldiers, and talks about a Double V campaign that will not only produce victory abroad but also achieve equality at home. When one angry black soldier says he is fighting for the chance "to kill me some white mens," Evans points out the reality of their continued powerlessness: "Killing white men is a gift you only get from other white men."

The next installment of the story, tellingly titled "The Passage," parallels the transitions that occur in the protagonists' lives (as the military subjects them to supersoldier experiments and ships them to Europe) and in their ancestors' experiences with the Middle Passage of slavery. Here, Morales and Baker present the black soldiers as nothing more than lab rats caught in a racist system that devalues their lives. As the government tests an experimental version of the supersoldier serum (which will later be perfected and used to transform the scrawny Steve Rogers into Captain America), the military refuses to desegregate blood supplies for white troops. The experiments continue, producing grisly results, one soldier literally exploding into little pieces. The government moves ahead with a cover-up, informing our heroes' families and friends that they have died accidentally, while their loved ones are actually treated with the supersoldier serum and survive.

The creators then more directly evoke the Middle Passage, illustrating the story of the soldiers as they ship to Europe. Echoing the human costs of the slave trade, one supersoldier dies en route. As the soldier suffers his last, painful moments, another soldier asks the veteran Evans about "the biggest battle you fought." Evans surprises them by talking about the Red Summer in Washington, DC, through which the creators excavate another touchstone of America's racial past. As Evans relates the story, after World

War I, black men were being beaten and lynched in the nation's capital, but "nobody—not the cops, President Wilson—lifted a finger to stop them." "That's when we decided," Evans says, "it was up to us," and he describes blacks arming themselves and fighting back, successfully enough to stop the lynching, "for a spell anyway." By the end of this sojourn, *Truth* has thoroughly entwined the racial crimes of America's not-so-distant past with slavery.

When the setting shifts to Europe, *Truth* likewise parallels American racism to that precipitating the Holocaust. At this point, Bradley stands as the lone survivor. As our hero parachutes into a Nazi concentration camp, the text highlights the parallels between German and American racism. Bradley's story is now told by Faith, who laments how the army turned her husband into a "tireless killer" and a "stranger." Through her retelling of her husband's tale, Faith compares his treatment to that of Jews at the hands of heinous Nazi scientists. Making the comparison explicit, she recalls the message army officials had for her husband: "Do not consider what we did to you, is what they didn't say." Bradley's capture by Germans further underlines the point. "Look at this!" one says, mockingly. "It would appear they sent Jesse Owens," evincing a casual racism not unlike that extant in the United States.

The story wraps up by shifting to the present, as Steve Rogers, the present-day Captain America, tries to piece together his origins, allowing the creators again to address the persistence of American racism. Cap eventually tracks down Damien Merritt, a bigoted soldier from World War II. Here, Baker draws Captain America more realistically (and heroically), while Merritt becomes more and more unrealistic in appearance as his racism is revealed, his character eventually looking more like an infected flesh wound than a real person. Stunned to learn from Merritt that there was a "black Captain America," Cap tracks down Colonel Walker Price, the racist who spearheaded the racial experiments. Price ties the story together by talking about the eugenics movement in early twentieth-century America, again emphasizing the connections between Nazi atrocities and American history.

But this coda of sorts also allows *Truth* and its creators to make a final point about American racism. Captain America tries to fashion a happy ending for this tale, but no such possibility really exists. He finds Faith, who wears a burka and lives in the Bronx, and she fills in the rest of the story. As it turns out, Bradley was rescued by sympathetic Germans, some of whom were African, and these rebels helped him get home. Upon his return, Bradley "was arrested and court-martialed. He got life . . . for stealing

Figure 6.10. *Truth*, published in 2004, presented the complexities of racism on levels rarely seen in comics, sketching out the long—if little discussed—history of racism in the United States. Driving the point home, the racist Merritt transforms in his depictions into an increasingly inhuman being. Flipping the theme of dehumanization on its head, *Truth* asked readers to reconsider the American past.

your costume [which he wore when attacking the concentration camp]." As Cap sits in stunned silence, Faith assures him, "It's not your fault." But Bradley did seventeen years in solitary, nonetheless, until President Eisenhower pardoned him, telling the family to keep his story secret. The serum has since taken its toll, rendering Bradley impotent and increasingly incapacitated, in a nod to the Tuskegee experiments that in many ways encompasses the entire series. As he waits to meet Isaiah, Cap sees photos on the family wall of Bradley with all kinds of black celebrities (including Muhammad Ali, Colin Powell, Nelson Mandela, Malcolm X, and Alex Haley, among others), revealing that the black community knows about Bradley, even if Cap and whites do not.

When the two men finally meet, Cap has the chance to try to make amends for centuries of racism. Understanding the enormity of these national sins and his inability to redress them, he apologizes, saying, "I can't say enough how sorry I am for what happened to you and your family." And Cap adds, "I wish I could undo all the suffering you've gone through. If I could've taken your place . . ." Finally, as "the smallest of consolations," Cap returns Bradley's tattered World War II–era uniform, and the old man smiles broadly. Faith takes a picture of the two men, perhaps to hang on the wall with the other luminaries and perhaps suggesting the possibility of a racial healing if Americans come to grips with their racist past. But that possibility remains, in *Truth*, only a possibility.

Employing ethnic replacement superheroes, comic creators embarked upon a campaign for inclusion in increasing numbers in the 1990s and beyond. As *Truth* suggested, whatever progress obtained in race relations remained bogged down in cultural anxieties and uncertainties rooted deeply in the American past. While some creators and readers seem to have assumed that these legacy heroes provided a sufficient answer to such questions that had long dogged Americans about race, replacements turned out to be a good deal more complicated. In retrospect, it is all too clear that just adding nonwhite crusaders—as was true with the superteams of the 1980s—hardly solved the problem. In the end, replacements worked or didn't work as a result of the care and effort put into their creation and use. When deployed carelessly and with little thought, the continuing power of stereotypes limited or even eliminated possibilities for progress. When treated as complex individuals, other replacements suggested significant progress. Whatever the case, some creators looked for different solutions as the twenty-first century arrived, preferring to move beyond replacements by either looking to the past or building new worlds to more effectively address issues of race in the United States.

CHAPTER 7

Something Old, Something New: Heroes Reborn and Reimagined, 1990–2015

In *A Different Mirror*, Ronald Takaki titles his chapter on the second half of the twentieth century "Through a Glass Darkly: Toward the Twenty-First Century." As the United States has now passed into the twenty-first century, Takaki, despite his acknowledging the difficulties of writing contemporary history, seems to have anticipated the ways in which the country would continue to be plagued by strife, racial and otherwise. The crises of the latter twentieth century — Rodney King, Reginald Denny, and more — were exacerbated, when the century turned, by the 9/11 attacks and subsequent "war on terror," Hurricane Katrina and its aftermath, and the Great Recession, to name but a few. Though this same period would also feature the election of America's first black president, the reality of race in American life in the first decades of the twenty-first century was, to say the least, vexed.

The stark and tumultuous nature of this era produced another tack by which comics sought to confront race. While the turn-of-the-century creators who deployed ethnic replacement heroes to address issues of multiculturalism often did so to express an idealized vision of US society, others based their work in a belief that superheroes should be grounded in reality, which led in turn to a more self-conscious interrogation of comics' racial past. This grounding in reality had its roots in the Marvel heroes of the early 1960s. As Stan Lee explained after the fact, "I try to make the characters seem as believable and realistic as possible. In order to do that, I have to place them in the real world, or, if the story is set in an imaginary world, I have to try to make that imaginary world as realistic-seeming as possible, so the character doesn't exist in a vacuum."[1] Here, Lee speaks more in generalized terms of character and world building when he discusses Marvel's grounding in realism. By the end of the century, comic creators concretized this goal as not just representing realistic worlds and characters but grounding those in the issues of the day.

For many, comics' turn to a greater—and grittier—realism is marked by the arrival of *Watchmen* (by Alan Moore and Dave Gibbons) and *Batman: The Dark Knight Returns* (by Frank Miller) in the mid-1980s. In both, the creators strove to make what has been regularly lauded as a different kind of comic art, one seen as transcending popular understandings of comics as kiddie fare starring brightly colored heroes. Ironically, for all that *Watchmen* and *The Dark Knight Returns* might be said to have done to elevate comics in the popular mind, they were hardly the first with such ambitions. Similar efforts at realism arrived prior to their publication, for example O'Neil and Adams's early 1970s run on *Green Lantern/Green Arrow*, whatever its flaws. These works have likewise been hailed for their deconstructions of superhero tropes and past (*Watchmen* more generally and Miller's *Dark Knight* specifically regarding Batman); but the near simultaneous publication of Marvel's *Squadron Supreme* (1985–1986) at least somewhat belies such claims as unique to these works. *Squadron Supreme* likewise took on the underlying assumptions of comic book heroism but did so much more fully dressed up in the bright colors and action long associated with the genre. Thus, comics in general (as opposed to two exceptional works) realized the potential they had always had to do more, especially in terms of creating complex, more fully realized worlds and characters that transcended two-dimensional storytelling. Such influence is still felt, even in standard comic book fare; more recently, for instance, the creator Jeph Loeb has written about reimagining what comic books might accomplish when the focus moves beyond just battles royal. In this way, Loeb explains, superhero tales, "when they're told well, . . . make us slow down and think about the situations that we're in and the people that we're affecting—at least the best stories do. . . . If we take that pause and really look at our lives and seek to be both inspired and inspirational—and a little less self-absorbed—we can make the world a much better place than it currently is. At least, I hope we can."[2]

Loeb's comments about the power of superhero tales hearkens back to those ideas of Adam Newton, Patrick Colm Hogan, Patrick Hamilton, and others discussed in the introduction that undergird this study. As they argue, literature has the effect of guiding and shaping our understandings of our world. Hogan aptly sums up that "literature is one of the primary means by which a culture represents to itself the ambient acts and ideas of daily life."[3] Frederick Luis Aldama and Derek Royal, in turn, extend such power to affect our constructions, particularly of difference, to the so-called lowbrow medium of comics. Whether reading *Ulysses* or Proust, a picture book or a teen novel, or, yes, even a comic book, Aldama argues, "readers' cognitive processes work in similar ways," not only to, as he continues, "transform fragments into wholes" but to understand that whole and its relevance to our experience.[4] In this, literature—including comics—functions as what Hogan, drawing from cognitive psychology, terms a "situation model," or what we represent in our minds as the world that thus guides our behavior. It is a model that both accommodates and assimilates experience in an ongoing and recursive process.[5] Such a process is inherent in Loeb's comment as well as in works like *Watchmen* and *The Dark Knight Returns*—and in stories in general—causing readers to pause and consider our impact on our world, hopefully for the better.

Such aspirations, whether conscious or not, spurred the creators in this chapter both to create new heroes and to reimagine past protagonists in an effort to come to grips with, among other things, race in the United States. In the 1990s, Image Comics and Milestone Comics rejected past characters altogether in creating new ethnic heroes—and, indeed, even new multicultural worlds—to address racial issues from new perspectives less encumbered by past baggage. The results of their efforts were mixed, as Image, for all its spirit of youthful rebellion, remained firmly entrenched in the problematic aspects of the DC/Marvel tradition. More successfully, Milestone both implicitly and explicitly engaged with comics' racialized past in its drive toward authenticity. In the ensuing decade, others similarly addressed this past, dusting off and revising 1970s "blaxploitation" heroes like Black Lightning, Luke Cage, and the Black Panther in efforts to elevate them beyond their stereotypical origins. As always, there were the less successful of these attempts, which continued to struggle to overcome longheld stereotypes as well as contemporary issues of race and ethnicity. But the more successful probed race relations by directly invoking these characters' dodgy pasts as a step toward creating human, well-developed, and more fully realized characters. Such efforts demonstrate comics' ability to transcend limited conceptions of race and ethnicity in fostering greater respect, tolerance, and equality.

Superheroes Reimagined: Image and Milestone Comics

While Marvel and DC could introduce ethnic replacements in a quest for multiculturalism, upstart Image Comics had no such back catalog to exploit. Founded in 1992 by some of the most popular comic book artists

Figure 7.1. The arrival of Image Comics might have portended the possibility of something new in comic books, but its initial fare looked more to the past than the future. *WildC.A.T.s*, for instance, mirrored much of the upstart company's superteams by including only one token nonwhite member. Here, Voodoo played to a long tradition of exoticized and sexualized ethnic characters.

of the day—including Todd McFarlane, Erik Larsen, Jim Lee, Rob Lie-feld, and Marc Silvestri—Image launched with creator-owned characters steeped in the superhero traditions of DC and particularly Marvel, including their limitations regarding diversity. The various team titles, including Liefeld's *Youngblood*, Silvestri's *Cyberforce*, and Lee's *WildC.A.T.s*, did little new to advance multiculturalism. The cover of *Youngblood* #1 (April 1992) hearkens back to the days of the single "token" black member, with Chapel the only recognizably nonwhite member. *Cyberforce* was even less diverse at first glance, as none of the team members manifest their ethnicity. Nor does this issue become less pronounced once they do; the Native American Ripclaw, the sole nonwhite member, is based in long-prevailing stereotypes of savagery and mysticism. Lee's *WildC.A.T.s* likewise featured the exoticized and objectified Voodoo as a single token member.

Image also featured two solo series with black protagonists that similarly fall short of their potential: Jim Valentino's *Shadowhawk* and Todd McFarlane's *Spawn*. *Shadowhawk* put the former district attorney Paul Johnstone behind a mask and accompanying armor that completely obscure any hint of his racial identity. Shadowhawk is likewise noted for his take-no-prisoners attitude. As Valentino explained, "Only in super hero comics do heroes not kill. I decided the character wouldn't kill . . . but he'd maim."[6] What Valentino saw as unique, of course, hardly was; the hero's predilection plays into the violence underlying the classic "buck" stereotype that had dogged racial representation from the early days of comics.

Both a more immediate and sustained hit, Todd McFarlane's *Spawn* featured the black Al Simmons as its protagonist. Moving on from his spectacularly successful run on *Spider-Man* at Marvel, McFarlane produced a spooky, supernatural story; however, it has not been positively received. One critic argues that Spawn demonized black men, while another contends that his disfigurement erased his racial identity.[7] And such critics largely have it right. While *Spawn* could have explored issues of race and identity, McFarlane just doesn't seem interested in doing so, at least not authentically.[8] Thus, the series begins with televised news coverage of the death of Simmons, a heroic marine who just so happened to be black. As the story progresses, Simmons's race seems largely irrelevant, the plot focusing more on revealing his past, which includes a deal with the devil to come back to life to see his wife. When Spawn takes off his mask and

Figure 7.2. While Spawn brought an African American superhero to the Image Universe, the character was often depicted as an ashy corpse or played for laughs, as here he can transform his appearance into something more human, but only if he is willing to be white. While such circumstances raised the possibility of addressing race, the comic mostly chose not to pursue such possibilities.

costume, however, he is corpse-like, with gray, ashy skin and talon-like fingers. He can use his powers to make himself look normal, but to his great unhappiness, he is now white. "This can't be," he shouts to no one in particular. "I'm a black man!" He chooses to look like a corpse instead, saying, "I won't stay like this. Not white. Someone's playing a bad joke, screwing with my mind. I just want to be me. But these friggin' powers won't work. Can't make me whole."

Here existed an opportunity to comment on race in America, but McFarlane generally plays this black/white twist as a gag, a clever idea worth using just because it's clever. Instead of any deep social critique, race is commodified, a running in-joke to entertain. Thus, after tracking down his wife, Spawn visits her in Queens, using his powers to look human — and white — again. He is still upset, complaining, "I look like some California beach bum. And of all the hair colors — why blonde?!" He is thrown, however, when he finds out that his wife and her new husband, Terry, have a daughter. A recap later reminds us how hard it is for Spawn "to cope with his so-called reality. That reality includes him being brought back from the dead; selling his soul; being given what seem to be unlimited powers; and getting shot five years into his future as a white man . . . when he is black." Thus, the end of the first story arc left Simmons without his wife, his identity, and his pride. The series, as with those launched by the other founding creators, left Image with little that contributed differently than the bulk of past comics to understanding race in the United States.

The founders of Milestone Comics had the same advantages and disadvantages of founding a new company and comic book world; unlike McFarlane and the others, they did something with it. Initially owned and controlled by Derek T. Dingle, Dwayne McDuffie, Denys Cowan, and Michael Davis, Milestone produced comics that DC printed and distributed.[9] The founders wanted to present a multicultural message in aesthetically and narratively pleasing comics. As McDuffie explained, "We could have done just African American comics because that is obviously the experience that we understand best, but we realize that that is only one of many possible viewpoints that we want to bring forward to our readers." In wanting also to show diversity within the African American community, McDuffie added, the company wanted to "break up the idea of a monolith."[10] Such intentions were also made manifest in the comics themselves, as evidenced by the aforementioned editorial regarding their universe's diversity in the first issue of *Blood Syndicate*.

Milestone received generally positive reviews for its comic books, although sales figures did not reflect a smashing success. Jeffrey A. Brown suggests that Milestone's appeal arose from the company's efforts to address (and redress) characters like the 1970s versions of Luke Cage, the Black Panther, and Black Lightning. As one father explained about the new line's superheroes, "These characters are maybe better, more realistic than guys like Cage. They're not spending all their time trying to be really black, but they're doing the same thing that the books I used to read were doing. They may be new versions of the old guys, but they let my kid dream about saving the world." In this way, the company focused on telling traditional superhero and adventure stories, only weaving in race and politics secondarily. Offering an alternative to the blaxploitation heroes of the past, Milestone's crusaders won using their brains just as often as their brawn, facilitating what Brown sees as a more forward-thinking expression of black masculinity. In doing so, Milestone intended to provide its young fans a more egalitarian and hopeful world.[11]

Of its various offerings, Milestone's *Icon* has prompted the most considerable scholarly debate. Adilifu Nama, who typically celebrates the possibilities in black comics, criticizes the title as patently imitative of Superman.[12] Brown disagrees, arguing instead that *Icon*'s parallels with Superman and the trappings of the superhero more generally allow the comic to challenge and revise these traditions based on a nonwhite conception of heroism.[13] By and large, despite problems at times, *Icon* generally lives up to Brown's celebration. The familiarity of the titular hero's origin hardly undermines what the writer McDuffie and the penciller M. D. Bright hoped to accomplish, as they first created two irreducibly complex characters in the series' chief protagonists, Icon and Rocket, and also deployed the dynamic between them to render a similarly irreducible picture of black experience.

This effort begins with the origin of Icon himself. As a massive spaceship seemingly self-destructs in outer space in 1839, a featureless humanoid launches itself to safety in an escape pod. The alien lands in the American South, where a slave finds him. When she touches the ship, the alien becomes a black infant, whom the woman adopts. The story then jumps forward to 1993, where the child, grown up to become the African American lawyer Augustus Freeman IV, sits in his very posh office, suggesting the former slave's newfound power. Freeman is a no-nonsense kind of guy and a staunch conservative.[14]

But the narrative then complicates this seeming one-dimensionality by tracing Freeman's vexed relationship to racism in the United States since the days of slavery, thus adding complexity to his initial depiction. As he recounts his rise to affluence and power, Freeman remarks that as he became accustomed to "that rarified air" of his life as a successful lawyer, he gradually lost touch with his racial identity, no longer "personally confronted by racism of any consequence" and no longer mingling "with black people of any kind." His social isolation led him, he ruefully admits, to believe in the United States "as the land of opportunity." Connecting his complacency to American history, Freeman notes, "I truly believed that the long fight for equality was won in 1964 with the signing of the Civil Rights Act. . . . I had become a pillar of the community, a staunch 'Republican,' a by-your-own-bootstraps, Booker T. Washington conservative." His experience in rising from slavery to power, indeed, makes him no longer sympathetic to arguments about the power of race in black lives.[15] Here, he espouses a version of the "American dream" tied to the "model-minority" idea that perniciously blames those who do not succeed for their failures, an ideology that Freeman will come to question.

McDuffie adds Rocket's perspective to counterbalance and thus further interrogate the stiffly upright Freeman and the experience he represents. Indeed, Raquel Ervin, a fifteen-year-old kid from the mean streets of Dakota, seems Freeman's antithesis in terms of her experiences and how they've shaped her. Hoping one day to be a writer but seeing few options to achieve her dream, young Ervin lets her boyfriend talk her into robbing what turns out to be Freeman's mansion. The heist fails when Freeman confronts the gang of black youths, subduing them but also revealing his superhuman abilities. After she returns home, Ervin compares her "crappy" life to Freeman's luxurious existence and decides that she now has an alternative. She visits Freeman a couple of days later, telling the stunned lawyer that she has a new plan for his life.[16]

Here, McDuffie utilizes Ervin/Rocket to contrast and thus complicate what Freeman/Icon represents. She wants him to become an inspirational superhero, having already sketched out costumes and decided on names—Icon and Rocket—but she wonders, "What do you stand for?" She also insists that she become his sidekick, "so that you never forget why you're doing it." In such comments, she serves as an agitation to Freeman, literally questioning him in the way her presence in general also does. Freeman, not surprisingly, resists, arguing, "People don't need any example, child. If you aren't doing well, you haven't tried hard enough. If you want a better life, don't look for examples, do what I did: pull yourself up by your own bootstraps." As she leaves, Raquel replies, "It's a lot easier to pull yourself up by your bootstraps, Mr. Man—if you already know how to fly!" Here, Raquel most directly challenges Freeman's ideology, to real effect. Although Raquel assumes she'll never see Freeman again, he re-

Figure 7.3. As Icon and Rocket head off on their first adventure, the complexity of both the African American past and the present are demonstrated, the younger Rocket aware of and wanting to confront institutional racism, the older (and ironically more naïve) Icon trusting in a system he does not understand.

turns two days later, having come to accept her proposal and, implicitly, her critique.[17]

Having set up the story and this dynamic between Icon/Freeman and Rocket/Ervin, McDuffie opens interesting possibilities for discussing race from different perspectives. Read this way, the complex relationship between Icon and Rocket exposes differences within the African American community as well as racism in the broader society. That this contrast underlies their hero/sidekick dynamic becomes clear as the pair head off to the inner city on their first adventure. Icon, confronted—almost as if for the first time—with trash, dilapidated buildings, filth, and poverty, asks, "How could they live like this?" But, his eyes already opening to a different view of the world, he quickly shifts from blaming the victim to considerations of his own complicity in the problem, asking, "How could I let them?" Icon then answers his own question damningly—as Bright's pencils focus on a shirtless child, a victim who has done nothing to earn his poverty and suffering—explaining, "I pretended that those who suffer under such conditions must have brought it upon themselves. And while they have lived without hope . . . I have lived a lie."[18]

Such realizations hardly transform Icon immediately, as one would expect, a further earmark of the series' complexity. Instead, on the cusp of their first adventure, Rocket quotes W. E. B. Du Bois (on the need for "exceptional men" to lead African Americans), and Freeman replies that he is "more of a Booker T. Washington man myself." McDuffie continues fleshing out their dynamic in this way as the pair encounter institutional racism. As they arrive, cops have already surrounded Dakota's city hall, and Icon decides to offer help. Rocket protests that this approach is "naïve," asking her partner, "You think the cops are sitting around waiting for a flying nigger to drop out of the sky and do their job for them?" But Icon is not worried, replying, "Watch your language. And don't assume everything is racial. If you want to do this you'll have to show respect for the authorities." Rocket is right, however, and when they land, a white cop tries to arrest them, despite Icon's assurance of help. Rocket quips, as the would-be superheroes find themselves surrounded by heavily armored cops, "I bet this never happens to Superman."[19]

The pair continue to confront very different realities as they work together. Following his initial "misunderstanding" with the authorities, Icon quickly becomes a Dakota City hero and even receives a key to the city. His speech at the event is classic Icon, apologizing for not using his powers earlier but now promising to challenge himself "to be of service to humanity." As he explains, holding tight to his individualistic view of the world, "I challenge you to challenge yourselves. You're all gifted with special abilities. Strive to live up to your potential as I will strive to live up to mine. I can fly—so can you." As he delivers this last line, Icon ascends into the heavens; the crowd is positively rapturous, blacks and whites alike inspired by their new hero.[20]

Rocket, meanwhile, finds out she is pregnant, a plot twist by which McDuffie further grounds his story in the real world. Readers feel her embarrassment when Ervin goes to buy a pregnancy test and as she fears Icon's judgment. The pregnancy also ratchets up tensions in her family, especially with her grandmother, who tells her granddaughter that she will not help to raise the child. Adrift from her family, things get even worse when Ervin's boyfriend abandons her, too.[21] The pregnancy also adds to the continuing disconnect between the teenager and Icon. At a seeming dead end in her life, Ervin even uncomfortably considers abortion. When she asks Freeman for advice, she is unhappy with his platitudes, angrily exclaiming, "You're not poor. You're not a woman. You could never understand the kind of decision I'm trying to make."[22]

While life circumstances separate Icon and Rocket, their shared African American history draws them together. When Icon describes his life on earth, he reveals his life in bondage and his decision to keep his powers secret as he helped slaves escape via the Underground Railroad. The biography that follows continually locates Freeman within the African American experience: fighting in the Civil War, graduating from Fisk University during Reconstruction, getting married during the Harlem Renaissance, living as an expat in France between the world wars. Rocket, as a result, gains a new appreciation of Freeman, explaining to the reader that Freeman's "life spans the breadth of the African-American experience. The things he's seen! The things he knows!"[23]

Having thus grounded *Icon* in African American history as well as the different dynamics of black experience in the United States, McDuffie moves to a second dimension of the series' accomplishments: a deconstruction of the stereotypes that continued to dominate the presentation of black superheroes. While he did so in various ways, his introduction of Buck Wild provided the most obvious analysis of the past. As Brown has written, this character—and a host of others associated with him—interrogate the often difficult history of black superheroes that Icon and other Milestone heroes strive to reinvent.[24]

Buck Wild arrives as a brilliant parody of Luke Cage and his blaxploitation origins, crashing through a window, glass flying as bullets ricochet off his impervious skin. He looks just like the early Cage, sporting a small Afro and a ridiculous tiara along with a yellow leotard without leggings, the shirt cut all the way down to the navel to show off his chiseled physique. As Buck enters, he screams, in his best over-the-top jive, "Alright you mother-lovin', finger-lickin' chicken pluckers! You done messed up now! 'Cause I'm Buck Wild, Mercenary Man!" The accompanying narration (by Buck) makes the connection to blaxploitation clear, lest anyone miss it. As he considers the 1972 Marvin Gaye soundtrack album *Trouble Man* (for the eponymous blaxploitation film) Buck ponders:

> The music's way better'n the movie it came from. It's like the soundtrack to my life. And I can't get it outta my head. The music or the pictures. Pimps in platform shoes. Big black studs. Fat, sloppy, rag-headed mammies. Bug-eyed jigaboos, runnin' from shadows. Drug dealers in fine clothes. Wit' fine hoes. The record's played out, alright, but nothin' new ever came along to take its place. So I keeps that song runnin' through my head. It ain't much.

It ain't even good. But it might be all there is. And that's better'n nothin'.
Ain't it?

Here, McDuffie presents a scathing critique of black images in film as well
as comic book history, from the early "pickaninnies" of World War II, who
were always scared and incompetent, to the alleged progress of Cage in
the 1970s, which continued to present inner-city stereotypes of pimps,
dealers, and whores. Just as Buck Wild cannot escape, McDuffie suggests,
African Americans find themselves trapped, too, by these stereotypical
and vacant images and narratives that continue to influence their—and
all Americans'—understandings.[25]

Nor is this the only way McDuffie invokes this past to subvert its reified
conceptions of black identity and experience. One such ever-present sig-
nifier of Buck's entrapment is the "jive" he speaks, a language meant to
capture what whites *think* blacks sound like. Paying further homage to
Cage, Buck Wild drops phrases like, "Sweet Easter!" or "And now I gots
to get paid!" When he meets Icon and Rocket for the first time, the ensuing
fight showcases both Buck's power and his way with words; he expresses
surprise colorfully—"Aunt Jemima's do-rag! You's about one tough son
of a biscuit!"—and anger directly—"You mother-huggin', flock-pluggin',
hogs-head cheese eaters!" Icon and Rocket are taken aback. Icon, the oh-
so-proper lawyer, observes, somewhat dryly, "His dialect is unfamiliar."
Rocket, as usual, is more direct: "I don't think it's slang, though. I think
it's brain damage."[26]

Buck Wild's origin story makes him seem all the more ridiculous to Icon
and Rocket, as McDuffie further mocks the circumstances that gave birth
to Luke Cage (and blaxploitation heroes more generally). As Buck explains,
it all began "when I wuz convicted for a crime I didn't commit. I plea bar-
gained down from the crime I really did do." Wanting to escape police brutality in prison, Buck volunteered for a cryogenic experiment that went
badly when the equipment exploded. As Buck explains, "Before the ex-
plosion, nuthin' had froze yet but my brain." While his brain remained
ever frozen in the early 1970s, the experiment endowed the new hero with
"tungsten-hard skin and belief-defyin' strength." Inspired by Icon and
Rocket, Buck wonders about what might have been. "Lookin' at you makes
me think," he explains. "Mebbe if I hadn't been frozen, I wouldn't have to
be like this."[27] Buck Wild's repeated references to being "frozen" are clearly
comments on the ways Luke Cage and other heroes of his era—as well as
their creators—remain trapped in a racially dodgy past.

Nor would Buck Wild only serve as a means to critique Luke Cage; he would also undermine the staunch, traditional (and classically white) heroism to which Icon himself played. After Icon returns to his home planet, Rocket asks Buck to take his place. Gone, of course, are the philosophical debates involving Du Bois and Washington; in their place, Buck does his best Icon impression, thus exposing his character as little more than a facade. He understands what is needed—"Real deep voice. Enunciate. Be pompous. Good grammar. No contractions."—but struggles to implement it. After defeating one gang, for example, Buck, dressed as Icon (although still sporting his trademark Afro), does a ridiculous Icon impersonation, saying, "'Twas nothing, noble law-enforcement officer. And my thanks to you for giving me your barber's business card." When Rocket tries to make Buck smarter by taking him to Third World Books, the plan backfires, changing Buck's lingo, but not necessarily for the better, as the "new" Icon now says things like, "I refuse to be held down by the white man's gravity." He also adopts "Kwanzaa!" as a rallying cry and lectures fellow African Americans for running a red light. "Don't you have any respect for your people?" he asks. "A black man invented the stoplight!"[28] If Buck Wild then is himself a parody of black heroes stuck in the past, he also manages to satirize Icon as a response to this past, one that smacks of artificiality.

After Buck Wild died defending the earth, his funeral service allowed McDuffie to complete his searching critique of the history of blacks in comic books. A minister fails to deliver a fitting eulogy—he can only point to the deceased's lack of intelligence, gentleness, charity, spirituality, and dignity, among a long list of shortcomings—before concluding that the hero "had no dignity. He had no friends. And he died without achieving any of his dreams."[29] It falls instead to Icon to eulogize the complicated hero in a way that doesn't overlook Buck's problems but also finds some good in him by placing him in his historical context. Looking to the past, Icon admits, "Years before I arrived, Buck Wild was already here, fighting the good fight." Importantly, Icon defends not only Buck but the blaxploitation heroes of the 1970s as well: "Although we may, from our current perspective, have found him crude and ill-informed, we cannot deny his importance. Intentions count as much as actions. And Buck was nothing if not well intentioned." Here, Icon serves to credit the intentions of not only Buck but those behind his source, Luke Cage. Icon literally reminds his audience that Buck "spent his life fighting for what is right. All the while struggling with questions of identity and public perception that we still do not have answers for. He reinvented himself time and again, searching for a comfortable way to present himself to the world. And while we winced on occasion at his speech and demeaning behavior, more often we cheered him on." Whatever his faults, Icon concludes, Buck, and those heroes he represents, were heroes "for those of us who had no heroes. Were it not for him, we wouldn't be here today."[30] Here, too, McDuffie gives voice to much the same about Luke Cage.

As Icon finishes, a number of Buck's old friends and enemies rise to speak, exposing Buck's long history of adopting other identities. Through this history, McDuffie makes clear that he extends his analysis not only to Luke Cage but to the other black heroes of the 1970s more generally. Through the eulogies delivered by characters who are themselves parodies of blaxploitation figures, Buck Wild becomes a symbolic parade of only slightly veiled DC and Marvel characters, including turns as Buck Goliath (modeled after Black Goliath), Jim Crow (a swipe at the Falcon), the Patriot (a ridiculous stand-in for Captain America), and Buck Lightning (instead of Black Lightning).[31] Finally, McDuffie turns his parodic eye to Marvel's supernatural figures: Buck is brought back to life as Buck Voodoo, complete with jungle drums in the background. Here, McDuffie sharply encompasses all these heroes within both his critiquing and crediting of what they did. Though Buck's death signals that his—and their—time is gone (at least in these flattened forms) so, too, does it acknowledge the significance they had.[32]

Another Milestone hero, Curtis Metcalf/Hardware, arrived with a sharp if less satirical edge of his own, an initially violent and aggressive character who first invoked and then escaped the stereotype of black rage by undergoing a crisis of conscience; however, anger was his first distinguishing trait. The story begins with a full-page splash featuring a title caption that tellingly proclaims, "Angry Black Man." Joining our hero midadventure, readers watch Hardware exact violent vengeance against his former benefactor's hired muscle, brutally working to take down a corrupt corporate empire. As he ruthlessly defeats the thugs, Hardware throws one helicopter pilot to his death. Afterward, Metcalf thinks, "People ask me all the time: 'Curt,' they say, 'why do you have such a bad attitude?' 'Why are you so angry?'" His answer: "I've got every right."[33]

Having established Metcalf's rage, McDuffie then complicates the hero by sketching in his origins, refusing to let readers become comfortable with what appears to be a standard comic book stereotype. Discovered at a science fair as "a twelve-year-old kid from a working-class neighborhood," Metcalf was taken in and mentored by the famous inventor Edwin Alva. Ultimately earning seven college degrees, Metcalf comes to work for Alva, who allows the wunderkind to explore his interests and make the corporate titan loads of money. Along the way, Metcalf sees Alva as both his best

Figure 7.4. While the debut of Hardware directly evoked long-held stereotypes of the African American man as a "buck" — here, the "Angry Black Man" in both text and image — the series worked thereafter to undermine such reductive and damaging understandings of the hero and, by extension, of African Americans more generally.

friend and a father figure. Thus, Metcalf expects no problems when he asks Alva to share in the profits being made. But Alva refuses, contradicting any sense of Curtis as family by reducing him to a mere employee and pet.[34] Here, then, Metcalf's anger starts to become less a stereotypical trait than a justified response to exploitation and discrimination. When authorities refuse to respond to Alva's reported criminality, Metcalf takes advantage of a forgotten underground lab at Alva's complex to create Hardware. He emerges as a hero invoking imagery not wholly free of suggestive tropes, entering a hallway totally naked, his chiseled physique totally exposed but for a few well-placed shadows. He steps first into his shell, a skintight sheathing that covers his body, again highlighting his physique, and then jumps down a long-abandoned elevator, suiting up on his way down.[35]

On his earliest adventures, Hardware is a killer, further problematizing his depiction. However, it isn't long before his predilection for violence precipitates his crisis. When his good friend Professor Barraki Young discovers what he's been doing, she is appalled. Metcalf realizes she is right but hardly swears off killing; he instead concludes that he must kill Alva. Still, Metcalf here begins to struggle with his conscience, and when he embarks on what he thinks to be his last mission, he no longer kills Alva's hired guards, instead choosing to subdue them. When he finally confronts Alva, however, the effect of his crisis appears muddled. Hardware reveals his plan to the villain. He has stolen all of Alva's journals, research notes, and computer files and plans to use this information to bring Alva down. Then, after Alva has hit rock bottom, Hardware will kill him. To make his point, Hardware stomps on Alva's leg, breaking it. In wanting to bring Alva down before killing him, Hardware seems hardly a hero.[36]

As he moves forward, Hardware does in fact become a kinder and gentler crusader, now trying to avoid casualties. He matures further, too, beginning to wrestle with hard questions about his actions. Racked by a growing guilt, Metcalf drifts into an uncomfortable sleep that ultimately solves his crisis of conscience and completes his redemption. In his nightmare, Metcalf first confronts the victims of his violence and realizes the consequences, for them, of his actions. He likewise becomes cognizant of their cost to himself: estrangement from his parents, subservience to Alva, and, again, failure to consider the ramifications of his actions. The dead victims of Hardware chime in, reminding him of his transgressions. When Metcalf still refuses to "wake up," his dream guide takes him to "school," reminding him of the origins of the superhero within African trickster tales, his own exploitation and casual disregard of women, and his spiritual emptiness and anger. The dream guide then delivers the key lesson: "We had our tantrum. It's time to move on. We know what we gotta do." Hardware replies (to himself), "I gotta wake up."[37]

Metcalf arises from his transformative dream, now a true hero and no longer burdened by the need for vengeance. He renounces anger; he further realizes and accepts responsibility for his actions and their consequences: "I can never undo the evil I've committed in the name of my vendetta. I can't make up for what I've done. But I can live up to my ideals from now on. I can do better. And so can Hardware." As with other modern non-

Figure 7.5. Milestone worked to create more fully human characters in a variety of ways. Here, in presenting the home of the hero Static, the images resist stock understandings of the ghetto that confined black heroes for much of comic book history. The hero and his family live a typical—as opposed to stereotypical—life in their comfortable, if not showy, abode.

white superheroes, Metcalf, in completing this redemptive arc, eschews old stereotypes, rising above them to become a more fully realized character, a human being instead of a stereotype.[38]

If *Hardware* created such a human character by subjecting Curtis Metcalf to a crisis of conscience, Milestone creators used the master-to-apprentice story arc to do the same for Virgil Hawkins, a.k.a. Static. Static's story immediately sets him in the pattern of Peter Parker. When he confronts a gang, the Five-Alarm Crew, that is harassing Frieda (Static's friend and unrequited crush), he directs Spider-Man-like quips at them, making others—rather than himself—the target of such troped humor. For instance, when a gang member curses, Static warns, "Watch your language! This is a family establishment." As he leaves, victorious, the oh-so-cool Static tells Frieda, "And when you talk about this to all your friends, be sure to mention my winning smile. I never hear enough about that." Here is a Spidey-esque teenage hero, heavy on swagger and armed with one-liners rather than subject to them.[39]

Static's personal life is likewise cast in this mold Marvel made famous. He and his family live in a decent neighborhood—not the despair-ridden ghettos of other comic book inner cities—and their place seems nice enough, if not spacious or expensive. While his dad is rather absent, the family seems to have warm and fairly typical—as opposed to stereotypical—relationships. Virgil hurries home to answer a phone call he knows is coming from Frieda, squabbling with his sister, who makes fun of him for being so anxious to talk to his crush. The next morning the reader sees a not-unexpected scene as Hawkins's mother harasses her son to get him moving for school.[40] At school, Hawkins seems a somewhat awkward nerd, but he also gets along with a diverse group of friends.

The fallout from Static's initial encounter with the Five-Alarm Crew reinforces his status as a neophyte hero, a necessary component of the master-to-apprentice narrative, and allows him to complete his redemptive arc. The gang kidnaps Frieda, using her as bait to cause Static to confront their leader, Hotstreak, who turns out to be a formidable opponent with fire and speed powers. After a brief struggle, the villain stands triumphant, pummeling Static with high-speed punches. Static falls to the ground, begging, "No . . . please . . . no more . . . ."[41] Hawkins thus has to prove himself, and he confronts the villain again, this time relying on his superior intelligence as he kicks "his sorry ass." Having figured out how Hotstreak's powers work—his superspeed generates heat, which he can then throw as fire—Static cuffs Hotstreak to the playground equipment before he can move, thus depriving him of both of his powers.[42]

Victorious as a hero, Static still finds himself beset by personal problems that Peter Parker knew all too well. Our hero, flush with success, asks Frieda out, but she demurs, seeing him only as a friend. Hawkins also struggles with his daily life as a teenager, unable to hold a job because his superheroing always gets in the way. His struggles are presented with gentle humor, as his boss lists his lame excuses for leaving work on earlier occasions. When Virgil corrects her on one lamely faked excuse, she says, "Congratulations! You can keep them all straight! Now you expect to rush off before you finish the first thing I ask. A new record! No sir!" Virgil leaves anyway, losing this job, too, walking home sadly after saving the day as Static, and thinking, "This never happens to Icon."[43]

Static eventually found himself facing a crisis of conscience that demanded he choose his future path. Confronted by Holocaust, formerly of Blood Syndicate, Static is tempted by his worldview. "You bust your ass cleaning up the neighborhood," Holocaust argues. "They owe you. Look at 'em. Can they fly? Toss lightning? Stop bullets? You risk your life every day for them? You gonna get something for it or give it away?" Holocaust also observes that "connections" give some a "birthright" to success denied to others, but their new powers "got their 'birthright' beat all to hell." As Holocaust talks, his fancy car travels through the impoverished neighborhood in which Hawkins lives and arrives at a palatial casino. As the two disembark, they are immediately mobbed by gorgeous women. Holocaust continues his sales pitch, saying, "This is how I'm livin'. Grab a taste." The villain then delivers his key message: "Like I say, if you don't take it, somebody else will. And if you ain't takin', you're gettin' took. Stick with me, and you'll do the taking."[44] Static ultimately rejects Holocaust's offer, deciding to serve humanity selflessly instead. Such hard choices, as had numerous times before, serve to humanize Virgil, who had begun to grow into his role as a superhero.

In these various ways, Milestone characters like Icon, Hardware, and Static reaped the benefits of coming wholly new into superhero popular culture. Their lack of baggage—beyond, such as in the case of Icon in particular, what of the past they consciously chose to engage—at least in part facilitated the ways in which these comics escaped from those persistent limitations. Remaining to be accomplished was a similar reinvigoration of established nonwhite heroes within this body of work.

Established Heroes: Reborn

The turn of the century thus also saw creators at Marvel and DC breathing new life into their black heroes from the 1970s to address issues of race. The complications of doing so arise in a brief scene in a 2006 issue of *Infinite Crisis*. In the midst of this DC event, the new Mister Terrific and Black Lightning come together. Black Lightning asks, incredulously, "So you really call yourself Mr. Terrific?" His ally's response cuts right to the racial politics of Black Lightning's origins: "You really call yourself *Black Lightning*?" Black Lightning, obviously feeling the need to explain himself to an upstart who doesn't understand the past (or at least the 1970s), shoots back, "Hey, back when I started in this business, I was the only one of us around." The exchange serves as a dual reminder regarding nonwhite heroes. On the one hand, those earlier heroes like Black Lightning wore, for better or worse, their racial identity on their sleeves. But on the other, they were trailblazing in opening possibilities for nonwhite heroes. This ambiguity perhaps facilitated the efforts of writers and artists at Marvel and DC who now sought to revamp these established characters for a new, more multicultural world, not wholly jettisoning their pasts but also not allowing their comic histories to limit them.[45]

As he was the first of such heroes, it makes sense that these attempts began with Marvel's Black Panther. While an important step forward, it almost didn't happen. As the writer Christopher Priest recalls, when asked to write a new Black Panther series, "I was a little horrified. . . . I mean, Black Panther? Who reads Black Panther? Black Panther? The guy with no powers? The guy in the back of the Avengers class photo, whose main job was to point and cry out, 'Look—a big scaly monster! Thor—go get him!' That guy?!" Priest's apprehensions didn't end there, understanding as he did that "minorities and female super heroes do not sell." Finally, writing a new series about the Black Panther meant entering a racially charged arena. As Priest explains, "The problem with race and popular media is, in most every 'black' movie or 'black' music CD you'll see or hear, there is some hostility directed towards whites. Now, were I a white man, I certainly wouldn't want to spend eight bucks to go see a film where white males are portrayed as stupid and are the butt of every joke, or where I am made to feel guilty about things I had nothing to do with, or prejudices I don't actually have." He also worried about falling into "White People Bashing, fueled by our race's legacy of anger and resentment by centuries-old unreparative wrongs. But this hostility polarizes rather than unites. There is no healing, and it limits our opportunities."[46]

Eventually talked into doing the series, Priest understood the need to adopt some nontraditional strategies in making a statement about race. Most importantly, he wanted "to make Panther so cool he transcends the racial divide here in America. Rather than try and force the readers to identify with a black character, I accepted the fact [that] a great many readers would not be able to overcome the race thing, and withdrew from the Panther entirely." Making Panther relatively silent helped—readers are not privy to his inner thoughts and motivations—but Priest knew he needed to do more if he were going to create "a book about a black king of a black nation who comes to a black neighborhood and not have it be a 'black' book." To accomplish this, Priest introduced Everett K. Ross, a white character who always says what he's thinking, no matter how politically incorrect, to "give voice to the skeptical readers and validate their doubts and fears about the series. And, best of all, he could amplify the Panther's mystery and overall enigma as his monologues would be, at best, a guess about Panther's whereabouts and motives."[47]

Ross also allowed Priest to invoke previous attitudes toward the Panther, in this way building them into his fiction in order to challenge them.

Thus, in the first story arc, "The Client," when Ross finds out in a flash-back that he will serve as the government liaison for the Panther's up-coming visit to the United States, he is less than impressed, arguing that the visit—not unlike the Black Panther generally—is important only be-cause "the guy is black." When pressed on the importance of the visit, Ross replies, "Whatever. He comes here all the time. Hangs out at the Avengers mansion—orders up some ribs. . . . I mean, think about it—he's got no powers or anything."[48]

Despite such disrespect, the Black Panther is an incredibly smart and effective superhero. Having to juggle a series of critical situations cooked up by Achebe (and ultimately the demon Mephisto)—that include scan-dals at the Wakanda-supported Tomorrow Fund (including the murder of a little girl) and a refugee crisis in Wakanda—T'Challa rises to the occa-sion, bringing the murderer to account, straightening out the foundation's scandals, outwitting the devil himself, and resolving the ethnic crisis in his homeland. As Ross observes, the Black Panther "wasn't nearly as naïve as everyone hoped he'd be. . . . I was finally starting to see the [Black Panther] was much more like the puppet master. Always one step ahead of the bad guys, and manipulating things to his advantage."[49]

In writing Black Panther in this style, Priest managed some problems better than others. On the positive side, he handles Zuri, T'Challa's assis-tant, effectively, using what he described as one of the Panther's support-ing cast of "soul brothers in diapers with bones through their noses" to dismantle stereotypes. At a state ball, the comic book pokes fun at old stereotypes of Africans, as Ross, in his rented tux, shares a table with Zuri, for whom, Ross observes, formal wear seemingly means "Even Bigger Dead Animal Slung Across Shoulder." Dressed in stereotypical "tribal" fashion, Zuri sports a huge bone at his throat along with garish gold jewelry. To top off the ensemble, a gorilla skull/skin covers his head and a leopard skin/skull is draped over his shoulder. Zuri also carries his spear, an odd choice for someone who could certainly choose from Wakanda's arsenal of high-tech weapons. Zuri's words reinforce his savage appearance. He asks, dis-appointedly, "This is a feast? Bah. There has been no bloodshed and the women are all clothed."

But Zuri is more than meets the eye as Priest undermines comic book stereotypes. Thus, a flashback reveals a college-age T'Challa dating a white girl, which angers some black students. The wise Zuri explains to T'Challa that the prejudice he just experienced not only is common here but is the reason for Wakanda's isolation. It is also Zuri, despite all the superficial stereotypes loaded upon him, who achieves a form of interracial understanding with a local cop, Tork. In battle, the two come to a multicultural appreciation of each other. As Zuri explains, "You know—for a scrawny white man, you are not completely useless in battle, Sergeant Tork!" The cop's reply—"Well, gee, comin' from a big, old, grits-and-catfish, Fred Sanford–looking soul brother like you, Zuri"—reveals that cooperation is possible, once long-held stereotypes and distrust are both acknowledged and dispelled.[50]

Priest struggles, however, with gender when the Dora Milaje arrive. Ross describes these wives-in-training as "Amazonian teenage karate chicks from two Wakandan tribes. Keeping them in his family as potential wives somehow kept the peace between the city dwellers and the tribal factions of the client's kingdom." The presentation of the two women, Okoye and Nakia, seems even more problematic when Ross goes on to note, "The girls were six feet tall and not quite legal age." As they first go to battle for T'Challa, the duo wear super short skirts that highlight their long legs and revealing tops that reveal their ample chests.

While Priest might very well have wanted to set up the idea, as he did with Zuri, of Wakanda's cultural difference, his choices in dealing with the Dora Milaje are potentially fraught. It is problematic that the girls speak only to the Panther and, even then, only in a language that no one else can understand. As Ross notes, in observing the way in which these African women are silenced, they left "the rest of the world to wonder what was on their minds." Although the narrative does reveal some background about Nakia, she is of course just one of many women that T'Challa juggles as love interests. Even after proving themselves in battle, the Dora Milaje are reduced to objects once again, as Ross sits in a limo with the two very young women, who change clothes in front of him without even noticing he is there. As they do so, Ross continues to emphasize their extreme youth, his voyeurism leading him to imagine "the sound of jail doors slamming shut."[51]

Whatever its struggle with gender, Priest's series wanted to, and often did, comment on multiculturalism. During his American adventures, the Black Panther confronts a race riot on the streets of New York and tries to talk the mob down. Here, the Panther delivers a plea for multiculturalism, reminding an angry black audience, "I am merely a man. As any other." When someone shouts back that this is not true, not in the United States, anyway, the Panther interrupts the speaker by noting that he is just a man "in any country—among all peoples! We should not become polarized by self-interest—but embrace our common humanity."[52] But Priest does not shy away from also identifying obstacles to such interracial accord. His

Figure 7.6. The Black Panther's rebirth in the twenty-first century allowed his creators to reclaim the hero, now as a spokesperson for multiculturalism, while also deconstructing aspects of his earlier depictions, such as in this sequence of panels where his alliances with white-dominated superteams are treated as a putative abandonment of nonwhites.

critique exposes politicians who playact their concern for race with empty public gestures. At a White House–sponsored reception for T'Challa in the series' second arc, Ross captures the cynicism of an event staged because it is "good politics to do something nice for the African-American community" in an election year. He further laments the lack of any black persons outside of the king, his entourage, and those waiting on them. A "quick call to Spike Lee's casting director" by Ross quickly diversifies the guests but does nothing to alleviate the cynical nature of this event, Ross summing up its superficiality by comparing it to a Benetton ad.[53] Ross's comment recalls bell hooks's laments about US culture and its treatment of difference, not by being subject to such a critique, but sharing it.

Priest did not just critique real-world politics; the author also worked to expose the ways in which such hypocrisy had been translated into past comic books.[54] As the Avengers step in to prevent a riot, Ross doubts the heroes. As he explains, "They called themselves the Avengers, which I had always assumed was Greek for 'Gaudily Dressed Borderline Fascists.'" Pushing his criticism further, Ross wonders what makes the Avengers different from radical militias, militant black groups, or even "the moral right wing." More crucially, the civil servant draws an important distinction between T'Challa and his erstwhile allies, noting that the former's "cat suit was largely ceremonial. It was a badge of office—not the expression of some chronic self-delusion." Here, Ross reverses T'Challa's traditional role as an Avenger, in which he seemed relegated to a lesser status. Instead, T'Challa stands, in the cynical Ross's view, as the more noble.

A similar effect is the result of Ross's running monologues that lead him (and the reader) to a logical question: Why, if the Panther was not a superhero like the others, did he join the Avengers? The hero answers this question when asked by Achebe, who notes that many wonder why he joined the Avengers, even though "in every photograph, these 'Avengers' have the king of the realm standing in the back" and "do not even honor you by addressing you as king." The Panther replies that the Avengers are his friends, "among whom there can be no issues of protocol." But he adds, in an unexpected twist, that he originally joined the Avengers so he could investigate them as a potential threat to Wakanda. After the battle, when the Avengers assume that the Panther was only bluffing Achebe by saying this, the Panther tells them that they are mistaken, and he walks off, leaving the chastised heroes silhouetted behind him, again lessening them while elevating him.

Much like the Black Panther, Luke Cage, another blaxploitation relic, would be dusted off in the early years of the twenty-first century. The writer Brian Michael Bendis, in both *Alias* (2001–2004) and *The New Avengers* (Vol. 1) beginning in 2005, would turn Cage from a slightly embarrassing figure to a mainstay in the Marvel pantheon. Nama, however, is quick to dismiss Cage's significance in this era, identifying him as a no-longer-relevant cultural symbol and little more than a guest star to service other characters' plots. Curiously, Nama focuses solely on the five-issue spin-off series, *House of M: Avengers* (2008), where Cage appears once again in his 1970s regalia alongside other 1970s Marvel heroes in an alternate universe.[55] But Nama neglects how Bendis, over the course of these two series, evolved the character beyond his blaxploitation origins into a much more fully realized figure. Thus, the Luke Cage in the yellow silk shirt, tiara, and chains is gone, now replaced by a new and symbolically superior hero.

However, such auspicious significance was not clearly in the offing when

Cage made his first appearance in *Alias* #1. When Jessica Jones, a former superhero turned hard-luck private detective, wakes up having passed out at Cage's bar, the former Power Man seems very much in blaxploitation mode, particularly in terms of his sexuality. When Jessica asks how he exists in a world that won't forget his somewhat embarrassing past, he replies, broadly grinning, "Who's gonna fuck with me? I'm the scariest nigga ever was!" He then offers to take her home, and Jessica's ensuing first-person narration places Cage in the role of the hypersexed "buck." As the artist Michael Gaydos depicts Jessica's clear anguish, she states, "This was the night that I let him do anything he wanted. And even though he'll know it's wrong, he'll smile to himself. He just won't be able to help it."[56] When, in the next issue, Jessica seeks Cage out at home for help on a case, she finds him with another woman. Cage is as dismissive with Jessica—telling her, "Come on, girl, get the fuck outta here[.] I'll hook up witchoo later"—as he is curt with his current lover, telling her there's no one at the door.[57] Issue #6 would further highlight Cage's rampant sexuality, as Carol Danvers (the former Ms. Marvel) identifies him as a "cape chaser" who has had sex with Spider-Woman, Tigra, and She-Hulk.[58]

But while these appearances trade on Cage's past as a blaxploitation figure, the series on the whole strives to move him beyond this reified image. As early as issue #3, readers saw Cage hiring Matt Murdock to bail Jessica out of jail. Luke and Jessica's conversation outside Murdock's office is full of a witty repartee that suggests a close relationship, Cage mocking her as "chicken" when she doesn't confront the visiting Black Widow, positing that it's "'cause she could wup your ass."[59] The upshot of these moments would come in the series' climactic story line, where Jessica confronted the villain Zebediah Killgrave (a.k.a. the Purple Man), who had years prior mentally controlled and humiliated her. Cage, in contrast to previous depictions, cares for her. When she crashes, drunk and a mess, in his apartment after learning a case she has taken on requires her to confront Killgrave, Cage takes her clothes to the cleaner and brings her coffee. More crucially, he provides a shoulder for her to lean on as she relates her history with Killgrave. Her revelations, too, prompt him to hold her and, by conversation's end, offer to confront Killgrave for her.[60]

Though she eventually confronts and defeats Killgrave on her own, the remainder of these scenes mark a profound shift in their relationship and thus in Cage's characterization. No longer is he the cape-chasing, smartass lothario; he is Jessica's friend. The series' final scene showcased the transformation of their relationship and, indeed, Cage. He is more awkward, hesitantly telling her, "I seem to be thinking about you . . . a lot,"

Figure 7.7. The capstone to the reinvention of the new Luke Cage was his impending fatherhood. With it, *Alias* completed a story arc that transformed Cage from long-held stereotypes of the "buck" into a human and more fully realized character. As he smiles about the next chapter in his life, Cage extinguished the pernicious traits that had for so long limited him.

and, "The thing of it is, is I've grown quite—I worry about you." And when Jessica reveals that she's pregnant with Luke's child, he is a happy father-to-be. The last image of Cage is him smiling and closing the series with, "Alright, then. New chapter."[61] Just as the pair has reached a new chapter in their lives, so too has the series turned a page on the depiction of Luke Cage, evolving him into a more nuanced and fully realized character.

Bendis built on this foundation—and revised the ways in which non-white members have been added to superhero teams—when the first volume of *The New Avengers* launched in 2005. Initially teaming up with Captain America, Iron Man, Spider-Man, and others, Cage immediately made clear that he would not accept the subordinate position on the new team that so many black heroes had previously occupied. As he explains to Cap, "But listen, I'm going to want to be heard. There's things I'm going to want a group like this to try—new ways of doing things. I want—I want to be heard."[62] Depicting Cage's "new ways of doing things" would have to wait until issue #17 of the series. There, he and the other New Avengers arrive in the Highland Park area of Detroit, depicted, between the pencil artist Mike Deodato Jr. and the colorist Dave Stewart, as a severely blighted neighborhood: crumbling buildings and junked cars populate the streets, and the entire area is cast in dour shades of brown. Cage takes charge, telling the team to spread out, and he himself orders a group of pushers off the streets, a command that they readily obey.

When a local news crew arrives, they approach Captain America for answers about their presence, but the hero instead directs them to Cage, who explains: "So when Captain America over there was nice enough to offer me a place on the Avengers, I said to the man that there's something I want to do differently than the Avengers had done before . . . and this is one of those. This is impact superhero work. Instead of sipping tea and playing X-Box and waiting for the next alien invasion—on our days off we're going to put on our happy suits . . . and we're coming to your neighborhood. And we are just going to stand there."[63] Here Cage turns the Avengers into a kind of community police force, asserting their presence as a deterrent to crime in the neediest areas. Cage also points out that their purpose isn't to serve notice only to those who prey on such areas, but also to those in

Figure 7.8. Luke Cage's transformation in *The New Avengers* also brought changes to the team, suggesting that superheroes had a much broader range of social obligations than had typically been assumed in comic books. Here, as the Avengers, under Cage's lead, arrive in Detroit, they point out systemic problems and, at least for this moment, commit themselves to building a better world.

power who allow such deprivation to exist (to leverage them into taking action). Far from a subordinate and marginalized presence on the team like so many before him, Cage becomes one of its leaders, and specifically a moral leader. He makes the Avengers do not only something different but also something more than they did in the past, using their presence not just to take down superpowered villains but to do good where there is the most good needing to be done.

Cage's position as the moral center of the Avengers was cemented as the team fell apart during the first *Civil War* crossover. Now married to Jessica Jones and helping raise their daughter, Cage confronts Iron Man, who has come to persuade him and Jessica to sign the newly passed Super-human Registration Act, which requires the divulgence of secret identities and mandates federal service for superheroes. Cage tells the Armored Avenger, "You're perverting it all. You're distorting the ideas you said we stand for to the point that when you're done with all of this . . . the ideas won't mean anything. You'll stand for nothing, except whatever 'they' tell you to." Cage is confirmed in his fears when, simply sitting peacefully in his Harlem apartment, he is attacked by SHIELD agents when the registration deadline passes.[64] Throughout, Cage speaks for the Avengers' (and Americans') ideals; it is Cage who argues for the civil liberties that Iron Man and the Registration Act threaten to stamp out. By issue's end, Cage has safely sent his wife and daughter abroad to wait out the conflict and joined Captain America's resistance. Husband, father, community activist, and moral center, Luke Cage has at this point far eclipsed his origins and their limitations, transforming not only himself but the often problematic role and status of ethnic superheroes within superteams such as the Avengers.

Christopher Priest's short-lived series *The Crew* also demonstrated the potential of superhero teams to present a more inclusive view of race while simultaneously revamping older characters. *The Crew* pulled together little used superheroes as it told the story of James Rhodes, formerly War Machine, as he pieced together a new team that included the third White Tiger (Kasper Cole), Junta (Manuel Diego Armand Vicente, here working under his alias, Danny Vincent, who, like Cole, previously debuted in Priest's *Black Panther*), and Josiah X (the son of Isaiah Bradley, the black Captain America). Nama argues that Rhodes, once removed from his War Machine armor, becomes an interesting character and that the African and Jewish White Tiger speaks to the possibilities of not only multiracial identity and relationships but also an America free of racial prejudice.[65] This argument fits all of the team members nicely, as they present human characters dealing with realistic and complex problems in thoughtful and intentional ways.

In issue #1 of *The Crew*, the writer Priest and the penciller Joe Bennet introduced the reader to a James Rhodes who has fallen on hard times, a life change that emphasizes his humanity.[66] His body, long abused in his adventures, appears to be in great shape, but his hair is graying, suggesting his age, and he takes painkillers. His sad-sack life also includes a series of failed or empty relationships and impending bankruptcy, made all the more embarrassing given that he once ran Stark Enterprises. Bottoming out, Rhodes tries to pawn what's left of his War Machine armor; unsuccessful, he also offers a nice Rolex. Our hero then immediately blows this money on an expensive dinner with a buxom but disinterested blonde. To make matters worse, Rhodes learns from the Brooklyn cop Marcy Howard that his sister is dead. If Rhodes had been working hard to avoid confronting the sad state of his life, he no longer can. He travels to New York to identify his sister's body but still resists reality, describing his sister as "a very bright college student." Howard, clearly one to deal with reality, sets our hero straight, bluntly reminding him, "Your sister was a crack fiend and a prostitute." "That too," Rhodes replies.

Investigating his sister's life, Rhodes goes to Little Mogadishu, a Brooklyn ghetto that seems to present the stereotypical inner city of the comic book world. Here, Rhodes finds the expected blighted neighborhood, filled with angry and suspicious people, all black. The local men, all pissed off at the world, carry automatic weapons, which they brandish openly in an obviously lawless part of the city. The women are either scantily clad or very pregnant. These flat characters exist in an environment that has been presented many times before, the mean streets full of run-down cars, tenement buildings, and litter. Rhodes, upon arrival, gets caught up in its violence. When a local resident insults his sister, Rhodes's fist smashes into his face, and he then beats down a slew of the thug's buddies. There hardly seems much progress here.

But with issues #2 and #3, the comic introduces more of the cast, important additions that help to populate the city with more fully developed characters, as White Tiger and Junta are complex characters struggling to find their places in the world.[67] The actions of Cole/White Tiger are not motivated by race; instead, he obsesses about money, trying to please his shopaholic and pregnant girlfriend by taking advantage of his powers, planning to use them to earn a promotion and pay raise as a cop. The self-interested Cole sees "the Mog" as "Hell" but also as an opportunity for career advancement. However self-interested he may initially appear, Cole is not beyond redemption, as demonstrated by his decision to save a crook even though it means delaying his economic ascension. Danny Vincent — much like Cole — seems to act primarily out of self-interest.[68] Like Rhodes,

Vincent has fallen on hard times, and he plays the con man to make ends meet. Reduced to sleuthing in divorce cases, the ever-resourceful Danny collects evidence of an extramarital affair for an angry wife and then offers to sabotage the evidence for the husband, being sure to collect money from both. As with the other "heroic" characters in this series, any sense of a simplistic moral center is initially hard to find.

The origin story of the final member of the cast, Josiah X, ties his biography as closely to post–World War II African American history as his father's was to the previous era.[69] Josiah, it turns out, is the result of army experiments to create a supersoldier from the genetic material of Isaiah Bradley, the black Captain America from Marvel's *Truth*, and Bradley's wife, Faith. Radicalized by a series of hardships—being orphaned as an infant, experiencing racism in the army when he fought in Vietnam, finding himself targeted by the government when it realizes his genetic inheritance—Josiah escapes, eventually to Harlem, where he lives as a black radical militant. As he pieces together the mystery of who he is, he eventually visits Faith, now Muslim, to confirm his story and meet his dad. He cannot stay—as the government continues to watch the Bradley household—so Josiah spends the next seventeen years living abroad and earning a living as a mercenary, killing "for profit." This lifestyle takes its toll, however, and Josiah eventually turns to Islam. When he returns to the Bradley household in the present, he meets Rhodes, Junta, and White Tiger and finds himself pulled into superheroing.

To this point, the story set forth in *The Crew* seems not too dissimilar from the fare offered by blaxploitation heroes like Luke Cage in the 1970s and even Blood Syndicate in the 1990s. All the characters seem morally flawed, and as they come together, they don't get along well, the narrator explaining bluntly, "The four men want nothing to do with each other."[70] The heroes also operate in the inner-city ghetto, our heroes' racial identities seemingly anchoring them to the urban frontier. But *The Crew* is different from older material like *Luke Cage* and *Blood Syndicate* in significant ways. Most importantly, this difference arises from Priest, who wrestles with old images and tropes, arguing with and contesting outdated ideas by engaging them and creating characters who are more human.

As the team begins to gel, Josiah X, for example, wrestles with a crisis of conscience, played out on the sidewalk in front of his mission. Holding the American flag in his arms, Josiah notes that flying it has caused tensions in the local Muslim community: "I have offended some of our brethren with this flag. While at the same time—I've inspired some people with it. Somewhere, between those extremes, is where I belong." As he struggles to

Figure 7.9. Josiah X's struggles to understand his country's past and present come to a climax at his inner-city mission. Holding an American flag, he debates where he belongs in America. The answers provided in *The Crew* suggest the complexities of such questions and potential answers for it in the early twenty-first-century United States.

find a middle ground—and perhaps some long-needed nuance in comics—Josiah asks a Muslim passerby what Captain America means to African Americans, and the response is grim: "To black people? Not much. All this rah-rah post-9-11 jingoism has a different meaning for us. This coalescing of America is exciting—but it's not our America that's being coalesced. We are, at best, observers through a chain link fence." The visitor argues that Cap is "a white icon. A great and noble man whose greatness and nobility are near exclusive to white America. You run around with that star on your chest, you'll come off as some sad also-ran. A wannabe. Captain blackface." When Josiah protests that "the first super soldier was a black man," his visitor responds, "Oral tradition. Urban myth. History is written by the dominant culture." Josiah, seemingly now determined to act, replies, "Yeah, but we know the truth. Maybe the star will inspire that."

With Josiah X now ready to act, the Crew finally come together, each character confronting life-defining decisions along the way.[71] As the fighting escalates and Rhodes is stabbed, Junta and White Tiger have to make important decisions about who they are. As White Tiger has to choose either to save Rhodes and the victims of violence all around them or to catch the villain Triage (the latter bringing him the promotion he so badly wants), he observes Josiah heroically carrying kids to safety. As White Tiger observes: "Josiah doesn't say much. This being his first night as a hero and all. Though we've never been friends, I can't help but notice — the decisions he's made. Without hesitation. Without figuring the consequences. While I run the numbers on whether or not to tie my shoes." White Tiger makes the redeeming choice, saving others' lives instead of advancing his own, a hero at last. Junta also makes a redemptive decision, turning Triage over to the cops instead of using the villain to get back into the black-ops game. Rhodes needs his absolution, too, and the story ends with him laying flowers on his sister's grave. Marcy Howard shows up, and Rhodes admits that his problems are "way worse" than his sister's. "But," he says, turning to Howard, "I'm getting better," and the two share a passionate kiss, suggesting hope that Rhodes might turn his life around as well. The redemptive nature of these characters' arcs also redeems them from being more of what plagued comics in the past. Their struggles are resolved in part, but by no means in whole, thus avoiding any simplistic moralizing that would ring false. Short-lived though it was, The Crew presents a concise narrative that does much to redeploy these characters in a much more complicated reality.

At DC, the writer Tony Isabella revived Black Lightning in the hopes of demonstrating that old characters and superhero tropes might be revised to suggest a more complex and inclusive America. Isabella, an early pioneer at writing ethnic characters, succeeds, although his tendency to sermonize, in combination with the weight of stereotypes and underdeveloped characters, occasionally limits his multicultural ambitions. While Marc Singer argues for a complexity in Isabella's explorations,[72] the sharp limits of liberalism so clearly present in the earliest attempts to diversify the casting of superheroes in the 1970s and 1980s sometimes echo here.

The ghetto in the Black Lightning series is full of threat and bereft of hope, highlighting real social problems.[73] Opening to television coverage of Brick City, a ghetto area, and its "long-neglected Carver neighborhood," which contains "some of the city's worst and most dilapidated public housing," Isabella and the artist Eddy Newell paint a bleak picture. Although the city has promised renovations, the black residents are skeptical, assuming a few cosmetic changes might occur before public officials lose interest; as one resident explains, "They start things they don't ever finish." Readers then tour Brick City, a typical comic book ghetto: dark, mostly deserted streets, run-down and boarded-up buildings, and dangerous-looking black men carrying guns. The lingo of the area is a classic version of a commodified "jive," with local gangbangers uttering things like, "I thought the chump was gonna turn white!" and, "One of you clowns wanna check on Deon out there? Boy shoulda been back for mo' product by now."

Quick and creative with curse words, the gang members live in a hopeless world beyond "the gleaming offices and the malls and hotels," and Isabella wants to explore this, at least in passing, from a critical perspective. As one resident describes it, "The establishment put these black people here, so they can keep a check on us. You know, like they did with the Indians. It's just brick buildings instead of teepees." Another adds, "The projects is the end of dreams." Isabella makes clear, too, that the residents of Brick City are not to blame for their situation, emphasizing that they "want to do things." As one laments, "We have poetry writers, dancers, and singers. My 73-year-old neighbor paints portraits of her friends. There are a lot of good people in these projects." Here Isabella delivers a progressive message about what deprivation and racism do to people, although his penchant for preaching instead of storytelling threatens to dilute the message.

Isabella also moves beyond a blaming-the-victim mentality in focusing on self-serving politicians who neglect the ghetto. In *Black Lightning*, Mayor Jackson Perry seems interested only in self-promotion. The black leader expresses upset at gang warfare not for its effects on children or the inner city but instead because it could sabotage his efforts to get state money to build a stadium. He is also leery of Black Lightning, not wanting to share the limelight with one whom he deems a lesser hero. Later, as Jackson prepares to visit Carver High, his advisor—suggesting how the mayor intends to trade on his race for political reward with both whites and blacks—tells the mayor to give his typical speech for this event: "The 'role model, stay in school, take control of the future' one." When the visit is cut short by a shooting, Jackson flees like a coward, clearly placing his own well-being over any desire to understand or help inner-city kids. Always worried about his reputation and political clout, Jackson later ramps up a war on drugs, dubbed "Operation City Storm," to further compete with Black Lightning for media coverage, as well as to cast further blame on drug abuse's victims.[74]

The mayor and the gangs present serious problems that Jefferson Pierce (a.k.a. Black Lightning) must solve. He does so, however, as an at times too perfect hero, failing to achieve the more fully realized humanity of contemporaneous black heroes at Marvel. Early in the series, this is certainly true of the hero in his civilian identity. He volunteers his time to help an elderly lady do her shopping. He also uses the trip to the grocery store to follow up with her grandson, who missed class the other day (as Pierce selflessly continues being a teacher in his post-Olympics career). As he brings the groceries in, the elderly lady invites him to dinner and says her niece will be there. The niece, Gail Harris, is absolutely gorgeous and a coworker of Pierce at Carver High; they haven't met at work yet, she explains, because she and the other first-year teachers have "been hiding in the faculty lounge" from the scary students. In contrast, the too-perfect Pierce carries on teaching in spite of this threat. As he explains to Gail after gang members have trashed his classroom, "Classrooms come and go. Education endures. I came here to teach—and I can do that whether I'm in a classroom or locker room—or out on the street." Not surprisingly, the seemingly perfect Pierce is a great teacher, pushing and inspiring his students, all the while—of course—earning Gail's admiration.[75] Issue #7 presents our hero and his crusade against crime about as starkly as possible: "High school teacher Jefferson Pierce, a man at war with the crime and ignorance that cripple his community, uses his electrifying abilities to take back the streets and show his city that one man can make a difference."[76] Making that difference, however, too often puts Black Lightning in an unrealistic moral light.

Isabella did take steps to complicate and humanize Black Lightning's character with a crisis of conscience in the aftermath of a school shooting that leaves fellow teacher Walter Kasko dead and Pierce severely wounded.[77] The recovering Pierce struggles with Kasko's death, thinking about how an overweight man who ate, smoked, and drank too much acted like a hero, sacrificing himself to save a student's life. "Walter moved," he thinks. "He threw himself across Lamar's body. He was probably dead before I was even hit once. Walter Kasko was a real hero." Pierce eventually works through his self-doubt with the help of his ex, Lynn, and in particular Samuel Daly, a lab technician at the hospital who was also Kasko's partner. Daly, who has discovered Pierce is a superhero, wants to know "why [Walter] died. Don't tell me he was a hero. Heroes die all the time and then they come back. . . . He's not coming back!" Pierce points out how Walter daily battled the "stupidity" of a world in which "kids shoot other kids over the color of a shirt." He encourages Daly to "be very angry, at this cruel and stupid world we live in. It deserves all the rage you can muster. But don't ever be angry at the man you loved. His kind of courage is the only hope we have." Here, Black Lightning props up himself as much as he does Daly.

While Isabella and Newell effectively complicate Pierce through his crisis of conscience, helping in the process to make Black Lightning a more human character, his adventures overall are too often grounded in stereotypical surroundings populated by stock characters.[78] This problem becomes especially clear in the three-part story of a gang summit meant to bring peace to the inner city. As a summit organizer publicizes his efforts, Isabella delivers a heavy-handed sermon on the causes of gang violence. "But peace on the streets isn't an issue of black or white or Asian or Hispanic," the activist explains. "Gang violence stems from a much wider problem, a community problem that requires community response. Gangs come from an urban underclass that has had the ladder of economic opportunity taken away from it. People outside the gangs don't under-stand that's what fostered all the drugs and the violence. The gangs think they got to sell drugs—it's the only occupation truly and readily open to them." While certainly well intentioned and raising important issues, the sermon-like quality of the presentation—Isabella lectures, but the story does little to illustrate how the system functions from the gang members' point of view—runs the risk of trivializing the message.

Indeed, instead of presenting more nuanced characters on the wrong side of the law, the gang summit goes badly and introduces readers to stereotypes instead of more fully realized characters. The gangbangers talk a commodified jive; while the readers' column in issue #2 praised the realism of such talk, it feels flat and forced here, as it does throughout the series. In the climax, set at a black church, all-out gang warfare looks certain, although Black Lightning helps to defuse it at the last minute. The story does not purport to present a totally happy ending. As Isa-bella makes clear—even as heroes, cops, and former gang members hold hands—the gangs still exist and will start killing each other again, "sooner or later." But Black Lightning sees at least some positive outcome, noting in reply, "They didn't kill each other today." Seemingly modeled on liberal fare as far back as the early 1970s and *Green Lantern/Green Arrow*, that is apparently all that can be hoped for; systemic change is not addressed, let alone attempted. Thus, Black Lightning's revival sometimes struggled to escape fully the same backward-looking ideology that other contempora-neous attempts eschewed.

Conclusion

The efforts of comic creators to present sustained images of humanized nonwhite superheroes anticipated a broader social struggle to see beyond race that the election and presidency of Barack Obama would soon reveal all too clearly. On the one hand, many Americans expressed a new optimism about race relations with Obama's election in 2008. Gallup polls taken the day after his election captured an ebullient mood, noting that 71 percent of those polled viewed Obama's victory as either the most important or one of the two or three most important advances for African Americans in the past century. Even those who voted for the Republican John McCain acknowledged the election's significance, 51 percent agreeing with the above assessment and only 14 percent selecting "not that important." Additionally, the poll suggested, Americans had become more sanguine about race relations, with just over two-thirds believing that problems "between blacks and whites" would "eventually be worked out." While the electoral afterglow certainly helped to boost these numbers, the results were built on past progress (as positive responses to this question had been trending upward for two years).[79]

But amidst such optimism, grounds for concern persisted. There existed a clear split between Obama and McCain supporters. When selecting terms to describe their emotional state, the difference was stark. Ninety-five percent of those who voted for the winner described themselves as proud and 93 percent as excited; those voting for the loser clocked in at 32 percent and 15 percent, respectively. In terms of negative emotions, Obama supporters selected pessimism to describe their feelings only 12 percent of the time; McCain voters registered a robust 60 percent. In addition to a clear divide amongst the electorate, the positive numbers undoubtedly reflected the first flush of victory and a new president; such "honeymoons" often don't last all that long.[80]

Any such "honeymoon," indeed, turned out to be short-lived, and a Gallup poll taken in the summer of 2015 suggested a starkly different view of race in America. The news had turned grim, and Gallup now reported that "Americans rate black-white relations much more negatively today than they have at any point in the past 15 years." Only 47 percent described black-white relations as "very good" or "somewhat good," a significant drop from the 70 percent who had as late as 2013. The positive ratings among whites had dropped twenty-seven points in that two-year period; the number had dropped fifteen points among African Americans. Even more startlingly, the 2015 result was the lowest in the fifteen years that this question had been asked. While 58 percent of Americans believed that "a solution will eventually be worked out"—a number unchanged since 2013—attitudes had clearly changed.[81]

This nosedive in attitudes about race relations most likely reflected a grim couple of years. Racial incidents multiplied quickly, generating a list that cannot be exhaustively covered here; a condensed compilation might start with the shooting death of Trayvon Martin in Sanford, Florida. Killed by the neighborhood-watch volunteer George Zimmerman, Martin's death generated national outrage and debate, the hoodie becoming a much-discussed symbol of racial danger (which the *Luke Cage* Netflix series to come would pointedly address). The public also suddenly became aware of police violence against nonwhites as a long list of cases piled up. Michael Brown's death in Ferguson, Missouri, on August 9, 2014, at the hands of a white police officer sparked protests and national debate. This national conversation and rioting were extended by the injury and later death of Freddie Gray Jr. while in police custody in Baltimore in April 2015. Other cases followed, including, among the better-known examples that later came to light, the deaths of seventeen-year-old Laquan McDonald in Chicago on October 20, 2014, and twelve-year-old Tamir Rice in Cleveland on November 22, 2014. By late 2015, fifteen officers had been charged nationwide with murder or manslaughter while on duty, a significant rise from the average of about five cases per year in the years leading up to 2015.[82]

But racism appeared in subtler ways, too, and Obama serves as a useful way to think about the resurgent power of race, especially in the ways in which the commander in chief had to tread carefully. Indeed, Obama often seemed to be in a no-win situation. Some African Americans, Steven Gray reminded *Time* readers, had doubted the racial authenticity of the president, given his upbringing in Hawaii and Indonesia. As he gained black support during primary season, Obama then had to deal with the white electorate over the issue of Reverend Jeremiah Wright Jr., whose harsh rhetoric in regard to racism forced the candidate to distance himself from Chicago's Trinity United Church of Christ, in part because whites failed to understand how black religion had long helped African Americans cope with the legacies of racism.[83] The Comedy Central show *Key and Peele* commented on how Obama had to control his reactions as president, too, to avoid appearing as a stereotypical "angry black man." Here, Keegan-Michael Key and Jordan Peele introduced the very human president's "anger translator" in a sketch that examined Obama's seemingly perpetual cool demeanor, perhaps a necessary defense mechanism for the black president.[84]

Even the election and presidency of Obama, it turns out, did not deliver Americans from their racist past. Certainly, progress had occurred, but hopes that the age of Obama would usher in a "postracial" America seem destined for disappointment. Race continued as a powerful force in the United States, and the increasing cases of police brutality served as a stark reminder that problems remained.

Coda: Born Again (and Again and Again . . . and Again and Again . . .)

When we started work on this project, in the summer of 2011, it seemed as if the conclusion was writing itself as DC prepared to relaunch its universe as "The New 52." In the wake of their *Flashpoint* event series, DC's nearly seventy-five-year-old superhero universe was scrapped and restarted, now merged with properties including Vertigo, DC's mature readers imprint, and Wildstorm, the universe started by Jim Lee at Image that DC had acquired in 1999. "The New 52" was trumpeted as an effort to promote, among other things, greater diversity in DC's publications. As the then vice president of sales Bob Wayne promised in a letter to comic store retailers, the fifty-two new titles published under this banner would "introduce readers to a more modern, diverse DC Universe, with some character variations in appearance, origin and age."[1] Joey Esposito at IGN.com celebrated the initiative, writing, "DC Comics is making a push in many different directions with their September initiative, and it's great to see that diversity and appeal to all readers is a primary focus."[2]

The creators involved in "The New 52" were just as enthusiastic about the emphasis on diversity. As Eric Wallace explained in an interview regarding his new *Mister Terrific* title (featuring the black Michael Holt version),

> That *Mister Terrific* #1 will bring a diverse character out of the sidelines and into the comic book spotlight is a big deal. Especially for diverse readers looking for diverse characters. As many comic book fans have pointed out, the "status quo" for superhero adventures are stories where diverse characters are always supporting characters to their non-diverse counterparts. Not with *Mister Terrific*. Michael's the star, and his world is chockfull of diverse characters. It's a deliberate attempt on the part of the creative team to craft a book that more accurately reflects the world we live in.[3]

With its clear emphasis on diversity, "The New 52" appeared like a natural end point for our project, in a way culminating the growing trend toward and respect for racial and ethnic difference that this project examines.

But, it turns out, "The New 52" was only the first of what would become a series of new initiatives, rebrandings, and relaunches that would occur—seemingly nonstop—at both DC and Marvel over the next several years. In response to the initial success of "The New 52," one year later Marvel began "Marvel NOW!," which launched twenty-eight new titles in October 2012 following their "Avengers vs. X-Men" crossover event. Less than two years later, a second wave—"All New Marvel NOW!"—introduced thirty-four new and rebranded series. In the first six months of 2015, both Marvel and DC would repurpose their lines yet again. The 2015 *Secret Wars* series merged the Marvel Universe proper and the alternate Ultimate Universe as part of what executives were now calling "All-New, All-Different Marvel," a branding that, in deliberately echoing the debut of the "all-new, all-different" *X-Men* in 1975, appeared to wear its intent regarding diversity on its sleeve. In June of the same year, DC would officially bring "The New 52" (at least as a brand) to an end. Following yet another universe-altering story line—*Convergence*—DC began its short-lived "DC You" initiative, which would preserve the continuity established in "The New 52" but also put a premium on storytelling and bringing new creators into DC's fold.[4] Since then, as hard as it may be to believe, the relaunches have continued. In 2016, DC began "DC Rebirth," which sought to restore some of the pre-*Flashpoint* continuity to its comic universe, and Marvel's *Generations* crossover in Summer 2017 led to "Marvel Legacy," a similar "back-to-basics" approach, returning established versions of characters like the Hulk, Wolverine, and Thor alongside their legacy replacements; by summer 2018, Marvel had launched yet another line-wide refurbishing: "Fresh Start."

Throughout these disparate efforts, a constant intention was achieving greater diversity in comics, in terms of both characters as well as those who create the comics themselves. Promoting *The Uncanny Avengers* (Vol. 1), one of the featured titles launched out of "Marvel NOW!," the writer Rick Remender described the series as having a "focus on human-mutant relations" and "a team that comprises a vision for the Marvel Universe's future."[5] The series did so by creating the so-called Avengers Unity Squad, which brought human and mutant heroes together, clearly playing on the "mutancy"-as-race metaphor in which *X-Men* had long traded. Marvel Executive Editor Tom Brevoort spoke more generally about the issues "Marvel NOW!" attempted to redress: "There's always room for more; there's always room for further diversity. Whether it's more Latino characters, or more Black characters, or more LGBT characters—you pretty much can pick any group of people, and as long as you're not talking about middle-aged white men like myself, they're probably underrepresented in the world of superhero comics."[6] With "DC You," promoters used buzzwords like "inclusive" and "accessible" to describe the line, further characterized as an effort to "embrace *all* our audiences, and to create product that . . . talks to everybody." Too, it brought minority creators to the fore, with Ming Doyle, Gene Luen Yang, and others contributing to titles.[7] Promotional images for "All-New, All-Different Marvel" similarly highlighted this line's emphasis on diversity, featuring such characters as the Black Panther, Sam Wilson now in the role of Captain America, a new nineteenth-century Red Wolf, the Miles Morales Spider-Man, and Ms. Marvel/Kamala Khan, a Pakistani American character who debuted in the "All-New Marvel NOW!" wave.

However laudable the goals of DC and Marvel, their almost hyperactive promotion of diversity has not produced uniformly progressive results. Of the two, DC's has seen the most mixed results. A significant number of titles released as part of "The New 52" included nonwhite characters. Ethnic protagonists headlined six solo titles in the first wave: *The Fury of Firestorm*, starring Jason Rusch; *Mister Terrific*, with Michael Holt; *Batwing*, which saw the Congolese police officer David Zavimbe as a new "Batman of Africa"; *Voodoo*, showcasing the stripper who debuted in Jim Lee's *WildC.A.T.s*; *Static Shock*, featuring Static from the Milestone imprint; and *Blue Beetle*, with Jaime Reyes. Additionally, various team titles strove for greater inclusion, as Cyborg was added to the founding roster of the Justice League while Vixen and the Chinese August General in Iron joined the Justice League International. The "New 52" version of the Teen Titans added several new minority characters to its roster as well: Bunker/Miguel Barragan, a gay Mexican teen; Solstice/Kiran Singh, an Indian girl; and the African American Skitter/Celine Patterson.

While such efforts were laudable, the titles featuring ethnic heroes were among the lowest selling and soonest canceled. *Mister Terrific* and *Static Shock* lasted a paltry eight issues before cancellation, while *Justice League International* and *Voodoo* only survived a year. Among those that lasted longer, *Blue Beetle* managed sixteen issues before folding, and *Fury of Firestorm* lasted twenty. *Batwing* was retooled after twenty issues, shifting the lead role from Zavimbe to Luke Fox, the son of longtime supporting character Lucius Fox, a move that only bought the title another fourteen issues. Nor were the fortunes any better for later titles featuring nonwhite

Figure 8.1. While DC's recent frenetically relaunched titles emphasized diversity and inclusion, they often fell prey to old racialized tropes in comics. The Teen Titan Skitter, for instance, underwent a physical transformation that both obscured her African American heritage and dehumanized her.

headliners, as both *Justice League of America's Vibe* and *Katana*, each of which started in the fourth wave of "New 52" releases in early 2013, managed only ten issues each before finding themselves on the chopping block. Both title characters, alongside the Muslim and replacement Green Lantern Simon Baz, were the minority members of the similarly short-lived *Justice League of America* (fourteen issues) launched in this wave as well.

Nor were the problems of these series limited to just their short runs. Inside the pages of these "New 52" titles were patterns that had long plagued superhero comics and their efforts toward diversity. The addition of Cyborg, for example, to the Justice League treats him as a "token" member as he joins an otherwise all-white cast. Other ethnic team members found their identities erased: the seemingly black Voodoo was revealed to be a cloned alien shape-shifter (thus playing into the trope of polymorphous ethnicity), and both Solstice and Skitter in *Teen Titans* underwent dramatic physical transformations—the former appearing as a humanoid nimbus of black energy and the other gaining an insect-like carapace— that completely obscured their race. And the very notion of a "Batman of Africa" in *Batwing* treats that entire continent as one homogenous entity.

Old stereotypes also abound. Voodoo was overtly sexualized, first appearing crawling on her hands and knees on a bill-strewn strip-club stage, her pendulous breasts fully on display in a miniscule string bikini. She is likewise wholly silent while she gyrates and strips, not actually speaking

until almost halfway through her debut.[8] Elements of the "buck" stereotype, largely absent in the hero who had appeared in the late 1990s, would
similarly underlie Mister Terrific's depiction in his series. In the third
issue, he nearly beats the villain Brainstorm to death when he reveals his
role in Holt's wife's death. The hero thinks, "I'm one of the smartest men in
the world, but I'm acting like a Neanderthal, a frightened caveman whose
only method for expressing pain ... is pure unadulterated rage. Is this who
I really am?"[9] This conflict would continue in the next two issues, where
Mister Terrific encountered the Kryl, an alien race similarly divided between advanced and "barbaric" tendencies; his advice to an intersex character about self-acceptance is as much for him as for the alien Py'lothia,
and rather problematically emphasizes this rage as an undeniable part of
who he is.[10]

Similar problems exist in the depiction of characters representing other
minorities in "The New 52." Though the writer Tony Bedard—himself of
Puerto Rican descent—sought to populate his *Blue Beetle* series with a
broad array of Latinx characters,[11] they remain rather homogenous and
stereotyped. The opening scene at Jaime Reyes's high school is replete with
a stereotypical machismo, as the Puerto Rican Joey talks about Jaime's
friend Brenda "begging to meet 'Little Joey,'" a comment that prompts
Paco—wearing a red bandana to signal his gang affiliation—to similarly
assert his masculinity: "Oye, menso! You wanna talk smack about Brenda,
you can tell it to me!"[12] This new volume of *Blue Beetle* likewise appears
guilty of promulgating an exoticized idea of Latinx identity and culture
in various ways. For example, Paco's dialogue demonstrates that propensity to constantly "spice" English with Spanish phrases and exclamations.
In addition, La Dama, Jaime's mafioso aunt, is both sexualized (she first
appears wearing a strapless, thigh-high-slit dress) and exoticized (by her
use of "blood magic"). Finally, the alien scarab empowering Jaime is revealed to have possessed an ancient warrior; when Jaime, now in deep
space, reawakens this warrior, he declares his intent to "shuck you like an
ear of maize!" Gone too, amidst this heavy-handed treatment of ethnic
identity, is the youthful optimism of Jaime's original incarnation, as this
version's origin story included Jaime violently impaling Paco on one of
his arm blades.[13] The *Katana* series is no less stereotypical despite its later
debut. Within the first two pages, the creators played on notions of Japanese honor and stoicism, as Katana laments her "stupid, dishonorable way
to die" at the hands of her opponent Coil; too, Coil mocks her: "Tsk. You
are riddled with emotion. So brittle. Easier to break than a twig." A flashback to the Japantown of San Francisco depicts a wooden building with

Figure 8.2. Released as part of DC's "New 52," this version of Vibe not only was a more positive step toward diversity than other similarly timed and intended relaunches, but also was far removed from the profoundly stereotypical version that debuted as part of the "Detroit Era" Justice League.

thatched roof that apparently exists in this imagined version of the modern metropolis.[14]

Vibe, in his solo series, however, represented some progress being made in the fourth wave of "The New 52." Not surprisingly, the series did so by presenting a less stereotyped, more humanized hero. The opening page featured the young Cisco Ramon with his older brothers Dante and Armando, each with their own motivations: the oldest, Armando, looking forward to the opportunity of college, Dante being skeptical, and Cisco already missing his eldest sibling. When a Parademon attacks the trio, Armando sacrifices himself to save Cisco, leaving him and a too-scared-to-act Dante to mourn.[15] Tapped by ARGUS, an arm of Homeland Security tasked with superhuman affairs, Vibe also undergoes the classic apprentice-to-master narrative arc as he slowly learns to wield his extradimensional powers, using them to track down a stray Parademon in the first issue as well as to take on the Teen Titans' Kid Flash.[16] Similarly, Vibe asserts his independence, first by helping the ARGUS prisoner Gypsy to escape and then returning to ARGUS at the end of the series, but on his own terms.[17] As well, unlike those of his predecessor Blue Beetle, Vibe's creators do not feel it necessary to "pepper" his dialogue with Spanish and thus avoid reifying his identity in the same way. Unfortunately, the progress represented by Vibe is more the exception than the rule in the efforts of "The New 52" to represent diversity.

Marvel was somewhat more successful at tackling diversity in the second decade of the twentieth century. They clearly meant to do so in *The Un-canny Avengers*, a flagship title of "Marvel NOW!" Uniting disparate X-Men with individual Avengers, the so-called Unity Squad was meant to heal rifts between humans and mutants recently exacerbated by a now-telepathic Red Skull. Not dodging the racial problems that remained present in American society, the team is initially defined by the tension that resulted from grafting these two groups together. In issue #5, the X-Man Rogue and the Avenger Wasp come into conflict as the former attempts to re-place a picture of the original Avengers with one of the X-Men's founder and mentor, Professor Charles Xavier. Wasp exclaims to Rogue, "Have I done something to offend you? Because if not—I'm about to." And when the chairman Havok/Alex Summers attempts a compromise on where to hang the paintings, Rogue retorts, "Let me know if you need suggestions on where you can stick it, Alex."[18] Hardly the image of unity and harmony the team intended.

This same issue would provoke further tension not just between the characters in the comics but between the comic and its readers. Later in issue #5, as the team holds a press conference announcing its formation, Havok removes his mask and leaps into the fray of identity politics, es-chewing the label "mutant": "In fact, I see the very word 'mutant' as divi-sive. Old thinking that serves to further separate us from our fellow man. We are all humans. Of one tribe. We are defined by our choices, not the makeup of our genes. So, please don't call us mutants. The 'M' word rep-resents everything I hate."[19] Andrew Wheeler of Comics Alliance, though recognizing the creators' intentions, excoriated the speech and issue for its rejection of minority identity. Far from promoting inclusion, Wheeler saw Havok's speech as an argument for, at best, assimilation and, at worst, erasure of minority identities, from race to gender to sexuality. He further criticized Remender's response to critics of the issue, whom Remender suggested "drown [themselves] in hobo piss" if they didn't like Havok's speech.[20]

The culmination of a massive epic (involving the Avengers villain Kang and the X-Men villain Apocalypse) allowed Remender to reach his ultimate

Figure 8.3. *The Uncanny Avengers* arrived clearly wanting to deliver a message about the importance of interracial amity. Although not without its missteps along the way, its final point was clear enough: if mankind could not overcome its artificially drawn racial differences, only doom could await it.

point, delivered as a somewhat preachy lesson on the importance of inter-racial understanding and amity. By issue #17, the heroes' well-intentioned effort at interracial accord has gone even more badly sideways, and readers literally watch the earth destroyed, in large part because the blended team of mutants and nonmutants fail to cooperate in the face of an apocalyptic threat. Thor, the sole earthly survivor of this tale, escapes to "Asgard-Space," where our distraught hero meets his father, Odin, and considers the cataclysm that has resulted from the failed attempt at interracial co-operation. When Thor suggests that the blame for this devastation rests with himself, Odin contradicts his son, arguing from a multicultural per-spective. Odin instead believes that the ultimate fault lies with humanity, a negative example from which Thor (and readers) should learn. As he ex-plains in delivering a sermon on the importance of human cooperation, "The denizens, and heroes, of Midgard allowed petty differences and petu-lant squabbling to stand in the way of their own future. There is a point in the evolution of any species where they must discard their tribal instincts and unite as one people. One cohesive representative of their world on the cosmic stage. This is the test of all life. To see their world relative to the stars. To finally absorb how meaningless their rage at their brothers and sisters truly is!" Odin goes on to explain that he had expected that the people of earth would unite in the face of this existential threat. "Yet," he preaches, "they continued to war over their trifling differences. Combat, their only means of survival. Too savage to be allowed to join the cosmic community." As a result, he resolutely concludes, "the true fault lies with men. Ragnarok was their choice." As Odin walks away on a bleak, empty surface, backgrounded by an ominous crimson-purple sky, Thor remains on bended knee (as he recedes in the reader's view), the silence of the last two panels emphasizing the desolation that surrounds him.[21]

Here, in only three pages, *The Uncanny Avengers* came to its point once again. Assembled by Captain America to serve as a multicultural super-team that would prove that "racial" differences did not have to separate people, the individual heroes had proved incapable of overcoming petty disagreements and unnecessary arguments. Unable to achieve multicultural unity, the story suggested, only doom could await humankind—an ominous and heavy-handed message, yes, but one that seemed to present clearly the intentions of the comic's creators.

The other tentpole for the original "Marvel NOW!" launch was the writer Jonathan Hickman's run on the other two main Avengers titles, *The Avengers* and *The New Avengers*. Here, too, the results are somewhat mixed. On the one hand, Hickman's eighteen-member roster in *The Avengers* included several nonwhite characters: the Falcon, Shang-Chi, Sunspot, Manifold (Eden Fesi, an Aboriginal Australian with teleportation powers), and Captain Universe, inhabiting the comatose body of black American Tamara Devoux. But though almost a full third of this lineup was nonwhite, the sprawling nature of the team—not to mention Hickman's plot—meant that many of them played only bit roles in the saga. Hickman was more successful in *The New Avengers*, where he included the Black Panther among the Illuminati, an assembly of power brokers working behind the scenes of the Marvel Universe that included Iron Man/Tony Stark, Mister Fantastic/Reed Richards, Dr. Stephen Strange, Namor the Sub-Mariner, the Inhuman king Black Bolt, and the Beast. Here, Hickman built upon the groundwork established years earlier in Christopher Priest's *Black Panther* series, depicting the African hero as a noble and powerful man equal to all others.

Other titles were even more successful in their efforts toward greater inclusion and representation. The "All-New Marvel NOW!" initiative introduced Robbie Reyes, a Latino character, in the role of Ghost Rider.[22] Even more auspicious was the debut of the new Pakistani American Ms. Marvel, Kamala Khan, written by G. Willow Wilson and championed by the editor Sana Amanat, both themselves Muslim Americans. Kamala represents yet another iteration of a young ethnic hero following in the Peter Parker/Spider-Man mode.[23] Exposed to the Inhumans' "terrigen mist," the New Jersey native develops the power to change shape, allowing her to grow to enormous or miniscule size, increase the size of her appendages, and take on the appearance of others (as she does immediately, transform-

Figure 8.4. Kamala Khan arrived as part of "All-New Marvel NOW!" and quickly achieved critical and commercial success. The *Ms. Marvel* series demonstrated the power of comic books to address fundamental issues of race, religion, and identity.

ing into the classic 1970s version of her favorite hero, Ms. Marvel/Carol Danvers). These plot-based struggles are paralleled by Kamala's struggles as a teenage Muslim girl in America, as she deals with the limits put on her by her fairly traditional parents and her religion, as well as ridicule or sometimes just misdirected sympathy from ignorant kids at school. But where Peter Parker learned a lesson about power and responsibility, Kamala learns a lesson about identity, coming to be, in a way she was not at the start of the series, comfortable with her own multifaceted identity. Indicative of the series' success are the honors it has received, earning in 2016 the second annual Dwayne McDuffie Award for Diversity in Comics, the 2016 Angoulême Prize for Best Series, and the 2015 Hugo Award for Best Graphic Story.

Another series spun out of this initiative, if not quite the critical and sales darling that was and continues to be *Ms. Marvel*, also marked important progress for the representation of diversity in comics: *The Mighty Avengers* (Vol. 2), by the writer Al Ewing and the artist Greg Land.[24] This series featured, for lack of a better term, a "minority Avengers" team, an idea that had percolated before at Marvel. As Tom Brevoort explained, he had long been "fielding questions about Marvel doing a team of 'Black Avengers' or any other group with a minority focus." However, he "always felt the concept was fake and forced, but the reality is that the people who are interested in these characters and want to see heroes that reflect them have a genuine point."[25] The series brought together numerous non-white heroes into a different kind of Avengers team: Luke Cage, Spectrum (the former Captain Marvel Monica Rambeau), the Blue Marvel (Dr. Adam Brashear), a new Power Man (Victor Alvarez, son of the Luke Cage antagonist Shades), a new White Tiger (Ava Ayala, sister of the original White Tiger), Blade (masquerading first as "Spider Hero" and then Ronin), and the Falcon. In this series, Ewing built on the foundation Brian Michael Bendis had previously established with Luke Cage, continuing to portray him as a family man first and a superhero second. Cage likewise remains concerned with accomplishing broader change for his daughter, as he explains in the series' first issue to the chafing Power Man: "This is not the world I want. Not for her. It needs to change. And I can do more about that. I can mean more." He makes a similar statement to the Falcon in issue #4, as he works to set up what is now a volunteer, not-for-profit operation: "We're here to fight what can't be fought alone, for the people who need us to, the ones who can't fight at all. If that ain't the definition of Avenger—well, I'm changing the damn definition right now." Here, as before in *The New Avengers*, Cage speaks to the idea of doing more than just waiting around for supervillains to attack; he wants his Avengers to work for social justice.

Nor was Luke Cage the sole member with a socially oriented motivation to join this team. As a result, all the characters among these so-called black Avengers were brought together by something more, and thus something less superficial, than their race. Both the new Power Man and White Tiger want to do more, the former perhaps more out of ego than anything else, while the latter strives to live up to the memory of her brother. Blue Marvel and Spectrum, in their own ways, possess a shared motivation: to contribute, to matter. Spectrum, largely in limbo since her Avengers days, describes herself in issue #1 as "trying to rebrand," thus reestablishing her heroic self; Blue Marvel had been similarly off the grid, isolating

Figure 8.5. Though short-lived, Marvel's *The Mighty Avengers* brought together a number of its nonwhite heroes—Luke Cage, Spectrum/Monica Rambeau, new versions of Power Man and White Tiger, and Blue Marvel, as pictured here—but did so in ways that felt organic rather than forced or based solely on their racial identity.

himself and abandoning his heroic identity after the loss of his family. As a result of their clear motivations, this was a team not just conglomerated due to their racial backgrounds (as, say, DC's earlier New Guardians had been), but instead assembled as a result of both their friendship as well as a deeply shared sense of common purpose. *The Mighty Avengers* was short-lived, becoming, after only fourteen issues, *Captain America and the Mighty Avengers* (with Sam Wilson in the role of the patriotic hero), which itself only ran for nine issues. But throughout its roughly two years of publication, the various iterations of *The Mighty Avengers*, like the new *Ms. Marvel*, spoke most fully to the potential of comics to achieve something other than their at best mixed and at times sordid racial past.

Which brings us to the present, or at least as near the present as the drafting of this coda can be. DC's "Rebirth" has faced backlash for representing a backward step in diversity, in relation to both its characters and its creators.[26] And it's hard to fault such accusations when, for example, the cover of *DC Comics Previews* for the relaunch included only three minority characters—the Simon Baz and Jessica Cruz Green Lanterns, as well as the black Wally West/Kid Flash—and they are much smaller figures behind the more prominent (and white) Batman, Wonder Woman, Superman, Batgirl, Robin, Superboy, Aquaman, and Harley Quinn. That being said, "Rebirth" still demonstrated some diversity, with Cyborg and Blue Beetle continuing their solo series; *New Super-Man* featuring a Chinese teenager, Kenan Kong, as its protagonist; *Green Lanterns* pairing Baz and Cruz; and a *Teen Titans* that includes the black versions of Kid Flash and Aqualad. However, the long-term prospects are less promising. *Cyborg*, *Blue Beetle*, and *New Super-Man* were eventually canceled. *Green Lanterns* continues, but with Baz and Cruz—though for a time also elevated to members in the Justice League—no longer headlining the title; so, too, does *Teen Titans*, but with only Kid Flash embodying diversity. More positive is the continued presence of Cyborg and John Stewart in *Justice League*, Mister Terrific's leadership role in *The Terrifics*, and, as part of DC's "New Age of Heroes" subtheme, Honor Guest headlining *Silencer*. However, the overall line does seem a bit of a retrenchment from earlier levels of diversity.

Marvel's recent efforts similarly appear mixed. The various subsequent "Marvel NOW!" waves, for their part, continued a clear emphasis on diversity. Under these initiatives, Marvel continued to publish a plethora of titles spotlighting nonwhite heroes: *America*, featuring America Chavez; *Captain America: Sam Wilson*, despite the simultaneous presence of Steve Rogers in the role; *Ghost Rider*, featuring the Reyes version; *The Invincible Iron Man*, featuring the African American Riri Williams as Ironheart; *Luke*

Cage; *Moon Girl and Devil Dinosaur*; *Ms. Marvel*, with Kamala Khan; *The Totally Awesome Hulk*, starring the Korean American genius Amadeus Cho as a new Green Goliath; and as part of the Spider-Man family of titles, *Prowler*, *Spider-Man* featuring Miles Morales, and *Silk*, starring the Korean American Cindy Moon. Perhaps the biggest launch was a new *Black Panther* series, written by the National Book Award winner and MacArthur Genius Grant recipient Ta-Nehisi Coates, that would spawn *World of Wakanda* and *Black Panther and the Crew* as spin-offs. As well, Marvel features diverse lineups in several of their team titles. *The Ultimates* by Al Ewing and Kenneth Rocafort and *Ultimates²* by Ewing and Travel Foreman team up the Black Panther, Spectrum, the Blue Marvel, and America Chavez to deal with cosmic-level threats and situations. The Sunspot-led *The New Avengers* and *US Avengers* also included Dr. Toni Ho as Iron Patriot and the time-traveling Danielle Cage among members, and the *All-New, All-Different Avengers* includes Captain America (Sam Wilson), Ms. Marvel (Kamala Khan), and Spider-Man (Miles Morales); this team later split into two titles: *The Avengers* led by Wilson's Captain America and *Champions*, which teamed Khan and Morales with Cho's Hulk. A *Power Man and Iron Fist* series by the writer David Walker and the artist Sanford Greene; *Occupy Avengers*, featuring a new version of Red Wolf; and a relaunched *Runaways* also contributed to this recent diversity at Marvel.

Like at DC, though, recent line-wide initiatives from Marvel have largely culled the representation of nonwhite heroes. Of the previously noted titles, only *Black Panther*, *Champions*, *Moon Girl and Devil Dinosaur*, *Ms. Marvel*, and *Runaways* continue as of the writing of this coda; the restoration of Psylocke to her Caucasian appearance is, on the other hand, a mostly welcome change, even if it still plays to old notions of race and sexuality.[27] To its credit, *Champions* added two more nonwhite characters—Ironheart/Riri Williams and the new Inuit hero Snowguard—to its already diverse lineup. As well, the most recent relaunch of *The Avengers* included Black Panther and the Reyes Ghost Rider among the team, and a new title featuring Shuri, Black Panther's sister, by the acclaimed author Nnedi Okorafor, debuted in October of 2018. However, Marvel's line appears just as retrenched from its previous diversity as DC's fare.

But the depiction of Marvel and DC superheroes is no longer limited to just the comics, as both are building their own film and television universes. The DC Universe, which has suffered a slow and fitful arrival, continues to struggle with issues of diversity, with the Christopher Nolan *Batman* trilogy and what has followed remaining predominantly white. Even when nonwhites appear, they tend to serve subordinate and at times

Figure 8.6. Though many of the diverse offerings from
the various "Marvel NOW!" initiatives ceased publication,
Champions, which brings together a number of Marvel's young,
nonwhite heroes—as seen in this image from the title's recap
page—continues the company's efforts toward inclusion.

stereotypical roles. In this way, Morgan Freeman's Lucius Fox simply
serves Batman, offering moral advice at times, to be certain, but always
acceding to the hero's decisions. *Suicide Squad* (2016) trumpeted a highly
diverse cast—Viola Davis, Will Smith, Adewale Akinnuoye-Agbaje, Jay
Hernandez, and Karen Fukuhara—but reduced the latter three (playing
Killer Croc, El Diablo, and Katana, respectively) to shallow ethnic stereotypes. Such fare too often hearkened backward to old presentations of
race. Even the well-received *Wonder Woman* (2017) stumbled, most obviously in assembling what was, in effect, a revival of the World War II–era

"All-American platoon," piecing together a multiethnic support team for the white heroine and Steve Trevor during the Great War. Most grating here is the laconic Chief's use of smoke signals to alert Wonder Woman in one scene, a callback to a long history of racialized depictions of Native Americans. *Justice League* (2017), too, replicated old patterns, adding Cyborg as the token nonwhite member in an otherwise Caucasian lineup and continuing to use Laurence Fishburne as Perry White (originated in 2013's *Man of Steel*) and thus in a supporting role.

Marvel's film universes are more fully developed as of this writing, and they have done better with racial diversity, although not without some problems. The *Spider-Man* films at Sony have been predominantly white (featuring Jamie Foxx as Electro in one movie), although the recent reboot features a somewhat more multicultural cast that includes Zendaya and Jacob Batalon. The *X-Men* franchise has been more successfully transferred to the screen at Fox, its mutant metaphor embracing sexuality as much as race in these films. The Marvel Cinematic Universe (MCU), which has grown to, at the time of this writing, twenty movies, has, on the one hand, made some significant efforts regarding diversity. It has introduced screen versions of James Rhodes/War Machine, Sam Wilson/Falcon, and Black Panther, the latter arriving to much acclaim and massive box office numbers in 2018 as the first nonwhite Marvel character to headline his own film.[28] An animated version of Miles Morales/Spider-Man added to this list in late 2018. Marvel has also diversified traditionally white characters (though not without controversy), casting Idris Elba as the Asgardian Heimdall, Tessa Thompson as Valkyrie, and, perhaps most famously, Samuel L. Jackson as Nick Fury. That's not to say the MCU has been without problems. Tilda Swinton's casting as the traditionally Asian Ancient One in *Doctor Strange* was widely lambasted, and the depiction of Mantis in the second *Guardians of the Galaxy* played on stereotypes of Asian submissiveness as well as the perpetual-foreigner trope.

The small screen has likewise borne witness to a veritable explosion of superhero series. DC's properties have become a cornerstone of the CW, debuting with *Arrow* in 2012, followed by *The Flash* (2015), *DC's Legends of Tomorrow* (2016), *Supergirl* (which debuted on CBS in 2015 before moving to the CW), and *Black Lightning* (2018). In many ways, as DC's television universe has developed, so too has its treatment of diversity. *Arrow*, with John Diggle as Spartan, and *The Flash*, with Cisco Ramon as Vibe, originally featured nonwhite characters as sidekicks to the titular heroes, but both cast members have since gone on to become full-fledged heroes and characters themselves. *Legends of Tomorrow* has included several nonwhite characters among its cast, beginning with Hawkgirl and Jefferson Jackson (as one half of Firestorm), and going on to comprise versions of Vixen, Isis, and Kid Flash. However, it is the two most recent series—*Supergirl* and *Black Lightning*—that have most fully embraced issues of identity, the former not only smartly encompassing race but gender and sexuality as well, and the latter sensitively depicting two generations of a black superhero family and their struggles.

Marvel's television adaptations have been more disparate in both nature and venue but just as concerted in treating issues of identity. ABC continues to host the first MCU show—*Agents of SHIELD* (2013)—and also presented the two seasons of the short-lived *Agent Carter* (2015) and a season of the even shorter-lived *Inhumans* (2017). Netflix has so far proven to be audiences' most consistent avenue for televised versions of Marvel properties: three seasons of *Daredevil* (2015), two each of *Jessica Jones* (2015), *Luke Cage* (2016), and *Iron Fist* (2017), and one of *The Punisher* (2017), as well as *The Defenders* (2017), a one-off event teaming up the first four heroes; however, with the cancellations of *Daredevil*, *Luke Cage*, and *Iron Fist* and no apparent plans beyond a third season of *Jessica Jones* and a second season of *Punisher*, Marvel's Netflix presence seems on the wane. In the last year, Marvel properties have debuted on FX (*Legion*, 2017), Fox (*The Gifted*, 2017), Hulu (*Runaways*, 2017), and Freeform (*Cloak and Dagger*, 2018). Across its various homes, Marvel television includes a nigh dizzying array of diversity, ranging from adapted to original characters: Daisy Johnson/Quake, Melinda May, Mack, Yo-Yo Rodriguez, and Ghost Rider/ Robbie Reyes on *Agents of SHIELD*, as well as Claire Temple, an African American Ben Urich, Misty Knight, Colleen Wing, Malcolm Ducasse, Oscar Arocho, Shades, Turk, Black Mariah, Cottonmouth, Diamondback, Bushmaster, and Nightshade across Marvel's Netflix offerings. Another adaptation of Marvel's X-Men, *The Gifted*, introduced updated versions of Thunderbird and Blink (played by the Korean American actress Jamie Chung), as well as Eclipse, a Latino hero invented for the series. The Hulu version of *Runaways* maintained the diversity of the original comic cast, and Freeform's *Cloak and Dagger* not only transplanted the characters from New York to New Orleans but has so far avoided the pitfalls inherent in the source material.

This recent past in superhero popular culture is both encouraging and disheartening, making it part and parcel of what superhero comics—much like American society writ large—have (and have not) been doing for over seventy years. That such struggles continue is hardly surprising. The election of Donald Trump in 2016 demonstrated the continued power of race and racism in American life. The candidate and then president—in describing Mexican immigrants as rapists and violent gang members; promising to build a wall spanning the United States' southern border; reacting blithely to racial violence in Charlottesville, Virginia; and deciding to separate children from parents in dealing with issues of undocumented immigration, to name but a few issues—has politicized and elevated race to the forefront of American politics again, confronting the optimism of multiculturalism with a much bleaker view of what diversity portends for the United States. And superhero popular culture, as it has since World War II (and now perhaps in its most ubiquitous position within US culture), will play a role—not simply in passively reflecting American attitudes toward race but in actively shaping them—in this ongoing debate, for good or for ill.

Notes

Introduction

1. In contrast, we echo Kate Polak's assertion that the gutter is better thought of "more as a space that creates the 'room' to imagine connections, rather than the space in which connections explicitly occur." See Polak, *Ethics in the Gutter*, 1.

2. The noted independent cartoonist Harvey Pekar, for instance, in compiling his volume of *Best American Comics*, eschews superhero comics, finding none of them "particularly good" and ultimately arguing that comics "don't have to be about costumed superheroes, cute little kids, and talking animals." Similarly, Hillary Chute and Marianne DeKoven include pre-twentieth-century painting and picture stories as well as name check early twentieth-century works like Winsor McCay's *Little Nemo* and George Herriman's *Krazy Kat* in their history of graphic narrative, but then skip over sixty years' worth of superhero comics to "today's graphic narrative." Finally, when Derek Parker Royal edited a special edition of *MELUS* on graphic narrative, superheroes were few and far between. See Pekar, Introduction, xvii, xxii; Chute and DeKoven, "Introduction," 768–769; Royal, "Introduction," 15.

3. Eisner, *Comics and Sequential Art*, xi, 2, 39.

4. Eisner, *Comics and Sequential Art*, 2, xi.

5. McCloud, *Understanding Comics*, 6, 9, 10–18.

6. McCloud, *Understanding Comics*, 3, 9, 45.

7. As the back-cover copy of their book proclaims, "Superhero comics are only one small component in a wealth of representations of black characters," a statement that implies such comics to be of a lesser worth amid this wealth. Gateward and Jennings, *Blacker the Ink*, back cover.

8. Hajdu, *Ten-Cent Plague*, 10–11, 25, 31.

9. Hajdu, *Ten-Cent Plague*, 25, 31.

10. Regalado, *Bending Steel*, 8.

11. G. Jones, *Men of Tomorrow*, xiv–xv.

12. G. Jones, *Men of Tomorrow*, xv, 62.

13. Wright, *Comic Book Nation*, ix–x, xiii.

14. Wall, *Inventing the "American Way,"* 115.

15. For the following discussion, see Remender and Acuña, "Apocalypse Twins."

16. Hennon, "Ms. Marvel."

17. See Rosberg, "Walker Talks *Shaft*."

18. Wright, *Comic Book Nation*, 110.

19. Singer, "'Black Skins' and White Masks," 109.

20. O'Neil, Foreword, 5–6.

21. Fingeroth, *Superman on the Couch*, 56.

22. Fingeroth, "Power and Responsibility," 125–126.

23. DeFalco, "Superheroes Are Made," 145.

24. Nama, *Super Black*, 9.

25. Singer, "'Black Skins' and White Masks," 107.

26. Dixon and Rivoche, "How Liberalism Became Kryptonite."

27. Nama, *Super Black*, 4, 8.

28. Fawaz, *New Mutants*, 3. For example, Fawaz celebrates the end of *The Fantastic Four* #1 and the team's birth as a "radical transformation of identity," and yet the final panel of this page depicts three members—Mister Fantastic, Invisible Girl, and the Human Torch—in their fully human forms while the Thing's transformed appearance is completely shrouded by a trench coat and hat. See Fawaz, 30–31.

29. Wright, *Comic Book Nation*, 287–293.

30. Newton, *Narrative Ethics*, 9.

31. Hogan, *Empire and Poetic Voice*, 2, 32.

32. P. Hamilton, *Of Space and Mind*, 13.

33. I. Gordon, *Comic Strips and Consumer Culture*, 108, 110–111.

34. I. Gordon, *Superman*, 17, 52.

35. Regalado, *Bending Steel*, 8–9.

36. Aldama, *Your Brain on Latino Comics*, 4, 11.

37. Royal, "Foreword," ix.

38. Regalado, *Bending Steel*, 8–9.

39. Chang, "Superman Is About to Visit," 42.

40. Bogle, *Toms, Coons, Mulattoes*.

41. Steve Englehart, Mike Friedrich, and Sal Buscema, "When a Legend Dies!," in Englehart, Gerber, et al., *Essential Captain America*.

42. Chris Claremont and John Byrne, "Cry for the Children!," in Claremont, Cockrum, and Byrne, *Uncanny X-Men Omnibus*, 608–609.

43. Steve Englehart and Frank Robbins, "Nomad: No More," in Englehart, Gerber, et al., *Essential Captain America*.

Chapter 1: "World's Finest"?

1. G. Jones, *Men of Tomorrow*, 86, 109–110, 113, 118, 121–125, 142, 174; Wright, *Comic Book Nation*, 7, 9–10, 12–14.

2. G. Jones, *Men of Tomorrow*, 165, 170.

3. Wright, *Comic Book Nation*, 18–19.

4. Wright, *Comic Book Nation*, 22–29, 33–35.

5. G. Jones, *Men of Tomorrow*, 231–232; Wright, *Comic Book Nation*, 31.

6. Wright, *Comic Book Nation*, 30, 35–37, 39, 53; see Cronin, *Was Superman a Spy?*, 135–136.

7. Wright, *Comic Book Nation*, 8–11; G. Jones, *Men of Tomorrow*, 218. As the war in Europe drew closer to the United States, comic books and their heroes increasingly joined the fight. The Sub-Mariner fought the crew of a submarine flying the swastika flag in February 1940. Captain America and the Human Torch faced down Nazi spies and saboteurs. Quality Comics introduced the Blackhawks, a diverse military aviation group (that included a character named Chop Chop, steeped in demeaning Chinese stereotypes). Leverett Gleason published *Daredevil Battles Hitler*, presenting a strong internationalist stance. See Wright, *Comic Book Nation*, 40–41, 44–45; Cronin, *Was Superman a Spy?*, 216.

8. Wright, *Comic Book Nation*, 53–55.

9. Jeffries, *Wartime America*, 120, 134.

10. R. Daniels, "Bad News from the Good War," 161.

11. R. Daniels, "Bad News from the Good War," 157, 163–164; Wall, *Inventing the "American Way*," 132–133, 149–150.

12. Jeffries, *Wartime America*, 133–139.

13. For Japanese American exile and incarceration, see R. Daniels, *Concentration Camps*; Murray, *What Did the Internment Mean?*

14. By February 16, 1942, those interned included 2,192 Japanese, 1,393 Germans, and 264 Italians. See Murray, *What Did the Internment Mean?*

15. Quoted in A. Austin, "Loyalty and Concentration Camps," 254–255.

16. Commission on Wartime Relocation and Internment of Civilians, *Personal Justice Denied*.

17. R. Daniels, "Bad News from the Good War," 164–165.

18. R. Daniels, "Bad News from the Good War," 165–166; Jeffries, *Wartime America*, 114, 141.

19. Roy Thomas, "Foreword," in Fox, *All Star Comics*, 5–9; Gardner Fox, Jack Burnley, Sheldon Moldoff, et al., *All Star Comics #12*, in Fox, *All Star Comics*, 71.

20. "Sneer Strikes," in Siegel, Ellsworth, et al., *Superman*, 154.

21. "Sneer Strikes," in Siegel, Ellsworth, et al., *Superman*, 169.

22. Kneitel, "Japoteurs"; "Sneer Strikes," in Siegel, Ellsworth, et al., *Superman*, 169. Superman's radio show, it is worth noting, used the same racist terminology. As Ian Gordon has reported, the Man of Steel's radio adventures included battles against both German and Japanese enemies; however, the Germans were labeled "Nazis," while the Japanese were "labeled racially." See I. Gordon, *Superman*, 155.

23. Sony Pictures Home Entertainment, *Batman*, chap. 13, "Eight Steps Down."

24. A. Austin, "Loyalty and Concentration Camps," 255–256.

25. Stan Lee and Al Gabriele, *Young Allies #3*, in S. Lee, Binder, et al., *Golden Age Young Allies*, 140.

26. Roy Thomas, "Foreword," in Fox, *All Star Comics*, 7.

27. Gardner Fox, Jack Burnley, Sheldon Moldoff, et al., *All Star Comics #12*, in Fox, *All Star Comics*, 68–69.

28. "Sneer Strikes," in Siegel, Ellsworth, et al., *Superman*, 154, 156, 158, 159.

29. Sony Pictures Home Entertainment, *Batman*, chap. 1, "The Electrical Brain"; chap. 4, "Slaves of the Rising Sun"; chap. 10, "Flying Spies"; chap. 11, "A Nipponese Trap"; chap. 12, "Embers of Evil"; chap. 15, "The Doom of the Rising Sun."

30. Kneitel, "Japoteurs." On "Japoteurs," see also A. Austin, "Superman Goes to War," 51–56.

31. "Sneer Strikes," in Siegel, Ellsworth, et al., *Superman*, 158.

32. Sony Pictures Home Entertainment, *Batman*, chap. 1, "The Electrical Brain."

33. Sony Pictures Home Entertainment, *Batman*, chap. 3, "The Mark of the Zombies"; chap. 5, "The Living Corpse"; chap. 11, "A Nipponese Trap"; chap. 13, "Eight Steps Down."

34. Kneitel, "Japoteurs."

35. Kneitel, "Japoteurs."

36. Timely Comics, *Captain America Comics*, 12.

37. Sony Pictures Home Entertainment, *Batman*, chap. 1, "The Electrical Brain"; chap. 12, "Embers of Evil."

38. The cave is seen in Sony Pictures Home Entertainment, *Batman*, chap. 1, "The Electrical Brain"; chap. 4, "Slaves of the Rising Sun"; and chap. 15, "The Doom of the Rising Sun." Captain America's adventures with the Japanese enemy led him not to a cave but to a cobwebbed cellar that might as well have been one. See Timely Comics, *Captain America Comics*, 10.

39. "Sneer Strikes," in Siegel, Ellsworth, et al., *Superman*, 158, 160; Sony Pictures Home Entertainment, *Batman*, chap. 1, "The Electrical Brain"; chap. 2, "The Bat's Cave"; chap. 13, "Eight Steps Down."

40. R. Lee, *Orientals*, 28–29.

41. Ma, *Deathly Embrace*, 5–6, 7, 15–16.

42. G. Jones, *Men of Tomorrow*, 29.

43. G. Jones, *Men of Tomorrow*, 82–85, 120–121; L. Daniels, *DC Comics*, 18.

44. G. Jones, *Men of Tomorrow*, 173; Wright, *Comic Book Nation*, 11.

45. Takaki, *Different Mirror*, 10–11, 54–55, 149–154. Takaki notes that Irish immigrants also used their race to their advantage in outcompeting Chinese Americans, becoming citizens and "blending into American society." In this way, Irish Americans claimed political and economic progress, but "often at the expense of the Chinese and blacks." See Takaki, *Different Mirror*, 9.

46. "Sneer Strikes," in Siegel, Ellsworth, et al., *Superman*, 157.

47. Kneitel, "Japoteurs."

48. Sony Pictures Home Entertainment, *Batman*, chap. 5, "The Living Corpse"; chap. 4, "Slaves of the Rising Sun."

49. Kneitel, "Japoteurs"; "Sneer Strikes," in Siegel, Ellsworth, et al., *Superman*, 155, 166; Gardner Fox, Jack Burnley, Cliff Young, et al., *All Star Comics* #11, in Fox, *All Star Comics*, 24.

50. Timely Comics, *Captain America Comics*, 6.

51. Gardner Fox, Jack Burnley, Cliff Young, et al., *All Star Comics* #11, in Fox, *All Star Comics*, 47–48, 25–26, 53–54, 55; and *All Star Comics* #12, in Fox, *All Star Comics*, 100, 114–115.

52. "Sneer Strikes," in Siegel, Ellsworth, et al., *Superman*, 155–156, 159, 166.

53. Sony Pictures Home Entertainment, *Batman*, chap. 1, "The Electrical Brain."

54. Gardner Fox, Jack Burnley, Sheldon Moldoff, et al., *All Star Comics* #12, in Fox, *All Star Comics*, 97–99, 110.

55. Timely Comics, *Captain America Comics*, table of contents, cover, 1, 7, 16.

56. Gardner Fox, Jack Burnley, Cliff Young, et al., *All Star Comics* #11, in Fox, *All Star Comics*, 35–37, 56–58.

57. Stan Lee and Al Gabriele, *Young Allies* #3, in S. Lee, Binder, et al., *Golden Age Young Allies*, 153, 164, 170, 176.

58. Stan Lee and Al Gabriele, *Young Allies* #3, in S. Lee, Binder, et al., *Golden Age Young Allies*, 152, 167, 173–175.

59. Sony Pictures Home Entertainment, *Batman*, chap. 15, "The Doom of the Rising Sun"; chap. 4, "Slaves of the Rising Sun."

60. Gardner Fox, Jack Burnley, Cliff Young, et al., *All Star Comics* #11, in Fox, *All Star Comics*, 18, 56.

61. Sony Pictures Home Entertainment, *Batman*, chap. 14, "The Executioner Strikes."

62. "Sneer Strikes," in Siegel, Ellsworth, et al., *Superman*, 167.

63. Timely Comics, *Captain America Comics*, 1, 5, 9.

64. "Sneer Strikes," in Siegel, Ellsworth, et al., *Superman*, 155, 160.

65. Sony Pictures Home Entertainment, *Batman*, chap. 3, "The Mark of the Zombies"; chap. 4, "Slaves of the Rising Sun"; chap. 9, "The Sign of the Sphinx."

66. Timely Comics, *Captain America Comics*, 2, 4.

67. Sony Pictures Home Entertainment, *Batman*, chap. 15, "The Doom of the Rising Sun"; chap. 4, "Slaves of the Rising Sun"; chap. 14, "The Executioner Strikes"; chap. 12, "Embers of Evil."

68. "Sneer Strikes," in Siegel, Ellsworth, et al., *Superman*, 159.

69. Kneitel, "Japoteurs."

70. Sony Pictures Home Entertainment, *Batman*, chap. 1, "The Electrical Brain"; chap. 4, "Slaves of the Rising Sun"; chap. 13, "Eight Steps Down"; chap. 15, "The Doom of the Rising Sun"; chap. 5, "The Living Corpse"; chap. 3, "The Mark of the Zombies."

71. Gardner Fox, Jack Burnley, Cliff Young, et al., *All Star Comics* #11, in Fox, *All Star Comics*, 10, 16.

72. Timely Comics, *Captain America Comics*, cover.

73. "Sneer Strikes," in Siegel, Ellsworth, et al., *Superman*, 156, 162, 163, 165, 167; Kneitel, "Japoteurs."

74. Gardner Fox, Jack Burnley, Cliff Young, et al., *All Star Comics* #11, in Fox, *All Star Comics*, 50, 80, 81.

75. Timely Comics, *Captain America Comics*, 1, 2.

76. "Sneer Strikes," in Siegel, Ellsworth, et al., *Superman*, 165. See also Stan Lee and Al Gabriele, *Young Allies* #3, in S. Lee, Binder, et al., *Golden Age Young Allies*, 145, 150, 163.

77. Gardner Fox, Jack Burnley, Cliff Young, et al., *All Star Comics* #11, in Fox, *All Star Comics*, 14–15, 17, 41, 45, 46; Gardner Fox, Jack Burnley, Sheldon Moldoff, et al., *All Star Comics* #12, in Fox, *All Star Comics*, 85.

78. Gardner Fox, Jack Burnley, Sheldon Moldoff, et al., *All Star Comics* #12, in Fox, *All Star Comics*, 10–11, 72–78.

79. Kneitel, "Japoteurs"; D. Gordon and Bowsky, "Eleventh Hour"; Sony Pictures Home Entertainment, *Batman*, chap. 3, "The Mark of the Zombies"; chap. 4, "Slaves of the Rising Sun"; chap. 6, "Poison Peril"; chap. 8, "Lured by Radium"; chap. 12, "Embers of Evil"; chap. 13, "Eight Steps Down"; chap. 14, "The Executioner Strikes."

80. Wright, *Comic Book Nation*, 45.

81. Wright, *Comic Book Nation*, 49, 54.

82. "Sneer Strikes," in Siegel, Ellsworth, et al., *Superman*, 162.

83. Yang and Liew, *Shadow Hero*, 154–158.

84. Gardner Fox, Jack Burnley, Sheldon Moldoff, et al., *All Star Comics* #12, in Fox, *All Star Comics*, 99–102.

85. Sony Pictures Home Entertainment, *Batman*, chap. 8, "Lured by Radium."

86. For the following discussion, see Ace Magazines, "Captain Courageous."

87. For the Atom's adventure, see Gardner Fox, Jack Burnley, Sheldon Moldoff, et al., *All Star Comics* #12, in Fox, *All Star Comics*, 85–90.

88. Michael Uslan, "Introduction," in S. Lee, Binder, et al., *Golden Age Young Allies*, vii. On images of African Americans in film, see Bogle, *Toms, Coons, Mulattoes*.

89. Otto Binder and Charles Nicholas Wojtkowski, *Young Allies* #1, in S. Lee, Binder, et al., *Golden Age Young Allies*, 11.

90. Otto Binder and Charles Nicholas Wojtkowski, *Young Allies* #1, 16, 40–41; *Young Allies* #2, 90, 105, 109; Stan Lee and Al Gabriele, *Young Allies* #3, 146; all in S. Lee, Binder, et al., *Golden Age Young Allies*.

91. Otto Binder and Charles Nicholas Wojtkowski, *Young Allies* #1, in S. Lee, Binder, et al., *Golden Age Young Allies*, 19–21. For another example, see, in the same volume, Binder and Wojtkowski, *Young Allies* #1, 4–8; *Young Allies* #2, 114.

92. Otto Binder and Charles Nicholas Wojtkowski, *Young Allies* #1, in S. Lee, Binder, et al., *Golden Age Young Allies*, 24–29.

93. Otto Binder and Charles Nicholas Wojtkowski, *Young Allies* #1, 49; *Young Allies* #2, 101; Stan Lee and Al Gabriele, *Young Allies* #3, 160; all in S. Lee, Binder, et al., *Golden Age Young Allies*. Any hope Whitewash Jones might have held for a progressive message about race in *Young Allies* was further doused by the arrival of Black Talon in issue #2. Described as the "greatest criminal mastermind of the age," Black Talon's origins are revealed early on when he meets a German baron who is shocked that the villain's hand is "black," even though "you are a white man??!!" Black Talon explains that his hand, "not a pretty sight," was crushed in a car accident years ago; a surgeon then attached "the hand of an African killer to my wrist." The narrator, to help uncomprehending readers, then adds that "Black Talon does not explain, or realize, that the corpuscles of the black killer's hand had crept into his blood-stream, making him the most feared and ruthless chieftain of the underworld." Here, the comic book looked to the past (and not the future) in terms of race relations, presenting a long-held myth that race mixing would corrupt and ultimately destroy the white race, as evidenced by Black Talon's fangs and claws. Black Talon, fitting a racial motif applied to the Japanese as well, repeatedly threatens white women in *Young Allies*, grabbing one by the hair and threatening to "wring your pretty neck." See *Young Allies* #2, in S. Lee, Binder, et al., *Golden Age Young Allies*, 72, 78, 85, 92, 129.

94. See Beebe and Taylor, *Green Hornet*; *Green Hornet Strikes Again*.

95. Beebe and Taylor, *Green Hornet*, chap. 1, "The Tunnel of Terror"; *Green Hornet Strikes Again*, chap. 7, "Death in the Clouds."

96. Beebe and Taylor, *Green Hornet*, chap. 13, "Doom of the Underworld"; chap. 3, "Flying Coffins"; chap. 6, "Highways of Peril"; chap. 11, "Disaster Rides the Rails"; *Green Hornet Strikes Again*, chap. 6, "The Fatal Flash"; chap. 3, "The Avenging Heavens."

97. Beebe and Taylor, *Green Hornet*, chap. 6, "Highways of Peril."

98. Similar patterns emerge in the adventures of the Crimson Avenger and his sidekick (and chauffeur), Wing. On the positive side, the Crimson Avenger's earliest adventure had Wing prodding the hero to a broader consciousness of and involvement in the world. On a less progressive note, however, Wing rather quickly devolved into a pile of ethnic clichés, developing a stereotyped accent and often fading away into silence in the Crimson Avenger's ensuing adventures. See "Crimson Avenger

(Travis)"; "Crimson Avenger I (Lee Travis)"; "Wing (Wing How)"; Dayton, "DC Comics History."

99. While examples are numerous, see especially: Beebe and Taylor, *Green Hornet*, chap. 1, "The Tunnel of Terror"; chap. 2, "The Thundering Terror"; chap. 3, "Flying Coffins"; chap. 4, "Pillar of Flame"; chap. 11, "Disaster Rides the Rails"; *Green Hornet Strikes Again*, chap. 1, "Flaming Havoc"; chap. 2, "The Plunge of Peril"; chap. 5, "Shattering Doom"; chap. 9, "The Tragic Crash!"

100. Beebe and Taylor, *Green Hornet*, chap. 2, "The Thundering Terror"; chap. 3, "Flying Coffins."

101. Gardner Fox, Jack Burnley, Cliff Young, et al., *All Star Comics* #11, in Fox, *All Star Comics*, 32.

102. "Sneer Strikes," in Siegel, Ellsworth, et al., *Superman*, 159, 167, 168.

103. Gardner Fox, Jack Burnley, Cliff Young, et al., *All Star Comics* #11, in Fox, *All Star Comics*, 25.

Chapter 2: Struggling for Social Relevance

1. Quoted in Bacevich, "Farewell, the American Century."

2. G. Jones, *Men of Tomorrow*, 301.

3. See Lawson and Payne, *Debating the Civil Rights Movement*, 99–138; Chafe, *Unfinished Journey*, 140–142.

4. Chafe, *Unfinished Journey*, 76–82, 82–93, 140–142.

5. Chafe, *Unfinished Journey*, 144–152.

6. Krenn, *Color of Empire*, 106.

7. G. Jones and Jacobs, *Comic Book Heroes*, 7–8; Wright, *Comic Book Nation*, 56–59, 61–65, 126–127, 134; G. Jones, *Men of Tomorrow*, 234, 236–237; Hajdu, *Ten-Cent Plague*, 110; Cronin, *Was Superman a Spy?*, 32; Savage, *Comic Books and America*, 75–77, 114.

8. Hajdu, *Ten-Cent Plague*, 39–45; Wright, *Comic Book Nation*, 86, 87, 88, 89–92; Nyberg, *Seal of Approval*, 1, 3, 15, 17–18; I. Gordon, *Comic Strips and Consumer Culture*, 135–137; I. Gordon, *Superman*, 20, 102.

9. See, for example, Wertham, *Seduction of the Innocent*, 100–105.

10. G. Jones, *Men of Tomorrow*, 273; Hajdu, *Ten-Cent Plague*, 235, 326; Wright, *Comic Book Nation*, 98, 102–104, 157–159, 161, 172–173, 179; Savage, *Comic Books and America*, 97; G. Jones and Jacobs, *Comic Book Heroes*, 10. See also Nyberg, "No Harm in Horror," 27–45. Wertham, in fact, had spoken out against comics in 1948 and 1951 before his starring turn in front of a US Senate committee in 1954. For details, see Nyberg, *Seal of Approval*, 32–36, 47–48, 50–84, 104, 110.

11. L. Daniels, *DC Comics*, 131; Wright, *Comic Book Nation*, 182; G. Jones and Jacobs, *Comic Book Heroes*, 4, 10, 22.

12. G. Jones and Jacobs, *Comic Book Heroes*, 3, 9–12.

13. Wright, *Comic Book Nation*, 183–186; G. Jones and Jacobs, *Comic Book Heroes*, 33–39, 75–77, 86–87; G. Jones, *Men of Tomorrow*, 285.

14. Robert Bernstein and Kurt Schaffenberger, "The Ugly Superman," *Superman's Girl Friend Lois Lane* 1, no. 8, in Siegel and Shuster, *Superman*, 55–56.

15. Freeman and Freeman, "Treasure of the Incas."

16. For the discussion that follows, see Bill Finger and Dick Sprang, "Bodyguards to Cleopatra!," *Detective Comics* #167, in Kane, *Batman: Vol. 8*, 167–179.

17. G. Jones and Jacobs, *Comic Book Heroes*, 55; G. Jones, *Men of Tomorrow*, 208.

18. Robert Kanigher and Ross Andru, "The Secret of Volcano Mountain," *Wonder Woman* #120, in Kanigher, Andru, and Esposito, *Wonder Woman*, vol. 2, 73, 79; Robert Kanigher and Ross Andru, "The Invasion of the Sphinx Creatures," *Wonder Woman* #113, in Kanigher, Andru, and Esposito, *Wonder Woman*, vol. 1, 403.

19. Robert Kanigher and Ross Andru, "The Wonder Woman Album," *Wonder Woman* #103, 140–143; "The Bridge of Crocodiles," *Wonder Woman* #110, 323–340; both in Kanigher, Andru, and Esposito, *Wonder Woman*, vol. 1.

20. Curt Swan, "Superboy and the Sleeping Beauty," *Superboy* #22, in DC Comics, *Greatest 1950s Stories*, 116–125.

21. D. Hamilton, "Drums of Death."

22. For the discussion that follows, see Bill Finger and Sheldon Moldoff, "The Origins of the Bat-Cave," *Batman Annual* #1, in DC Comics, *Batman Annuals*, 10, 51–62.

23. For the discussion that follows, see France Herron and Sheldon Moldoff, "Batman–Indian Chief," *Batman Annual* #2, in DC Comics, *Batman Annuals*, 12, 118–127.

24. Robert Kanigher and Ross Andru, "The Secret of Volcano Mountain," *Wonder Woman* #120, in Kanigher, Andru, and Esposito, *Wonder Woman*, vol. 2, 73, 79.

25. Robert Kanigher and Ross Andru, "Wonder Tot and Mister Genie," *Wonder Woman* #126, 216; "Secret of Mister Genie's Magic Turban," *Wonder Woman* #130, 320–333; in Kanigher, Andru, and Esposito, *Wonder Woman*, vol. 2; "The Kite of Doom," 9–12; "The Human Lightning," 62–72; "Last Day of the Amazons" 311–312; in Kanigher and Andru, *Wonder Woman*, vol. 3.

26. For the discussion that follows, see Robert Kanigher and Ross Andru, "I—the Bomb," *Wonder Woman* #157, in DC Comics, *Showcase Presents: Wonder Woman*, 6–30.

27. For the discussion that follows, see Robert Kanigher and Ross Andru, "The Fury of Egg Fu," *Wonder Woman* #158, in DC Comics, *Showcase Presents: Wonder Woman*, 31–47.

28. Egg Fu the Fifth arrived the following year to carry on the dehumanized Chinese threat. See Robert Kanigher and Ross Andru, "The Sinister Scheme of Egg Fu," *Wonder Woman* #166, in DC Comics, *Showcase Presents: Wonder Woman*, 231–243.

29. Wright, *Comic Book Nation*, 121, 123; Benton, *Comic Book in America*, 54; Cronin, *Was Superman a Spy?*, 138.

30. Mort Lawrence, "The Girl Who Was Afraid!," *Men's Adventures* #27, in Romita, Ayers, and Everett, *Atlas Era Heroes*, 10–16.

31. John Romita, "The Green Dragon!," *Captain America* #78, in Romita, Ayers, and Everett, *Atlas Era Heroes*, 111–116.

32. Examples of such street scenes can be found in S. Lee and Kirby, "The Coming of . . . the Sub-Mariner!," *The Fantastic Four* #6, in *Marvel Masterworks: Fantastic Four*, vol. 1, 127, 137; "The Mysterious Molecule Man!," *The Fantastic Four* #20, in *Marvel Masterworks: Fantastic Four*, vol. 2, 283; "Unus, the Untouchable!," *The X-Men* #8, in *Marvel Masterworks: X-Men*, 172.

33. S. Lee and Kirby, "The End of the Fantastic Four!," *The Fantastic Four* #9, in *Marvel Masterworks: Fantastic Four*, vol. 1, 201–225.

34. S. Lee and Kirby, "Prisoners of the Pharaoh!," *The Fantastic Four* #19, in *Marvel Masterworks: Fantastic Four*, vol. 2, 244–266.

35. Stan Lee, R. Berns, and Don Heck, "The Mad Pharaoh!," *Tales of Suspense* #44, in S. Lee, Heck, Kirby, et al., *Invincible Iron Man*, 70–83.

36. S. Lee and Kirby, "Prisoners of the Pharaoh!," *The Fantastic Four* #19, in *Marvel Masterworks: Fantastic Four*, vol. 2, 244–266.

37. S. Lee and Jack Kirby, "The Master Plan of Doctor Doom!," *The Fantastic Four* #23, in *Marvel Masterworks: Fantastic Four*, vol. 3, 51–56; Stan Lee and Dick Ayers, "A Fortress in the Desert Sands!," *Sgt. Fury and His Howling Commandos* #16, in S. Lee, Kirby, and Ayers, *Essential Sgt. Fury*, 11–14.

38. Stan Lee and Jack Kirby, "Their Darkest Hour!," *The Avengers* #7, in S. Lee, Kirby, and Heck, *Avengers Omnibus*, 155–178.

39. Dick Ayers, "Playing with Fire!," *Captain America* #78, 118–122; "In Korea!," *Human Torch* #38, 191–196; in Romita, Ayers, and Everett, *Atlas Era Heroes*.

40. John Romita, "Kill Captain America," *Men's Adventures* #28, 36–43; "Captain America," *Captain America* #77, 98–104; in Romita, Ayers, and Everett, *Atlas Era Heroes*.

41. John Romita, "Come to the Commies!," *Captain America* #76, in Romita, Ayers, and Everett, *Atlas Era Heroes*, 72–77.

42. Roy Thomas, "Introduction," in Maneely et al., *Atlas Era Black Knight*; Michael J. Vassallo, "Joe Maneely: Adventure Comics," in Maneely et al., *Atlas Era Black Knight*.

43. Al Feldstein and Joe Maneely, "The Coming of the Yellow Claw," *The Yellow Claw* #1, in Maneely et al., *Atlas Era Black Knight*, 131–137.

44. Stan Lee and Dick Ayers, "On to Okinawa!," *Sgt. Fury and His Howling Commandos* #10, 3–5, 13–14; "The Man Who Failed!," *Sgt. Fury and His Howling Commandos* #23, 1–7; in S. Lee, Kirby, and Ayers, *Essential Sgt. Fury*.

45. Wright, *Comic Book Nation*, 207–209.

46. For the discussion that follows, see Stan Lee and Jack Kirby, "The Hordes of General Fang," *The Incredible Hulk* #5, in S. Lee, Kirby, and Ditko, *Incredible Hulk*, 112–124.

47. For the discussion that follows, see Stan Lee, Larry Lieber, and Don Heck, "Iron Man Is Born!," *Tales of Suspense* #39, in S. Lee, Heck, Kirby, et al., *Invincible Iron Man*, 1–13.

48. For the discussion that follows, see Stan Lee and Don Heck, "When the Commissar Commands!," *The Avengers* #18, in S. Lee, Kirby, and Heck, *Avengers Omnibus*, 414–436.

49. Stan Lee, "Introduction," in S. Lee and Heck, *Invincible Iron Man*, vi.

50. For the discussion that follows, see S. Lee and Heck, "The Origin of the Mandarin!," *Tales of Suspense* #62, in *Invincible Iron Man*, 174–186.

51. Stan Lee and Don Heck, "The Hands of the Mandarin!," *Tales of Suspense* #50, in S. Lee, Kirby, Heck, et al., *Invincible Iron Man*, 174–187.

52. S. Lee and Heck, "The Mandarin's Revenge!" *Tales of Suspense* #54, in *Invincible Iron Man*, 42–55.

53. S. Lee and Heck, "No One Escapes the Mandarin!," *Tales of Suspense* #55, in *Invincible Iron Man*, 56–69.

54. Stan Lee and Don Heck, "The Hands of the Mandarin!," *Tales of Suspense* #50, in S. Lee, Kirby, Heck, et al., *Invincible Iron Man*, 174–187.

55. S. Lee and Heck, "The Mandarin's Revenge!," *Tales of Suspense* #54, in *Invincible Iron Man*, 42–55.

56. Stan Lee and Don Heck, "The Hands of the Mandarin!," *Tales of Suspense* #50,

in S. Lee, Kirby, Heck, et al., *Invincible Iron Man*, 174–187; "The Mandarin's Revenge!," *Tales of Suspense* #54, 42–55; "The Death of Tony Stark!," *Tales of Suspense* #61, 160–173; in S. Lee and Heck, *Invincible Iron Man*.

57. Stan Lee and Don Heck, "The Hands of the Mandarin!," *Tales of Suspense* #50, in S. Lee, Kirby, Heck, et al., *Invincible Iron Man*, 174–187.

58. Chafe, *Unfinished Journey*, 155–164.

59. Chafe, *Unfinished Journey*, 201–209.

60. Wright, *Comic Book Nation*, 61–65, 126–127; G. Jones and Jacobs, *Comic Book Heroes*, 25–26; I. Gordon, *Superman*, 156–158.

61. Cronin, *Was Superman a Spy?*, 14; G. Jones, *Men of Tomorrow*, 242. For a synopsis of the story, see Lantz, "Superman Radio Series."

62. L. Daniels, *DC Comics*, 108–109; G. Jones, *Men of Tomorrow*, 241, 258–259.

63. For the discussion that follows, see Fielding, "Riddle of the Chinese Jade."

64. Dennis O'Neil, Foreword, 5–6; Michael Uslan, "Introduction," in Kane and Uslan, *Batman in the Fifties*, 5, 8; G. Jones and Jacobs, *Comic Book Heroes*, 27–28; Wright, *Comic Book Nation*, 59–60.

65. Don Cameron and Bob Kane, "The Phantom of the Library," *Detective Comics* #106, in Kane, *Batman: Vol. 5*, 46–57.

66. Warner Home Video, *Batman*.

67. Bill Finger and Lew Sayre Schwartz, "The Man Behind the Red Hood," *Detective Comics* #168, in Kane, *Batman: Vol. 8*, 180–193.

68. Al Feldstein and Joe Maneely, "The Coming of the Yellow Claw," *The Yellow Claw* #1, 131–137; "Free Agent," *The Yellow Claw*, #1, 139–144; "The Yellow Claw," *The Yellow Claw*, #1, 150–155; Jack Kirby, "Concentrate on Chaos," *The Yellow Claw* #2, 157–161; "The Mystery of Cabin 361," *The Yellow Claw* #2, 183–187; all in Maneely et al., *Atlas Era Black Knight*.

69. For the discussion that follows, see John Romita, "The Man with No Face!," *Captain America* #77, in Romita, Ayers, and Everett, *Atlas Era Heroes*, 85–90.

70. The story's final confrontation showcases Captain America caring for Wing paternalistically. High above the city on a rooftop, the villainous Man with No Face reveals that he is Wing's twin brother, before hurling himself over the edge of the building to commit suicide. Cap keeps this newfound information secret from Wing, however, as the corpse's face is mangled beyond recognition. The white hero paternalistically knows what's best and explains to Wing only that "from now on, your brother's life is no longer in any danger! Take my word for it!" The expressionless Wing's response—"That's good enough for me, Captain!"—underscores his subordinate position. While Chinese Americans might be good guys, as was the case here, they remained clearly inferior to their white counterparts.

71. G. Jones and Jacobs, *Comic Book Heroes*, 48–50, 66, 68–71, 89, 94; Wright, *Comic Book Nation*, 201–204, 210, 213–215, 223–224; G. Jones, *Men of Tomorrow*, 285, 296–297, 299, 301; Howe, *Marvel Comics*, 16–17.

72. Wright, *Comic Book Nation*, 200–201, 215–217, 219, 220; G. Jones and Jacobs, *Comic Book Heroes*, 66; Howe, *Marvel Comics*, 90.

73. Stan Lee, "When the Golden Avenger Was Gray," in S. Lee, Kirby, Heck, et al., *Invincible Iron Man* (originally written in 1975).

74. Cronin, "When We First Met."

75. G. Jones and Jacobs, *Comic Book Heroes*, 59–62; G. Jones, *Men of Tomorrow*, 296–297; Wright, *Comic Book Nation*, 180, 210–212.

76. S. Lee and Ditko, "Bring Back My Goblin to Me!," *The Amazing Spider-Man* #27, in *Marvel Masterworks*, 165.

77. S. Lee and Ditko, "The Menace of the Molten Man!," *The Amazing Spider-Man* #28, in *Marvel Masterworks*, 188–190; Stan Lee and Steve Ditko, "If This Be My Destiny . . . !," *The Amazing Spider-Man* #31, 8–9, 11, 13; "When Falls the Meteor!," *The Amazing Spider-Man* #36, 109–110; "Just a Guy Named Joe!," *The Amazing Spider-Man* #38, 157, 161; in S. Lee, Ditko, and Romita, *Amazing Spider-Man*.

78. S. Lee and Ditko, "Never Step On a Scorpion!," *The Amazing Spider-Man* #29, in *Marvel Masterworks*, 224–225. See also Stan Lee and Steve Ditko, "The Thrill of the Hunt!," *The Amazing Spider-Man* #34, in S. Lee, Ditko, and Romita, *Amazing Spider-Man*, 71.

79. S. Lee and Ditko, "The Man in the Crime-Master's Mask!," *The Amazing Spider-Man* #26, in *Marvel Masterworks*, 135; Stan Lee and Steve Ditko, "Once Upon a Time, There Was a Robot . . . !," *The Amazing Spider-Man* #37, 129; "The Final Chapter!," *The Amazing Spider-Man* #33, 58, 61; in S. Lee, Ditko, and Romita, *Amazing Spider-Man*.

80. Stan Lee and Jack Kirby, "Seven Against the Nazis!," *Sgt. Fury and His Howling Commandos* #1, in S. Lee, Kirby, and Ayers, *Essential Sgt. Fury*, 1–4.

81. Stan Lee and Jack Kirby, "Midnight on Massacre Mountain!," *Sgt. Fury and His Howling Commandos* #3, in S. Lee, Kirby, and Ayers, *Essential Sgt. Fury*, 3, 4.

82. Stan Lee and Jack Kirby, "7 Doomed Men!," *Sgt. Fury and His Howling Commandos* #2, 1, 4; "Midnight on Massacre Mountain!," *Sgt. Fury and His Howling Commandos* #3, 1; in S. Lee, Kirby, and Ayers, *Essential Sgt. Fury*.

83. Stan Lee and Jack Kirby, "Lord Ha-Ha's Last Laugh!," *Sgt. Fury and His Howling Commandos* #4, in S. Lee, Kirby, and Ayers, *Essential Sgt. Fury*, 17.

84. Stan Lee and Jack Kirby, "Seven Against the Nazis!," *Sgt. Fury and His Howling Commandos* #1, in S. Lee, Kirby and Ayers, *Essential Sgt. Fury*, 18.

85. For the discussion that follows, see Stan Lee and Jack Kirby, "The Fangs of the Fox!," *Sgt. Fury and His Howling Commandos* #6, in S. Lee, Kirby, and Ayers, *Essential Sgt. Fury*, 1–23.

86. S. Lee and Kirby, "X-Men," *The X-Men* #1, in *Marvel Masterworks: X-Men*, 10.

87. S. Lee and Kirby, "The Brotherhood of Evil Mutants," *The X-Men* #4, in *Marvel Masterworks: X-Men*, 82.

88. S. Lee and Kirby, "No One Can Stop the Vanisher," *The X-Men* #2, in *Marvel Masterworks: X-Men*, 35.

89. S. Lee and Kirby, "X-Men," *The X-Men* #1, in *Marvel Masterworks: X-Men*, 77.

90. S. Lee and Kirby, "Unus, the Untouchable!," *The X-Men* #8, in *Marvel Masterworks: X-Men*, 168–189.

91. For the discussion that follows, see Stan Lee, Jack Kirby, and Jay Gavin, a.k.a. Werner Roth, "Among Us Stalk . . . the Sentinels!," *The X-Men* #14, in S. Lee, Kirby, Thomas, et al., *X-Men*, 63–83.

92. Stan Lee, Jack Kirby, and Jay Gavin, a.k.a. Werner Roth, "Prisoners of the Mysterious Master Mold!," *The X-Men* #15, in S. Lee, Kirby, Thomas, et al., *X-Men*, 84–104.

93. Stan Lee, Jack Kirby, and Jay Gavin, a.k.a. Werner Roth, "The Supreme Sacrifice!," *The X-Men* #16, in S. Lee, Kirby, Thomas, et al., *X-Men*, 105–125.

94. S. Lee and Kirby, "The Fantastic Four!," *The Fantastic Four* #1, in *Marvel Masterworks: Fantastic Four*, vol. 1, 9.

95. Stan Lee, "Introduction," in S. Lee and Kirby, *Marvel Masterworks: Fantastic*

Four, vol. 2, vi; S. Lee and Kirby, "The Hate-Monger!," *The Fantastic Four* #21, in *Marvel Masterworks: Fantastic Four*, vol. 3, 1–22.

96. S. Lee and Kirby, "Bedlam at the Baxter Building!," *The Fantastic Four Annual* #3, in *Marvel Masterworks: Fantastic Four*, vol. 5, 63–86.

Chapter 3: "We're All Brothers!"

1. Warner Home Video, *All-New Super Friends Hour: Season One*, vol. 2, "Prejudice."
2. Patterson, *Grand Expectations*, 311.
3. See Chafe, *Unfinished Journey*, 98–99.
4. Hodgson, *America in Our Time*, 7.
5. DeKoven, *Utopia Limited*, 210–211.
6. Chafe, *Unfinished Journey*, 290.
7. Killian, "Race Relations," 1–13.
8. Horton, *Race*, 14.
9. Horton, *Race*, 121, 122.
10. Horton, *Race*, 134, 138.
11. Dennis O'Neil, Introduction, 4–5.
12. Wright, *Comic Book Nation*, 233–234.
13. J. Moore, "Education of Green Lantern," 263, 277; Wright, *Comic Book Nation*, 234.
14. O'Neil, Introduction, 6, 7.
15. O'Neil and Adams, "No Evil Shall Escape My Sight!," in *Green Lantern*, 13.
16. O'Neil and Adams, "No Evil Shall Escape My Sight!," in *Green Lantern*, 15–16, 21–23, 25–27.
17. O'Neil and Adams, "No Evil Shall Escape My Sight!," in *Green Lantern*, 11.
18. O'Neil and Adams, "Journey to Desolation!," in *Green Lantern*, 54.
19. O'Neil and Adams, "Ulysses Star Is Alive!," in *Green Lantern*, 94.
20. O'Neil and Adams, "Ulysses Star Is Alive!," in *Green Lantern*, 97.
21. O'Neil and Adams, "No Evil Shall Escape My Sight!," in *Green Lantern*, 14.
22. O'Neil and Adams, "Journey to Desolation!," in *Green Lantern*, 42.
23. O'Neil and Adams, "Ulysses Star Is Alive!," in *Green Lantern*, 87–88.
24. O'Neil and Adams, "Death Be My Destiny!," in *Green Lantern*, 141.
25. O'Neil and Adams, "No Evil Shall Escape My Sight!," in *Green Lantern*, 28, 30.
26. O'Neil and Adams, "No Evil Shall Escape My Sight!," in *Green Lantern*, 32.
27. O'Neil and Adams, "Ulysses Star Is Alive!," in *Green Lantern*, 103.
28. O'Neil and Adams, ". . . And a Child Shall Destroy Them!," in *Green Lantern*, 183.
29. Black Canary similarly dramatizes racism as a moral/ethical struggle. Canary provides medical care on the Native American reservation. As Nama explains, Black Canary's "action implied that personal reflection was an equal or possibly more important and effective step toward eliminating racism than organized political confrontation of institutional racism." Nama, *Super Black*, 16.
30. O'Neil and Adams, "Snowbirds Don't Fly!," in *Green Lantern*, 243.
31. O'Neil and Adams, "They Say It'll Kill Me . . . But They Won't Say When!," in *Green Lantern*, 268–269.
32. Patell, *Negative Liberties*, xiv, xv.

33. O'Neil and Adams, "Ulysses Star Is Alive!," in *Green Lantern*, 103.

34. O'Neil and Adams, "They Say It'll Kill Me . . . But They Won't Say When!," in *Green Lantern*, 267.

35. Smiley, "Say It Ain't So," 61.

36. See S. Lee and Heck, "Sign of the Serpent," 9.

37. Gardner Fox and Mike Sekowsky, "Man, Thy Name Is—Brother!," in Fox, Sekowsky, and Greene, *Justice League*, 154.

38. Gardner Fox and Mike Sekowsky, "Indestructible Creatures of Nightmare Island!," in Fox, Sekowsky, and Sachs, *Justice League*, 238.

39. Kanigher and Roth, "Indian Death Charge," 14.

40. S. Lee and Colan, "Brother, Take My Hand," 20.

41. The series never identifies Chen's nationality. All it mentions about him is that "his troops have fought ours [the United States'] on the battlefield in Asia" and that he is the leader "of a hostile Oriental nation." S. Lee and Heck, "Sign of the Serpent," 15; S. Lee and Heck, "To Smash a Serpent," 6.

42. S. Lee and Heck, "To Smash a Serpent," 6.

43. S. Lee and Heck, "To Smash a Serpent," 7.

44. S. Lee and Heck, "Sign of the Serpent," 5.

45. S. Lee and Heck, "Sign of the Serpent," 12.

46. S. Lee and Heck, "Sign of the Serpent," 12.

47. At this time, SHIELD stood for "Supreme Headquarters, International Espionage, Law-Enforcement Division." It has since been changed to "Strategic Hazard Intervention Espionage Logistics Directorate" in the comic book Marvel Universe and "Strategic Homeland Intervention, Enforcement and Logistics Division" in the Marvel television and movie universes.

48. S. Lee and Heck, "Sign of the Serpent," 14.

49. Thomas and Adams, "Hell on Earth," 3.

50. Conway and Adams, "Evening's Wait," 6.

51. Conway and Adams, "Evening's Wait," 1–2.

52. Conway and Adams, "Evening's Wait," 2.

53. Conway and Adams, "Evening's Wait," 9.

54. Gardner Fox and Mike Sekowsky, "Man, Thy Name Is—Brother!," in Fox, Sekowsky, and Greene, *Justice League*, 164–166.

55. Kanigher and Roth, "Indian Death Charge," 4, 5.

56. Kanigher and Roth, "Indian Death Charge," 6, 8, 12.

57. Bob Haney and Gil Kane, "Skis of Death!," in DC Comics, *Showcase Presents: Teen Titans*, 157.

58. Bob Haney and Gil Kane, "Skis of Death!," in DC Comics, *Showcase Presents: Teen Titans*, 161.

59. Robert Kanigher and Nick Cardy, "The Titans Kill a Saint?," in DC Comics, *Showcase Presents: Teen Titans*, 200.

60. Bogle, *Toms, Coons, Mulattoes*, 178.

61. Robert Kanigher and Nick Cardy, "A Penny for a Black Star," in DC Comics, *Showcase Presents: Teen Titans*, 224.

62. Bogle, *Toms, Coons, Mulattoes*, 7.

63. Steve Skeates and George Tuska, "A Mystical Realm, A World Gone Mad," in DC Comics, *Showcase Presents: Teen Titans*, 356.

64. Bob Haney and George Tuska, "A Titan Is Born," in DC Comics, *Showcase Presents: Teen Titans*, 485.

65. Levitz and Rozakis, "Man Who Toppled the Titans," 2.

66. Rozakis and Novick, "You Can't Say No," 2.

67. Rozakis and Novick, "You Can't Say No," 8, 9.

68. Thomas and Giacoia, "Sting of the Serpent," 2.

69. Robbins and Andru, "Flying Samurai," 9.

70. Robbins and Andru, "Flying Samurai," 2, 3.

71. Robbins and Andru, "Flying Samurai," 3.

72. Robbins and Andru, "Flying Samurai," 5.

73. Robbins and Andru, "Flying Samurai," 11.

74. Robbins and Andru, "Flying Samurai," 4.

75. Robbins and Andru, "Flying Samurai," 9.

76. Robbins and Andru, "Flying Samurai," 16, 17.

77. Robbins and Andru, "Flying Samurai," 7, 13, 22.

78. Robbins and Andru, "Attack of the Samuroids," 6–7, 23.

79. Robbins and Andru, "Flying Samurai," 4.

80. Robbins and Andru, "Flying Samurai," 8.

81. Robbins and Andru, "Flying Samurai," 3.

82. Robbins and Andru, "Attack of the Samuroids."

83. Horton, *Race*, 140.

84. Gardner Fox and Mike Sekowsky, "Man, Thy Name Is—Brother!," in Fox, Sekowsky, and Greene, *Justice League*, 161.

85. Gardner Fox and Mike Sekowsky, "Man, Thy Name Is—Brother!," in Fox, Sekowsky, and Greene, *Justice League*, 164–165.

86. Robert Kanigher and Nick Cardy, "A Penny for a Black Star," in DC Comics, *Showcase Presents: Teen Titans*, 217, 225.

87. Thomas and Adams, "Hour for Thunder," 8–9.

88. S. Lee and Colan, "Brother, Take My Hand," 14.

89. Kanigher and Roth, "Indian Death Charge," 14.

90. Kanigher and Roth, "I Am Curious," 2–4.

91. Kanigher and Roth, "I Am Curious," 4.

92. Kanigher and Roth, "I Am Curious," 5–6.

93. Kanigher and Roth, "I Am Curious," 7–8, 9.

94. Kanigher and Roth, "I Am Curious," 11, 13.

95. Kanigher and Roth, "I Am Curious," 14.

96. Gardner Fox and Mike Sekowsky, "Man, Thy Name Is—Brother!," in Fox, Sekowsky, and Greene, *Justice League*, 161.

97. Gardner Fox and Mike Sekowsky, "Man, Thy Name Is—Brother!," in Fox, Sekowsky, and Greene, *Justice League*, 155, 172.

98. Gardner Fox and Mike Sekowsky, "Indestructible Creatures of Nightmare Island!," in Fox, Sekowsky, and Sachs, *Justice League*, 215.

99. Gardner Fox and Mike Sekowsky, "Indestructible Creatures of Nightmare Island!," in Fox, Sekowsky, and Sachs, *Justice League*, 238.

100. Gardner Fox and Mike Sekowsky, "Indestructible Creatures of Nightmare Island!," in Fox, Sekowsky, and Sachs, *Justice League*, 219.

101. Gardner Fox and Mike Sekowsky, "Indestructible Creatures of Nightmare Island!," in Fox, Sekowsky, and Sachs, *Justice League*, 219.

102. Steve Skeates and Nick Cardy, "Greed . . . Kills!," in DC Comics, *Showcase Presents: Teen Titans*; Steve Skeates and Dick Dillin, "The Computer That Captured a Town!," in DC Comics, *Showcase Presents: Teen Titans*; S. Lee and Heck, "To Smash a Serpent," 6, 20.

103. Goodwin and Tuska, "Replacement"; "From This Conflict."

104. Goodwin and Heck, "Fury of the Firebrand," 5.

105. Goodwin and Heck, "Fury of the Firebrand," 6.

106. Goodwin and Heck, "Fury of the Firebrand," 15.

107. Goodwin and Heck, "Fury of the Firebrand," 20.

108. Gardner Fox and Mike Sekowsky, "Indestructible Creatures of Nightmare Island!," in Fox, Sekowsky, and Sachs, *Justice League*, 238.

109. Gardner Fox and Mike Sekowsky, "Man, Thy Name Is—Brother!," in Fox, Sekowsky, and Greene, *Justice League*, 176.

110. Steve Skeates and Dick Dillin, "The Computer That Captured a Town!," in DC Comics, *Showcase Presents: Teen Titans*, 468.

111. Haney and Saaf, "Litchburg Graveyard," 17.

112. Thomas and Adams, "Hour for Thunder," 10.

113. S. Lee and Heck, "To Smash a Serpent," 20.

Chapter 4: Guess Who's Coming to Save You?

1. Nama, *Super Black*, 11.

2. Aldama, *Latinx Superheroes*, 17.

3. Chafe, *Unfinished Journey*, 166–167.

4. Chafe, *Unfinished Journey*, 167.

5. See, for example, Gonzales, *Mexicanos*; and Neate, *Tolerating Ambiguity*.

6. Kilpatrick, *Celluloid Indians*, 66; Chafe, *Unfinished Journey*, 167–168.

7. Takaki, *Different Mirror*, 399–400.

8. Bogle, *Toms, Coons, Mulattoes*, 95.

9. Bogle, *Toms, Coons, Mulattoes*, 236.

10. Kilpatrick, *Celluloid Indians*, 65–66, 71.

11. Berg, *Latino Images in Film*, 111–112.

12. Bogle, *Toms, Coons, Mulattoes*, 17–18.

13. Eisner, *Graphic Storytelling*, 11–14. It's important to note that Eisner, in this discussion, deals more with occupational and genre-specific stereotypes than with racial or ethnic ones, though they all share a not unproblematic basis in physical appearance that goes untroubled by Eisner.

14. Royal, "Introduction," 7–8.

15. Gardner, "Same Difference," 133–35.

16. Abrams, "Primitivism and Progress," 244.

17. Hogue, *Race, Modernity, Postmodernity*, 2–4.

18. Achebe, "An Image of Africa," 2–3, 13.

19. Brown, "Panthers and Vixens," 142.

20. S. Lee and Kirby, "The Black Panther!," in *Marvel Masterworks: Fantastic Four*, 24, 29.

21. S. Lee and Kirby, "The Black Panther!," in *Marvel Masterworks: Fantastic Four*, 30.

22. S. Lee and Kirby, "The Black Panther!," in *Marvel Masterworks: Fantastic Four*, 30.

23. S. Lee and Kirby, "The Black Panther!," in *Marvel Masterworks: Fantastic Four*, 36.

24. S. Lee and Kirby, "The Black Panther!," in *Marvel Masterworks: Fantastic Four*, 24, 27, 29.

25. S. Lee and Kirby, "The Way It Began . . . !," in *Marvel Masterworks: Fantastic Four*, 43–44.

26. Don McGregor, "Panther's Chronicles," in McGregor, Buckler, and Graham, *Black Panther*, vii.

27. Abrams, "Primitivism and Progress," 244.

28. Don McGregor and Rich Buckler, "Panther's Rage," in McGregor, Buckler, and Graham, *Black Panther*, 5.

29. Don McGregor and Rich Buckler, "Malice by Crimson Moonlight," in McGregor, Buckler, and Graham, *Black Panther*, 38.

30. Don McGregor and Billy Graham, "Once You Slay the Dragon!," in McGregor, Buckler, and Graham, *Black Panther*, 91.

31. Don McGregor and Billy Graham, "Blood Stains on Virgin Snow!," in McGregor, Buckler, and Graham, *Black Panther*, 110.

32. Don McGregor and Billy Graham, "The God Killer," in McGregor, Buckler, and Graham, *Black Panther*, 127.

33. Don McGregor and Billy Graham, "And All Our Past Decades Have Seen Revolutions!," in McGregor, Buckler, and Graham, *Black Panther*, 175.

34. Len Wein and Dave Cockrum, "Second Genesis!," in Claremont, Cockrum, and Byrne, *Uncanny X-Men Omnibus*, 17–18.

35. Chris Claremont and Dave Cockrum, "Night of the Demon!," in Claremont, Cockrum, and Byrne, *Uncanny X-Men Omnibus*, 102.

36. Chris Claremont and Dave Cockrum, "Like a Phoenix, from the Ashes!," in Claremont, Cockrum, and Byrne, *Uncanny X-Men Omnibus*, 200.

37. Chris Claremont and John Byrne, "Home Are the Heroes!," in Claremont, Cockrum, and Byrne, *Uncanny X-Men Omnibus*, 343, 353.

38. Chris Claremont and John Byrne, "Desolation," in Claremont, Cockrum, and Byrne, *Uncanny X-Men Omnibus*, 449, 453.

39. Len Wein and Gene Colan, "Brother Voodoo!," in Marvel Comics, *Essential Marvel Horror*.

40. Nama, *Super Black*, 107.

41. Len Wein and Gene Colan, "Baptism of Fire!," in Marvel Comics, *Essential Marvel Horror*.

42. Len Wein and Gene Colan, "Brother Voodoo!," in Marvel Comics, *Essential Marvel Horror*.

43. Len Wein and Gene Colan, "Baptism of Fire!," in Marvel Comics, *Essential Marvel Horror*.

44. Lein Wein and Gene Colan, "March of the Dead!," in Marvel Comics, *Essential Marvel Horror*.

45. Fox and Shores, "Golden Grave," 26.

46. Sheyahshe, *Native Americans in Comic Books*, 55, 79.

47. Chris Claremont and John Byrne, "Shoot-Out at the Stampede!," in Claremont, Cockrum, and Byrne, *Uncanny X-Men Omnibus*, 581.

48. Fox and Shores, "Golden Grave," 15; "King Cycle," 19.

49. Fox and Shores, "Red Wolf," 14.

50. Fox and Shores, "Golden Grave," 21.

51. Levitz and Sherman, "Dazzling Debut," 8, 10.

52. Bogle, *Toms, Coons, Mulattoes*, 12–13, 241–242.

53. Archie Goodwin and George Tuska, "Out of Hell—A Hero!," in Thomas, Romita, et al., *Essential Luke Cage*.

54. Archie Goodwin and George Tuska, "Out of Hell—A Hero!," in Thomas, Romita, et al., *Essential Luke Cage*.

55. Archie Goodwin and George Tuska, "Vengeance Is Mine!," in Thomas, Romita, et al., *Essential Luke Cage*.

56. Bogle, *Toms, Coons, Mulattoes*, 235.

57. For the discussion that follows, see Archie Goodwin and George Tuska, "Out of Hell—A Hero!," in Thomas, Romita, et al., *Essential Luke Cage*.

58. Steve Englehart, Gerry Conway, and Billy Graham, "Knights and White Satin!," in Thomas, Romita, et al., *Essential Luke Cage*.

59. O'Neil and Adams, "Beware My Power!," in *Green Lantern*, 271.

60. O'Neil and Adams, "Beware My Power!," in *Green Lantern*, 276.

61. O'Neil and Adams, "Beware My Power!," in *Green Lantern*, 278, 281, 284.

62. O'Neil and Adams, "Beware My Power!," in *Green Lantern*, 282–283.

63. Marv Wolfman and Gene Colan, "His Name Is . . . Blade!," in Conway, Goodwin, et al., *Tomb of Dracula*, 199, 202, 204, 212.

64. Chris Claremont and Tony DeZuniga, "The Night Josie Harper Died!," in Wolfman, Claremont, DeZuniga, et al., *Blade*.

65. Marv Wolfman and Gene Colan, "Night of the Screaming House!," in Conway, Goodwin, et al., *Tomb of Dracula*, 247.

66. See Bogle, *Toms, Coons, Mulattoes*, 222; Marv Wolfman and Gene Colan, "Night of the Screaming House!," in Conway, Goodwin, et al., *Tomb of Dracula*, 248.

67. Marv Wolfman and Gene Colan, "A Night for the Living . . . A Morning for the Dead!," in Wolfman, Claremont, Colan, et al., *Tomb of Dracula*, 10–11.

68. Isabella and Von Eeden, "Black Lightning," 1, 2–3.

69. Isabella and Von Eeden, "Black Lightning," 5.

70. Isabella and Von Eeden, "Merlyn Means Murder," 1–5, 12–15.

71. O'Neil and Nasser, "Magnetic Menace," 7–8, 17.

72. Bogle, *Toms, Coons, Mulattoes*, 236.

73. Isabella and Von Eeden, "One Man's Poison," 6.

74. Isabella and Von Eeden, "Nobody Beats a Superman," 12.

75. Isabella and Von Eeden, "Every Hand Against Them," 6.

76. Conway and Dillin, "Plague of Monsters," 11, 17.

77. Bogle, *Toms, Coons, Mulattoes*, 251. DC introduced a literal "black super-woman"—or, to be more precise, a black "wonder woman"—in a three-part story line in *Wonder Woman* (Vol. 1) #204–206 (February, April, and July 1973), debuting Nubia. However, a reader would not know she was black from her introductory cover, where she stands completely armored from head to toe, sword poised to stab a prone Wonder Woman beneath her. Issue #205 featured a backup story entitled "The Mystery of Nubia!" in which she demonstrated the readiness for battle and violence typical of the black superwoman. As two black men—wearing no more than loincloths—battle for the right to claim her, Nubia intervenes to fight for herself.

When her male opponent asks, "How can you hope to compete with me? I AM A MAN!" Nubia immediately disarms him, describing him as "just another ordinary human—helpless as a babe—waiting to be slaughtered!" Kanigher and Heck, "Mystery of Nubia," 5–6.

78. Rozakis and Novick, "You Can't Say No," 5.

79. Rozakis and Delbo, "Daddy's Little Crimefighter," 8.

80. Rozakis and Delbo, "Raid of the Rocket-Rollers," 8, 10.

81. Tony Isabella and Arvell Jones, "Daughters of the Death-Goddess," in Claremont, Byrne, et al., *Essential Iron Fist*.

82. Chris Claremont and John Byrne, "A Duel of Iron!," in Claremont, Byrne, et al., *Essential Iron Fist*.

83. Bogle, *Toms, Coons, Mulattoes*, 7–8.

84. O'Neil and Adams, *Green Lantern*, 280.

85. Steve Englehart, Gerry Conway, and Billy Graham, "Knights and White Satin!," in Thomas, Romita, et al., *Essential Luke Cage*.

86. Kirby, "King Solomon's Frog!," in *Black Panther*, 11, 13.

87. Kirby, "Race Against Time," 43, 47–48; "Friends or Foes," 66, in *Black Panther*.

88. Gary Friedrich and John Romita, "And in the End . . ." and "Power to the People," in S. Lee, Friedrich, et al., *Essential Captain America*.

89. Bogle, *Toms, Coons, Mulattoes*, 39.

90. See, for instance, S. Lee and Ditko, "Spidey Strikes Back!," in *Great Responsibility*, 29.

91. S. Lee and Ditko, "The End of Spider-Man!," in *Great Responsibility*, 17.

92. S. Lee and Kirby, "Where Stalks the Sandman?," in *Fantastic Four Omnibus*, 9.

93. Dennis O'Neil and Dick Dillin, "Plague of the Galactic Jest-Master," in DC Comics, *Justice League*, 3.

94. Roy Thomas and Don Heck, "The Coming of Sunfire!," in Thomas, Adams, Friedrich, et al., *X-Men Omnibus*, 773–774.

95. Englehart and Starlin, "Shang-Chi," 19.

96. O'Neil and Estrada, "Arena of No Exit," 8, 14.

97. Englehart and Brown, "Night of the Swordsman," 10, 28.

98. Wu, *Yellow*, 79; Chen and Yoo, *Asian American Issues Today*, 645.

99. Englehart and Starlin, "Midnight Brings," 1–2, 14.

100. Levitz and Estrada, "My World Begins," 6–7.

101. Levitz and Estrada, "My World Begins," 8–9.

102. Jameson and Estrada, "International Dooms," 2–3.

103. R. Lee, *Orientals*, 28–29.

104. Ma, *Deathly Embrace*, 5–6, 7, 15–16.

105. R. Lee, *Orientals*, 9–10.

106. Englehart and Heck, "Lion God," 12.

107. O'Neil and Estrada, "Arena of No Exit," 8.

108. O'Neil and Estrada, "Slay the Blind Dragon," 7.

109. O'Neil and Estrada, "Preying Mantis," 5.

110. O'Neil and Estrada, "Arena of No Exit," cover, 1, 16.

111. Englehart and Buscema, "Divide," 13; "Bewitched," 7.

112. Englehart and Buscema, "Bewitched," 17, 31.

113. O'Neil and Estrada, "To Catch an Assassin," 9.

114. Howe, *Marvel Comics*, 160.

115. Englehart and Cockrum, "Blast from the Past," 9.

116. Englehart and Brown, "Night of the Swordsman," 17, 18.

117. Aldama, *Latinx Superheroes*, 11–17.

118. Berg, *Latino Images in Film*, 76.

119. Mantlo and Buscema, "Like a Tiger," 17.

120. Mantlo and Buscema, "Tiger in a Web," 13.

121. Mantlo and Robbins, "Tiger and the Fly," 6–7.

122. Mantlo and Buscema, "My Friend, My Foe," 30; Mantlo and Mooney, "Carrion," 11.

123. Stan Lee and Gene Colan, "The Coming of . . . the Falcon!," in S. Lee, Kirby, Steranko, et al., *Essential Captain America*.

124. Stan Lee and Gene Colan, "Crack-Up on Campus!," in S. Lee, Kirby, Steranko, et al., *Essential Captain America*.

125. Chris Claremont and John Byrne, "Cry for the Children!," in Claremont, Cockrum, and Byrne, *Uncanny X-Men Omnibus*, 604.

126. Isabella and Tuska, "Black Goliath," 2.

127. Archie Goodwin and George Tuska, "Out of Hell—A Hero!," in Thomas, Romita, et al., *Essential Luke Cage*.

128. Chris Claremont and John Byrne, "Cry for the Children!," in Claremont, Cockrum, and Byrne, *Uncanny X-Men Omnibus*, 604–605.

129. Thomas and Buscema, "Man-Ape," 8.

130. Isabella and Von Eeden, "Nobody Beats a Superman," 12.

131. O'Neil and Nasser, "Magnetic Menace," 12.

132. Stern and Cowan, "White Tiger," 22, 23.

133. Stan Lee and Gene Colan, "They Call Him—Stone-Face!," in S. Lee, Friedrich, et al., *Essential Captain America*; see Thomas and Buscema, "Heroes for Hire," 5–6; and Isabella and Von Eeden, "Black Lightning."

134. Mantlo and Mooney, "Zoo Story," 14.

135. Stan Lee and John Romita, "The Badge and the Betrayal!," in S. Lee, Friedrich, et al., *Essential Captain America*.

136. Isabella and Von Eeden, "Black Lightning," 6.

137. Thomas and Buscema, "Behold," 7.

138. Thomas and Buscema, "Heroes for Hire," 12–13.

139. Mantlo and Buscema, "Like a Tiger," 3.

140. Stan Lee and Gene Colan, "The Fate of . . . the Falcon!," in S. Lee, Kirby, Steranko, et al., *Essential Captain America*.

141. Stan Lee and Gene Colan, "The Fate of . . . the Falcon!," in S. Lee, Kirby, Steranko, et al., *Essential Captain America*.

142. Isabella and Von Eeden, "Fear and Loathing," 4.

143. Thomas and Buscema, "Coming of Red Wolf," 7, 18.

144. Thomas and Buscema, "Coming of Red Wolf," 20.

145. Mantlo and Buscema, "Like a Tiger," 6.

146. Thomas and Giacoia, "Sting of the Serpent," 16.

147. Chafe, *Unfinished Journey*, 306.

148. Stan Lee and Gene Colan, "The Fate of . . . the Falcon!," in S. Lee, Kirby, Steranko, et al., *Essential Captain America*.

149. Stan Lee and Gene Colan, "Madness in the Slums!," in S. Lee, Friedrich, et al., *Essential Captain America*.

150. Stan Lee and Gene Colan, "They Call Him—Stone-Face!," in S. Lee, Friedrich, et al., *Essential Captain America*.

151. Gary Freidrich and John Romita, "Power to the People!," in S. Lee, Friedrich, et al., *Essential Captain America*.

152. Gary Freidrich and John Romita, "Power to the People!," in S. Lee, Friedrich, et al., *Essential Captain America*.

153. Gary Freidrich and John Romita, "Power to the People!," in S. Lee, Friedrich, et al., *Essential Captain America*.

154. Stan Lee, Gary Friedrich, and John Romita, "HYDRA Over All!," in S. Lee, Friedrich, et al., *Essential Captain America*.

155. Stan Lee, Gary Friedrich, and John Romita, "HYDRA Over All!," in S. Lee, Friedrich, et al., *Essential Captain America*.

156. Bates and Grell, "Hero Who Hated the Legion," 1.

157. Bates and Grell, "Hero Who Hated the Legion," 4.

158. Bates and Grell, "Hero Who Hated the Legion," 7–8.

159. Bates and Grell, "Hero Who Hated the Legion," 12.

160. Len Wein and Dave Cockrum, "Second Genesis!," in Claremont, Cockrum, and Byrne, *Uncanny X-Men Omnibus*, 12.

161. Len Wein and Dave Cockrum, "Second Genesis!," in Claremont, Cockrum, and Byrne, *Uncanny X-Men Omnibus*, 12–13.

162. Chris Claremont and John Byrne, "Wanted: Wolverine! Dead or Alive!," in Claremont, Cockrum, and Byrne, *Uncanny X-Men Omnibus*, 556.

163. Chris Claremont and John Byrne, "Shoot-Out at the Stampede!," in Claremont, Cockrum, and Byrne, *Uncanny X-Men Omnibus*, 581.

164. Chris Claremont and John Byrne, "Rage!," in Claremont, Byrne, and Cockrum, *Uncanny X-Men Omnibus*, 234.

165. Fox and Shores, "Red Wolf," 1, 7, 10, 11, 12.

166. Fox and Shores, "Red Wolf," 14–15, 16, 19.

167. Everett and Friedrich, "Atomic Samurai," 3; Friedrich and Tuska, "Night of the Rising Sun," 17.

168. Mantlo and Buscema, "Like a Tiger," 3; Mantlo and Robbins, "Tiger and the Fly," 6–7.

Chapter 5: "Something for Everyone"

1. For coverage of this aspect of the comic, see, for example, Wright, *Comic Book Nation*, 263.

2. Len Wein and Dave Cockrum, "Second Genesis!," in Claremont, Cockrum, and Byrne, *Uncanny X-Men Omnibus*, 24; Chris Claremont and Dave Cockrum, "Deathstar, Rising!," in Claremont, Cockrum, and Byrne, *Uncanny X-Men Omnibus*, 148.

3. Michelinie and Byrne, "Matter of Heroes," 15.

4. Fawaz, *New Mutants*, 4–5.

5. Carrington, *Speculative Blackness*, 90.

6. Chafe, *Unfinished Journey*, 453, 456, 459, 467.

7. Hollinger, *Postethnic America*, 92.

8. Hollinger, *Postethnic America*, 96.

9. Hollinger, *Postethnic America*, 2, 98, 100, 101.

10. Hollinger, *Postethnic America*, x, 8, 32.

11. Sollors, *Beyond Ethnicity*, 12.

12. Sollors, *Beyond Ethnicity*, 186; Hollinger, *Postethnic America*, 8.

13. hooks, *Black Looks*, 21, 23.

14. Hollinger, *Postethnic America*, 34.

15. Alaimo, "Multiculturalism," 163.

16. Michelinie and Byrne, "Redoubtable Return," 8.

17. Michelinie and Byrne, "Death on the Hudson," 9; Gruenwald et al., "Call of the Mountain Thing," 2; Michelinie and Pérez, "Interlude."

18. Gruenwald et al., "Nights of Wundagore," 13–14, 16; Gruenwald et al., "Call of the Mountain Thing," 16; Mantlo and Byrne, "Elementary," 9; Grant, Stern, and Byrne, "Heart of Stone," 1, 13; Michelinie and Buscema, "Battleground," 8, 13.

19. Gruenwald et al., "Call of the Mountain Thing," 4, 5.

20. Mantlo and Byrne, "Elementary," 13.

21. Michelinie and Byrne, "Death on the Hudson," 8.

22. Michelinie and Pérez, "Interlude," 3.

23. Wolfman and Pérez, "Today," 13–15.

24. Wolfman and Pérez, "Fearsome Five," 9.

25. Wolfman and Pérez, "Fearsome Five," 14.

26. Wolfman and Pérez, "Day in the Lives," 10–11.

27. Wolfman and Pérez, "Today," 18.

28. Wolfman and Swan, "Trigon Lives," 14.

29. Wolfman and Pérez, "Where Nightmares Begin," 9–10.

30. Wolfman and Pérez, "Where Nightmares Begin," 3, 13.

31. Nicieza and Bagley, "From the Ground Up!," in *New Warriors Omnibus*, 1–2.

32. Tom DeFalco and Ron Frenz, "Introducing . . . the New Warriors!," in Nicieza and Bagley, *New Warriors Omnibus*, 45, 55; Nicieza and Bagley, "Mirror Moves," in *New Warriors Omnibus*, 81–82.

33. Tom DeFalco and Ron Frenz, "Introducing . . . the New Warriors!," in Nicieza and Bagley, *New Warriors Omnibus*, 49.

34. Nicieza and Bagley, "I Am, Therefore I Think," 93, "Genetech Potential," 111, in *New Warriors Omnibus*.

35. Nicieza and Bagley, "Mirror Moves," 52, "Genetech Potential," 126, in *New Warriors Omnibus*.

36. Hama and Ryan, "Wind from the East," 4, 7.

37. Giffen, DeMatteis, and Maguire, "Winning Hand," 3.

38. Aldama, *Your Brain on Latino Comics*, 33.

39. Englehart and Milgrom, "The Search for the Thing!," in *Sins of the Past*, 8.

40. Steve Englehart and Al Milgrom, "Quest for Cats!," 203, "A Bird in the Hand!," 253, in Englehart, Milgrom, and Howell, *Family Ties*.

41. Steve Englehart and Al Milgrom, "Hot Pursuit," in Englehart, Milgrom, and Howell, *Family Ties*, 292; Englehart and Milgrom, "The Search for the Thing!," in *Sins of the Past*, 5.

42. Ostrander, Wein, and Byrne, "Breach of Faith," 10; "Send for . . . the Suicide Squad," 17.

43. Ostrander and McDonnell, "Trial by Blood," 4.

44. Ostrander and McDonnell, "The Final Price," 2, 4, 8–9; "Blood and Snow," 7.

45. Claremont and Romita, "Nightcrawler's Inferno," 5; Claremont and Byrne, "Mind Out of Time," 9.

46. Claremont and Anderson, "Ou, La, La," 10, 16; Claremont and Cockrum, "First Blood," 6.

47. Claremont and Cockrum, "Gold Rush," 3, 5.

48. Claremont and Leonardi, "Duel," 14, 20.

49. Chris Claremont and John Romita Jr., "The Morning After," 26; Chris Claremont, John Romita Jr., and Bret Blevins, "Massacre", 66; both in Claremont, Simonson, et al., *Mutant Massacre*.

50. Chris Claremont and Mark Silvestri, "Unfinished Business," in Simonson, David, et al., *Fall of the Mutants*, 402.

51. Chris Claremont and Jim Lee, "First Strike," in Claremont, Simonson, Lee, et al., *X-Tinction Agenda*, 100–103, 108, 266.

52. Stern and Romita Jr., "Who's That Lady?," 2–4.

53. Stern and Romita Jr., "Who's That Lady?," 9–10, 12.

54. Stern and S. Buscema, "Testing," 3; Stern and Milgrom, "Trial and Error," 3–4; Stern and Milgrom, "Final Curtain," 3; Stern and Milgrom, "Up from the Depths"; Stern and J. Buscema, "Eve of Destruction"; Stern and J. Buscema, "Command Decision"; Stern and J. Buscema, "If Wishes Were Horses."

55. For the origins of her conflict with Blackout, see Stern and Milgrom, "I Want to Be an Avenger"; and Stern and Milgrom, "Meltdowns and Mayhem." For her confrontation with Nebula and her gang, see Stern and J. Buscema, "Legacy of Thanos."

56. Bogle, *Toms, Coons, Mulattoes*, 271–272; Nama, *Super Black*, 67.

57. Fawaz, *New Mutants*, 169.

58. David Michelinie and John Byrne, "At the Mercy of My Friends!," 60; David Michelinie and John Romita Jr., "The Old Man and the Sea Prince!," 105; both in Michelinie, Layton, and Romita, *Iron Man*.

59. O'Neil and Kirby, "Claws of the Dragon," 7; O'Neil and Estrada, "Time to Be a Whirlwind," 7.

60. Dennis and Durañona, "Coming of a Dragon," 4.

61. Stan Lee and John Romita, "It Happens in Harlem!," in S. Lee, Friedrich, et al., *Essential Captain America*.

62. Steve Englehart and Sal Buscema, "Enter: Solaar!," in Englehart, Gerber, et al., *Essential Captain America*.

63. Nama, *Super Black*, 58, 88.

64. Chris Claremont and John Byrne, "Fist of Iron—Heart of Stone!," "Seagate Is a Lonely Place to Die!," in McGregor, Mantlo, et al., *Essential Luke Cage*.

65. Ed Hannigan and Lee Elias, "Heroes for Hire!," in Claremont, Duffy, et al., *Essential Power Man*.

66. Mary Jo Duffy and Trevor Von Eeden, "The Scarab's Sting!," in Claremont, Duffy, et al., *Essential Power Man*.

67. Chris Claremont and John Byrne, "Freedom!," in Claremont, Duffy, et al., *Essential Power Man*.

68. Chris Claremont and Mike Zeck, "A Night on the Town," in Claremont, Duffy, et al., *Essential Power Man*.

69. Mary Jo Duffy and Trevor Von Eeden, "The Scarab's Sting!," in Claremont, Duffy, et al., *Essential Power Man*.

70. Jo Duffy and Kerry Gammill, "Luck and Death," in Claremont, Duffy, et al., *Essential Power Man.*

71. Mantlo and Leonardi, "True Confessions!," in *Cloak and Dagger*, 81, 86.

72. Mantlo and Hannigan, "Cloak and Dagger," 3.

73. Mantlo and Hannigan, "Cloak and Dagger," 4–5, 6–7.

74. Mantlo and Frenz, "Hunters and the Hunted," 4.

75. Mantlo and Frenz, "Hunters and the Hunted," 7.

76. Mantlo and Leonardi, "Hope," in *Cloak and Dagger*, 20.

77. Mantlo and Hannigan, "Cloak and Dagger," 3.

78. Mantlo and Leonardi, "Sinners All," 19.

79. Mantlo and Leonardi, "Faith," in *Cloak and Dagger*, 14.

80. Mantlo and Leonardi, "Have You Seen Your Mother," 2.

81. Mantlo and Milgrom, "Crime and Punishment," 20.

82. Mantlo and Leonardi, "Bellyful of Blues!," in *Cloak and Dagger*, 29.

83. Nama, *Super Black*, 85.

84. Mantlo and Leonardi, "Bellyful of Blues!," 33, "Dark Is My Love, and Deadly!," 55, in *Cloak and Dagger*.

85. Nama, *Super Black*, 86.

86. Mantlo and Leonardi, "True Confessions!," in *Cloak and Dagger*, 80.

87. Mantlo and Leondari, "Dagger's Light," 2.

88. Mantlo and Blevins, "All in the Family," 5.

89. T. Austin and Vosburg, "Agony Is Ecstasy," 17.

90. Warner Home Video, *All-New Super Friends Hour: Season One*, vol. 1, "The Whirlpool"; *All-New Super Friends Hour: Season One*, vol. 2, "Day of the Rats."

91. Warner Home Video, *All-New Super Friends Hour: Season One*, vol. 1, "The Antidote."

92. Warner Home Video, *All-New Super Friends Hour: Season One*, vol. 2, "Alaska Peril."

93. Warner Home Video, *All-New Super Friends Hour: Season One*, vol. 1, "Fire."

94. Warner Home Video, *Super Friends! Legacy of Super Powers*, "Bazarowurld."

95. hooks, *Black Looks*, 21–22.

96. Len Wein and Dave Cockrum, "Second Genesis!," in Claremont, Cockrum, and Byrne, *Uncanny X-Men Omnibus*, 42–45.

97. Len Wein and Dave Cockrum, "Second Genesis!," in Claremont, Cockrum, and Byrne, *Uncanny X-Men Omnibus*, 24, 31.

98. Len Wein and Dave Cockrum, "Second Genesis!," in Claremont, Cockrum, and Byrne, *Uncanny X-Men Omnibus*, 20.

99. Chris Claremont and Dave Cockrum, "The Doomsmith Scenario!," 49, "Warhunt!," 83–84, in Claremont, Cockrum, and Byrne, *Uncanny X-Men Omnibus*.

100. hooks, *Black Looks*, 21, 23.

101. Chris Claremont and Dave Cockrum, "Warhunt!," in Claremont, Cockrum, and Byrne, *Uncanny X-Men Omnibus*, 70.

102. Chris Claremont and Dave Cockrum, "Warhunt!," 72, "Deathstar Rising!," 149, 150, 156, in Claremont, Cockrum, and Byrne, *Uncanny X-Men Omnibus*.

103. Chris Claremont and Dave Cockrum, "Deathstar Rising!," in Claremont, Cockrum, and Byrne, *Uncanny X-Men Omnibus*, 149.

104. Chris Claremont and Dave Cockrum, "Warhunt!," in Claremont, Cockrum, and Byrne, *Uncanny X-Men Omnibus*, 69, 74.

105. Sheyashe, *Native Americans in Comic Books*, 106.

106. Claremont and Cockrum, "Rogue Storm," 16.

107. Claremont and Anderson, "Chutes and Ladders," 3–4, 11.

108. Claremont and Cockrum, "Binary Star," 5, 18.

109. Claremont and Smith, "To Have and Have Not," 19; Claremont and Romita Jr., "Two Girls Out," 5–6; Claremont and Romita Jr., "Warhunt 2," 12.

110. Fawaz, *New Mutants*, 234–235.

111. Claremont and McLeod, "Renewal," in *New Mutants Classic*, 11.

112. Claremont and McLeod, "Renewal," in *New Mutants Classic*, 18, 38.

113. Claremont and McLeod, "Renewal," in *New Mutants Classic*, 20, 26.

114. Claremont and McLeod, "Renewal," 41, "Sentinels," 81, 95, in *New Mutants Classic*.

115. Claremont and McLeod, "Renewal," in *New Mutants Classic*, 8.

116. Chris Claremont and Sal Buscema, "Heroes," in Claremont and McLeod, *New Mutants Classic*, 192.

117. Claremont and McLeod, "Renewal," in *New Mutants Classic*, 50, 54.

118. Claremont and McLeod, "Initiation," in *New Mutants Classic*, 57, 61.

119. Claremont and McLeod, "Renewal," in *New Mutants Classic*, 25.

120. R. Lee, *Orientals*, 11.

121. Claremont and McLeod, "Renewal," 27, "Sentinels," 98, in *New Mutants Classic*.

122. Claremont and McLeod, "Renewal," in *New Mutants Classic*, 14.

123. Claremont and McLeod, "Renewal," in *New Mutants Classic*, 59.

124. Chris Claremont and Sal Buscema, "Who's Scaring Stevie?," in Claremont and McLeod, *New Mutants Classic*, 158.

125. Claremont and McLeod, "Nightmare," in *New Mutants Classic*, 103.

126. Claremont and McLeod, "Flying Down to Rio!," in *New Mutants Classic*, 228; Chris Claremont and Bob McLeod, "Sunstroke," in Claremont and Buscema, *New Mutants Classic*, 102; Claremont and Sienkiewicz, "Shadowman," in *New Mutants Classic*, 180.

127. Warner Home Video, *Challenge of the Super Friends*, "Invasion of the Fearians."

128. Warner Home Video, *Challenge of the Super Friends*, "The Time Trap."

129. Warner Home Video, *Challenge of the Super Friends*, "Super Friends: Rest in Peace," "Fairy Tale of Doom."

130. Warner Home Video, *Challenge of the Super Friends*, "The Time Trap," "Wanted: The Super Friends," "Secret Origins of the Super Friends," "Swamp of the Living Dead."

131. Aldama, *Your Brain on Latino Comics*, 33.

132. Conway and Patton, "End of the Justice League," 28.

133. Conway and Patton, "End of the Justice League," 32.

134. Conway and Patton, "'Rebirth' Part Two," 13.

135. Conway and Patton, "'Rebirth' Part One," 8; Conway and Tuska, "Battle Cry," 9.

136. Conway and Patton, "Savage Symphony," 13–14.

137. Englehart and Staton, "New Guardians," 2.

138. Aldama, *Your Brain on Latino Comics*, 35.

139. Englehart and Staton, "New Guardians," 4, 16–17.

140. Bates and Staton, "Whiter Shade of Peril," 5.

141. DC Comics, New Guardians letters page, *New Guardians* 1, no. 12.

142. Englehart, Bates, and Staton, "Blow in the Wind," 7; Bates and Staton, "Heartlands," 10, 16.

143. DC Comics, New Guardians letters page, *New Guardians* 1, no. 6; New Guardians letters page, *New Guardians* 1, no. 11.

144. Bates, Dooley, and Broderick, "Dawn Light," 21.

145. Singer, "'Black Skins' and White Masks," 112.

146. Milestone Comics, editorial, 13.

147. Aldama, *Your Brain on Latino Comics*, 47.

148. Velez, McDuffie, and ChrisCross, "Blood Battle," 16.

149. McDuffie, Velez, and Von Eeden, "America Eats," 2, 3.

150. Velez, McDuffie, Jones, et al., "Thicker Than Blood," 23.

151. McDuffie, Velez, and Von Eeden, "America Eats," 16–19.

152. Velez, McDuffie, Jones, et al., "Thicker than Blood," 24.

153. Wayne, "There Goes the Neighborhood."

154. For example, as Triathlon's membership is discussed, he points to a picture of the Falcon when he served as the team's "token" member and asks, "So . . . what do you think they're talking about?" See Busiek and Pérez, "New Order."

Chapter 6: Replacement Heroes and the Quest for Inclusion

1. Learning Network, "May 1, 1992."

2. Takaki, *Different Mirror*, 4.

3. Sanchez, "Face the Nation," 1010.

4. Johns and Morales, "Who Do You Trust?," in *Fair Play*, 48.

5. Baron, McLaurin, and Mayerik, "Escape from New York," 2–9.

6. Baron, McLaurin, and Mayerik, "Escape from New York," 10, 13–14.

7. Baron, McLaurin, and Mayerik, "Escape from New York," 10–11, 13.

8. Baron, McLaurin, and Mayerik, "Crackdown," 1, 7–8.

9. Baron, McLaurin, and Mayerik, "Crackdown," 11, 15; "Fade to White," 7, 9–10.

10. Claremont and Silvestri, "Crash and Burn," 14.

11. Claremont and Lee, "Key That Breaks," 14.

12. Claremont and Lee, "Key That Breaks," 19, 31.

13. Claremont and Lee, "Lady Mandarin," 1–9.

14. Claremont and Lee, "Lady Mandarin," 17–19.

15. Claremont and Lee, "Broken Chains," 25.

16. Claremont and Silvestri, "Harriers Hunt," 1–19.

17. J. Lee and Byrne, "Blowback," 2–3; J. Lee and Lobdell, "Tooth and Claw," 8–10; J. Lee and Byrne, "Not So Big Easy," 16–17; Nicieza and Kubert, "Skinning of Souls," 13–14.

18. Nicieza and Bagley, "Bug Bites Back," 22.

19. Nicieza and Adlard, "Life Sentences," 39.

20. Nicieza and Bagley, "Targeted for Death," 14.

21. Nicieza and Zircher, "New Beginnings," 13–14.

22. See Goodwin and Tuska, "Replacement"; O'Neil and McDonnell, "Blackout."

23. Len Kaminski and Kevin Hopgood, "Legacy of Iron," 102–104, 110; Len Kaminski and Kevin Hopgood, "Ashes to Ashes," 127, 131; Len Kaminski and Tom Morgan, "The Light at the End," 258, 268–269; all in Marvel Comics, *Invincible Iron Man*.

24. Len Kaminski and Kevin Hopgood, "Meltdown," 173–175; Len Kaminski and Tom Morgan, "The Light at the End," 249; Len Kaminski and Kevin Hopgood, "Ashes to Ashes," 146; all in Marvel Comics, *Invincible Iron Man*.

25. Len Kaminski and Kevin Hopgood, "Meltdown," in Marvel Comics, *Invincible Iron Man*, 180–181.

26. Len Kaminski and Kevin Hopgood, "War Machine," 59–62, "Put the Hammer Down," 82, "Legacy of Iron," 111, "Judgement Day," 315, 317–318, in Marvel Comics, *Invincible Iron Man*; Abnett, Lanning, and Ross, "Avengers West Coast."

27. Matthew Sturges, Freddie Williams II, and Howard Porter, "Glory Days"; Matthew Sturges and Freddie Williams II, "Constellations"; both in Sturges, Porter, and Williams, *JSA All-Stars*.

28. Matthew Sturges, Freddie Williams II, and Howard Porter, "Glory Days," in Sturges, Porter, and Williams, *JSA All-Stars*.

29. Gray, Palmiotti, and Acuña, "First Strike," 1–5.

30. Gray, Palmiotti, and Acuña, "First Strike," 6–20; "A Call to Arms," 1–4.

31. Gray, Palmiotti, and Acuña, "Traitors and Patriots," 10–11; "Liberty and Justice," 1–21.

32. Gray, Palmiotti, and Acuña, "A Call to Arms," 5.

33. Gray, Palmiotti, and Acuña, "A Call to Arms," 5; "Returning of Champions," 16–17, 19.

34. Wolfman and Pérez, "And Thus Shall the World Die," in *Crisis on Infinite Earths*, 103–105.

35. Wolfman and Pérez, "And Thus Shall the World Die," in *Crisis on Infinite Earths*, 110–111.

36. Wolfman and Pérez, "Three Deaths, Three Earths," 150, 158, "Beyond the Silent Night," 210–222, in *Crisis on Infinite Earths*.

37. Wolfman and Pérez, "Beyond the Silent Night," 210–222, "Final Crisis," 349, in *Crisis on Infinite Earths*.

38. Thomas and McFarlane, "Shadows at Midnight," 8–9.

39. Aldama, *Latinx Superheroes*, 28.

40. Thomas, Thomas, and McFarlane, "Business as Usual," 15–18.

41. Thomas and McFarlane, "Shadows at Midnight," 11; Thomas, Thomas, and McFarlane, "Business as Usual," 10, 23–24.

42. Wolfman and Pérez, "Beyond the Silent Night," in *Crisis on Infinite Earths*, 177–178.

43. Wolfman and Pérez, "War Zone," in *Crisis on Infinite Earths*, 259.

44. R. Daniels, *Asian America*, 317–321.

45. Gail Simone, Grant Morrison, and John Byrne, "Indivisible," in Simone, Byrne, et al., *Life in Miniature*, 12–14.

46. Gail Simone and John Byrne, "Binding Energies," 63–72; Gail Simone and Eddy Barrows, "Aggressive Ideologies," 81; both in Simone, Byrne, et al., *Life in Miniature*.

47. Gail Simone and John Byrne, "Indivisible," 16, 25–27, "Binding Energies," 66–72, in Simone, Byrne, et al., *Life in Miniature*.

48. Simone and Norton, "Never Too Small to Hit the Big Time," in *Hunt for Ray Palmer*, 12; Gail Simone and Mike Norton, "The Man Who Swallowed Eternity: Part I," in Simone, Norton, and Barrows, *Future/Past*, 21.

49. Gail Simone, Mike Norton, and Andy Smith, "The Atom and the Amazon! Part 2," in Simone, Remender, et al., *Small Wonder*, 47, 75; Gail Simone, Grant Morri-

son, and John Byrne, "Indivisible," in Simone, Byrne, et al., *Life in Miniature*, 16; Gail Simone and Mike Norton, "The Man Who Swallowed Eternity: Part I," in Simone, Norton, and Barrows, *Future/Past*, 14, 18.

50. Gail Simone, Grant Morrison, and John Byrne, "Indivisible," 17–18, 27–28; Gail Simone and John Byrne, "Atomic Shell," 42–43; Gail Simone and Eddy Barrows, "Aggressive Ideologies," 96; Gail Simone and Eddy Barrows, "Redline Shift," 116; all in Simone, Byrne, et al., *Life in Miniature*.

51. Takaki, *Different Mirror*, 2; Schlesinger, *Disuniting of America*, 120.

52. Schlesinger, *Disuniting of America*, 119, 121–122, 127, 131, 133.

53. Takaki, *Different Mirror*, 3, 6, 14, 17.

54. S. Lee and Ditko, "Spider-Man!," in *Great Power*, 15.

55. Louise Simonson and Jon Bogdanove, "Steel," in Jurgens et al., *Return of Superman*, 46–49.

56. Louise Simonson and Jon Bogdanove, "Prolog," in Jurgens et al., *Return of Superman*, 4–5.

57. Louise Simonson and Jon Bogdanove, "Steel," in Jurgens et al., *Return of Superman*, 49; Simonson and Bogdanove, "Wrought Iron," 6–8; Simonson and Batista, "Challenge," 2.

58. Roger Stern and Jackson Guice, "Who Is the Hero True?," 214; Louise Simonson and Jon Bogdanove, "Ambush!," 131; Louise Simonson and Jon Bogdanove, "The Return!," 311; all in Jurgens et al., *Return of Superman*.

59. Simonson and Bogdanove, "Wrought Iron," 2.

60. Simonson and Bogdanove, "Wrought Iron," 1.

61. Simonson and Batista, "Retaliation," 4.

62. Louise Simonson and Jon Bogdanove, "Ambush!," 131–133, "Steel," 55, in Jurgens et al., *Return of Superman*; Simonson and Fosco, "Bad News," 1.

63. Louise Simonson and Jon Bogdanove, "Steel," 58–59, "Ambush!," 149, in Jurgens et al., *Return of Superman*; Simonson and Bogdanove, "Wrought Iron," 5.

64. Louise Simonson and Jon Bogdanove, "Ambush!," 142–145; Roger Stern and Jackson Guice, "Who Is the Hero True?," 210, 214, 222; Louise Simonson and Jon Bogdanove, "Blast Off!," 414–415; all in Jurgens et al., *Return of Superman*.

65. Simonson and Batista, "In the Beginning," 17.

66. Louise Simonson and Jon Bogdanove, "The Return!," 310–311, 321, "Blast Off!," 405, 411, in Jurgens et al., *Return of Superman*.

67. Simonson and Batista, "In the Beginning," 1–2.

68. Simonson and Bogdanove, "Wrought Iron," 22.

69. Simonson and Batista, "Retaliation," 22.

70. Simonson and Batista, "Collision Course," 7.

71. Simonson and Fosco, "Bad News," 14; Michelinie and Larocque, "Seeking Spirit," 7.

72. S. Moore and Igle, *Firestorm*, 40.

73. Jolley and ChrisCross, "Eye Contact," 4–5.

74. Jolley and ChrisCross, "Eye Contact, 1–4; "Everybody Wants You," 3–7.

75. Jolley and ChrisCross, "Eye Contact," 8–13.

76. Jolley and ChrisCross, "Eye Contact," 7.

77. Jolley and ChrisCross, "Eye Contact," 2–7; "Empowered," 15; "Everybody Wants You, Part 2," 1–2.

78. Jolley and ChrisCross, "Joyride," 11–21.

79. Jolley and ChrisCross, "Joyride," 21; Jolley and ChrisCross, "Everybody Wants You," 14; Jolley and ChrisCross, "Everybody Wants You, Part 2," 22; S. Moore and Igle, *Firestorm*, 37, 78.

80. David Goyer, Geoff Johns, and Stephen Sadowski, "Time's Assassin," 161; David Goyer, Geoff Johns, and Stephen Sadowski, "Wild Hunt," 108; David Goyer, Geoff Johns, and Buzz, "Split," 132; David Goyer, Geoff Johns, and Buzz, "The Blood-Dimmed Tide," 143–146; all in Goyer, Johns, Sadowski, et al., *Darkness Falls*. David Goyer, Geoff Johns, and Stephen Sadowski, "Cold Comfort," 31, "Into the Labyrinth," 83, in Goyer and Johns, *Return of Hawkman*.

81. David Goyer, Geoff Johns, and Buzz, "The Blood-Dimmed Tide," in Goyer, Johns, Sadowski, et al., *Darkness Falls*, 143–146; David Goyer, Geoff Johns, and Stephen Sadowski, "Divide and Conquer," in Goyer and Johns, *Return of Hawkman*, 14–17; Johns and Morales, "Thunderstruck," in *Fair Play*, 74–76.

82. David Goyer, Geoff Johns, and Stephen Sadowski, "Icarus Fell," in Goyer and Johns, *Return of Hawkman*, 197.

83. David Goyer, Geoff Johns, and Stephen Sadowski, "Seven Devils," in Goyer and Johns, *Return of Hawkman*, 224–225.

84. Dwayne McDuffie, Gregory Wright, and Jackson Guice, "The Brains of the Outfit," 17–18, "Jesus Saves," 72, in McDuffie, Wright, et al., *Deathlok*.

85. Dwayne McDuffie, Gregory Wright, and Jackson Guice, "The Brains of the Outfit," 21–28, "Jesus Saves," 72–73, in McDuffie, Wright, et al., *Deathlok*.

86. Dwayne McDuffie, Gregory Wright, and Jackson Guice, "The Brains of the Outfit," in McDuffie, Wright, et al., *Deathlok*, 31–40.

87. Dwayne McDuffie, Gregory Wright, and Jackson Guice, "The Brains of the Outfit," in McDuffie, Wright, et al., *Deathlok*, 49–59.

88. Dwayne McDuffie, Gregory Wright, and Jackson Guice, "Jesus Saves," in McDuffie, Wright, et al., *Deathlok*, 63–68.

89. Dwayne McDuffie, Gregory Wright, and Jackson Guice, "Jesus Saves," 107; Dwayne McDuffie, Gregory Wright, and Denys Cowan, "Dam If He Don't," 117–140; both in McDuffie, Wright, et al., *Deathlok*.

90. Dwayne McDuffie, Gregory Wright, and Jackson Guice, "Ryker's Island," in McDuffie, Wright, et al., *Deathlok*, 141–203.

91. Johns, Jimenez, et al., *Infinite Crisis*, 5, 87, 117, 144–146.

92. Johns, Jimenez, et al., *Infinite Crisis*, 175–176.

93. Giffen, Rogers, and Hamner, "Blue Monday," in *Blue Beetle*, 8–10, 12–14.

94. Keith Giffen, John Rogers, and Cully Hamner, "Blue Monday," 25; Keith Giffen, John Rogers, Cynthia Martin, and Phil May, "The Past Is Another Country," 57–58; both in Giffen, Rogers, and Hamner, *Blue Beetle*, 57–58.

95. Giffen, Rogers, and Hamner, "Person of Interest," in *Blue Beetle*, 75–76.

96. Keith Giffen, John Rogers, and Cully Hamner, "Person of Interest," 86–89, 94; Keith Giffen, John Rogers, and Duncan Rouleau, "Secrets, Part I," 117; both in Giffen, Rogers, and Hamner, *Blue Beetle*.

97. For the discussion that follows, see Bendis and Pichelli, *Spider-Man*.

98. See Aldama, *Latinx Superheroes*, 83–84.

99. For the discussion that follows, see Morales and Baker, *Truth*.

Chapter 7: Something Old, Something New

1. S. Lee, "More Than Normal," 116.
2. Loeb, "Making the World," 121, 123; see also Quesada, "Extraordinary," 148.
3. Hogan, *Empire and Poetic Voice*, 2.
4. Aldama, *Why the Humanities Matter*, 247.
5. Hogan, *Cognitive Science*, 40–42.
6. Khoury, *Image Comics*, 134.
7. Nama, *Super Black*, 132–136; Morrison, *Supergods*, 248.
8. For the discussion that follows, see McFarlane, *Spawn*.
9. Reginald Hudlin, "Introduction," in McDuffie and Bright, *Hero's Welcome*; Brown, *Black Superheroes*, 26–27, 51–52; G. Jones and Jacobs, *Comic Book Heroes*, 354; Howe, *Marvel Comics*, 346.
10. Brown, *Black Superheroes*, 28–32.
11. Brown, *Black Superheroes*, 40–41, 153–161, 166, 178, 180–183, 189, 196.
12. Nama, *Super Black*, 93–99.
13. Brown, *Black Superheroes*, 36–38, 49, 157, 184.
14. McDuffie and Bright, "By Their Own Bootstraps," in *Hero's Welcome*, 9–14.
15. Dwayne McDuffie and Mark Bright, "Testify," in McDuffie, Bright, and Gustovich, *Mothership Connection*, 175–176.
16. McDuffie and Bright, "By Their Own Bootstraps," in *Hero's Welcome*, 14–24.
17. McDuffie and Bright, "By Their Own Bootstraps," in *Hero's Welcome*, 23–25.
18. McDuffie and Bright, "By Their Own Bootstraps," in *Hero's Welcome*, 26–27.
19. McDuffie and Bright, "By Their Own Bootstraps," in *Hero's Welcome*, 27–30.
20. McDuffie and Bright, "By Their Own Bootstraps," 48–53, "Payback," 55–73, 74–76, "Great Expectations," 88–99, in *Hero's Welcome*.
21. McDuffie and Bright, "Payback," 77–78, "May We Bang You?," 101, 109–111, 119–120, in *Hero's Welcome*.
22. Dwayne McDuffie, Erica Helene, and M. D. Bright, "The Moment of Truth," in McDuffie and Bright, *Hero's Welcome*, 150, 157–159, 165.
23. McDuffie and Bright, "Entelechy," in *Hero's Welcome*, 182–183, 189–191.
24. Brown, *Black Superheroes*, 163.
25. Dwayne McDuffie and Mark Bright, "It's Always Christmas," in McDuffie, Bright, and Gustovich, *Mothership Connection*, 7–9.
26. Dwayne McDuffie and Mark Bright, "It's Always Christmas," in McDuffie, Bright, and Gustovich, *Mothership Connection*, 7–9, 8–9, 17–19.
27. Dwayne McDuffie and Mark Bright, "It's Always Christmas," in McDuffie, Bright, and Gustovich, *Mothership Connection*, 7–9, 21–28.
28. Dwayne McDuffie and Mark Bright, "It's Always Christmas," 7–9, 28, "If You Ain't Gonna Get It On," 85, "The Cinderella Theory," 104, 112–123, in McDuffie, Bright, and Gustovich, *Mothership Connection*.
29. Dwayne McDuffie and Mark Bright, "It's Always Christmas," 7–9, "The Buck Passes," 231–237, in McDuffie, Bright, and Gustovich, *Mothership Connection*.
30. Dwayne McDuffie and Mark Bright, "It's Always Christmas," 7–9, "The Buck Passes," 237–239, in McDuffie, Bright, and Gustovich, *Mothership Connection*.
31. Dwayne McDuffie and Mark Bright, "It's Always Christmas," 7–9, "The Buck Passes," 237–239, in McDuffie, Bright, and Gustovich, *Mothership Connection*.

32. Dwayne McDuffie and Mark Bright, "It's Always Christmas," 7–9, "The Buck Passes," 247–253, in McDuffie, Bright, and Gustovich, *Mothership Connection*.

33. McDuffie and Cowan, "Angry Black Man," in *Hardware*, 7–15.

34. McDuffie and Cowan, "Angry Black Man," in *Hardware*, 16–20.

35. McDuffie and Cowan, "Angry Black Man," in *Hardware*, 21–24.

36. McDuffie and Cowan, "Reprisals," 32–50, "Angry Black Man," 27, "Confrontations," 54–72, in *Hardware*.

37. Dwayne McDuffie and Denys Cowan, "That Obscure Object of Desire," 101–103, "Guilty," 158–162; Dwayne McDuffie and J. J. Birch, "Rest in Peace," 165–185; in McDuffie and Cowan, *Hardware*.

38. Dwayne McDuffie and J. J. Birch, "Rest in Peace, 185–186, in McDuffie and Cowan, *Hardware*.

39. Dwayne McDuffie, Robert L. Washington III, and John Paul Leon, "Burning Sensation," in McDuffie, Washington, et al., *Static Shock*, 6–12.

40. Dwayne McDuffie, Robert L. Washington III, and John Paul Leon, "Burning Sensation," in McDuffie, Washington, et al., *Static Shock*, 13–17.

41. Dwayne McDuffie, Robert L. Washington III, and John Paul Leon, "Burning Sensation," in McDuffie, Washington, et al., *Static Shock*, 18–28.

42. Dwayne McDuffie, Robert L. Washington III, and John Paul Leon, "Everything But the Girl," in McDuffie, Washington, et al., *Static Shock*, 47–51.

43. Dwayne McDuffie, Robert L. Washington III, and John Paul Leon, "Everything But the Girl," 51, "Pounding the Pavement," 58–59, in McDuffie, Washington, et al., *Static Shock*.

44. Dwayne McDuffie, Robert L. Washington III, and John Paul Leon, "Playing with Fire," in McDuffie, Washington, et al., *Static Shock*, 63–74, 78–97.

45. Johns, Jimenez, et al., *Infinite Crisis*, 188.

46. Christopher Priest, "Introduction," in Priest, Texeira, and Evans, *Black Panther*.

47. Christopher Priest, "Introduction," in Priest, Texeira, and Evans, *Black Panther*.

48. Christopher Priest and Mark Texeira, "The Client," in Priest, Texeira, and Evans, *Black Panther*.

49. Christopher Priest and Mark Texeira, "The Client," "Invasion," "Original Sin," "The Price"; Christopher Priest and Vince Evans, "Lord of the Damned"; all in Priest, Texeira, and Evans, *Black Panther*. Christopher Priest and Joe Jusko, "Hunted," "Caged," "That Business with the Avengers"; Christopher Priest and Mike Manley, "Enemy of the State," "Enemy of the State: Book Two," "Enemy of the State: Book Three"; Christopher Priest and Mark Bright, "Enemy of the State: Conclusion"; all in Priest, Jusko, et al., *Black Panther*.

50. Christopher Priest and Mark Texeira, "The Client," "Invasion," "Original Sin," "The Price"; Christopher Priest and Vince Evans, "Lord of the Damned"; all in Priest, Texeira, and Evans, *Black Panther*. Christopher Priest and Joe Jusko, "Hunted," "Caged," "That Business with the Avengers"; Christopher Priest and Mike Manley, "Enemy of the State," "Enemy of the State: Book Two," "Enemy of the State: Book Three"; Christopher Priest and Mark Bright, "Enemy of the State: Conclusion"; all in Priest, Jusko, et al., *Black Panther*.

51. Christopher Priest and Mark Texeira, "The Client," "Invasion," "Original Sin," "The Price"; Christopher Priest and Vince Evans, "Lord of the Damned"; all in Priest, Texeira, and Evans, *Black Panther*.

52. Christopher Priest and Joe Jusko, "Hunted," in Priest, Jusko, et al., *Black Panther*.

53. Christopher Priest and Joe Jusko, "Hunted," in Priest, Jusko, et al., *Black Panther*.

54. Christopher Priest and Joe Jusko, "That Business with the Avengers," in Priest, Jusko, et al., *Black Panther*.

55. Nama, *Super Black*, 65–66.

56. Bendis and Gaydos, "Issue 1," in *Alias Omnibus*.

57. Bendis and Gaydos, "Issue 2," in *Alias Omnibus*.

58. Bendis and Gaydos, "Issue 6," in *Alias Omnibus*.

59. Bendis and Gaydos, "Issue 3," "Issue 15," in *Alias Omnibus*.

60. Brian Michael Bendis, Michael Gaydos, and Mark Bagley, "Issue 25," "Issue 26," in Bendis and Gaydos, *Alias Omnibus*.

61. Bendis and Gaydos, "Issue 28," in *Alias Omnibus*.

62. Bendis and Finch, "Breakout."

63. Bendis and Deodato, "Collective."

64. Bendis and Yu, "New Avengers."

65. Nama, *Super Black*, 122.

66. For the discussion that follows, see Priest and Bennet, "Big Trouble, Part 1."

67. For the discussion that follows, see Priest and Bennet, "Big Trouble, Part 2."

68. For the discussion that follows, see Priest and Bennet, "Big Trouble, Part 3."

69. For the discussion that follows, see Priest and Bennet, "Big Trouble, Part 5."

70. For the discussion that follows, see Priest and Bennet, "Big Trouble, Part 6."

71. For the discussion that follows, see Priest and Bennet, "Big Trouble, Part 7."

72. Singer, "'Black Skins' and White Masks," 112.

73. For the discussion that follows, see Isabella and Newell, "Weekend Report."

74. Isabella and Newell, "Weekend Report"; "Teachers."

75. Isabella and Newell, "Weekend Report"; "Teachers"; "Students."

76. Isabella and Newell, "Weekend Report"; Isabella, Newell, Batista, et al., "Season of the Warrior."

77. For the discussion that follows, see Isabella and Newell, "Lessons"; "Blowed Away."

78. For the discussion that follows, see Isabella and Newell, "Return of the Warlord"; Isabella, Newell, Batista, et al., "Season of the Warrior"; Isabella, Cariello, et al., "Armies of the Street."

79. Newport, "Obama Election."

80. Newport, "Obama Election."

81. J. Jones, "Black-White Relations."

82. Kaste, "Since Ferguson."

83. S. Gray, "Obama's Election."

84. Blair, "For 'Black Nerds Everywhere.'"

Coda

1. Melrose, "DC Announces Post-'Flashpoint.'"

2. Esposito, "Exclusive."

3. Hyde, "Eric Wallace."

4. Rogers, "DC Reveals Major Changes."

5. Frannich, "Marvel's New Beginning."

6. Ching, "Brevoort on 'Silver Surfer.'"

7. See Rogers, "DC Reveals Major Changes."

8. Ron Marz and Sami Basri, "Part 1," in Marz, Basri, and Williamson, *Voodoo*.

9. Eric Wallace and Scott Clark, "Haunted," in Wallace, Gugliotta, and Faucher, *Mister Terrific*.

10. Eric Wallace and Gianluca Gugliotta, "In Veritas," in Wallace, Gugliotta, and Faucher, *Mister Terrific*.

11. See Campbell, "Bilingual 'Blue Beetle.'"

12. Tony Bedard and Ig Guara, "Part 1," in Bedard, Guara, Mayer, et al., *Blue Beetle*.

13. Tony Bedard and Ig Guara, "Part 2," in Bedard, Guara, Mayer, et al., *Blue Beetle*; Tony Bedard and Ig Guara, "Scarabworld!," in Bedard, Guara, and Takara, *Blue Beetle*; Tony Bedard and Ig Guara, "Part 3," in Bedard, Guara, Mayer, et al., *Blue Beetle*.

14. Ann Nocenti and Alex Sanchez, "Way of the Outsider," in Nocenti, Sanchez, and Richards, *Katana*.

15. Geoff Johns, Andrew Kreisberg, and Pete Woods, "Not-So-Secret Origin," in Gates et al., *Vibe*.

16. Geoff Johns, Andrew Kreisberg, and Pete Woods, "Not-So-Secret Origin"; Geoff Johns, Andrew Kreisberg, Pete Woods, and Andres Guinaldo, "Why Me?"; both in Gates et al., *Vibe*.

17. Sterling Gates and Pete Woods, "Suicide Solution"; Sterling Gates and Derlis Santacruz, "Clean Out Your Desk"; both in Gates et al., *Vibe*.

18. Remender and Coipel, "Let the Good Times Roll."

19. Remender and Coipel, "Let the Good Times Roll."

20. Wheeler, "Avengers Assimilate."

21. Remender and McNiven, "Ragnarok Now," 23–25.

22. Smith, and Moore, *All-New Ghost Rider*.

23. For the following discussion, see Wilson and Alphona, *Ms. Marvel*.

24. For the following discussion, see Ewing and Land, *Mighty Avengers*.

25. Phegley, "Marvel Adds 'Mighty.'"

26. See, for example, King, "Jimmy Olsen"; and Terror, "Lack of Diversity."

27. Zub and Silas, *Hunt for Wolverine*.

28. As of the writing of this chapter, *Black Panther* is the most successful movie (in terms of unadjusted box office receipts) not only in the Marvel Cinematic Universe but in all of superhero films. See A. Rosenberg, "Black Panther."

Bibliography

Abnett, Dan, Andy Lanning, and Dave Ross. "The Avengers West Coast Are Finished!" *Avengers West Coast* 1, no. 102. Marvel Comics, January 1994.

Abrams, M. H. "Primitivism and Progress." In *A Glossary of Literary Terms*, 244–246. 7th ed. Boston: Heinle and Heinle, 1999.

Ace Magazines. "Captain Courageous." *Four Favorites* 1, no. 9. Ace Magazines, 1943.

Achebe, Chinua. "An Image of Africa." *Research in African Literatures* 9, no. 1 (Spring 1978): 1–15.

Alaimo, Stacy. "Multiculturalism and Epistemic Rupture: The Vanishing Acts of Guillermo Gómez-Peña and Alfredo Véa Jr." *MELUS* 25, no. 2 (Summer 2000): 163–185.

Aldama, Frederick Luis. *Latinx Superheroes in Mainstream Comics*. Tucson: University of Arizona Press, 2017.

———, ed. *Multicultural Comics: From "Zap" to "Blue Beetle."* Austin: University of Texas Press, 2010.

———. *Why the Humanities Matter: A Commonsense Approach*. Austin: University of Texas Press, 2008.

———. *Your Brain on Latino Comics: From Gus Arriola to Los Bros Hernandez*. Austin: University of Texas Press, 2009.

Austin, Allan W. "Loyalty and Concentration Camps in America: The Japanese American Precedent and the Internal Security Act of 1950." In *Last Witnesses: Reflections on the Wartime Internment of Japanese Americans*, edited by Erica Harth, 253–270. New York: St. Martin's Press Griffin, 2001.

———. "Projecting Japanese American Exile and Incarceration: Ethnicity, the Enemy, and Mass Incarceration in Film during World War II." In *2004–2005 Film and History CD-ROM Annual*. Cleveland, OK: Film and History Center, 2006.

———. "Superman Goes to War: Teaching Japanese American Exile and Incarceration with Film." *Journal of American Ethnic History* 30, no. 4 (Summer 2011): 51–56.

Austin, Terry, and Mike Vosburg. "Agony Is Ecstasy." *The Mutant Misadventures of Cloak and Dagger* 1, no. 6. Marvel Comics, October 1989.

Bacevich, Andrew J. "Farewell, the American Century: Rewriting the Past and Adding In What's Been Left Out." TomDispatch.com, April 28, 2009. tomdispatch .com/post/175065.

Baron, Mike, Marcus McLaurin, and Val Mayerik. "Crackdown." *The Punisher* 2, no. 61. Marvel Comics, March 1992.

———. "Escape from New York." *The Punisher* 2, no. 60. Marvel Comics, February 1992.

———. "Fade to White." *The Punisher* 2, no. 62. Marvel Comics, April 1992.

Barr, Mike W., and Jim Aparo. *Showcase Presents: Batman and the Outsiders.* Vol. 1. New York: DC Comics, 2007.

Bates, Cary, Dave Cockrum, Mike Grell, Jim Shooter, and Bill Draut. *Showcase Presents: Legion of Super-Heroes.* Vol. 5. New York: DC Comics, 2014.

Bates, Cary, Kevin Dooley, and Pat Broderick. "Dawn Light." *The New Guardians* 1, no. 12. DC Comics, September 1989.

Bates, Cary, and Mike Grell. "The Hero Who Hated the Legion." *Superboy* 1, no. 216. DC Comics, April 1976.

Bates, Cary, and Joe Staton. "Heartlands." *The New Guardians* 1, no. 7. DC Comics, February 1989.

———. "A Whiter Shade of Peril." *The New Guardians* 1, no. 8. DC Comics, April 1989.

Bedard, Tony, Ig Guara, J. P. Mayer, and Roy Jose. *Blue Beetle Volume 1: Metamorphosis.* New York: DC Comics, 2012.

Bedard, Tony, Ig Guara, and Márcio Takara. *Blue Beetle Volume 2: Blue Diamond.* New York: DC Comics, 2013.

Beebe, Ford, and John Rawlins, dirs. *The Green Hornet Strikes Again.* 1941. DVD. New York: Universal Pictures, 2009.

Beebe, Ford, and Ray Taylor, dirs. *The Green Hornet.* 1940. DVD. New York: Universal Pictures, 2009.

Bendis, Brian Michael, and Mike Deodato Jr. "The Collective" (Part One). *The New Avengers* 1, no. 17. Marvel Comics, May 2006.

Bendis, Brian Michael, and David Finch. "Breakout!" (Part Three). *The New Avengers* 1, no. 3. Marvel Comics, March 2005.

Bendis, Brian Michael, and Michael Gaydos. *Alias Omnibus.* 2nd ed. New York: Marvel Comics, 2014.

Bendis, Brian Michael, and Sara Pichelli. *Ultimate Comics: Spider-Man.* New York: Marvel Comics, 2012.

Bendis, Brian Michael, and Leinil Yu. "New Avengers: Disassembled" (Part Two). *The New Avengers* 1, no. 22. Marvel Comics, September 2006.

Benton, Mike. *The Comic Book in America: An Illustrated History.* Dallas: Taylor, 1993.

Berg, Charles Ramírez. *Latino Images in Film: Stereotypes, Subversion, and Resistance.* Austin: University of Texas Press, 2002.

Blair, Elizabeth. "For 'Black Nerds Everywhere,' Two Comedy Heroes." NPR, January 27, 2012. npr.org/2012/01/27/145838407/for-black-nerds-everywhere-two -comedy-heroes.

Bogle, Donald. *Toms, Coons, Mulattoes, Mammies, and Bucks: An Interpretive History of Blacks in American Films.* 4th ed. New York: Continuum, 2007.

Brown, Jeffrey A. *Black Superheroes, Milestone Comics, and Their Fans.* Jackson: University Press of Mississippi, 2000.

———. "Panthers and Vixens: Black Superheroines, Sexuality, and Stereotypes in Contemporary Comic Books." In *Black Comics: Politics of Race and Representation*, edited by Sheena C. Howard and Ronald L. Jackson II, 133–149. London: Bloomsbury, 2013.

Busiek, Kurt, and George Pérez. "New Order." *The Avengers* 3, no. 27. Marvel Comics, April 2000.

Campbell, Josie. "Bedard Brings a Bilingual 'Blue Beetle' to the DCU." CBR.com, October 3, 2011. cbr.com/bedard-brings-a-bilingual-blue-beetle-to-the-dcu.

Carrington, André M. *Speculative Blackness: The Future of Race in Science Fiction.* Minneapolis: University of Minnesota Press, 2016.

Chafe, William. *The Unfinished Journey: America since World War II.* 6th ed. New York: Oxford University Press, 2007.

Chang, Gordon. "'Superman Is About to Visit the Relocation Centers' and the Limits of Wartime Liberalism." *Amerasia* 19, no. 1 (1993): 37–59.

Chen, Edith Wen-Chu, and Grace J. Yoo, eds. *Encyclopedia of Asian American Issues Today.* Vol. 1. Santa Barbara, CA: ABC-CLIO, 2010.

Ching, Albert. "Brevoort on 'Silver Surfer,' 'Uncanny Avengers,' and Diversity in Marvel Now!" CBR.com, March 10, 2014. cbr.com/brevoort-on-silver-surfer-uncanny-avengers-diversity-in-marvel-now.

Chute, Hillary, and Marianne DeKoven. "Introduction: Graphic Narrative." *Modern Fiction Studies* 52, no. 4 (Winter 2006): 767–782.

Claremont, Chris, and Brent Anderson. "Chutes and Ladders!" *The Uncanny X-Men* 1, no. 160. Marvel Comics, August 1982.

———. "Ou, La, La . . . Badoon!" *X-Men Annual* 1, no. 5. Marvel Comics, 1981.

Claremont, Chris, and Sal Buscema. *The New Mutants Classic.* Vol. 2. New York: Marvel Comics, 2007.

Claremont, Chris, and John Byrne. "Mind Out of Time!" *The Uncanny X-Men* 1, no. 142. Marvel Comics, February 1981.

Claremont, Chris, John Byrne, and Dave Cockrum. *The Uncanny X-Men Omnibus.* Vol. 2. New York: Marvel Comics, 2016.

Claremont, Chris, John Byrne, et al. *Essential Iron Fist.* Vol. 1. New York: Marvel Comics, 2005.

Claremont, Chris, and Dave Cockrum. "Binary Star!" *The Uncanny X-Men* 1, no. 164. Marvel Comics, December 1982.

———. "First Blood." *The Uncanny X-Men* 1, no. 155. Marvel Comics, March 1982.

———. "Gold Rush!" *The Uncanny X-Men* 1, no. 161. Marvel Comics, September 1982.

———. "Rogue Storm!" *The Uncanny X-Men* 1, no. 147. Marvel Comics, July 1981.

Claremont, Chris, Dave Cockrum, and John Byrne. *The Uncanny X-Men Omnibus.* Vol. 1. New York: Marvel Comics, 2013.

Claremont, Chris, Jo Duffy, John Byrne, Mike Zeck, Kerry Gamill, et al. *Essential Power Man and Iron Fist.* Vol. 1. New York: Marvel Comics, 2007.

Claremont, Chris, and Jim Lee. "Broken Chains." *The Uncanny X-Men* 1, no. 258. Marvel Comics, February 1990.

———. "The Key That Breaks the Locke." *The Uncanny X-Men* 1, no. 256. Marvel Comics, December 1989.

———. "Lady Mandarin." *The Uncanny X-Men* 1, no. 257. Marvel Comics, January 1990.

Claremont, Chris, and Rick Leonardi. "Duel!" *The Uncanny X-Men* 1, no. 201. Marvel Comics, January 1986.

Claremont, Chris, and Bob McLeod. *The New Mutants Classic.* Vol. 1. New York: Marvel Comics, 2006.

Claremont, Chris, and John Romita Jr. "Nightcrawler's Inferno." *X-Men Annual* 1, no. 4. Marvel Comics, 1980.

———. "Two Girls Out to Have Fun!" *The Uncanny X-Men* 1, no. 189. Marvel Comics, January 1985.

———. "Warhunt 2." *The Uncanny X-Men* 1, no. 193. Marvel Comics, May 1985.

Claremont, Chris, and Bill Sienkiewicz. *The New Mutants Classic*. Vol. 3. New York: Marvel Comics, 2008.

Claremont, Chris, and Marc Silvestri. "Crash and Burn." *The Uncanny X-Men* 1, no. 255. Marvel Comics, December 1989.

———. "Harriers Hunt." *The Uncanny X-Men* 1, no. 261. Marvel Comics, May 1990.

Claremont, Chris, Louise Simonson, Jim Lee, Rob Liefeld, Jon Bogdanove, Rick Leonardi, and Marc Silvestri. *X-Men: X-Tinction Agenda*. New York: Marvel Comics, 2011.

Claremont, Chris, Louise Simonson, Walter Simonson, Ann Nocenti, John Romita Jr., Terry Shoemaker, Bret Blevins, Jackson Guice, Sal Buscema, Jon Bogdanove, et al. *X-Men: Mutant Massacre*. New York: Marvel Comics, 2009.

Claremont, Chris, and Paul Smith. "To Have and Have Not." *The Uncanny X-Men* 1, no. 173. Marvel Comics, September 1983.

Commission on Wartime Relocation and Internment of Civilians. *Personal Justice Denied: Report of the Commission on Wartime Relocation and Internment of Civilians*. Seattle: University of Washington Press, 1997.

Conway, Gerry, and Neal Adams. "An Evening's Wait for Death!" *Amazing Adventures* 1, no. 7. Marvel Comics, July 1971.

Conway, Gerry, and Dick Dillin. "A Plague of Monsters." *Justice League of America* 1, no. 174. DC Comics, January 1980.

Conway, Gerry, Archie Goodwin, Gardner Fox, Marv Wolfman, and Gene Colan. *The Tomb of Dracula*. Vol. 1. New York: Marvel Comics, 2010.

Conway, Gerry, and Chuck Patton. "The End of the Justice League!" *Justice League of America Annual* 1, no. 2. DC Comics, 1984.

———. "'Rebirth' Part One: 'Gang War.'" *Justice League of America* 1, no. 233. DC Comics, December 1984.

———. "'Rebirth' Part Two: 'Claws.'" *Justice League of America* 1, no. 234. DC Comics, January 1985.

———. "Savage Symphony." *Justice League of America* 1, no. 238. DC Comics, May 1985.

Conway, Gerry, and George Tuska. "Battle Cry." *Justice League of America* 1, no. 242. DC Comics, September 1985.

"Crimson Avenger (Travis)." Comic Vine Character Wiki, n.d. Accessed January 21, 2016. comicvine.gamespot.com/crimson-avenger-travis/4005-11175.

"Crimson Avenger I (Lee Travis)." Unofficial Guide to the DC Universe, n.d. Accessed January 21, 2016. dcuguide.com/w/Crimson_Avenger_(Lee_Travis).

Cronin, Brian. *Was Superman a Spy? And Other Comic Book Legends Revealed*. New York: Penguin, 2009.

———. "When We First Met—More Agents of S.H.I.E.L.D." CBR.com, September 23, 2014. cbr.com/when-we-first-met-more-agents-of-s-h-i-e-l-d.

Daniels, Les. *Batman: The Complete History*. San Francisco: Chronicle Books, 1998.

———. *DC Comics: Sixty Years of the World's Favorite Comic Book Heroes*. Boston: Bullfinch Press, 1995.

Daniels, Roger. *Asian America: Chinese and Japanese in the United States since 1850*. Seattle: University of Washington Press, 1988.

———. "Bad News from the Good War: Democracy at Home during World War II." In *The Home-Front War: World War II and American Society*, edited by Kenneth Paul O'Brien and Lynn Hudson Parsons, 157–171. Westport, CT: Greenwood Press, 1995.

———. *Concentration Camps, North America: Japanese in the United States and Canada during World War II*. Malabar, FL: Robert E. Krieger, 1981.

Dayton, Deejay. "DC Comics History: Crimson Avenger (Early Golden Age)." Comic Book Bin, April 29, 2015. comicbookbin.com/Crimson_Avenger002.html.

DC Comics. *The Batman Annuals: Volume 1*. New York: DC Comics, 2009.

———. *The Greatest 1950s Stories Ever Told*. New York: DC Comics, 1990.

———. *Justice League of America Archives*. Vol. 10. New York: DC Comics, 2012.

———. New Guardians letters page. *The New Guardians* 1, no. 6. DC Comics, Holiday 1988.

———. New Guardians letters page. *The New Guardians* 1, no. 11. DC Comics, August 1989.

———. New Guardians letters page. *The New Guardians* 1, no. 12. DC Comics, September 1989.

———. *Showcase Presents: Teen Titans*. Vol. 2. New York: DC Comics, 2007.

———. *Showcase Presents: Wonder Woman*. Vol. 4. New York: DC Comics, 2011.

———. *Superman in the Fifties*. New York: DC Comics, 2002.

DeFalco, Tom. "Superheroes Are Made." In *What Is a Superhero?*, edited by Robin S. Rosenberg and Peter Coogan, 139–146. Oxford, UK: Oxford University Press, 2013.

DeKoven, Marianne. *Utopia Limited: The Sixties and the Emergence of the Postmodern*. Durham, NC: Duke University Press, 2004.

Dennis, Jim, and Leopoldo Durañona. "Coming of a Dragon!" *Richard Dragon, Kung-Fu Fighter* 1, no. 1. DC Comics, May 1975.

Dixon, Chuck, and Ron Marz. *Green Lantern: Emerald Allies*. New York: DC Comics, 2000.

Dixon, Chuck, and Paul Rivoche. "How Liberalism Became Kryptonite for Superman: A Graphic Tale of Modern Comic Books' Descent into Moral Relativism." *Wall Street Journal*, June 8, 2014. wsj.com/articles/dixon-and-rivoche-how -liberalism-became-kryptonite-for-superman-1402265792.

Eisner, Will. *Comics and Sequential Art: Principles and Practices from the Legendary Cartoonist*. New York: W. W. Norton, 2008.

———. *Graphic Storytelling and Visual Narrative: Principles and Practices from the Legendary Cartoonist*. New York: W. W. Norton, 2008.

Englehart, Steve, Cary Bates, and Joe Staton. "Blow in the Wind." *The New Guardians* 1, no. 2. DC Comics, October 1988.

Englehart, Steve, and Bob Brown. "All the Sounds and Sights of Death!" *The Avengers* 1, no. 126. Marvel Comics, August 1974.

———. "Below Us the Battle!" *The Avengers* 1, no. 115. Marvel Comics, September 1973.

———. "Night of the Swordsman." *The Avengers* 1, no. 114. Marvel Comics, August 1973.

Englehart, Steve, and Sal Buscema. "Bewitched, Bothered, and Dead!" *The Avengers* 1, no. 128. Marvel Comics, October 1974.

———. "Divide . . . and Conquer." *The Defenders* 1, no. 9. Marvel Comics, October 1973.

———. "The Reality Problem!" *The Avengers* 1, no. 130. Marvel Comics, December 1974.

Englehart, Steve, and Dave Cockrum. "A Blast from the Past!" *Giant-Size Avengers* 1, no. 2. Marvel Comics, November 1974.

Englehart, Steve, Steve Gerber, Tony Isabella, Mike Friedrich, John Warner, Sal Buscema, Alan Weiss, Frank Robbins, Herb Trimpe, et al. *Essential Captain America.* Vol. 4. New York: Marvel Comics, 2008.

Englehart, Steve, and Don Heck. "The Lion God Lives!" *The Avengers* 1, no. 112. Marvel Comics, June 1973.

Englehart, Steve, and Al Milgrom. *The Avengers: West Coast Avengers — Sins of the Past.* New York: Marvel Comics, 2011.

Englehart, Steve, Al Milgrom, and Richard Howell. *The Avengers: West Coast Avengers — Family Ties.* New York: Marvel Comics, 2011.

Englehart, Steve, and Jim Starlin. "Midnight Brings Dark Death!" *Special Marvel Edition* 1, no. 16. Marvel Comics, February 1974.

———. "Shang-Chi, Master of Kung Fu!" *Special Marvel Edition* 1, no. 15. Marvel Comics, December 1973.

Englehart, Steve, and Joe Staton. "The New Guardians." *The New Guardians* 1, no. 1. DC Comics, September 1988.

Esposito, Joey. "Exclusive: DC Focuses On Diversity in Batman Titles." IGN, June 6, 2011. ign.com/articles/2011/06/06/exclusive-dc-focuses-on-diversity-in -batman-titles.

Everett, Bill. "Comes Now . . . the Decision!" *Sub-Mariner* 1, no. 54. Marvel Comics, October 1972.

Everett, Bill, and Mike Friedrich. "The Attack of the Atomic Samurai!" *Sub-Mariner* 1, no. 52. Marvel Comics, August 1972.

Ewing, Al, and Greg Land. *Mighty Avengers Volume 1: No Single Hero.* New York: Marvel Comics, 2014.

Fawaz, Ramzi. *The New Mutants: Superheroes and the Radical Imagination of American Comics.* New York: New York University Press, 2016.

Fielding, Richard. "The Riddle of the Chinese Jade." Directed by Tommy Carr. *Adventures of Superman,* 1951. Burbank, CA: Warner Home Video, 2006.

Fingeroth, Danny. "Power and Responsibility . . . and Other Reflections on Superheroes." In *What Is a Superhero?,* edited by Robin S. Rosenberg and Peter Coogan, 125–128. Oxford, UK: Oxford University Press, 2013.

———. *Superman on the Couch: What Superheroes Really Tell Us about Ourselves and Our Society.* New York: Continuum, 2004.

Fox, Gardner. *All Star Comics: Archives, Vol. 3.* New York: DC Comics, 1997.

Fox, Gardner, Mike Sekowsky, and Sid Greene. *Justice League of America: Archives, Vol. 7.* New York: DC Comics, 2001.

Fox, Gardner, Mike Sekowsky, and Bernard Sachs. *Justice League of America: Archives, Vol. 5.* New York: DC Comics, 1999.

Fox, Gardner, and Syd Shores. "Echo from a Golden Grave!" *Red Wolf* 1, no. 7. Marvel Comics, May 1973.

———. "King Cycle Deals Death!" *Red Wolf* 1, no. 8. Marvel Comics, July 1973.

———. "Red Wolf!" *Marvel Spotlight* 1, no. 1. Marvel Comics, November 1971.

Frannich, Darren. "Marvel's New Beginning: Witness Marvel Now!" EW.com, July 3, 2012. ew.com/article/2012/07/03/marvel-now-jean-grey-exclusive.

Freeman, Ben, and Peter Freeman. "Treasure of the Incas." Directed by Lee Sholem. *Adventures of Superman*, 1951. Burbank, CA: Warner Home Video, 2006.

Friedrich, Mike, and George Tuska. "Night of the Rising Sun!" *Iron Man* 1, no. 68. Marvel Comics, June 1974.

Gardner, Jared. "Same Difference: Graphic Alterity in the Work of Gene Luen Yang, Adrian Tomine, and Derek Kirk Kim." In *Multicultural Comics: From "Zap" to "Blue Beetle,"* edited by Frederick Luis Aldama, 133–147. Austin: University of Texas Press, 2010.

Gates, Sterling, Pete Woods, Geoff Johns, Andres Guinaldo, and Derlis Santacruz. *Justice League of America's Vibe, Volume 1: Breach*. New York: DC Comics, 2014.

Gateward, Frances, and John Jennings, eds. *The Blacker the Ink: Constructions of Black Identity in Comics and Sequential Art*. New Brunswick, NJ: Rutgers University Press, 2015.

Giffen, Keith, J. M. DeMatteis, and Kevin Maguire. "Winning Hand." *Justice League* 1, no. 4. DC Comics, May 1987.

Giffen, Keith, John Rogers, and Cully Hamner. *Blue Beetle: Shellshocked*. New York: DC Comics, 2006.

Gonzales, Manuel. *Mexicanos: A History of Mexicans in the United States*. Bloomington: University of Indiana Press, 2009.

Goodwin, Archie, and Don Heck. "The Fury of the Firebrand!" *Iron Man* 1, no. 27. Marvel Comics, July 1970.

Goodwin, Archie, and George Tuska. "From This Conflict . . . Death!" *Iron Man* 1, no. 22. Marvel Comics, February 1970.

———. "The Replacement!" *Iron Man* 1, no. 21. Marvel Comics, January 1970.

Gordon, Dan, and Willard Bowsky, dirs. "Eleventh Hour." 1942. DVD. *Max Fleisher's Superman, 1941–1942*. Burbank, CA: Warner Bros., 2009.

Gordon, Ian. *Comic Strips and Consumer Culture, 1890–1945*. Washington, DC: Smithsonian Institution Press, 1998.

———. *Superman: The Persistence of an American Icon*. New Brunswick, NJ: Rutgers University Press, 2017.

Goyer, David S., and Geoff Johns. *JSA: The Return of Hawkman*. New York: DC Comics, 2002.

Goyer, David S., Geoff Johns, Stephen Sadowski, Buzz, Marcos Martin, and Michael Bair. *JSA: Darkness Falls*. New York: DC Comics, 2002.

Grant, Steven, Roger Stern, and John Byrne. "Heart of Stone." *The Avengers* 1, no. 190. Marvel Comics, December 1979.

Gray, Justin, Jimmy Palmiotti, and Daniel Acuña. "A Call to Arms." *Uncle Sam and the Freedom Fighters* 1, no. 4. DC Comics, December 2006.

———. "First Strike." *Uncle Sam and the Freedom Fighters* 1, no. 3. DC Comics, November 2006.

———. "Liberty and Justice for All." *Uncle Sam and the Freedom Fighters* 1, no. 8. DC Comics, April 2007.

———. "The Returning of Champions." *Uncle Sam and the Freedom Fighters* 1, no. 6. DC Comics, February 2007.

Gray, Steven. "What Obama's Election Really Means to Black America." Time.com, November 6, 2008. content.time.com/time/nation/article/0,8599,1857222,00 .html.

Gruenwald, Mark, Steven Grant, David Michelinie, and John Byrne. "The Call of the Mountain Thing!" *The Avengers* 1, no. 187. Marvel Comics, September 1979.

———. "Nights of Wundagore!" *The Avengers* 1, no. 186. Marvel Comics, August, 1979.

Hajdu, David. *The Ten-Cent Plague: The Great Comic-Book Scare and How It Changed America*. New York: Farrar, Straus, and Giroux, 2008.

Hama, Larry, and Paul Ryan. "Starting Line-Up." *The Avengers* 1, no. 329. Marvel Comics, February 1991.

———. "Wind from the East." *The Avengers* 1, no. 326. Marvel Comics, November 1990.

Hamilton, Dick. "Drums of Death." Directed by Lee Sholem. *Adventures of Superman*, 1951. Burbank, CA: Warner Home Video, 2006.

Hamilton, Patrick L. *Of Space and Mind: Cognitive Mappings of Contemporary Chicano/a Fiction*. Austin: University of Texas Press, 2011.

Haney, Bob, and Art Saaf. "What Lies in Litchburg Graveyard?" *Teen Titans* 1, no. 41. DC Comics, October 1972.

Hatfield, Charles, Jeet Heer, and Kent Worcester, eds. *The Superhero Reader*. Jackson: University Press of Mississippi, 2012.

Hennon, Blake. "'Ms. Marvel'; G. Willow Wilson, Sana Amanat on Kamala's Transformation." Hero Complex, *Los Angeles Times*, March 27, 2014. herocomplex .latimes.com/comics/ms-marvel-g-willow-wilson-sana-amanat-on-kamalas -transformation/#/0.

Hodgson, Godfrey. *America in Our Time*. New York: Doubleday, 1976.

Hogan, Patrick Colm. *Cognitive Science, Literature, and the Arts: A Guide for Humanists*. New York: Routledge, 2003.

———. *Empire and Poetic Voice: Cognitive and Cultural Studies of Literary Tradition and Colonialism*. Albany: State University of New York Press, 2004.

Hogue, W. Lawrence. *Race, Modernity, Postmodernity: A Look at the History and the Literatures of People of Color Since the 1960s*. Albany: State University of New York Press, 1996.

Hollinger, David A. *Postethnic America: Beyond Multiculturalism*. Revised ed. New York: Basic Books, 2005.

hooks, bell. *Black Looks: Race and Representation*. Boston: South End Press, 1992.

Horton, Carol A. *Race and the Making of American Liberalism*. Oxford, UK: Oxford University Press, 2005.

Howard, Sheena C., and Ronald L. Jackson II, eds. *Black Comics: Politics of Race and Representation*. London: Bloomsbury, 2013.

Howe, Sean. *Marvel Comics: The Untold Story*. New York: HarperCollins, 2012.

Hyde, David. "Eric Wallace on Mr. Terrific." *The Source*, DC Comics, July 6, 2011. dccomics.com/blog/2011/07/06/eric-wallace-on-mr-terrific.

Isabella, Tony, Octavio Cariello, David Zimmerman, and Eddy Newell. "Armies of the Street." *Black Lightning* 2, no. 8. DC Comics, September 1995.

Isabella, Tony, and Eddy Newell. "Blowed Away." *Black Lightning* 2, no. 5. DC Comics, June 1995.

———. "Lessons." *Black Lightning* 2, no. 4. DC Comics, May 1995.

———. "Return of the Warlord." *Black Lightning* 2, no. 6. DC Comics, July 1995.

———. "Students." *Black Lightning* 2, no. 3. DC Comics, April 1995.

———. "Teachers." *Black Lightning* 2, no. 2. DC Comics, March 1995.

———. "The Weekend Report." *Black Lightning* 2, no. 1. DC Comics, February 1995.

Isabella, Tony, Eddy Newell, Chris Batista, and Sergio Cariello. "Season of the Warrior." *Black Lightning* 2, no. 7. DC Comics, August 1995.

Isabella, Tony, and George Tuska. "Black Goliath." *Black Goliath* 1, no. 1. Marvel Comics, February 1976.

Isabella, Tony, and Trevor Von Eeden. "Black Lightning." *Black Lightning* 1, no. 1. DC Comics, April 1977.

———. "Every Hand Against Them." *Black Lightning* 1, no. 3. DC Comics, July 1977.

———. "Fear and Loathing at Garfield High." *Black Lightning* 1, no. 9. DC Comics, May 1978.

———. "Merlyn Means Murder." *Black Lightning* 1, no. 2. DC Comics, May 1977.

———. "Nobody Beats a Superman!" *Black Lightning*. 1, no. 5. DC Comics, November 1977.

———. "One Man's Poison." *Black Lightning* 1, no. 6. DC Comics, January 1978.

Jameson, Barry, and Ric Estrada. "Death-Duel on Orando." *Karate Kid* 1, no. 10. DC Comics, October 1977.

———. "The International Dooms of Major Disaster." *Karate Kid* 1, no. 2. DC Comics, June 1976.

———. "The Rage of Yesterday's Lost!" *Karate Kid* 1, no. 4. DC Comics, October 1976.

Jeffries, John W. *Wartime America: The World War II Home Front.* Chicago: Ivan R. Dee, 1996.

Johns, Geoff, Phil Jimenez, George Pérez, Jerry Ordway, Ivan Reis, and Andy Lanning. *Infinite Crisis.* New York: DC Comics, 2006.

Johns, Geoff, and Rags Morales. *JSA: Fair Play.* New York: DC Comics, 2003.

Johnson, Jeffrey K. *Super-History: Comic Book Superheroes and American Society, 1938 to the Present.* Jefferson, NC: McFarland, 2012.

Jolley, Dan, and ChrisCross. "Empowered." *Firestorm* 3, no. 3. DC Comics, September 2004.

———. "Everybody Wants You." *Firestorm* 3, no. 4. DC Comics, October 2004.

———. "Everybody Wants You, Part 2." *Firestorm* 3, no. 5. DC Comics, November 2004.

———. "Eye Contact." *Firestorm* 3, no. 1. DC Comics, July 2004.

———. "Joyride." *Firestorm* 3, no. 6. DC Comics, December 2004.

Jones, Gerard. *Men of Tomorrow: Geeks, Gangsters, and the Birth of the Comic Book.* New York: Basic Books, 2004.

Jones, Gerard, and Will Jacobs. *The Comic Book Heroes: The First History of Modern Comic Books, from the Silver Age to the Present.* Rocklin, CA: Prima Press, 1997.

Jones, Jeffrey M. "Americans' Views of Black-White Relations Deteriorate." Gallup, August 6, 2015. news.gallup.com/poll/184484/americans-views-black-white-re lations-deteriorate.aspx.

Jurgens, Dan, Karl Kesel, Roger Stern, Louise Simonson, Gerard Jones, Tom Grummett, Jackson Guice, Jon Bogdanove, and Mark Bright. *The Return of Superman.* New York: DC Comics, 1993.

Kane, Bob. *Batman: Archives, Vol. 5.* New York: DC Comics, 2001.

———. *Batman: Archives, Vol. 8.* New York: DC Comics, 2012.

Kane, Bob, and Michael Uslan. *Batman in the Fifties.* New York: DC Comics, 2002.

Kanigher, Robert, and Ross Andru. *Showcase Presents: Wonder Woman.* Vol. 3. New York: DC Comics, 2009.

Kanigher, Robert, Ross Andru, and Mike Esposito. *Showcase Presents: Wonder Woman.* Vol. 1. New York: DC Comics, 2007.

———. *Showcase Presents: Wonder Woman.* Vol. 2. New York: DC Comics, 2008.

Kanigher, Robert, and Don Heck. "The Mystery of Nubia!" *Wonder Woman* 1, no. 205. DC Comics, March–April 1973.

Kanigher, Robert, and Werner Roth. "I Am Curious (Black)!" *Superman's Girl Friend Lois Lane* 1, no. 106. DC Comics, November 1970.

———. "Indian Death Charge!" *Superman's Girl Friend Lois Lane* 1, no. 110. DC Comics, May 1971.

Kaste, Martin. "Since Ferguson, a Rise in Charges against Police Officers." NPR, November 25, 2015. npr.org/2015/11/25/457415588/since-ferguson-a-rise-in-charges-against-police-officers.

Khoury, George. *Image Comics: The Road to Independence.* Raleigh, NC: TwoMorrows, 2007.

Killian, Lewis M. "Race Relations and the Nineties: Where Are the Dreams of the Sixties?" *Social Forces* 69, no. 1 (September 1990): 1–13.

Kilpatrick, Jacquelyn. *Celluloid Indians: Native Americans and Film.* Lincoln: University of Nebraska Press, 1999.

King, Kyle. "Jimmy Olsen, Rebirth and Diversity in DC Comics." ComiConverse, March 6, 2016. comiconverse.com/jimmy-olsen-rebirth-diversity-dc-comics-8907.

Kirby, Jack. *Black Panther by Jack Kirby.* Vol. 1. New York: Marvel Comics, 2005.

Kneitel, Seymour, dir. "Japoteurs." 1942. DVD. *Max Fleisher's Superman, 1941–1942,* Burbank, CA: Warner Bros., 2009.

Krenn, Michael L. *The Color of Empire: Race and American Foreign Relations.* Washington, DC: Potomac Books, 2006.

Lantz, James. "Superman Radio Series — Story Reviews: 1946; The Clan of the Fiery Cross." Superman Homepage, n.d. Accessed April 9, 2013. supermanhomepage.com/radio/radio.php?topic=radio-reviews/070146-fierycross.

Lawson, Steven F., and Charles M. Payne. *Debating the Civil Rights Movement, 1945–1968.* Lanham, MD: Rowman and Littlefield, 2006.

Learning Network. "May 1, 1992: Rodney King Asks, 'Can We All Get Along?'" Learning Network, *New York Times,* May 1, 2012. learning.blogs.nytimes.com/2012/05/01/may-1-1992-victim-rodney-kings-asks-can-we-all-get-along/?_r=0.

Lee, Jim, and John Byrne. "Blowback." *X-Men* 2, no. 5. Marvel Comics, February 1992.

———. "The Not So Big Easy." *X-Men* 2, no. 9. Marvel Comics, June 1992.

Lee, Jim, and Scott Lobdell. "Tooth and Claw." *X-Men* 2, no. 8. Marvel Comics, May 1992.

Lee, Robert G. *Orientals: Asian Americans in Popular Culture.* Philadelphia: Temple University Press, 1999.

Lee, Stan. "More Than Normal, But Believable." In *What Is a Superhero?*, edited by Robin S. Rosenberg and Peter Coogan, 115–118. Oxford, UK: Oxford University Press, 2013.

Lee, Stan, Otto Binder, Al Gabriele, and Charles Nicholas. *Marvel Masterworks: Golden Age Young Allies*. Vol. 1. New York: Marvel Comics, 2009.

Lee, Stan, and Gene Colan. "Brother, Take My Hand!" *Daredevil* 1, no. 47. Marvel Comics, December 1969.

Lee, Stan, and Steve Ditko. *Marvel Masterworks: The Amazing Spider-Man*. Vol. 3. New York: Marvel Comics, 2009.

———. *The Amazing Spider-Man Epic Collection: Great Power*. Vol. 1. New York: Marvel Comics, 2016.

———. *The Amazing Spider-Man Epic Collection: Great Responsibility*. Vol. 2. New York: Marvel Comics, 2016.

Lee, Stan, Steve Ditko, and John Romita. *Marvel Masterworks: The Amazing Spider-Man*. Vol. 4. New York: Marvel Comics, 2010.

Lee, Stan, Gary Friedrich, Gerry Conway, Steve Englehart, Gene Colan, John Romita, Gil Kane, Sal Buscema, et al. *Essential Captain America*. Vol. 3. New York: Marvel Comics, 2006.

Lee, Stan, and Don Heck. *Marvel Masterworks: The Invincible Iron Man*. Vol. 2. New York: Marvel Comics, 2012.

———. "The Sign of the Serpent!" *The Avengers* 1, no. 32. Marvel Comics, September 1966.

———. "To Smash a Serpent!" *The Avengers* 1, no. 33. Marvel Comics, October 1966.

Lee, Stan, Don Heck, Jack Kirby, and Steve Ditko. *Marvel Masterworks: The Invincible Iron Man*. Vol. 1. New York: Marvel Comics, 2010.

Lee, Stan, and Jack Kirby. *Fantastic Four Omnibus*. Vol. 3. New York: Marvel Comics, 2015.

———. *Marvel Masterworks: The Fantastic Four*. Vol. 1. New York: Marvel Comics, 2009.

———. *Marvel Masterworks: The Fantastic Four*. Vol. 2. New York: Marvel Comics, 2009.

———. *Marvel Masterworks: The Fantastic Four*. Vol. 3. New York: Marvel Comics, 2010.

———. *Marvel Masterworks: The Fantastic Four*. Vol. 5. New York: Marvel Comics, 2010.

———. *Marvel Masterworks: The Fantastic Four*. Vol. 6. New York: Marvel Comics, 2007.

———. *Marvel Masterworks: The X-Men*. Vol. 1. New York: Marvel Comics, 2002.

Lee, Stan, Jack Kirby, and Dick Ayers. *Essential Sgt. Fury and His Howling Commandos*. Vol. 1. New York: Marvel Comics, 2011.

Lee, Stan, Jack Kirby, and Steve Ditko. *Marvel Masterworks: The Incredible Hulk*. Vol. 1. New York: Marvel Comics, 2009.

Lee, Stan, Jack Kirby, and Don Heck. *Avengers Omnibus*. Vol. 1. New York: Marvel Comics, 2011.

Lee, Stan, Jack Kirby, Jim Steranko, et al. *Essential Captain America*. Vol. 2. New York: Marvel Comics, 2002.

Lee, Stan, Jack Kirby, Roy Thomas, and Werner Roth. *Marvel Masterworks: The X-Men*. Vol. 2. New York: Marvel Comics, 2009.

Lepore, Jill. *The Secret History of Wonder Woman*. New York: Random House, 2015.

Levitz, Paul, and Ric Estrada. "My World Begins in Yesterday." *Karate Kid* 1, no. 1. DC Comics, April 1976.

Levitz, Paul, and Bob Rozakis. "The Man Who Toppled the Titans." *Teen Titans* 1, no. 44. DC Comics, November 1976.

Levitz, Paul, and James Sherman. "The Dazzling Debut of Dawnstar!" *Superboy and the Legion of Super-Heroes* 1, no. 226. DC Comics, April 1977.

Loeb, Jeph. "Making the World a Better Place." In *What Is a Superhero?*, edited by Robin S. Rosenberg and Peter Coogan, 119–124. Oxford, UK: Oxford University Press, 2013.

Lobdell, Scott, and Chris Bachalo. "Dead Silence." *Generation X* 1, no. 3. Marvel Comics, January 1995.

———. "Searching." *Generation X* 1, no. 2. Marvel Comics, December 1994.

Lobdell, Scott, Stan Lee, and Chris Bachalo. "The Teeth of Our Skin." *Generation X* 1, no. 17. Marvel Comics, July 1996.

Ma, Sheng-mei. *The Deathly Embrace: Orientalism and Asian American Identity.* Minneapolis: University of Minnesota Press, 2000.

Maneely, Joe, Jack Kirby, Stan Lee, Al Feldstein, Fred Kida, and Syd Shores. *Marvel Masterworks: Atlas Era Black Knight/Yellow Claw.* Vol. 1. New York: Marvel Comics, 2009.

Mantlo, Bill, and Brett Blevins. "All in the Family." *Strange Tales* 2, no. 2. Marvel Comics, May 1987.

Mantlo, Bill, and Sal Buscema. ". . . Like a Tiger in the Night!" *Peter Parker, the Spectacular Spider-Man* 1, no. 9. Marvel Comics, August 1977.

———. "My Friend, My Foe!" *Peter Parker, the Spectacular Spider-Man* 1, no. 18. Marvel Comics, May 1978.

———. "Tiger in a Web!" *Peter Parker, the Spectacular Spider-Man* 1, no. 10. Marvel Comics, September 1977.

Mantlo, Bill, and John Byrne. "Elementary, Dear Avengers." *The Avengers* 1, no. 188. Marvel Comics, October 1979.

Mantlo, Bill, and Ron Frenz. "The Hunters and the Hunted!" *Marvel Team-Up Annual* 1, no. 6. Marvel Comics, 1983.

Mantlo, Bill, and Ed Hannigan. "Cloak and Dagger." *Peter Parker, the Spectacular Spider-Man* 1, no. 64. Marvel Comics, March 1981.

Mantlo, Bill, and Rick Leonardi. *Cloak and Dagger: Child of Darkness, Child of Light.* New York: Marvel Comics, 2009.

———. "Dagger's Light." *Marvel Fanfare* 1, no. 19. Marvel Comics, March 1984.

———. "Have You Seen Your Mother Baby—Standing in the Shadows?" *Cloak and Dagger* 2, no. 2. Marvel Comics, September 1985.

———. "Sinners All!" *Cloak and Dagger* 2, no. 1. Marvel Comics, July 1985.

Mantlo, Bill, and Al Milgrom. "Crime and Punishment!" *Peter Parker, the Spectacular Spider-Man* 1, no. 82. Marvel Comics, September 1983.

Mantlo, Bill, and Jim Mooney. "A Zoo Story." *Peter Parker, the Spectacular Spider-Man* 1, no. 32. Marvel Comics, July 1979.

———. "Carrion, My Wayward Son!" *Peter Parker, the Spectacular Spider-Man* 1, no. 18. Marvel Comics, December 1978.

Mantlo, Bill, and Frank Robbins. "The Tiger and the Fly!" *The Human Fly* 1, no. 8. Marvel Comics, April 1978.

Marvel Comics. *Essential Marvel Horror.* Vol. 2. New York: Marvel Comics, 2008.

———. *The Invincible Iron Man: War Machine.* New York: Marvel Comics, 2008.

Marz, Ron, Sami Basri, and Josh Williamson. *Voodoo Volume 1: What Lies Beneath.* New York: DC Comics, 2012.

McCloud, Scott. *Understanding Comics: The Invisible Art.* New York: HarperCollins, 1994.

McDuffie, Dwayne, and M. D. Bright. *Icon: A Hero's Welcome.* New York: DC Comics, 2009.

McDuffie, Dwayne, M. D. Bright, and Mike Gustovich. *Icon: Mothership Connection.* New York: DC Comics, 2010.

McDuffie, Dwayne, and Denys Cowan. *Hardware: The Man in the Machine.* New York: DC Comics, 2010.

McDuffie, Dwayne, Ivan Velez Jr., and Trevor Von Eeden. "America Eats Her Young." *Blood Syndicate* 1, no. 1. DC Comics, April 1993.

McDuffie, Dwayne, Robert L. Washington, John Paul Leon, Denys Cowan, Derek T. Dingle, and Michael Davis. *Static Shock! Rebirth of the Cool.* New York: DC Comics, 2009.

McDuffie, Dwayne, Gregory Wright, Jackson Guice, and Denys Cowan. *Deathlok: The Living Nightmare of Michael Collins.* New York: Marvel Comics, 2012.

McFarlane, Todd. *Spawn: Beginnings.* Fullerton, CA: Image Comics, 1999.

McGregor, Don, Rich Buckler, and Billy Graham. *Marvel Masterworks: The Black Panther.* Vol. 1. New York: Marvel Comics, 2010.

McGregor, Don, Bill Mantlo, Marv Wolfman, Steve Englehart, Chris Claremont, George Tuska, Sal Buscema, Frank Robbins, Marie Severin, John Byrne, Mike Zeck, et al. *Essential Luke Cage, Power Man.* Vol. 2. New York: Marvel Comics, 2006.

Melrose, Kevin. "DC Announces Post-'Flashpoint' Details, Relaunches All Titles." CBR .com, May 31, 2011. cbr.com/dc-announces-post-flashpoint-details-relaunches -all-titles.

Michelinie, David, and Sal Buscema. "Battleground: Pittsburgh!" *The Avengers* 1, no. 193. Marvel Comics, March 1980.

Michelinie, David, and John Byrne. "Back to the Stone Age!" *The Avengers* 1, no. 191. Marvel Comics, January 1980.

———. "Death on the Hudson!" *The Avengers* 1, no. 184. Marvel Comics, June 1979.

———. "On the Matter of Heroes!" *The Avengers* 1, no. 181. Marvel Comics, March 1978.

———. "The Redoubtable Return of Crusher Creel!" *The Avengers* 1, no. 183. Marvel Comics, May 1979.

Michelinie, David, and Greg Larocque. "The Seeking Spirit." *Steel* 2, no. 17. DC Comics, July 1995.

Michelinie, David, Bob Layton, and John Romita Jr. *Iron Man by Michelinie, Layton, and Romita, Jr. Omnibus.* Vol. 1. New York: Marvel Comics, 2013.

Michelinie, David, and George Pérez. "Interlude." *The Avengers* 1, no. 194. Marvel Comics, April 1980.

Milestone Comics. Editorial. *Blood Syndicate* 1, no. 1. DC Comics, April 1993.

Moore, Jesse T. "The Education of Green Lantern: Culture and Ideology." *The Journal of American Culture* 26, no. 2 (May 2003): 263–278.

Moore, Stuart, and Jamal Igle. *Firestorm: The Nuclear Man—Reborn.* New York: DC Comics, 2007.

Morales, Robert, and Kyle Baker. *Truth: Red, White & Black.* New York: Marvel Comics, 2004.

Morrison, Grant. *Supergods: What Masked Vigilantes, Miraculous Mutants, and a Sun God from Smallville Can Teach Us about Being Human*. New York: Spiegel and Grau, 2012.

Murray, Alice Yang. *What Did the Internment of Japanese Americans Mean?* Boston: Bedford/St. Martin's, 2000.

Nama, Adilifu. *Super Black: American Pop Culture and Black Superheroes*. Austin: University of Texas Press, 2011.

National Allied Publications. *Detective Comics*. Vol. 1, no. 1. National Allied Publications, March 1937.

Neate, Wilson. *Tolerating Ambiguity: Ethnicity and Community in Chicano/a Writing*. New York: Peter Lang, 1998.

Newport, Frank. "Americans See Obama Election as Race Relations Milestone." Gallup, November 7, 2008. news.gallup.com/poll/111817/americans-see-obama -election-race-relations-milestone.aspx.

Newton, Adam Zachary. *Narrative Ethics*. Cambridge, MA: Harvard University Press, 1995.

Nicieza, Fabian, and Charlie Adlard. "Life Sentences." *Thunderbolts: Life Sentences* 1, no. 1. Marvel Comics, July 2001.

Nicieza, Fabian, and Mark Bagley. "The Bug Bites Back!" *Thunderbolts* 1, no. 37. Marvel Comics, April 2000.

———. *The New Warriors Omnibus*. Vol. 1. New York: Marvel Comics, 2013.

———. "Targeted for Death!" *Thunderbolts* 1, no. 38. Marvel Comics, May 2000.

Nicieza, Fabian, and Andy Kubert. "A Skinning of Souls." *X-Men* 2, no. 17. Marvel Comics, February 1993.

Nicieza, Fabian, and Patrick Zircher. "New Beginnings." *Thunderbolts* 1, no. 51. Marvel Comics, June, 2001.

Nocenti, Ann, Alex Sanchez, and Cliff Richards. *Katana Volume 1: Soul Taker*. New York: DC Comics, 2014.

Nyberg, Amy Kiste. "'No Harm in Horror': Ethical Dimensions of the Postwar Comic Book Controversy." In *Comics as Philosophy*, edited by Jeff McLaughlin, 27–45. Jackson: University Press of Mississippi, 2005.

———. *Seal of Approval: The History of the Comics Code*. Jackson: University Press of Mississippi, 1998.

O'Neil, Dennis. Foreword to *Batman: Archives, Vol. 5*. New York: DC Comics, 2001.

———. Introduction to *Green Lantern/Green Arrow, Vol. 1*. New York: DC Comics, 2004.

O'Neil, Dennis, and Neal Adams. *Green Lantern/Green Arrow*. New York: DC Comics, 2012.

O'Neil, Dennis, and Ric Estrada. "The Arena of No Exit!" *Richard Dragon, Kung-Fu Fighter* 1, no. 5. DC Comics, December/January 1975/1976.

———. "The Preying Mantis!" *Richard Dragon, Kung-Fu Fighter* 1, no. 9. DC Comics, June 1976.

———. "Slay the Blind Dragon." *Richard Dragon, Kung-Fu Fighter* 1, no. 8. DC Comics, May 1976.

———. "A Time to Be a Whirlwind!" *Richard Dragon, Kung-Fu Fighter* 1, no. 4. DC Comics, November 1975.

———. "To Catch an Assassin!" *Richard Dragon, Kung-Fu Fighter* 1, no. 13. DC Comics, February 1977.

O'Neil, Dennis, and Jack Kirby. "Claws of the Dragon!" *Richard Dragon, Kung-Fu Fighter* 1, no. 3. DC Comics, September 1975.

O'Neil, Dennis, and Luke McDonnell. "Blackout!" *Iron Man* 1, no. 169. Marvel Comics, April 1983.

O'Neil, Dennis, and Mike Nasser. "Lure of the Magnetic Menace." *World's Finest* 1, no. 260. DC Comics, December/January 1979/1980.

Ostrander, John, and Luke McDonnell. "Blood and Snow" (Part One). *Suicide Squad* 1, no. 11. DC Comics, March 1988.

———. "The Final Price." *Suicide Squad* 1, no. 9. DC Comics, January 1988.

———. "Trial by Blood." *Suicide Squad* 1, no. 1. DC Comics, May 1987.

Ostrander, John, Len Wein, and John Byrne. "Breach of Faith!" *Legends* 1, no. 2. DC Comics, December 1986.

———. "Send for . . . the Suicide Squad!" *Legends* 1, no. 3. DC Comics, January 1987.

Patell, Cyrus R. K. *Negative Liberties: Morrison, Pynchon, and the Problem of Liberal Ideology.* Durham, NC: Duke University Press, 2001.

Patterson, James T. *Grand Expectations: The United States, 1945–1974.* New York: Oxford University Press, 1996.

Pekar, Harvey. Introduction to *The Best American Comics 2006*, edited by Harvey Pekar and Anne Elizabeth Moore, xv–xxiii. Boston: Houghton Mifflin, 2006.

Phegley, Kiel. "Marvel Adds 'Mighty' New 'Avengers' Series." CBR.com, June 7, 2013. cbr.com/marvel-adds-mighty-new-avengers-series.

Polak, Kate. *Ethics in the Gutter: Empathy and Historical Fiction in Comics.* Columbus: Ohio State University Press, 2017.

Priest, Christopher, and Joe Bennet. "Big Trouble in Little Mogadishu, Part 1: Rhodey." *The Crew* 1, no. 1. Marvel Comics, July 2003.

———. "Big Trouble in Little Mogadishu, Part 2: Kasper." *The Crew* 1, no. 2. Marvel Comics, August 2003.

———. "Big Trouble in Little Mogadishu, Part 3: Danny." *The Crew* 1, no. 3. Marvel Comics, September 2003.

———. "Big Trouble in Little Mogadishu, Part 5: Josiah." *The Crew* 1, no. 5. Marvel Comics, November 2003.

———. "Big Trouble in Little Mogadishu, Part 6: Triage." *The Crew* 1, no. 6. Marvel Comics, December 2003.

———. "Big Trouble in Little Mogadishu, Part 7: The Crew." *The Crew* 1, no. 7. Marvel Comics, January 2004.

Priest, Christopher, Joe Jusko, Mike Manley, and Mark Bright. *Black Panther: Enemy of the State.* New York: Marvel Comics, 2002.

Priest, Christopher, Mark Texeira, and Vince Evans. *Black Panther: The Client.* New York: Marvel Comics, 2001.

Quesada, Joe. "Extraordinary." In *What Is a Superhero?*, edited by Robin S. Rosenberg and Peter Coogan, 147–152. Oxford, UK: Oxford University Press, 2013.

Regalado, Aldo J. *Bending Steel: Modernity and the American Superhero.* Jackson: University Press of Mississippi, 2015.

Remender, Rick, and Daniel Acuña. "The Apocalypse Twins, Part II." *Uncanny Avengers* 1, no. 7. Marvel Comics, June 2013.

Remender, Rick, and Olivier Coipel. "Let the Good Times Roll." *Uncanny Avengers* 1, no. 5. Marvel Comics, May 2013.

Remender, Rick, and Steve McNiven. "Ragnarok Now." *Uncanny Avengers* 1, no. 17. Marvel Comics, April 2014.

Reynolds, Richard. *Super Heroes: A Modern Mythology*. Jackson: University Press of Mississippi, 1994.

Robbins, Frank, and Ross Andru. "The Attack of the Samuroids." *The Flash* 1, no. 181. DC Comics, August 1968.

———. "The Flying Samurai." *The Flash* 1, no. 180. DC Comics, June 1968.

Rogers, Vaneta. "DC Reveals Major Changes, New Direction for Comic Book Line." *Newsarama*, February 6, 2015. newsarama.com/23456-dc-reveals-major-changes -new-direction-for-comic-book-line.html.

Romita, John, Dick Ayers, and Bill Everett. *Marvel Masterworks: Atlas Era Heroes*. Vol. 2. New York: Marvel Comics, 2008.

Rosberg, Caitlin. "David F. Walker Talks *Shaft*, *Cyborg*, and a Changing Industry." A.V. Club, *Onion*, July 22, 2015. aux.avclub.com/article/david-f-walker-talks-shaft -cyborg-and-changing-ind-222118.

Rosenberg, Adam. "'Black Panther' Is Officially the Biggest Superhero Movie in U.S. Box Office History." Mashable, March 24, 2018. yahoo.com/news/apos-black -panther-apos-officially-171632096.html.

Rosenberg, Robin S., and Peter Coogan, eds. *What Is a Superhero?* Oxford, UK: Oxford University Press, 2013.

Royal, Derek Parker. "Foreword; or Reading Within the Gutter." In *Multicultural Comics: From "Zap" to "Blue Beetle,"* edited by Frederick Luis Aldama, ix–xi. Austin: University of Texas Press, 2010.

———. "Introduction: Coloring America; Multi-Ethnic Engagements with Graphic Narrative." *MELUS* 32, no. 3 (Fall 2007): 7–22.

Rozakis, Bob, and Jose Delbo. "Daddy's Little Girl Crimefighter!" *Teen Titans* 1, no. 48. DC Comics, June 1977.

———. "Raid of the Rocket-Rollers." *Teen Titans* 1, no. 49. DC Comics, August 1977.

Rozakis, Bob, and Irv Novick. "You Can't Say No to the Angel of Death! (Or Can You?)." *Teen Titans* 1, no. 45. DC Comics, December 1976.

Saffel, Steve. "Editorial." *Generation X Collector's Preview* 1, no. 1. Marvel Comics, October 1994.

Sanchez, George. "Face the Nation: Race, Immigration, and the Rise of Nativism in Late Twentieth Century America." *International Migration Review* 31, no. 4 (Winter 1997): 1009–1030.

Saunders, Ben. *Do the Gods Wear Capes? Spirituality, Fantasy, and Superheroes*. London: Bloomsbury, 2011.

Savage, William W. *Comic Books and America, 1945–1954* Norman: University of Oklahoma Press, 1990.

Schlesinger, Arthur M., Jr. *The Disuniting of America: Reflections on a Multicultural Society*. New York: W. W. Norton, 1992.

Sheyahshe, Michael A. *Native Americans in Comic Books: A Critical Study*. Jefferson, NC: McFarland, 2008.

Siegel, Jerry, Whitney Ellsworth, Joe Shuster, Wayne Boring, et al. *Superman: The Golden Age Dailies, 1942–1944*. San Diego, CA: IDW, 2016.

Siegel, Jerry, and Joe Shuster. *Superman in the Fifties*. New York: DC Comics, 2002.

Simone, Gail, John Byrne, Eddy Barrows, and Trevor Scott. *The All-New Atom: Life in Miniature*. New York: DC Comics, 2007.

Simone, Gail, and Mike Norton. *The All-New Atom: The Hunt for Ray Palmer*. New York: DC Comics, 2007.

Simone, Gail, Mike Norton, and Eddy Barrows. *The All-New Atom: Future/Past*. New York: DC Comics, 2007.

Simone, Gail, Rick Remender, Pat Olliffe, and Mike Norton. *The All-New Atom: Small Wonder*. New York: DC Comics, 2008.

Simonson, Louise, and Chris Batista. "The Challenge!" *Steel* 2, no. 8. DC Comics, September 1994.

———. "Collision Course." *Steel* 2, no. 6. DC Comics, July 1994.

———. "In the Beginning." *Steel* 2, no. 0. DC Comics, October 1994.

———. "Retaliation." *Steel* 2, no. 5. DC Comics, June 1994.

Simonson, Louise, and Jon Bogdanove. "Bad Company." *Steel* 2, no. 3. DC Comics, April 1994.

———. "Turf War." *Steel* 2, no. 2. DC Comics, March 1994.

———. "Wrought Iron." *Steel* 2, no. 1. DC Comics, February 1994.

Simonson, Louise, Peter David, Chris Claremont, Walter Simonson, June Brigman, Todd McFarlane, Marc Silvestri, and Bret Blevins. *X-Men: The Fall of the Mutants*. New York: Marvel Comics, 2011.

Simonson, Louise, and Frank Fosco. "Bad News." *Steel* 2, no. 9. DC Comics, November 1994.

Singer, Marc. "'Black Skins' and White Masks: Comic Books and the Secret of Race." *African American Review* 36, no. 1 (Spring 2002): 107–119.

Smiley, Jane. "Say It Ain't So, Huck." *Harper's Magazine* 292, no. 1748 (1996): 61–67.

Smith, Felipe, and Tradd Moore. *All-New Ghost Rider* 1, no. 1. Marvel Comics, May 2014.

Sollors, Werner. *Beyond Ethnicity: Consent and Descent in American Culture*. New York: Oxford University Press, 1986.

Sony Pictures Home Entertainment. *Batman—The Complete 1943 Movie Serial Collection*. DVD. Sony Pictures Home Entertainment, 2005.

Stern, Roger, and John Buscema. "Command Decision." *The Avengers* 1, no. 279. Marvel Comics, May 1987.

———. "Eve of Destruction!" *The Avengers* 1, no. 265. Marvel Comics, March 1986.

———. "If Wishes Were Horses . . . !" *The Avengers* 1, no. 294. Marvel Comics, August 1988.

———. "The Legacy of Thanos!" *The Avengers* 1, no. 255. Marvel Comics, May 1985.

Stern, Roger, and Sal Buscema. "Testing . . . 1 . . . 2 . . . 3!" *The Avengers* 1, no. 227. Marvel Comics, January 1983.

Stern, Roger, and Denys Cowan. "A Killer Elite!" *Peter Parker, the Spectacular Spider-Man* 1, no. 50. Marvel Comics, January 1980.

———. "The White Tiger." *Peter Parker, the Spectacular Spider-Man* 1, no. 49. Marvel Comics, December 1980.

Stern, Roger, and Al Milgrom. Final Curtain!" *The Avengers* 1, no. 229. Marvel Comics, March 1983.

———. "I Want to Be an Avenger!" *The Avengers* 1, no. 236. Marvel Comics, October 1983.

———. "Meltdowns and Mayhem!" *The Avengers* 1, no. 237. Marvel Comics, November 1983.

———. "Trial and Error!" *The Avengers* 1, no. 228. Marvel Comics, February 1983.

———. "Up from the Depths!" *The Avengers* 1, no. 231. Marvel Comics, May 1983.

Stern, Roger, and John Romita Jr. "Who's That Lady?" *Amazing Spider-Man Annual* 1, no. 16. Marvel Comics, October 1982.

Sturges, Lilah, Howard Porter, and Freddie E. Williams. *JSA All-Stars: Glory Days.* New York: DC Comics, 2011.

Takaki, Ronald. *A Different Mirror: A History of Multicultural America.* New York: Back Bay Books, 1993.

Terror, Jude. "Report: Lack of Diversity in DC #Rebirth Announcement Direct Result of March Madness Tournament." Outhousers, March 28, 2016. theouthousers .com/index.php/news/134891-report-lack-of-diversity-in-dc-rebirth-announce ments-direct-result-of-march-madness-tournament.html.

Thomas, Roy, and Neal Adams. "Hell on Earth!" *Amazing Adventures* 1, no. 6. Marvel Comics, May 1971.

———. "An Hour for Thunder!" *Amazing Adventures* 1, no. 8. Marvel Comics, September 1971.

Thomas, Roy, Neal Adams, Gary Friedrich, et al. *The X-Men Omnibus.* Vol. 2. New York: Marvel Comics, 2011.

Thomas, Roy, and Rich Buckler. "Nuklo—The Invader That Time Forgot!" *Giant-Size Avengers* 1, no. 1. Marvel Comics, August 1974.

Thomas, Roy, and John Buscema. "Behold . . . the Vision!" *The Avengers* 1, no. 57. Marvel Comics, October 1968.

———. "The Coming of Red Wolf!" *The Avengers* 1, no. 80. Marvel Comics, September 1970.

———. "Heroes for Hire!" *The Avengers* 1, no. 77. Marvel Comics, June 1970.

Thomas, Roy, and Sal Buscema. "The Man-Ape Always Strikes Twice!" *The Avengers* 1, no. 78. Marvel Comics, July 1970.

Thomas, Roy, and Frank Giacoia. "The Sting of the Serpent." *The Avengers* 1, no. 73. Marvel Comics, February 1970.

Thomas, Roy, and Todd McFarlane. "Shadows at Midnight." *Infinity Inc.* 1, no. 21. DC Comics, December 1985.

Thomas, Roy, John Romita, Archie Goodwin, Steve Englehart, Gerry Conway, Tony Isabella, Len Wein, George Tuska, and Billy Graham. *Essential Luke Cage, Power Man.* Vol. 1. New York: Marvel Comics, 2005.

Thomas, Roy, Dann Thomas, and Todd McFarlane. "Business as Usual." *Infinity Inc.* 1, no. 25. DC Comics, April 1986.

Thomas, Roy, and Herb Trimpe. *Marvel Masterworks: The Incredible Hulk.* Vol. 6. New York: Marvel Comics, 2011.

Timely Comics. *Captain America Comics* 1, no. 13. Timely Comics, 1942. read.marvel .com/#/book/20531.

Velez, Ivan, Jr., Dwayne McDuffie, and ChrisCross. "Blood Battle." *Blood Syndicate* 1, no. 3. DC Comics, June 1993.

Velez, Ivan, Jr., Dwayne McDuffie, Arvell Jones, et al. "Thicker Than Blood." *Blood Syndicate* 1, no. 4. DC Comics, July 1993.

Wall, Wendy L. *Inventing the "American Way": The Politics of Consensus from the New Deal to the Civil Rights Movement.* Oxford, UK: Oxford University Press, 2008.

Wallace, Eric, Gianluca Gugliotta, and Wayne Faucher. *Mister Terrific Volume 1: Mind Games.* New York: DC Comics, 2012.

Warner Home Video. *Batman: The Complete Television Series*. Blu-ray Disc. Burbank, CA: Warner Home Video, 2014.

———. *The All-New Super Friends Hour: Season One*. Vol. 1. DVD. Burbank, CA: Warner Home Video, 2008.

———. *The All-New Super Friends Hour: Season One*. Vol. 2. DVD. Burbank, CA: Warner Home Video, 2009.

———. *Challenge of the Super Friends: Season One*. DVD. Burbank, CA: Warner Home Video, 2004.

———. *Super Friends! A Dangerous Fate*. DVD. Burbank, CA: Warner Home Video, 2013.

———. *Super Friends! Legacy of Super Powers*. DVD. Burbank, CA: Warner Home Video, 2013.

———. *Super Friends: The Lost Episodes*. DVD. Burbank, CA: Warner Home Video, 2009.

Wayne, Matt. "There Goes the Neighborhood." *Blood Syndicate* 1, no. 35. DC Comics, February 1996.

Wertham, Fredric. *Seduction of the Innocent*. New York: Main Road Books, 2004.

Whaley, Deborah Elizabeth. *Black Women in Sequence: Re-inking Comics, Graphic Novels, and Anime*. Seattle: University of Washington Press, 2016.

Wheeler, Andrew. "Avengers Assimilate: Identity Politics in 'Uncanny Avengers.'" *Comics Alliance*, March 29, 2013. comicsalliance.com/uncanny-avengers-5-rick-remender-identity-politics-mutants.

Wilson, G. Willow, and Adrian Alphona. *Ms. Marvel Volume 1: No Normal*. New York: Marvel Comics, 2014.

"Wing (Wing How)." Unofficial Guide to the DC Universe, n.d. Accessed January 21, 2016. dcuguide.com/w/Wing_(Wing_How).

Wolfman, Marv, Chris Claremont, Gene Colan, and Don Heck. *The Tomb of Dracula*. Vol. 3. New York: Marvel Comics, 2010.

Wolfman, Marv, Chris Claremont, Tony DeZuniga, and Gene Colan. *Blade the Vampire-Slayer: Black and White*. New York: Marvel Comics, 2004.

Wolfman, Marv, and George Pérez. *Crisis on Infinite Earths*. New York: DC Comics, 2000.

———. "A Day in the Lives . . . ." *The New Teen Titans* 1, no. 8. DC Comics, June 1981.

———. "The Fearsome Five!" *The New Teen Titans* 1, no. 3. DC Comics, January 1981.

———. "Today . . . the Terminator!" *The New Teen Titans* 1, no. 2. DC Comics, December 1980.

———. "Where Nightmares Begin!" *DC Comics Presents* 1, no. 26. DC Comics, October 1980.

Wolfman, Marv, and Curt Swan. "Trigon Lives!" *The New Teen Titans* 1, no. 5. DC Comics, March 1981.

Wright, Bradford. *Comic Book Nation: The Transformation of Youth Culture in America*. Baltimore: Johns Hopkins University Press, 2001.

Wu, Frank. *Yellow: Race in America beyond Black and White*. New York: Basic Books, 2003.

Yang, Gene Luen, and Sonny Liew. *The Shadow Hero*. New York: First Second, 2014.

Zub, Jim, and Thony Silas. *The Hunt for Wolverine: Mystery in Madripoor* 1, no. 4. Marvel Comics, October 2018.

Index

King, Rodney, 216, 218, 255
Kirby, Jack, 20, 21, 63–64, 78, 79, 81, 84, 105, 131, 153; as Jake Kurtzberg, 7
Knight, Misty: in comics, 127, 152–153, 194; Netflix, 309
Kong, Kenan, 305
Kroef, Janwillem, 210, 211

La Dama, 247, 297
Lady Shiva, 127, 155, 158–159
Land, Greg, 303
Lane, Lois, 26, 28, 29, 39, 40, 41, 55, 56, 75, 100, 107–108, 115, 118
La Raza Unida, 128
Larsen, Erik, 258
League of the Unicorn, 33, 35, 38
Lee, Ganke, 248, 249
Lee, Jim, 214, 222, 258, 293, 295
Lee, Robert G., 30, 157, 204
Lee, Stan, 7, 70, 78, 79, 81, 82–86, 103, 105, 255; as Lieber, Stanley, 7
Legion (TV), 309
Legion of Super-Heroes, The, 127, 142, 156, 169–170
Legion of Super-Heroes, The, 215
Lepore, Jill, 5
liberalism, 10, 21, 40, 51, 74, 78, 89–90, 114, 118, 119, 120, 143, 175, 177, 191, 223, 286, 289; in *Green Lantern/Green Arrow*, 92–95, 98, 99, 289; in *Iron Man*, 121–124; postwar, 16, 89, 90–91, 102, 203, 239; World War II, 22, 23, 25
Liebowitz, Jack, 7
Liefeld, Rob, 258
Lincoln, Willie, 100, 115, 116, 119
Little Moon, 100, 107, 115
Little Raven/Little Eagle, 59–60
Loeb, Jeph, 256, 257
Lone Eagle, Johnny, 107, 119
Luce, Henry, 50
Luke Cage, Hero for Hire, 1, 143, 145, 194, 284
Luke Cage (Marvel NOW!) 305–306
Luke Cage (Netflix), 291, 309
Luke, Keye, 47
Lynne, Monica, 134

M/Monet St. Croix, 215
Mach-2/Abe Jenkins, 223–224
Magma, 205
Magneto, 83
Major Hoy, 69–70, 72
Malcolm X, 83, 253
Mandarin, 70–72, 86, 222
Maneely, Joe, 67
Manelli, Dino, 80, 81
Manifold/Eden Fesi, 301
Man of Steel, 308
Mantis: in comics, 127, 155–156, 157–160, 221; in MCU, 308
Man with No Face, 77, 320n
March, Eddie, 122–124, 224
Martian Manhunter, 100, 185, 207, 208
Martin, Trayvon, 291
Marvel Cinematic Universe (MCU), 308, 309, 342n
Marvel Comics, 1, 14–18, 20, 51, 63, 65, 66, 68, 72–73, 78, 87, 89, 99, 114, 115, 125, 127, 138, 143, 148, 152, 162, 174, 177, 191, 192, 196, 205, 214, 220, 223, 224, 232, 243, 255, 256, 257, 258, 271, 273, 288, 293, 299, 301, 306; All-New, All-Different Marvel, 294–295; All New Marvel NOW!, 294, 295, 301–302; Marvel Legacy, 294; Marvel NOW!, 294–295, 299–302, 305, 307. *See also* Atlas Comics; Timely Comics
Marvel (TV), 309
Masquerade, 212, 213, 214
Maus, 3
Maxwell, Robert, 8–9
May, Melinda, 309
Mayerik, Val, 218
McCain, John, 290
McCloud, Scott, 4
McClure Syndicate, 19
McDonald, Laquan, 291
McDuffie, Dwayne, 243, 260, 261–268; award, 302
McFarlane, Todd, 258, 259–260
McGregor, Don, 133–134, 153
McLaurin, Marcus, 218
Mendinao, 134, 136
Mighty Avengers, The, 303–305

About the Authors

ALLAN W. AUSTIN is a professor of history at Misericordia University in Dallas, Pennsylvania. His books include *Quaker Brotherhood: Interracial Activism and the American Friends Service Committee, 1917–1950* (University of Illinois Press, 2012) and *From Concentration Camp to Campus: Japanese American Students and World War II* (University of Illinois Press, 2004). He coedited *Asian American History and Culture: An Encyclopedia* (M. E. Sharpe, 2010) and *Space and Time: Essays on Visions of History in Science Fiction and Fantasy Television* (McFarland, 2010).

PATRICK L. HAMILTON is an associate professor of English at Misericordia University in Dallas, Pennsylvania. His published works include *Of Space and Mind: Cognitive Mappings of Contemporary Chicano/a Fiction* (University of Texas Press, 2011) and essays in *Graphic Borders: Latino Comic Books Past, Present, and Future* (University of Texas Press, 2016) and *Multicultural Comics: From "Zap!" to "Blue Beetle"* (University of Texas Press, 2011).